Classics in CONSUMER BEHAVIOR

THE PPC MARKETING SERIES

Louis E. Boone, Consulting Editor

Louis E. Boone, The University of Tulsa
CLASSICS IN CONSUMER BEHAVIOR

Louis E. Boone, The University of Tulsa
James C. Johnson, St. Cloud State University
MARKETING CHANNELS, Second Edition

James C. Johnson, St. Cloud State University
READINGS IN CONTEMPORARY PHYSICAL
DISTRIBUTION, Second Edition

James C. Johnson, St. Cloud State University
Donald F. Wood, San Francisco State University
CONTEMPORARY PHYSICAL DISTRIBUTION

Stephen K. Keiser, The University of Delaware
Max E. Lupul, California State University, Northridge
MARKETING INTERACTION: A DECISION GAME

Howard A. Thompson, Eastern Kentucky University
THE GREAT WRITINGS IN MARKETING

Classics in
CONSUMER
BEHAVIOR

Louis E. Boone
The University of Tulsa

SELECTED READINGS
TOGETHER WITH THE AUTHORS'
OWN RETROSPECTIVE COMMENTS

BOOKS

Tulsa
Oklahoma

TO G. *Edward Kiser*, SCHOLAR AND FRIEND

ISBN 0–87814–030–1

Library of Congress No. 76–57505

Boone, Louis E.
    Classics in Consumer Behavior
Tulsa, Okla.   Petroleum Publishing Co.
1977 Fall   L58
                              10 dec 76

1 2 3 4 5   82 81 80 79 78

Contributors

Ralph I. Allison
Raymond A. Bauer
James A. Bayton
Peter D. Bennett
Francis S. Bourne
Richard P. Coleman
Scott M. Cunningham
Harry L. Davis
Saxon Graham
Harrison L. Grathwohl
Edward L. Grubb
Mason Haire
Edward T. Hall
John A. Howard
Subhash C. Jain
Harold H. Kassarjian
George Katona
Daniel Katz
Elihu Katz
Jerome B. Kernan
Philip Kotler

Alfred A. Kuehn
Robert J. Lavidge
Sidney J. Levy
Pierre Martineau
A. H. Maslow
John J. Painter
Robert A. Peterson
Fred D. Reynolds
Stuart U. Rich
Thomas S. Robertson
S. Prakash Sethi
J. N. Sheth
Tamotsu Shibutani
James E. Stafford
Gary A. Steiner
W. T. Tucker
Kenneth P. Uhl
Yoram Wind
Robert E. Witt
Lawrence H. Wortzel

Preface

The very existence of *Classics in Consumer Behavior* is testimony to the phenomenal strides in the study of the consumer and consumer decision-making. Early attempts by marketing professors to implement the marketing concept in their curricula led to the addition of scholars from psychology, sociology, economics, and anthropology to business administration faculties. Their ranks have more recently increased as new professors thoroughly grounded in the behavioral sciences have emerged from doctoral programs. New courses in Consumer Behavior and the Behavioral Sciences in Marketing have appeared in both graduate and undergraduate programs. Consumer Behavior is currently the fastest growing area in marketing.

Interest in Consumer Behavior as a discipline has been accompanied by a deluge of published research. Thousands of articles dealing with some aspect of the consumer decision process have appeared in the past ten years. Several textbooks and a dozen anthologies have been published since 1968.

The selections in *Classics In Consumer Behavior* were chosen on the following bases: (1) fundamental contributions, (2) reflections of the views of influential scholars, (3) ability to stimulate thought and new research, and (4) skill in presentation of ideas and concepts. In short, these are selections to which every serious marketing student should be exposed.

Classics in Consumer Behavior should prove a valuable supplement in any course in Consumer Behavior, Marketing Theory, or Marketing and the Behavioral Sciences. The accompanying Instructor's Manual provides summaries of each selection as well as discussion and objective questions. A matrix correlating selections in the book with chapters in major Consumer Behavior texts is also included. Discussion questions for each selection are also included at the end of each section in the book.

I have been fortunate in obtaining the assistance of a number of marketing colleagues in making suggestions and reviewing the preliminary selections. I should like to express my appreciation to Professors Bob C. Hamm, Oklahoma State University; Tom Ivey, University of Southern Mississippi; Walter P. Gorman, University of Tennessee;

James C. Johnson, St. Cloud State University; Joseph Barry Mason, University of Alabama; C. P. Rao and John E. Swan, University of Arkansas; and Howard A. Thompson, Eastern Kentucky University. Finally, I would thank the guest experts who added their insights to a number of the landmark writings in our discipline.

Tulsa, Oklahoma   LOUIS E. BOONE
January, 1977

Contents

Part I.
Introduction

Successful implementation of the marketing concept requires an understanding of consumer behavior. Marketing investigators have long recognized that understanding consumer behavior requires a knowledge of *human behavior* and have been ardent students of the behavioral sciences in the search for insights into the mental processes involved in consumer decision making.

In the first selection psychologist Sidney J. Levy emphasizes the symbolic connotations underlying products, ideas, and services. As the consumer becomes less functionally oriented, the consumer-oriented firm must understand the symbolism of its product offerings and attempt to match them with customer needs.

The second selection dates back more than a quarter-century and stands out as a pioneering attempt to employ scientific methodology in analyzing consumer behavior. The Haire shopping list study awakened marketers to deep-rooted symbolic meanings attributed to ordinary household products. Even though the profile of the instant coffee purchaser has softened with time, these changes add emphasis to the importance of understanding consumer behavior over time.

The "mother" science of demand analysis is microeconomics with its assumptions of rationality and explanations of demand in terms of diminishing marginal utility and indifference curves. George Katona modifies traditional economic theory in the third selection by including such factors as attitudes and motives into an approach that he terms *economic psychology.*

In the final selection in Part I, Professor Philip Kotler develops five models of consumer behavior from the theories of Marshall, Pavlov, Freud, Veblen, and Hobbes and applies each to marketing.

1. Symbols By Which We Buy

The science and practice of marketing have recently been infused with new life. There are many reasons for this. One of the core reasons is that behavior in the market place has become increasingly elaborated. The great multiplicity of goods, the burgeoning of new products, and their eager fruition in the consumers' homes, have moved our society to a point where practical considerations in the purchase of goods are often not given the central attention that was true in the past. The modern marketplace—exemplified so dramatically in the vast supermarket, whether called food, drug, or furniture store—reminds us daily of the marketing revolution that has come about.

In these new settings, with their astonishing arrays of merchandise, their frozen, prepackaged, precooked foods; their plastic containers; their polyethylene gadgets; and their intellectual appliances that can thoughtfully govern their own behavior—what kind of consumer is conjured into being? It is hardly an economic man—especially since there is a lot of evidence that he does not buy economically; is often vague about the actual price he pays for something; has few standards for judging the quality of what he buys; and often winds up not using it anyway! This is not just a joke. The point I am making is that nowadays when people shop, they buy relatively lavishly. They still talk about price and quality and durability, since these are regarded as sensible traditional values. At the same time, they know that other factors influence them, and they believe these to be legitimate influences. This point is worth some emphasis since there are many who disapprove of the fact that purchases may be made on grounds they think are insubstantial. The fact that people don't buy their furniture to last 20 years may be deplored as a sign of the lightheadedness of our times; on the other hand, such massive, stoutly made furniture may be dismissed from the home at the behest of other values in comfortable living and changing tastes.

Not only do people not want furniture such as grandmother used to

Reprinted by permission of the author and publisher from Lynn H. Stockman (ed.) Advancing Marketing Efficiency, *published by the American Marketing Association (1959), pp. 409–416.*

cherish; they also know that practical considerations can hardly determine their choice between Post or Kellogg, between Camels or Luckies, between Buick or Oldsmobile, between Arpege or Chanel. They know that package color and television commercials, newspaper and magazine ads incline them toward one preference or another—and when they can't really tell the difference among competitive brands of the same product, they don't believe that any of them should necessarily go out of business for being unable to distinguish his product.

At the heart of all this is the fact that the consumer is not as functionally oriented as he used to be, if he ever really was. The esthetic preferences that were there have changed somewhat—we no longer go in for stained glass lamps and antimacassars, although the latter were probably more attractive than transparent couch covers; and the diversity of choices that are now possible in the ways people can spend their money makes for a diversity of reasons for the choices. When people talk about the things they buy and why they buy them, they show a variety of logics. They refer to convenience, inadvertence, family pressures, other social pressures, complex economic reasonings, advertising, pretty colors, a wide range of feelings and wishes. They are trying to satisfy many aims and circumstances. The pleasure they gain from buying objects is ever more playful—less the question, do I need this? more the ideas, do I want it? do I like it? Answering these questions takes the definition of goods into new realms—at least new in the sense that they are studied more nowadays. The things people buy are seen to have personal and social meanings in addition to their functions. Modern goods are recognized as psychological things, as symbolic of personal attributes and goals, as symbolic of social patterns and strivings. In this sense, all commercial objects have a symbolic character, and making a purchase involves an assessment—implicit or explicit—of this symbolism, to decide whether or not it fits. Energy (and money) will be given when the symbols are appropriate ones, and denied or given parsimoniously when they are not. What determines their appropriateness?

A symbol is appropriate—and the product will be used and enjoyed when it joins with, meshes with, adds to, reinforces, the way the consumer thinks about himself. In the broadest sense, each person aims to enhance his sense of self, to behave in ways that are consistent with a set of ideas he has about the kind of person he is or wants to be. Prescott Lecky has written an interesting essay on how people behave in consistence with their self-concepts.[1] The variety of goods available permits more ways of living than was ever the case. Because of their symbolic nature, consumer goods can be chosen with less conflict or indecision than would otherwise be the case. Buridan's ass starved to death equi-

[1] Prescott Lecky, *Self-consistency* (New York: Island Press, 1945).

distant between two piles of attractive hay; he wouldn't have had the problem if one pile and been a bit more asinine—let's say—than the other. Our choices are made easier—either more routine, or more impulsive, seemingly—because one object is symbolically more harmonious to our goals, feelings, and self-definitions than is another. The difference may not be a large one, nor a very important one, in the manufacture or advertising of the products; but it may be big enough to dictate a constant direction of preference in the indulgence of one's point of view. There is then more well with the world when the bathroom tissue is pastel blue, the car a large one, the newspaper a tabloid size, the trousers with pleats, and so on. It becomes increasingly fashionable to be a connoisseur or gourmet of *some* kind, to consume with one or another standard of discrimination at work.

Research helps to identify the kinds of symbols utilized in the market, and the intensity with which they operate as determinants of purchases. Because some people don't like the idea that such things as feelings and symbols are influential in situations which they feel should be more purely utilitarian, they dislike research that investigates such ideas and meanings. Sometimes they even blame the research for having caused the phenomena, as though a microscope were responsible for the goodness or badness of the bacteria it examines.

In several years of research into the symbolic nature of products, or brands, of institutions and media of communication, much has been shown of the way consumers are able to gauge subtly and grossly the symbolic language of these objects, and to translate them into meanings for themselves. They understand that darker colors are symbolic of more "respectable" products, that pastel colors mean softness, youthfulness, femininity; that yellows and browns are manly, that red is exciting and provocative. They "know" that science means technical merits and an interest in quality and probably less enjoyment; that theatrical references imply glamour and the suspension of staid criteria. They think that Winston Churchill would be good testimony for cigars, whiskey, and books; and if they are very average consumers they are apt to miss (or ignore) the point of a Springmaid sheet ad altogether.

One of the most basic dimensions of symbolism is gender. Almost all societies make some differential disposition of the sexes, deciding who will do what; which objects will be reserved to men and which to women. They usually find it hard to evade thinking of inanimate things as male or female. Through such personalization, vessels tend to become feminine—and motherly if they are big enough. Men are challenged by the virgin forest which must be raped of its resources; they fall in love with their ships and cars, giving them women's names. And such places and objects are reserved for men, relatively speaking.

In America there has been complaint that some of this differentiation is fading, that women get more like men, and men shift to meet them, in a movement toward homogeneous togetherness. No doubt hunting and agricultural societies make sharper distinction between what is masculine and what is feminine. Still, products and behaviors tend to be more one or the other, and is minutely graded ways. Probably all cigarette brands could be placed on a continuum of degrees of gender, as one of their complex symbolic patternings. The same is true for musical compositions, and the recorded interpretations of any one of them, of cheeses and the brand versions of each kind.

These sexual definitions may seem absurd at times, and often are of modest influence in one or another choice. But they are at work and form a natural part of, for instance, the housewife's logic (and teaching) as she makes her selections in the food store and serves her family. She sums it up by thinking of what will please her husband's preference, what a growing boy should have, what is just right for a girl's delicate tastes. Since smoothness is generally understood to be more feminine, as foods go, it seems fitting that girls should prefer smooth peanut butter and boys the chunky. While the overlap is great, a cultivated society teaches such a discrimination, and the children, being attentive to their proper sex roles, learn it early. Families work busily at such indoctrination of symbolic appropriateness. One little 6-year-old boy protested in an interview how he had never liked peanut butter, but that his mother and sister had always insisted that he did, and now he loved it. Apparently a violent bias in favor of peanut butter is suitable to little boys, and may be taken as representing something of the rowdy boyishness of childhood, as against more restrained and orderly foods.

Similarly, in a recent study of a pair of cheese advertisements for a certain cheese, one wedge of it was shown in a setting of brown wooden cutting board, dark bread, and a glimpse of a chess game. The cheese wedge was depicted standing erect on its smallest base. Although no people were shown, consumers interpreted the ad as part of a masculine scene, men playing a game, being served a snack. The same cheese was also shown in a setting with lighter colors, a suggestion of a floral bowl, with the wedge lying flat on one of its longer sides. This was interpreted by consumers as a feminine scene, probably with ladies lunching in the vicinity. Each ad worked to convey a symbolic impression of the product, to modify or enhance the beliefs already held about it. Symbols of gender are among the most readily recognized. Most people are usually quite alert to whether something is addressed to them as a man or as a woman. Similarly, symbols of age are familiar. Teenagers are quite sensitive to communications which imply childishness. Presented with a layout showing a family going on a picnic, their reaction is apt to be, "Kid stuff." They are trying to break away from the family bosom. While they might actually enjoy a family picnic, the scene symbolizes restraint, being unable to get away to be with people their own age. Clothing is quite carefully graded in people's eyes; we normally judge within a few years' span whether some garment is fitted to the age of the wearer. Women are particularly astute (and cruel) in this, but men also observe when a pin-striped suit is too mature for one wearer, or when an outfit is too young for a man who should be acting his age.

Symbols of social participation are among the most dramatic factors in marketing. Most goods say something about the social world of the people who consume them. Debate goes on now whether automobiles are still related to people's social wishes or strivings, because some motivation research brought this rather well-known fact to the fore, and because some advertising has taken rather self-conscious account of it. This hardly changes the fact that cars say prominent things about their owners, and are likely to continue to do so. Like it or not, there are social class groupings formed by the ways people live, the attitudes they have, the acceptance and exclusiveness of their associations. The things they own are partly chosen to attest to their social positions, in one way or another. The possession of mink is hardly a matter of winter warmth alone, as all women know who wear mink with slacks while strolling at a beach resort. The social stature of mink—and its downgrading—leads us to marvel that it is now sold at Sears. But then, Sears has upgraded itself and become more middle class too. Shopping at Sears is symbolic of a certain chic among many middle class people who used to regard it as much more working class. Now they boast that Sears is especially suitable for certain kinds of merchandise, and their candor in saying they shop there is not matter-of-fact but is laughing, as if to point out that it is an amusing quirk in one's social behavior.

Membership in one social class or another tends to affect one's general outlook, modes of communication, concreteness of thinking and understanding.[2] Advertising often says different things to people of different social levels. A perfume ad showing an anthropological mask and swirling colors is likely to be incomprehensible to many working class women, whereas New Yorker readers will at least pretend they grasp the symbolism. On the other hand, working class women will accept a crowded, dark, screaming sale advertisement as meaning urgency and potential interest, while higher status women will ignore it as signaling inferiority. Sometimes, the symbolism becomes confined to a social class subgroup: even some upper middle class people aren't sure what is being said in various modern liquor ads with their groups of sinister men, their red shoes, and handsome males riding sidesaddle. Even while suspecting the symbolic language may be gibberish, they have

2 Leonard Schatzman and Anselm Strauss, "Social Class and Modes of Communication," *The American Journal of Sociology*, January, 1955, Vol. LX, No. 4.

some undercurrent of anxiety about not being part of the ingroup who use these "nonsense syllables" to tell each other about vodka. Since, as Susanne Langer discusses so well, symbolizing is a natural human function, it is not reserved to such formal categories as gender, age, and social status.[3] Any given complex of acts, gestures, movements, pictures, words, will signify much to the consumer. From commercials and ads, from television shows and editorial materials, the viewer or reader concludes about the meanings being offered. These meanings may correspond to the advertiser's intention—although often they are separate from, in addition to, or even contrary to his aim. A striking instance of such contradictory communication was an advertisement with a headline claiming the product was worth the 1¢ more that it cost when compared to its competitors. Housewives interpreted this claim as a sign of cheapness; they needed only to see the 1¢ in the headline to believe it was "one of those penny deals." Merely the idea of talking about 1¢ suggested cheapening, even to those readers who understood literally what was said. The literal aim had been to refer to the greater worth of the product; the symbolic means used were poor.

⟳ As consumers, we buy our way through a welter of symbols reflecting taste patterns, and the multitudes of human qualities we want to attach to ourselves. Just to refer to some of these symbolic poles brings images to our minds of "what that's like." The Ivy League cluster of symbols organizes purchases in one direction; being a subordinate is a broad identification, but it starts one's purchasing ideas moving in certain lines. Name your own suburb, and they leap into rather sharp focus. Neighbors are quite acute judges of the symbolic significance of how money is spent; they are quick to interpret the appropriateness of your spending pattern for the community, the kind of people you are, making reasonable or unreasonable deductions from books, liquor, power mowers, cars, and the gifts your children give at birthday parties.

Some objects we buy symbolize such personal qualities as self-control, others expose our self-indulgence. We reason in these directions about people who drink and smoke or who don't—and such reasoning will play a role in our choices of doing one or the other. A hard mattress is readily justified on pragmatic grounds of health, sound sleep, and the like; but people recognize the austere self-denial at work that will also strengthen the character. Then again, soft drinks may quench thirst, but people know that they are also buying an indulgent moment, a bit of ease, a lowering of adult restraints.

An outstanding dimension of symbolic guidance to consumers is that of conventionality versus self-expression. Some purchases are very

[3] Susanne K. Langer, *Philosophy in a New Key* (The New American Library of World Literature, Inc., New York, 1942).

conventional—a quart of milk, for instance. Others are conventional, but allow room for individuality—dishes, cups, silverware, let's say. Books become quite personal purchases, by and large. So, no one thinks much if you have milk on your table; (at least, they reason only generally about children)—it's different when you order a glass of milk at a businessmen's lunch. They also expect dishes, but may acquire the taste demonstrated by the pattern. They will respect you personally for *Dr. Zhivago* on the coffee table, and perhaps raise an eyebrow at *Lolita*.

A whole treatise could be written on the symbolic dimension of formality-informality. A great many of our decisions to buy take into account the degree of formal or informal implication of the object. Housewives are constantly gauging the place of hot dogs, the gifts they are giving, the tablecloth they plan to use, with an eye to how informal things are or they want them to be. The movement toward informality has been a fundamental one in recent years, governing the emphasis on casualness in clothes, backyard and buffet meals, staying at motels, and bright colors—with some current overtone of reaction to this and seeking of contrast again in the direction of more graciousness in living, a new interest in the elegance of a black car, a wish for homes with dining rooms, and greater individual privacy.

As this indicates, among all the symbols around us, bidding for our buying attention and energy, there are general trends that seem to fit the spirit of the time more aptly. Every so often there comes along a new symbol, one which makes a leap from the past into the present and has power because it captures the spirit of the present and makes other ongoing symbols old-fashioned. The Pepsi-Cola girl was a symbol of this sort. She had precursors, of course, but she distinctly and prominently signified a modern phantasy and established an advertising style, one somewhat removed from the Clabber girl.

I have touched on only a few of the varieties of symbols encountered in the identification of goods in the marketplace, especially as these become part of the individual identities of consumers. The topic is as ramified as our daily lives and behaviors, and everyone handles symbols of these sorts with relative little strain. Nevertheless, the interactions that go on around the symbols by which we buy are likely to involve the difficulties of all communications, and warrant study. Talking about symbols often involves discussion of much that is obvious or easily apparent—and most of us think we say what we mean. But much marketing and advertising thinking goes on with little actual regard given to the kinds of symbolic meanings that are so intrinsic to consumer viewpoints. Greater attention to these modes of thought will give marketing management and research increased vitality, adding to their own practical and symbolic merits.

RETROSPECTIVE COMMENT

The article "Symbols By Which We Buy" was also printed in the *Harvard Business Review* (July–August, 1959) under the title, "Symbols for Sale," and was subsequently anthologized in several marketing collections of readings. Interest in the topic was part of the growing attention given in the late 1940's and 1950's by people in the marketing field to ideas and methods of the behavioral sciences. Elaborating on the concept of product and brand imagery, the purpose of the article was to emphasize and discuss the subjective import of what people buy, in its symbolic variety, compared to the traditional weight placed on practical product features and economic motives.

Re-reading the article prompts these thoughts. To enhance the timeliness of the subject, great stress was placed on the rising incomes of the period and the consequent role of increased choices available to consumers. This argument implies that goods and services take on symbolic significance only when people are affluent, that something called symbolism is added on after more basic goals are met, *a la* the Maslow hierarchy of needs. In actuality, as was noted, the symbolic issues are always present, even during times of recession, energy crisis, etc., affecting people's perceptions of themselves, their situations, and the things they buy. That is,

1. Symbolizing is a basic mode of intellectual functioning.
2. Recession affects people unevenly, so that adaptations are made with reference to relative economic status and the perceived appropriateness of public market actions.
3. Even people at a poverty level are cognizant of the personal and social implications of their marketing behavior and are guided by them.

In less affluent times and places, choices do constrict, such as fewer color variations in some objects, fewer models in a product line, and less discretion in how one can spend money, with changes in emphasis on what kinds of symbols to choose. Small cars attest to one's recognition of energy problems and economic virtue; and Cadillac introduces the nuance of a smaller expensive car represented by the Seville. The various distinctions of sex, age, and social class are still at work, shifting content somewhat as fashions change in how to be female, young, or upper class. The changes in the symbols of everyday life are evident in a few outdated references in the article. *Look* magazine died, *Lolita* was replaced by *Fear of Flying*, and the "recent Pepsi-Cola Girl" was supplanted by the Pepsi Generation and other campaigns.

More generally, analysis of symbolism remains a neglected aspect of marketing study. By and large relegated to the esoteric mysteries of anthropology or a blaming of Freud or Jung, symbolism is just barely touched on in some marketing textbooks as important to the sphere of communications. Some look on it as a temporary byproduct of the 1950's. Occasionally an article in the *Journal of Marketing* takes some relatively explicit account of symbolism as a factor in marketing behavior (e.g., Edward M. Tauber's "Why Do People Shop?" *Journal of Marketing*, October, 1972, pp. 46–49). But the *Journal of Marketing Research* suggests little academic study in this direction. In private marketing research studies and some advertising agency work, one can find a livelier awareness and use of the richness and complexities of symbolic thinking. Perhaps this situation symbolizes the fact that the field of marketing is still young, with many potential areas for developing further insight.—*Sidney J. Levy*

2. Projective Techniques in Marketing Research

Mason Haire

It is a well accepted maxim in merchandizing that, in many areas, we are selling the sizzle rather than the steak. Our market research techniques, however, in many of these same areas, are directed toward the steak. The sizzle is the subjective reaction of the consumer; the steak the objective characteristics of the product. The consumer's behavior will be based on the former rather than the latter set of characteristics. How can we come to know them better?

When we approach a consumer directly with questions about his reaction to a product we often get false and misleading answers to our questions. Very often this is because the question which we heard ourselves ask was not the one (or not the only one) that the respondent heard. For example: A brewery made two kinds of beer. To guide their merchandizing techniques they wanted to know what kind of people drank each kind, and particularly, what differences there were between the two groups of consumers. A survey was conducted which led up to the questions "Do you drink ——— beer?" (If *yes*) "Do you drink the *Light* or *Regular*?" (These were the two trade names under which the company marketed.) After identifying the consumers of each product it was possible to find out about the characteristics of each group so that appropriate appeals could be used, media chosen, etc.

An interesting anomaly appeared in the survey data, however. The interviewing showed (on a reliable sample) that consumers drank *Light* over *Regular* in the ratio of 3 to 1. The company had been producing and selling Regular over Light for some time in a ratio of 9 to 1. Clearly, the attempt to identify characteristics of the two kinds was a failure. What made them miss so far?

When we say "Do you drink *Light* or *Regular*?" we are at once asking which brand is used, but also, to some extent, saying "Do you drink the regular run-of-the-mill product or do you drink the one that is more refined and shows more discrimination and taste?" The preponderance of "Light" undoubtedly flows from this kind of distortion.

Reprinted from the Journal of Marketing, *published by the American Marketing Association (April 1950), pp. 649–656.*

When we ask questions of this sort about the product we are very often asking also about the respondent. Not only do we say "What is ———— product like?" but, indirectly "What are *you* like?" Our responses are often made up of both elements inextricably interwoven. The answers to the second question will carry clichés and stereotypes, blocks, inhibitions, and distortions, whenever we approach an area that challenges the person's idea of himself.

There are many things that we need to know about a consumer's reaction to a product that he can not tell us because they are to some extent socially unacceptable. For instance, the snob appeal of a product vitally influences its sale, but it is a thing that the consumer will not like to discuss explicitly. In other cases the consumer is influenced by motives of which he is, perhaps, vaguely aware, but which he finds difficult to put into words. The interviewer-respondent relationship puts a good deal of pressure on him to reply and to make sense in his reply. Consequently, he gives us stereotypical responses that use clichés which are commonly acceptable but do not necessarily represent the true motives. Many of our motives do not, in fact, "make sense," and are not logical. The question-answer relation demands sense above all. If the response does not represent the true state of affairs the interviewer will never know it. He will go away. If it does not make sense it may represent the truth, but the respondent will feel like a fool and the interviewer will not go away. Much better produce a cliché and be rid of him.

THE NATURE OF PROJECTIVE TESTS

Still other kinds of motives exist of which the respondent may not be explicitly conscious himself. The product may be seen by him as related to things or people or values in his life, or as having a certain role in the scheme of things, and yet he may be quite unable, in response to a direct question, to describe these aspects of the object. Nevertheless, these characteristics may be of great importance as motives. How can we get at them?

Clinical psychologists have long been faced with a parallel set of problems. It is quite usual for a patient to be unable or unwilling to tell the therapist directly what kinds of things are stirring in his motivational pattern. Information about these drives are of vital importance to the process of cure, so a good deal of research has been directed towards the development of techniques to identify and define them. The development of projective techniques as diagnostic tools has provided one of the most useful means to uncover such motivations, and the market researcher can well afford to borrow their essentials from the therapist.

Basically, a projective test involves presenting the subject with an ambiguous stimulus—one that does not quite make sense in itself—and asking him to make sense of it. The theory is that in order to make it make sense he will have to add to it—to fill out the picture—and in so doing he projects part of himself into it. Since we know what was in the original stimulus we can quite easily identify the parts that were added, and, in this way, painlessly obtain information about the person.

Examples of these tests come readily to hand. Nearly everyone is familiar with the Rorschach Test, in which a subject is shown a series of ink-blots and asked to tell what they look like. Here the stimulus is incomplete in itself, and the interpretation supplied by the patient provides useful information. This test yields fairly general answers about the personality, however, and often we would like to narrow down the area in which the patient is supplying information.

The Thematic Apperception Test offers a good example of this function. Let us suppose that with a particular patient we have reason to suppose that his relation to figures of authority is crucial to his therapeutic problem. We can give him a series of pictures where people are shown, but where the relationship of authority or the characteristics of the authoritarian figure are not complete. He is asked to tell a story about each picture. If in each story the subordinate finally kills the figure of authority we have certain kinds of knowledge; if, on the other hand, he always builds the story so the subordinate figure achieves a secure and comfortable dependence, we have quite different information. It is often quite impossible to get the subject to tell us these things directly. Either he cannot or will not do so. Indirectly, however, he will tell us how he sees authority. Can we get him, similarly, to tell us how a product looks to him in his private view of the world?

APPLICATION OF PROJECTIVE TEST IN MARKET RESEARCH

Let us look at an example of this kind of thing in market research. For the purposes of experiment a conventional survey was made of attitudes toward Nescafé, an instant coffee. The questionnaire included the questions "Do you use instant coffee?" (If *No*) "What do you dislike about it?" The bulk of the unfavorable responses fell into the general area "I don't like the flavor." This is such an easy answer to a complex question that one may suspect it is a stereotype, which at once gives a sensible response to get rid of the interviewer and conceals other motives. How can we get behind this facade?

In this case an indirect approach was used. Two shopping lists were prepared. They were identical in all respects, except that one list specified Nescafé and one Maxwell House Coffee. They were administered to alternate subjects, with no subject knowing of the existence of the other list. The instructions were "Read the shopping list below. Try to project yourself into the situation as far as possible until you can more or less characterize the woman who bought the groceries. Then write a brief description of her personality and character. Wherever possible indicate what factors influenced your judgment."

Shopping List I
Pound and a half of hamburger
2 loaves Wonder bread
bunch of carrots
1 can Rumford's Baking Powder
Nescafé instant coffee
2 cans Del Monte peaches
5 lbs. potatoes

Shopping List II
Pound and a half of hamburger
2 loaves Wonder bread
bunch of carrots
1 can Rumford's Baking Powder
1 lb. Maxwell House Coffee (Drip Ground)
2 cans Del Monte peaches
5 lbs. potatoes

Fifty people responded to each of the two shopping lists given above. The responses to these shopping lists provided some very interesting material. The following main characteristics of their descriptions can be given:

1. 48 per cent of the people described the woman who bought Nescafé as lazy; 4 per cent described the woman who bought Maxwell House as lazy.

2. 48 per cent of the people described the woman who bought Nescafé as failing to plan household purchases and schedules well; 12 per cent described the woman who bought Maxwell House this way.

3. 4 per cent described the Nescafé woman as thrifty; 16 per cent described the Maxwell House woman as thrifty. 12 per cent described the Nescafé woman as spendthrift; 0 per cent described the Maxwell House woman this way.

4. 16 per cent described the Nescafé woman as not a good wife; 0 per cent described the Maxwell House woman this way. 4 per cent described the Nescafé woman as a good wife; 16 per cent described the Maxwell House woman as a good wife.

A clear picture begins to form here. Instant coffee represents a departure from "home-made" coffee, and the traditions with respect to caring for one's family. Coffee-making is taken seriously, with vigorous proponents for laborious drip and filter-paper methods, firm believers in coffee boiled in a battered sauce pan, and the like. Coffee drinking is a form of intimacy and relaxation that gives it a special character.

On the one hand, coffee making is an art. It is quite common to hear a woman say, "I can't seem to make good coffee," in the same way that one might say, "I can't learn to play the violin." It is acceptable to confess this inadequacy, for making coffee well is a mysterious touch that belongs, in a shadowy tradition, to the plump, aproned figure who is a little lost outside her kitchen but who has a sure sense in it and among its tools.

On the other hand, coffee has a peculiar role in relation to the household and the home-and-family character. We may well have a picture, in the shadowy past, of a big black range that is always hot with baking and cooking, and has a big enamelled pot of coffee warming at the back. When a neighbor drops in during the morning, a cup of coffee is a medium of hospitality that does somewhat the same thing as cocktails in the later afternoon, but does it in a broader sphere.

These are real and important aspects of coffee. They are not physical characteristics of the product, but they are real values in the consumer's life, and they influence his purchasing. We need to know and assess them. The "labor-saving" aspect of instant coffee, far from being an asset, may be a liability in that it violates these traditions. How often have we heard a wife respond to "This cake is delicious!" with a pretty blush and "Thank you—I made it with such and such a prepared cake mix." This response is so invariable as to seem almost compulsive. It is almost unthinkable to anticipate a reply "Thank you, I made it with Pillsbury's flour, Fleischman's yeast, and Borden's milk." Here the specifications are unnecessary. All that is relevant is the implied "I made it"—the art and the credit are carried directly by the verb that covers the process of mixing and processing the ingredients. In ready-mixed foods there seems to be a compulsive drive to refuse credit for the product, because the accomplishment is not the housewife's but the company's.

In this experiment, as a penalty for using "synthetics" the woman who buys Nescafé pays the price of being seen as lazy, spendthrift, a poor wife, and as failing to plan well for her family. The people who rejected instant coffee in the original direct question blamed its flavor. We may well wonder if their dislike of instant coffee was not to a large extent occasioned by a fear of being seen by one's self and others in the role they projected onto the Nescafé woman in the description. When asked directly, however, it is difficult to respond with this. One can not say, "I don't use Nescafé because people will think I am lazy and not a good wife." Yet we know from these data that the feeling regarding laziness and shiftlessness was there. Later studies (reported below) showed that it determined buying habits, and that something could be done about it.

ANALYSIS OF RESPONSES

Some examples of the type of response received will show the kind of material obtained and how it may be analyzed. Three examples of each group are given below.

DESCRIPTIONS OF A WOMAN WHO BOUGHT, AMONG OTHER THINGS, MAXWELL HOUSE COFFEE

I'd say she was a practical, frugal woman. She bought too many potatoes. She must like to cook and bake as she included baking powder. She must not care much about her figure as she does not discriminate about the food she buys.

The woman is quite influenced by advertising as signified by the specific name brands on her shopping list. She probably is quite set in her ways and accepts no substitutes.

I have been able to observe several hundred women shoppers who have made very similar purchases to that listed above, and the only clue that I can detect that may have some bearing on her personality is the Del Monte peaches. This item when purchased singly along with the other more staple foods indicates that she may be anxious to please either herself or members of her family with a "treat." She is probably a thrifty, sensible housewife.

DESCRIPTIONS OF A WOMAN WHO BOUGHT, AMONG OTHER THINGS, NESCAFÉ INSTANT COFFEE

This woman appears to be either single or living alone. I would guess that she had an office job. Apparently, she likes to sleep late in the morning, basing my assumption on what she bought such as Instant Coffee which can be made in a hurry. She probably also has can [sic] peaches for breakfast, cans being easy to open. Assuming that she is just average, as opposed to those dazzling natural beauties who do not need much time to make up, she must appear rather sloppy, taking little time to make up in the morning. She is also used to eating supper out, too. Perhaps alone rather than with an escort. An old maid probably.

She seems to be lazy, because of her purchases of canned peaches and instant coffee. She doesn't seem to think, because she bought two loaves of bread, and then baking powder, unless she's thinking of making cake. She probably just got married.

I think the woman is the type who never thinks ahead very far—the type who always sends Junior to the store to buy one item at a time. Also she is fundamentally lazy. All the items, with possible exception of the Rumford's, are easily prepared items. The girl may be an office girl who is just living from one day to the next in a sort of haphazard sort of life.

As we read these complete responses we begin to get a feeling for the picture that is created by Nescafé. It is particularly interesting to notice that the Nescafé woman is protected, to some extent, from the opprobrium of being lazy and haphazard by being seen as a single "office girl"—a role that relieves one from guilt for not being interested in the home and food preparation.

The references to peaches are significant. In one case (Maxwell House) they are singled out as a sign that the woman is thoughtfully preparing a "treat" for her family. On the other hand, when the Nescafé woman buys them it is evidence that she is lazy, since their "canned" character is seen as central.

In terms of the sort of results presented above, it may be useful to demonstrate the way these stories are coded. The following items are extracted from the six stories quoted:

Maxwell House	*Nescafé*
1. practical	1. single
frugal	office girl
likes to cook	sloppy
2. influenced by advertising	old maid
set in her ways	2. lazy
3. interested in family	does not plan
thrifty	newlywed
sensible	3. lazy
	does not plan
	office girl

Items such as these are culled from each of the stories. Little by little categories are shaped by the content of the stories themselves. In this way the respondent furnishes the dimensions of analysis as well as the scale values on these dimensions.

SECOND TEST

It is possible to wonder whether it is true that the opprobrium that is heaped on the Nescafé woman comes from her use of a device that represents a short-cut and labor-saver in an area where she is expected to embrace painstaking time-consuming work in a ritualistic way. To test this a variation was introduced into the shopping lists. In a second experiment one hundred and fifty housewives were tested with the form given above, but a sample was added to this group which responded to a slightly different form. If we assume that the rejection in the first experiment came from the presence of a feeling about synthetic shortcuts we might assume also that the addition of one more shortcut to both lists would bring the Maxwell House woman more into

Table 2.1. PERSONALITY CHARACTERISTICS ASCRIBED TO USERS OF PREPARED FOODS

If They Use	No Prepared Food (Maxwell House alone)		Nescafé (alone)		Maxwell House (plus Pie Mix)		Nescafé (plus Pie Mix)	
They are seen as:	Num-ber	Per Cent	Num-ber	Per Cent	Num-ber	Per Cent	Num-ber	Per Cent
Not Economical	12	17	24	32	6	30	7	35
Lazy	8	11	46	62	5	25	8	40
Poor Personality and Appearance	28	39	39	53	7	35	8	40
N-	72		74		20		20	

line with the Nescafé woman, since the former would now have the same guilt that the Nescafé woman originally had, while the Nescafé woman, already convicted of evading her duties, would be little further injured.

In order to accomplish this a second prepared food was added to both lists. Immediately after the coffee in both lists the fictitious item, "Blueberry Fill Pie Mix" was added. The results are shown in the accompanying table.

It will be seen immediately, in the first two columns, that the group to whom the original form of the list were given showed the same kind of difference as reported above in their estimates of the two women. The group with an additional prepared food, however, brought the Maxwell Coffee woman down until she is virtually undistinguishable from the Nescafé. There seems to be little doubt but that the prepared-food-character, and the stigma of avoiding housewifely duties is responsible for the projected personality characteristics.

RELATION TO PURCHASING

It is still relevant to ask whether the existence of these feelings in a potential consumer is related to purchasing. It is hypothesized that these personality descriptions provide an opportunity for the consumer to project hopes and fears and anxieties that are relevant to the way the product is seen, and that they represent important parts of her motivation in buying or not buying. To test this hypothesis, a small sample of fifty housewives, comparable in every way to the group just referred to, was given the original form of the shopping list (Nescafé only). In addition to obtaining the personality description, the inter-

Table 2.2.

The woman who buys Nescafé is seen as:	By Women Who Had Instant Coffee in the House (N = 32)		By Women Who Did Not Have Instant Coffee in the House (N = 18)	
	Number	Per Cent	Number	Per Cent
Economical **	22	70	5	28
Not economical	0	0	2	11
Can not cook or does not like to **	5	16	10	55
Plans balanced meals *	9	29	2	11
Good housewife, plans well, cares about family **	9	29	0	0
Poor housewife, does not plan well, does not care about family *	5	16	7	39
Lazy *	6	19	7	39

*A single asterisk indicates that differences this great would be observed only 5 times out of 100 in repeated samplings of a population whose true difference is zero.

**A double asterisk indicates that the chances are 1 in 100. We are justified in rejecting the hypothesis that there is no difference between the groups.

viewer, on a pretext, obtained permission to look at her pantry shelves and determine personally whether or not she had instant coffee of any brand. The results of this investigation are shown in the accompanying table.

The trend of these data shows conclusively that if a respondent sees the woman who buys Nescafé as having undesirable traits, she is not likely to buy instant coffee herself. The projected unacceptable characteristics go with failure to buy, and it does not seem unwarranted to assume that the association is causal.

Furthermore, these projected traits are, to some extent, additive. For instance, if a respondent describes the woman as having one bad trait only, she is about twice as likely not to have instant coffee. However, if she sees her as having two bad traits, and no good ones (e.g., lazy, can not cook), she is about three times as likely not to have instant coffee as she is to have it. On the other hand, if she sees her as having two good traits (e.g., economical, cares for family), she is about six times as likely to have it as not.

It was pointed out earlier that some women felt it necessary to "excuse" the woman who bought Nescafé by suggesting that she lived alone and hence could not be expected to be interested in cooking, or that she had a job and did not have time to shop better. Women who had instant coffee in the house found excuses almost twice as often as those who did not use instant coffee (12 out of 32, or 42 per cent, against 4 out of 18, or 22 per cent). These "excuses" are vitally important for merchandizing. The need for an excuse shows there is a barrier to buying in the consumer's mind. The presence of excuses shows that there is a way around the barrier. The content of the excuses themselves provides valuable clues for directing appeals toward reducing buying resistance.

CONCLUSION

There seems to be no question that in the experimental situation described here:

1. Motives exist which are below the level of verbalization because they are socially unacceptable, difficult to verbalize cogently, or unrecognized.

2. These motives are intimately related to the decision to purchase or not to purchase, and

3. It is possible to identify and assess such motives by approaching them indirectly.

Two important general points come out of the work reported. The first is in the statement of the problem. It is necessary for us to see a product in terms of a set of characteristics and attributes which are part of the consumer's "private world," and as such may have no simple relationship to characteristics of the object in the "real" world. Each of us lives in a world which is composed of more than physical things and people. It is made up of goals, paths to goals, barriers, threats, and the like, and an individual's behavior is oriented with respect to these characteristics as much as to the "objective" ones. In the area of merchandizing, a product's character of being seen as a path to a goal is usually very much more important as a determinant of purchasing than its physical dimensions. We have taken advantage of these qualities in advertising and merchandizing for a long time by an intuitive sort of "playing-by-ear" on the subjective aspects of products. It is time for a systematic attack on the problem of the phenomenological description of objects. What kinds of dimensions are relevant to this world of goals and paths and barriers? What kind of terms will fit the phenomenological characteristics of an object in the same sense that the centimetre-gram-second system fits its physical dimensions? We need to know the answers to such questions, and the psychological definitions of valued objects.

The second general point is the methodological one that it is possible, by using appropriate techniques, to find out from the respondent what the phenomenological characteristics of various objects may be. By and large, a direct approach to this problem in terms of straightforward questions will not yield satisfactory answers. It is possible, however, by the use of indirect techniques, to get the consumer to provide, quite unselfconsciously, a description of the value-character of objects in his environment.

RETROSPECTIVE COMMENT

In his famous study, Professor Haire *stressed* two points: the "sizzle" —the role of phenomenological attributes in consumer choice—and the need for consumer researchers to use indirect techniques to discover subjectively-defined product attributes. He *demonstrated* these points in the context of attitudes toward instant coffee.

Few consumer researchers would quibble with Haire's first point. People do tend to react to things as they view them and their views may not perfectly correspond to objectively-defined reality. Today, one of the most accelerating fashions in consumer research is the use of the highly cognitive, information processing approach to discover consumers' views of products and environments and how they integrate and use these views in an ongoing, dynamic decision-making process.

Haire's second point is equivocable. While indirect methods such as projective techniques have proved useful in eliciting from consumers the character of a product, so have direct methods. For instance, another instant coffee study showed that direct techniques could reveal findings similar to those found by Haire [5]. Today, both direct and indirect techniques are in constant use by consumer researchers.

Not surprisingly, the contextual findings of Haire's study—attitudes toward instant coffee and its users—have changed. A number of replications in the U.S. and in Norway have shown that the instant coffee user is no longer seen as being a lazy spendthrift or a poor wife who fails to plan well for her family; rather she may be viewed as more typical than the user of drip-grind coffee [1,2,3,4]. The shift in contextual findings over a twenty-five-year period can be understood in terms of the compatibility of the product with the times. Convenience foods enjoy widespread acceptance today—instant coffee is compatible with today's life styles whereas it was incompatible during the late 1940's when Haire conducted his study.

Thus, in offering a contemporary perspective, I would allow that while his contextual findings have changed, his general approach still is applicable to consumer research—it isn't the only game in town, however.—*Dr. Fred D. Reynolds*, Associate Professor of Marketing, University of Georgia

REFERENCES

ARNDT, JOHAN. Haire's Shopping List Revisited. *Journal of Advertising Research*, Vol. 13 (October 1973), 57–61.

HILL, CONRAD R. Haire's Classic Instant Coffee Study—18 Years Later. *Journalism Quarterly*, Vol. 45 (1968), 466–72.

SHETH, JAGDISH N. Projective Attitudes Toward Instant Coffee in Late Sixties. *Markedskommunikasjon*, Vol. 8, (1971), 73–79.

WEBSTER, FREDERICK E., JR., and Fredrick von Pechmann. A Replication of the "Shopping List" Study. *Journal of Marketing*, Vol. 34 (April 1970), 61–63.

WESTFIELD, R. L., Harper W. Boyd, Jr., and Donald T. Campbell. The Use of Structured Techniques in Motivation Research. *Journal of Marketing*, Vol. 22 (October 1957), 134–39.

3. Rational Behavior and Economic Behavior

George Katona

While attempts to penetrate the boundary lines between psychology and sociology have been rather frequent during the last few decades, psychologists have paid little attention to the problems with which another sister discipline, economics, is concerned. One purpose of this paper is to arouse interest among psychologists in studies of economic behavior. For that purpose it will be shown that psychological principles may be of great value in clarifying basic questions of economics and that the psychology of habit formation, of motivation, and of group belonging may profit from studies of economic behavior.

A variety of significant problems, such as those of the business cycle or inflation, of consumer saving or business investment, could be chosen for the purpose of such demonstration. This paper, however, will be concerned with the most fundamental assumption of economics, the principle of rationality. In order to clarify the problems involved in this principle, which have been neglected by contemporary psychologists, it will be necessary to contrast the most common forms of methodology in psychology and to discuss the role of empirical research in the social sciences.

THEORY AND HYPOTHESES

Economic theory represents one of the oldest and most elaborate theoretical structures in the social sciences. However, dissatisfaction with the achievements and uses of economic theory has grown considerably during the past few decades on the part of economists who are interested in what actually goes on in economic life. And yet leading sociologists and psychologists have recently declared "Economics is today,

George Katona, "Rational Behavior and Economic Behavior," Psychological Review, *Vol. 60 (1953), pp. 307–318. Copyright 1953 by the American Psychological Association, and reproduced by permission.*

in a theoretical sense, probably the most highly elaborated, sophisticated, and refined of the disciplines dealing with action."[1]

To understand the scientific approach of economic theorists, we may divide them into two groups. Some develop an a priori system from which they deduce propositions about how people *should* act under certain assumptions. Assuming that the sole aim of businessmen is profit maximization, these theorists deduce propositions about marginal revenues and marginal costs, for example, that are not meant to be suited for testing. In developing formal logics of economic action, one of the main considerations is elegance of the deductive system, based on the law of parsimony. A wide gap separates these theorists from economic research of an empirical-statistical type which registers what they call aberrations or deviations, due to human frailty, from the norm set by theory.

A second group of economic theorists adheres to the proposition that it is the main purpose of theory to provide hypotheses that can be tested. This group acknowledges that prediction of future events represents the most stringent test of theory. They argue, however, that reality is so complex that it is necessary to begin with simplified propositions and models which are known to be unreal and not testable.[2] Basic among these propositions are the following three which traditionally have served to characterize the economic man or the rational man:

1. The principle of complete information and foresight. Economic conditions—demand, supply, price, etc.—are not only given but also known to the rational man. This applies as well to future conditions about which there exists no uncertainty, so that rational choice can always be made. (In place of the assumption of certainty of future developments, we find nowadays more frequently the assumption that risks prevail but the probability of occurrence of different alternatives is known; this does not constitute a basic difference.)

---

[1] The quotation is from an introductory general statement signed by T. Parsons, E. A. Shils, G. W. Allport, C. Kluckhohn, H. A. Murray, R. R. Sears, R. C. Sheldon, S. A. Stouffer, and E. C. Tolman. The term "action" is meant to be synonymous with "behavior."

[2] A variety of methods used in economic research differ, of course, from those employed by the two groups of economic theorists. Some research is motivated by dissatisfaction with the traditional economic theory; some is grounded in a systematization greatly different from traditional theory (the most important example of such systematization is national income accounting); some research is not clearly based on any theory; finally, some research has great affinity with psychological and sociological studies.

2. The principle of complete mobility. There are no institutional or psychological factors which make it impossible, or expensive, or slow, to translate the rational choice into action.

3. The principle of pure competition. Individual action has no great influence on prices because each man's choice is independent from any other person's choice and because there are no "large" sellers or buyers. Action is the result of individual choice and is not group-determined.

Economic theory is developed first under these assumptions. The theorists then introduce changes in the assumptions so that the theory may approach reality. One such step consists, for instance, of introducing large-scale producers, monopolists, and oligopolists, another of introducing time lags, and still another of introducing uncertainty about the probability distribution of future events. The question raised in each case is this: Which of the original propositions need to be changed, and in what way, in view of the new assumptions?

The fact that up to now the procedure of gradual approximation to reality has not been completely successful does not invalidate the method. It must also be acknowledged that propositions were frequently derived from unrealistic economic models which were susceptible to testing and stimulated empirical research. In this paper we shall point to a great drawback of this method of starting out with a simplified a priori system and making it gradually more complex and more real—by proceeding in this way one tends to lose sight of important problems and to disregard them.

The methods most commonly used in psychology may appear at first sight to be quite similar to the methods of economics which have just been described. Psychologists often start with casual observations, derive from them hypotheses, test those through more systematic observations, reformulate and revise their hypotheses accordingly, and test them again. The process of hypotheses-observations-hypotheses-observations often goes on with no end in sight. Differences from the approach of economic theory may be found in the absence in psychological research of detailed systematic elaboration prior to any observation. Also, in psychological research, findings and generalizations in one field of behavior are often considered as hypotheses in another field of behavior. Accordingly, in analyzing economic behavior[3] and trying to understand rationality, psychologists can draw on (a) the theory of learning and thinking, (b) the theory of group belonging, and (c) the theory of motivation. This will be done in this paper.

[3] The expression "economic behavior" is used in this paper to mean behavior concerning economic matters (spending, saving, investing, pricing, etc.). Some economic theorists use the expression to mean the behavior of the "economic man," that is, the behavior postulated in their theory of rationality.

HABITUAL BEHAVIOR AND GENUINE DECISION MAKING

In trying to give noneconomic examples of "rational calculus," economic theorists have often referred to gambling. From some textbooks one might conclude that the most rational place in the world is the Casino in Monte Carlo where odds and probabilities can be calculated exactly. In contrast, some mathematicians and psychologists have considered scientific discovery and the thought processes of scientists as the best examples of rational or intelligent behavior.[4] An inquiry about the possible contributions of psychology to the analysis of rationality may then begin with a formulation of the differences between (a) associative learning and habit formation and (b) problem solving and thinking.

The basic principle of the first form of behavior is repetition. Here the argument of Guthrie holds: "The most certain and dependable information concerning what a man will do in any situation is information concerning what he did in that situation on its last occurrence." This form of behavior depends upon the frequency of repetition as well as on its recency and on the success of past performances. The origins of habit formation have been demonstrated by experiments about learning nonsense syllables, lists of words, mazes, and conditioned responses. Habits thus formed are to some extent automatic and inflexible.

In contrast, problem-solving behavior has been characterized by the arousal of a problem or question, by deliberation that involves reorganization and "direction," by understanding of the requirements of the situation, by weighing of alternatives and taking their consequences into consideration and, finally, by choosing among alternative courses of action.[5] Scientific discovery is not the only example of such procedures; they have been demonstrated in the psychological laboratory as well as in a variety of real-life situations. Problem solving results in action which is new rather than repetitive; the actor may have never behaved in the same way before and may not have learned of any others having behaved in the same way.

---

[4] Reference should be made first of all to Max Wertheimer who in his book *Productive Thinking* (17) uses the terms "sensible" and "intelligent" rather than "rational." Since we are mainly interested here in deriving conclusions from the psycholology of thinking, the discussion of psychological principles will be kept extremely brief (see 6 and 8, Chap. 3, 4).

[5] Cf. the following statement by a leading psychoanalyst: "Rational behavior is behavior that is effectively guided by an understanding of the situation to which one is reacting" (3, p. 16). French adds two steps that follow the choice between alternative goals, namely, commitment to a goal and commitment to a plan to reach a goal.

Some of the above terms, defined and analyzed by psychologists, are also being used by economists in their discussion of rational behavior. In discussing, for example, a manufacturer's choice between erecting or not erecting a new factory, or raising or not raising his prices or output, reference is usually made to deliberation and to taking the consequences of alternative choices into consideration. Nevertheless, it is not justified to identify problem-solving behavior with rational behavior. From the point of view of an outside observer, habitual behavior may prove to be fully rational or the most appropriate way of action under certain circumstances. All that is claimed here is that the analysis of two forms of behavior—habitual versus genuine decision making—may serve to clarify problems of rationality. We shall proceed therefore by deriving six propositions from the psychological principles. To some extent, or in certain fields of behavior, these are findings or empirical generalizations; to some extent, or in other fields of behavior, they are hypotheses.

1. Problem-solving behavior is a relatively rare occurrence. It would be incorrect to assume that everyday behavior consistently manifests such features as arousal of a problem, deliberation, or taking consequences of the action into consideration. Behavior which does not manifest these characteristics predominates in everyday life and in economic activities as well.

2. The main alternative to problem-solving behavior is not whimsical or impulsive behavior (which was considered the major example of "irrational" behavior by nineteenth century philosophers). When genuine decision making does not take place, habitual behavior is the most usual occurrence: people act as they have acted before under similar circumstances, without deliberating and choosing.

3. Problem-solving behavior is recognized most commonly as a deviation from habitual behavior. Observance of the established routine is abandoned when in driving home from my office, for example, I learn that there is a parade in town and choose a different route, instead of automatically taking the usual one. Or, to mention an example of economic behavior: Many businessmen have rules of thumb concerning the timing for reorders of merchandise; yet sometimes they decide to place new orders even though their inventories have not reached the usual level of depletion (for instance, because they anticipate price increases), or not to order merchandise even though the level has been reached (because they expect a slump in sales).

4. Strong motivational forces—stronger than those which elicit habitual behavior—must be present to call forth problem-solving behavior. Being in a "crossroad situation," facing "choice points," or perceiving that something new has occurred are typical instances in which we are

motivated to deliberate and choose. Pearl Harbor and the Korean aggression are extreme examples of "new" events; economic behavior of the problem-solving type was found to have prevailed widely after these events.

5. Group belonging and group reinforcement play a substantial role in changes of behavior due to problem solving. Many people become aware of the same events at the same time; our mass media provide the same information and often the same interpretation of events to groups of people (to businessmen, trade union members, sometimes to all Americans). Changes in behavior resulting from new events may therefore occur among very many people at the same time. Some economists (for instance, Lord Keynes) argued that consumer optimism and pessimism are unimportant because usually they will cancel out; in the light of sociopsychological principles, however, it is probable, and has been confirmed by recent surveys, that a change from optimistic to pessimistic attitudes or vice versa, sometimes occurs among millions of people at the same time.

6. Changes in behavior due to genuine decision making will tend to be substantial and abrupt, rather than small and gradual. Typical examples of action that results from genuine decisions are cessation of purchases or buying waves, the shutting down of plants or the building of new plants, rather than an increase or decrease of production by 5 or 10 per cent.[6]

Because of the preponderance of individual psychological assumptions in classical economics and the emphasis placed on group behavior in this discussion, the change in underlying conditions which has occurred during the last century may be illustrated by a further example. It is related—the author does not know whether the story is true or fictitious—that the banking house of the Rothschilds, still in its infancy at that time, was one of the suppliers of the armies of Lord Wellington in 1815. Nathan Mayer Rothschild accompanied the armies and was present at the Battle of Waterloo. When he became convinced that Napoleon was decisively defeated, he released carrier pigeons so as to transmit the news to his associates in London and reverse the commodity position of his bank. The carrier pigeons arrived in London before the news of the victory became public knowledge. The profits thus reaped laid, according to the story, the foundation to the outstanding position of the House of Rothschild in the following decades.

The decision to embark on a new course of action because of new events was then made by one individual for his own profit. At present,

[6] Some empirical evidence supporting these six propositions in the area of economic behavior has been assembled by the Survey Research Center of the University of Michigan.

news of a battle, or of change of government, or of rearmament programs, is transmitted in short order by press and radio to the public at large. Businessmen—the manufacturers or retailers of steel or clothing, for instance—usually receive the same news about changes in the price of raw materials or in demand, and often consult with each other. Belonging to the same group means being subject to similar stimuli and reinforcing one another in making decisions. Acting in the same way as other members of one's group or of a reference group have acted under similar circumstances may also occur without deliberation and choice. New action by a few manufacturers will, then, frequently or even usually not be compensated by reverse action on the part of others. Rather the direction in which the economy of an entire country moves —and often the world economy as well—will tend to be subject to the same influences.

After having indicated some of the contributions which the application of certain psychological principles to economic behavior may make, we turn to contrasting that approach with the traditional theory of rationality. Instead of referring to the formulations of nineteenth century economists, we shall quote from a modern version of the classical trend of thought. The title of a section in a recent article by Kenneth J. Arrow is "The Principle of Rationality." He describes one of the criteria of rationality as follows: "We can imagine the individual as listing, once and for all, all conceivable consequences of his actions in order of his preference for them". We are first concerned with the expression "all conceivable consequences." This expression seems to contradict the principle of selectivity of human behavior. Yet habitual behavior is highly selective since it is based on (repeated) past experience, and problem-solving behavior likewise is highly selective since reorganization is subject to a certain direction instead of consisting of trial (and error) regarding all possible avenues of action.

Secondly, Arrow appears to identify rationality with consistency in the sense of repetition of the same choice. It is part and parcel of rational behavior, according to Arrow, that an individual "makes the same choice each time he is confronted with the same set of alternatives."[7] Proceeding in the same way on successive occasions appears, however, a characteristic of habitual behavior. Problem-solving behavior, on the other hand, is flexible. Rationality may be said to reflect adaptability and ability to act in a new way when circumstances demand it, rather than to consist of rigid or repetitive behavior.

Thirdly, it is important to realize the differences between the con-

[7] In his recent book Arrow adds after stating that the economic man "will make the same decision each time he is faced with the same range of alternatives": "The ability to make consistent decisions is one of the symptoms of an integrated personality."

cepts action, decision, and choice. It is an essential feature of the approach derived from considering problem-solving behavior that there is action without deliberate decision and choice. It then becomes one of the most important problems of research to determine under what conditions genuine decision and choice occur prior to an action. The three concepts are, however, used without differentiation in the classical theory of rationality and also, most recently, by Parsons and Shils. According to the theory of these authors, there are "five discrete choices (explicit or implicit) which every actor makes before he can act"; before there is action "a decision must always be made (explicitly or implicitly, consciously or unconsciously)".

There exists, no doubt, a difference in terminology, which may be clarified by mentioning a simple case: Suppose my telephone rings; I lift the receiver with my left hand and say, "Hello." Should we then argue that I made several choices, for instance, that I decided not to lift the receiver with my right hand and not to say "Mr. Katona speaking"? According to our use of the terms decision and choice, my action was habitual and did not involve "taking consequences into consideration."[8] Parsons and Shils use the terms decision and choice in a different sense, and Arrow may use the terms "all conceivable consequences" and "same set of alternatives" in a different sense from the one employed in this paper. But the difference between the two approaches appears to be more far-reaching. By using the terminology of the authors quoted, and by constructing a theory of rational action on the basis of this terminology, fundamental problems are disregarded. If every action by definition presupposes decision making, and if the malleability of human behavior is not taken into consideration, a one-sided theory of rationality is developed and empirical research is confined to testing a theory which covers only some of the aspects of rationality.

This was the case recently in experiments devised by Mosteller and Nogee. These authors attempt to test basic assumptions of economic theory, such as the rational choice among alternatives, by placing their subjects in a gambling situation (a variation of poker dice) and compelling them to make a decision, namely, to play or not to play against the experimenter. Through their experiments the authors prove that "it is feasible to measure utility experimentally" but they do not shed

[8] If I have reason not to make known that I am at home, I may react to the ringing of the telephone by fright, indecision, and deliberation (should I lift the receiver or let the telephone ring?) instead of reacting in the habitual way. This is an example of problem-solving behavior characterized as deviating from habitual behavior. The only example of action mentioned by Parsons and Shils, "a man driving his automobile to a lake to go fishing," may be habitual or may be an instance of genuine decision making.

light on the conditions under which rational behavior occurs or on the inherent features of rational behavior. Experiments in which making a choice among known alternatives is prescribed do not test the realism of economic theory.

MAXIMIZATION

Up to now we have discussed only one central aspect of rationality—means rather than ends. The end of rational behavior, according to economic theory, is maximization of profits in the case of business firms and maximization of utility in the case of people in general.

A few words, first, on maximizing profits. This is usually considered the simpler case because it is widely held (a) that business firms are in business to make profits and (b) that profits, more so than utility, are a quantitative, measurable concept.

When empirical research, most commonly in the form of case studies, showed that businessmen frequently strove for many things in addition to profits or in place of profits, most theorists were content with small changes in their systems. They redefined profits so as to include long-range profits and what has been called nonpecuniary or psychic profits. Striving for security or for power was identified with striving for profits in the more distant future; purchasing goods from a high bidder who was a member of the same fraternity as the purchaser, rather than from the lowest bidder—to cite an example often used in textbooks—was thought to be maximizing of nonpecuniary profits. Dissatisfaction with this type of theory construction is rather widespread. For example, a leading theorist wrote recently:

> If *whatever* a business man does is explained by the principle of profit maximization—because he does what he likes to do, and he likes to do what maximizes the sum of his pecuniary and non-pecuniary profits—the analysis acquires the character of a system of definitions and tautologies, and loses much of its value as an explanation of reality (13, p. 526).

The same problem is encountered regarding maximization of utility. Arrow defines rational behavior as follows: ". . . among all the combinations of commodities an individual can afford, he chooses that combination which maximizes his utility or satisfaction" and speaks of the "traditional identification of rationality with maximization of some sort". An economic theorist has recently characterized this type of definition as follows:

> The statement that a person seeks to maximize utility is (in many versions) a tautology: it is impossible to conceive of an observational

phenomenon that contradicts it. . . . What if the theorem is contradicted by observation: Samuelson says it would not matter much in the case of utility theory; I would say that it would not make the slightest difference. For there is a free variable in his system: the tastes of consumers. . . . Any contradiction of a theorem derived from utility theory can always be attributed to a change of tastes, rather than to an error in the postulates or logic of the theory.[9]

What is the way out of this difficulty? Can psychology, and specifically the psychology of motivation, help? We may begin by characterizing the prevailing economic theory as a single-motive theory and contrast it with a theory of multiple motives. Even in case of a single decision of one individual, multiplicity of motives (or of vectors or forces in the field), some reinforcing one another and some conflicting with one another, is the rule rather than the exception. The motivational patterns prevailing among different individuals making the same decision need not be the same; the motives of the same individual who is in the same external situation at different times may likewise differ. This approach opens the way (*a*) for a study of the relation of different motives to different forms of behavior and (*b*) for an investigation of changes in motives. Both problems are disregarded by postulating a single-motive theory and by restricting empirical studies to attempts to confirm or contradict that theory.

The fruitfulness of the psychological approach may be illustrated first by a brief reference to business motivation. We may rank the diverse motivational patterns of businessmen by placing the striving for high immediate profits (maximization of short-run profits, to use economic terminology; charging whatever the market can bear, to use a popular expression) at one extreme of the scale. At the other extreme we place the striving for prestige or power. In between we discern striving for security, for larger business volume, or for profits in the more distant future. Under what kinds of business conditions will motivational patterns tend to conform with the one or the other end of the scale? Preliminary studies would seem to indicate that the worse the business situation is, the more frequent is striving for high immediate profits, and the better the business situation is, the more frequent is striving for nonpecuniary goals.

Next we shall refer to one of the most important problems of consumer economics as well as of business-cycle studies, the deliberate choice between saving and spending. Suppose a college professor receives a raise in his salary or makes a few hundred extra dollars through

---

[9] The quotation refers specifically to Samuelson's definition but also applies to that of Arrow.

a publication. Suppose, furthermore, that he suggests thereupon to his wife that they should buy a television set, while the wife argues that the money should be put in the bank as a reserve against a "rainy day." Whatever the final decision may be, traditional economic theory would hold that the action which gives the greater satisfaction was chosen. This way of theorizing is of little value. Under what conditions will one type of behavior (spending) and under what conditions will another type of behavior (saving) be more frequent? Psychological hypotheses according to which the strength of vectors is related to the immediacy of needs have been put to a test through nationwide surveys over the past six years.[10] On the basis of survey findings the following tentative generalization was established: Pessimism, insecurity, expectation of income declines or bad times in the near future promote saving (putting the extra money in the bank), while optimism, feeling of security, expectation of income increases, or good times promote spending (buying the television set, for instance).

Psychological hypotheses, based on a theory of motivational patterns which change with circumstances and influence behavior, thus stimulated empirical studies. These studies, in turn, yielded a better understanding of past developments and also, we may add, better predictions of forthcoming trends than did studies based on the classical theory (see footnote 10). On the other hand, when conclusions about utility or rationality were made on an a priori basis, researchers lost sight of important problems.[11]

DIMINISHING UTILITY, SATURATION, AND ASPIRATION

Among the problems to which the identification of maximizing utility with rationality gave rise, the measurability of utility has been prominent. At present the position of most economists appears to be that while interpersonal comparison of several consumers' utilities is not possible, and while cardinal measures cannot be attached to the utilities

[10] In the Surveys of Consumer Finances, conducted annually since 1946 by the Survey Research Center of the University of Michigan for the Federal Reserve Board and reported in the *Federal Reserve Bulletin*. See also 8 and a forthcoming publication of the Survey Research Center on consumer buying and inflation during 1950–52.

[11] It should not be implied that the concepts of utility and maximization are of no value for empirical research. Comparison between maximum utility as determined from the vantage point of an observer with the pattern of goals actually chosen (the "subjective maximum"), which is based on insufficient information, may be useful. Similar considerations apply to such newer concepts as "minimizing regrets" and the "minimax."

of one particular consumer, ordinal ranking of the utilities of each individual can be made. It is asserted that I can always say either that I prefer *A* to *B*, or that I am indifferent to having *A* or *B*, or that I prefer *B* to *A*. The theory of indifference curves is based on this assumption.

In elaborating the theory further, it is asserted that rational behavior consists not only of preferring more of the same goods to less ($2 real wages to $1, or two packages of cigarettes to one package, for the same service performed) but also of deriving diminishing increments of satisfaction from successive units of a commodity.[12] In terms of an old textbook example, one drink of water has tremendous value to a thirsty traveler in a desert; a second, third, or fourth drink may still have some value but less and less so, an *n*th drink (which he is unable to carry along) has no value at all. A generalization derived from this principle is that the more of a commodity or the more money a person has, the smaller are his needs for that commodity or for money, and the smaller his incentives to add to what he has.

In addition to using this principle of saturation to describe the behavior of the rational man, modern economists applied it to one of the most pressing problems of contemporary American economy. Prior to World War II the American people (not counting business firms) owned about 45 billion dollars in liquid assets (currency, bank deposits, government bonds) and these funds were highly concentrated among relatively few families; most individual families held no liquid assets at all (except for small amounts of currency). By the end of the year 1945, however, the personal liquid-asset holdings had risen to about 140 billion dollars and four out of every five families owned some bank deposits or war bonds. What is the effect of this great change on spending and saving? This question has been answered by several leading economists in terms of the saturation principle presented above. "The rate of saving is . . . a diminishing function of the wealth the individual holds" because "the availability of liquid assets raises consumption generally by reducing the impulse to save."[13] More specifically: a person who owns nothing or very little will exert himself greatly to acquire some reserve funds, while a person who owns much will have much smaller incentives to save. Similarly, incentives to increase one's income are said to weaken with the amount of income. In other words, the strength of motivation is inversely correlated with the level of achievement.

In view of the lack of contact between economists and psychologists, it is hardly surprising that economists failed to see the relevance for

[12] This principle of diminishing utility was called a "fundamental tendency of human nature" by the great nineteenth century economist, Alfred Marshall.

[13] The last quotation is from the publication of the U. S. Department of Commerce, *Survey of Current Business*, May 1950, p. 10.

their postulates of the extensive experimental work performed by psychologists on the problem of levels of aspiration. It is not necessary in this paper to describe these studies in detail. It may suffice to formulate three generalizations as established in numerous studies of goal-striving behavior:

1. Aspirations are not static, they are not established once for all time.
2. Aspirations tend to grow with achievement and decline with failure.
3. Aspirations are influenced by the performance of other members of the group to which one belongs and by that of reference groups.

From these generalizations hypotheses were derived about the influence of assets on saving which differed from the postulates of the saturation theory. This is not the place to describe the extensive empirical work undertaken to test the hypotheses. But it may be reported that the saturation theory was not confirmed; the level-of-aspiration theory likewise did not suffice to explain the findings. In addition to the variable "size of liquid-asset holdings," the studies had to consider such variables as income level, income change, and savings habits. (Holders of large liquid assets are primarily people who have saved a high proportion of their income in the past!) [14]

The necessity of studying the interaction of a great number of variables and the change of choices over time leads to doubts regarding the universal validity of a one-dimensional ordering of all alternatives. The theory of measurement of utilities remains an empty frame unless people's established preferences of A over B and of B over C provide indications about their probable future behavior. Under what conditions do people's preferences give us such clues, and under what conditions do they not? If at different times A and B are seen in different contexts—because of changed external conditions or the acquisition of new experiences—we may have to distinguish among several dimensions.

The problem may be illustrated by an analogy. Classic economic theory postulates a one-dimensional ordering of all alternatives; Gullup asserts that answers to questions of choice can always be ordered on a yes—uncertain (don't know)—no continuum; are both arguments subject to the same reservations? Specifically, if two persons give the same answer to a poll question (e.g., both say "Yes, I am for sending American troops to Europe" or "Yes, I am for the Taft-Hartley Act") may they mean different things so that their identical answers do not permit any conclusions about the similarity of their other attitudes and their

[14] The empirical work was part of the economic behavior program of the Survey Research Center under the direction of the author.

behavior? Methodologically it follows from the last argument that yes-no questions need to be supplemented by open-ended questions to discern differences in people's level of information and motivation. It also follows that attitudes and preferences should be ascertained through a multi-question approach (or scaling) which serves to determine whether one or several dimensions prevail.

ON THEORY CONSTRUCTION

In attempting to summarize our conclusions about the respective merits of different scientific approaches, we might quote the conclusions of Arrow which he formulated for social science in general rather than for economics:

> To the extent that formal theoretical structures in the social sciences have not been based on the hypothesis of rational behavior, their postulates have been developed in a manner which we may term *ad hoc*. Such propositions . . . depend, of course, on the investigator's intuition and common sense.

The last sentence seems strange indeed. One may argue the other way around and point out that such propositions as "the purpose of business is to make profits" or "the best businessman is the one who maximizes profits" are based on intuition or supposed common sense, rather than on controlled observation. The main problem raised by the quotation concerns the function of empirical research. There exists an alternative to developing an axiomatic system into a full-fledged theoretical model in advance of testing the theory through observations. Controlled observations should be based on hypotheses, and the formulation of an integrated theory need not be delayed until all observations are completed. Yet theory construction is part of the process of hypothesis-observation-revised hypothesis and prediction-observation, and systematization should rely on some empirical research. The proximate aim of scientific research is a body of empirically validated generalizations and not a theory that is valid under any and all circumstances.

The dictum that "theoretical structures in the social sciences must be based on the hypothesis of rational behavior" presupposes that it is established what rational behavior is. Yet, instead of establishing the characteristics of rational behavior a priori, we must first determine the conditions a_1, b_1, c_1 under which behavior of the type x_1, y_1, z_1 and the conditions a_2, b_2, c_2 under which behavior of the type x_2, y_2, z_2 is likely to occur. Then, if we wish, we may designate one of the forms of behavior as rational. The contributions of psychology to this process are not solely methodological; findings and principles about noneconomic behavior provide hypotheses for the study of economic behavior. Likewise, psychology can profit from the study of economic behavior because many aspects of behavior, and among them the problems of rationality, may be studied most fruitfully in the economic field.

This paper was meant to indicate some promising leads for a study of rationality, not to carry such study to its completion. Among the problems that were not considered adequately were the philosophical ones (rationality viewed as a value concept), the psychoanalytic ones (the relationships between rational and conscious, and between irrational and unconscious), and those relating to personality theory and the roots of rationality. The emphasis was placed here on the possibility and fruitfulness of studying forms of rational behavior, rather than the characteristics of *the* rational man. Motives and goals that change with and are adapted to circumstances, and the relatively rare but highly significant cases of our becoming aware of problems and attempting to solve them, were found to be related to behavior that may be called truly rational.

RETROSPECTIVE COMMENT

More than 20 years have passed since I wrote this essay. In the meantime I have conducted numerous studies on economic behavior and have written three books on psychological economics. There are reasons for both satisfaction and dissatisfaction with developments in these 20 years.

To speak of the dissatisfactions first, many economic theorists and even econometricians still start out by presenting a model of rational behavior and of maximization of utilities; the model is then stepwise modified so as to approximate "real" conditions. This procedure usually does not do justice to the powerful influence of subjective factors in economic decisions.

On the other hand, we know much more today than 20 years ago of the circumstances under which rational and calculating behavior or other forms of sensible and intelligent behavior occur. To illustrate newly won insights by an example of both theoretical and practical importance, I refer to consumer response to inflation. It has been postulated by theorists that rational people, when they expect prices to go up, will stock up and hoard in order to beat inflation. But in the U.S. during the last 25 years, this form of behavior was found to occur rarely and only under the influence of specific threatening developments. Most usually, anxiety about price increases makes for uncertainty, malaise, and misgivings which paralyze action. People then respond to inflationary expectations by spending less and saving more, rather than by spending more and saving less. This is not rational, as economists define the term, but it is sensible and explainable by psychological considerations.—*George Katona*

REFERENCES

ARROW, K. J. Mathematical models in the social sciences. In D. Lerner, & H. D. Lasswell (Eds.), *The policy sciences*. Stanford: Stanford Univer. Press, 1951.

ARROW, K. J. *Social choice and individual values*. New York: Wiley, 1951.

FRENCH, T. M. *The integration of behavior*. Vol. I. Chicago: Univ. of Chicago Press, 1952.

GUTHRIE, E. R. *Psychology of learning*. New York: Harper, 1935.

HABERLER, G. *Prosperity and depression*. (3rd Ed.) Geneva: League of Nations, 1941.

KATONA, G. *Organizing and memorizing*. New York: Columbia Univer. Press, 1940.

KATONA, G. Psychological analysis of business decisions and expectations. *Amer. economic Rev.*, 1946, 36, 44–63.

KATONA, G. *Psychological analysis of economic behavior*. New York: McGraw-Hill, 1951.

KEYNES, J. M. *The general theory of employment, interest and money*. New York: Harcourt, Brace, 1936.

KLEIN, L. R. Assets, debts, and economic behavior. In *Studies in income and wealth*, Vol. 14. New York: National Bureau of Economic Research, 1951.

KLEIN, L. R. Estimating patterns of savings behavior from sample survey data. *Econometrica*, 1951, 19, 438–454.

LEWIN, K., *et al.* Level of aspiration. In J. McV. Hunt (Ed.), *Personality and the behavior disorders*. New York: Ronald, 1944.

MACHLUP, F. Marginal analysis and empirical research. *Amer. economic Rev.*, 1946, 36, 519–555.

MOSTELLER, F., & Nogee, P. An experimental measurement of utility. *J. political Economy*, 1951, 59, 371–405.

PARSONS, T., & Shils, E. A. (Eds.). *Toward a general theory of action*. Cambridge, Mass.: Harvard Univer. Press, 1951.

STIGLER, G. J. Rev. of P. A. Samuelson's *Foundations of economic analysis*. *J. Amer. statist. Ass.*, 1948, 43, 603–605.

WERTHEIMER, M. *Productive thinking*. New York: Harper, 1945.

4. Behavioral Models for Analyzing Buyers

Philip Kotler

In times past, management could arrive at a fair understanding of its buyers through the daily experience of selling to them. But the growth in the size of firms and markets has removed many decision-makers from direct contact with buyers. Increasingly, decision-makers have had to turn to summary statistics and to behavioral theory, and are spending more money today than ever before to try to understand their buyers.

Who buys? How do they buy? And why? The first two questions relate to relatively overt aspects of buyer behavior, and can be learned about through direct observation and interviewing.

But uncovering *why* people buy is an extremely difficult task. The answer will tend to vary with the investigator's behavioral frame of reference.

The buyer is subject to many influences which trace a complex course through his psyche and lead eventually to overt purchasing responses. This conception of the buying process is illustrated in Figure 1. Various influences and their modes of transmission are shown at the left. At the right are the buyer's responses in choice of product, brand, dealer, quantities, and frequency. In the center stands the buyer and his mysterious psychological processes. The buyer's psyche is a "black box" whose workings can be only partially deduced. The marketing strategist's challenge to the behavioral scientist is to construct a more specific model of the mechanism in the black box.

Unfortunately no generally accepted model of the mechanism exists. The human mind, the only entity in nature with deep powers of understanding, still remains the least understood. Scientists can explain planetary motion, genetic determination, and molecular behavior. Yet they have only partial, and often partisan, models of *human* behavior.

Nevertheless, the marketing strategist should recognize the potential interpretative contributions of different partial models for explaining

Reprinted by permission of the author and publisher from the Journal of Marketing, *published by the American Marketing Association, Vol. 29 (October 1965), pp. 37–45.*

buyer behavior. Depending upon the product, different variables and behavioral mechanisms may assume particular importance. A psychoanalytic behavioral model might throw much light on the factors operating in cigarette demand, while an economic behavioral model might be useful in explaining machine-tool purchasing. Sometimes alternative models may shed light on different demand aspects of the same product.

What are the most useful behavioral models for interpreting the transformation of buying influences into purchasing responses? Five different models of the buyer's "black box" are presented in the present article, along with their respective marketing applications: (1) the Marshallian model, stressing economic motivations; (2) the Pavlovian model, learning; (3) the Freudian model, psychoanalytic motivations; (4) the Veblenian model, social-psychological factors; and (5) the Hobbesian model, organizational factors. These models represent radically different conceptions of the mainsprings of human behavior.

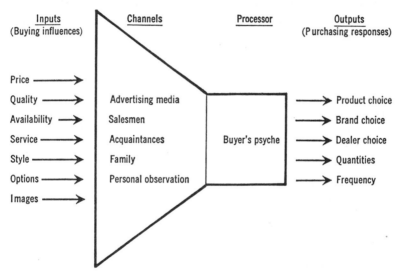

Figure 4.1. THE BUYING PROCESS CONCEIVED AS A SYSTEM OF INPUTS AND OUTPUTS.

THE MARSHALLIAN ECONOMIC MODEL

Economists were the first professional group to construct a specific theory of buyer behavior. The theory holds that purchasing decisions are the result of largely "rational" and conscious economic calculations. The individual buyer seeks to spend his income on those goods that will deliver the most utility (satisfaction) according to his tastes and relative prices.

The antecedents for this view trace back to the writings of Adam Smith and Jeremy Bentham. Smith set the tone by developing a doctrine of economic growth based on the principle that man is motivated by self-interest in all his actions.[1] Bentham refined this view and saw man as finely calculating and weighing the expected pleasures and pains of every contemplated action.[2]

Bentham's "felicific calculus" was not applied to consumer behavior (as opposed to entrepreneurial behavior) until the late 19th century. Then, the "marginal-utility" theory of value was formulated independently and almost simultaneously by Jevons[3] and Marshall[4] in England, Menger[5] in Austria, and Walras[6] in Switzerland.

Alfred Marshall was the greatest consolidator of the classical and neoclassical tradition in economics; and his synthesis in the form of demand-supply analysis constitutes the main source of modern microeconomic thought in the English-speaking world. His theoretical work aimed at realism, but his method was to start with simplifying assumptions and to examine the effect of a change in a single variable (say, price) when all other variables were held constant.

He would "reason out" the consequences of the provisional assumptions and in subsequent steps modify his assumptions in the direction of more realism. He employed the "measuring rod of money" as an indicator of the intensity of human psychological desires. Over the years his methods and assumptions have been refined into what is now known as *modern utility theory*: economic man is bent on maximizing his utility, and does this by carefully calculating the "felicific" consequences of any purchase.

> As an example, suppose on a particular evening that John is considering whether to prepare his own dinner or dine out. He estimates that a restaurant meal would cost $2.00 and a home-cooked meal 50 cents. According to the Marshallian model, if John expects less than four times as much satisfaction from the restaurant meal as the home-cooked meal, he will eat at home. The economist typically is not concerned with how these relative preferences are formed by John, or how they may be psychologically modified by new stimuli.
>
> Yet John will not always cook at home. The principle of diminishing marginal utility operates. Within a given time interval—say, a week—the

---

[1] Adam Smith, *An Inquiry into the Nature and Causes of the Wealth of Nations*, 1776 (New York: The Modern Library, 1937).

[2] Jeremy Bentham, *An Introduction to the Principles of Morals and Legislation*, 1780 (Oxford, England: Clarendon Press, 1907).

[3] William S. Jevons, *The Theory of Political Economy* (New York: The Macmillan Company, 1871).

[4] Alfred Marshall, *Principles of Economics*, 1890 (London: The Macmillan Company, 1927).

[5] Karl Menger, *Principles of Economics*, 1871 (Glencoe, Illinois: Free Press, 1950).

[6] Leon Walras, *Elements of Pure Economics*, 1874 (Homewood, Illinois: Richard D. Irwin, Inc., 1954).

utility of each additional home-cooked meal diminishes. John gets tired of home meals and other products become relatively more attractive.

John's *efficiency* in maximizing his utility depends on the adequacy of his information and his freedom of choice. If he is not perfectly aware of costs, if he misestimates the relative delectability of the two meals, or if he is barred from entering the restaurant, he will not maximize his potential utility. His choice processes are rational, but the results are inefficient.

MARKETING APPLICATIONS OF MARSHALLIAN MODEL

Marketers usually have dismissed the Marshallian model as an absurd figment of ivory-tower imagination. Certainly the behavioral essence of the situation is omitted, in viewing man as calculating the marginal utility of a restaurant meal over a home-cooked meal.

Eva Mueller has reported a study where only one-fourth of the consumers in her sample bought with any substantial degree of deliberation.[7] Yet there are a number of ways to view the model.

From one point of view the Marshallian model is tautological and therefore neither true nor false. The model holds that the buyer acts in the light of his best "interest." But this is not very informative.

A second view is that this is a *normative* rather than a *descriptive* model of behavior. The model provides logical norms for buyers who want to be "rational." Although the consumer is not likely to employ economic analysis to decide between a box of Kleenex and Scotties, he may apply economic analysis in deciding whether to buy a new car. Industrial buyers even more clearly would want an economic calculus for making good decisions.

A third view is that economic factors operate to a greater or lesser extent in all markets, and, therefore, must be included in any comprehensive description of buyer behavior.

Furthermore, the model suggests useful behavioral hypotheses such as: (a) The lower the price of the product, the higher the sales. (b) The lower the price of substitute products, the lower the sales of this product; and the lower the price of complementary products, the higher the sales of this product. (c) The higher the real income, the higher the sales of this product, provided that it is not an "inferior" good. (d) The higher the promotional expenditures, the higher the sales.

The validity of these hypotheses does not rest on whether *all* individuals act as economic calculating machines in making their purchasing decisions. For example, some individuals may buy *less* of a product when its price is reduced. They may think that the quality has gone

---

[7] Eva Mueller, "A Study of Purchase Decisions," Part 2, *Consumer Behavior, The Dynamics of Consumer Reaction*, edited by Lincoln H. Clark (New York: New York University Press, 1954), pp. 36–87.

down, or that ownership has less status value. If a majority of buyers view price reductions negatively, then sales may fall, contrary to the first hypothesis.

But for most goods a price reduction increases the relative value of the goods in many buyers' minds and leads to increased sales. This and the other hypotheses are intended to describe average effects.

The impact of economic factors in actual buying situations is studied through experimental design or statistical analyses of past data. Demand equations have been fitted to a wide variety of products—including beer, refrigerators, and chemical fertilizers.[8] More recently, the impact of economic variables on the fortunes of different brands has been pursued with significant results, particularly in the case of coffee, frozen orange juice, and margarine.[9]

But economic factors alone cannot explain all the variations in sales. The Marshallian model ignores the fundamental question of how product and brand preferences are formed. It represents a useful frame of reference for analyzing only one small corner of the "black box."

THE PAVLOVIAN LEARNING MODEL

The designation of a Pavlovian learning model has its origin in the experiments of the Russian psychologist Pavlov, who rang a bell each time before feeding a dog. Soon he was able to induce the dog to salivate by ringing the bell whether or not food was supplied. Pavlov concluded that learning was largely an associative process and that a large component of behavior was conditioned in this way.

Experimental psychologists have continued this mode of research with rats and other animals, including people. Laboratory experiments have been designed to explore such phenomena as learning, forgetting, and the ability to discriminate. The results have been integrated into a stimulus-response model of human behavior, or as someone has "wise-cracked," the substitution of a rat psychology for a rational psychology.

The model has been refined over the years, and today is based on four central concepts—those of *drive, cue, response,* and *reinforcement.*[10]

[8] See Erwin E. Nemmers, *Managerial Economics* (New York: John Wiley & Sons, Inc., 1962), Part II.

[9] See Lester G. Telser, "The Demand for Branded Goods as Estimated from Consumer Panel Data," *Review of Economics and Statistics*, Vol. 44 (August, 1962), pp. 300–324; and William F. Massy and Ronald E. Frank, "Short Term Price and Dealing Effects in Selected Market Segments," *Journal of Marketing Research*, Vol. 2 (May, 1965), pp. 171–185.

[10] See John Dollard and Neal E. Miller, *Personality and Psychotherapy* (New York: McGraw-Hill Book Company, Inc., 1950), Chapter III.

Drive. Also called needs or motives, drive refers to strong stimuli internal to the individual which impels action. Psychologists draw a distinction between primary physiological drives—such as hunger, thirst, cold, pain, and sex—and learned drives which are derived socially —such as cooperation, fear, and acquisitiveness.

Cue. A drive is very general and impels a particular response only in relation to a particular configuration of cues. Cues are weaker stimuli in the environment and/or in the individual which determine when, where, and how the subject responds. Thus, a coffee advertisement can serve as a cue which stimulates the thirst drive in a housewife. Her response will depend upon this cue and other cues, such as the time of day, the availability of other thirst-quenchers, and the cue's intensity. Often a relative change in a cue's intensity can be more impelling than its absolute level. The housewife may be more motivated by a 2-cents-off sale on a brand of coffee than the fact that this brand's price was low in the first place.

Response. The response is the organism's reaction to the configuration of cues. Yet the same configuration of cues will not necessarily produce the same response in the individual. This depends on the degree to which the experience was rewarding, that is, drive-reducing.

Reinforcement. If the experience is rewarding, a particular response is reinforced; that is, it is strengthened and there is a tendency for it to be repeated when the same configuration of cues appears again. The housewife, for example, will tend to purchase the same brand of coffee each time she goes to her supermarket so long as it is rewarding and the cue configuration does not change. But if a learned response or habit is not reinforced, the strength of the habit diminishes and may be extinguished eventually. Thus, a housewife's preference for a certain coffee may become extinct if she finds the brand out of stock for a number of weeks.

Forgetting, in contrast to extinction, is the tendency for learned associations to weaken, not because of the lack of reinforcement but because of nonuse.

Cue configurations are constantly changing. The housewife sees a new brand of coffee next to her habitual brand, or notes a special price deal on a rival brand. Experimental psychologists have found that the same learned response will be elicited by similar patterns of cues; that is, learned responses are *generalized*. The housewife shifts to a similar brand when her favorite brand is out of stock. This tendency toward generalization over less similar cue configurations is increased in proportion to the strength of the drive. A housewife may buy an inferior coffee if it is the only brand left and if her drive is sufficiently strong.

A counter-tendency to generalization is *discrimination*. When a housewife tries two similar brands and finds one more rewarding, her ability to discriminate between similar cue configurations improves. Discrimination increases the specificity of the cue-response connection, while generalization decreases the specificity.

MARKETING APPLICATIONS OF PAVLOVIAN MODEL

The modern version of the Pavlovian model makes no claim to provide a complete theory of behavior—indeed, such important phenomena as perception, the subconscious, and interpersonal influence are inadequately treated. Yet the model does offer a substantial number of insights about some aspects of behavior of considerable interest to marketers.[11]

An example would be in the problem of introducing a new brand into a highly competitive market. The company's goal is to extinguish existing brand habits and form new habits among consumers for its brand. But the company must first get customers to try its brand; and it has to decide between using weak and strong cues.

Light introductory advertising is a weak cue compared with distributing free samples. Strong cues, although costing more, may be necessary in markets characterized by strong brand loyalties. For example, Folger went into the coffee market by distributing over a million pounds of free coffee.

To build a brand habit, it helps to provide for an extended period of introductory dealing. Furthermore, sufficient quality must be built into the brand so that the experience is reinforcing. Since buyers are more likely to transfer allegiance to similar brands than dissimilar brands (generalization), the company should also investigate what cues in the leading brands have been most effective. Although outright imitation would not necessarily effect the most transference the question of providing enough similarity should be considered.

The Pavlovian model also provides guide lines in the area of advertising strategy. The American behaviorist, John B. Watson, was a great exponent of repetitive stimuli; in his writings man is viewed as a creature who can be conditioned through repetition and reinforcement to respond in particular ways.[12] The Pavlovian model emphasizes the de-

[11] The most consistent application of learning-theory concepts to marketing situations is found in John A. Howard, *Marketing Management: Analysis and Planning* (Homewood, Illinois: Richard D. Irwin, Inc., revised edition, 1963).

[12] John B. Watson, *Behaviorism* (New York: The People's Institute Publishing Company, 1925).

sirability of repetition in advertising. A single exposure is likely to be a very weak cue, hardly able to penetrate the individual's consciousness sufficiently to excite his drives above the threshold level.

Repetition in advertising has two desirable effects. It "fights" forgetting, the tendency for learned responses to weaken in the absence of practice. It provides reinforcement, because after the purchase the consumer becomes selectively exposed to advertisements of the product.

The model also provides guide lines for copy strategy. To be effective as a cue, an advertisement must arouse strong drives in the person. The strongest product-related drives must be identified. For candy bars, it may be hunger; for safety belts, fear; for hair tonics, sex; for automobiles, status. The advertising practitioner must dip into his cue box—words, colors, pictures—and select that configuration of cues that provide the strongest stimulus to these drives.

THE FREUDIAN PSYCHOANALYTIC MODEL

The Freudian model of man is well known, so profound has been its impact on 20th century thought. It is the latest of a series of philosophical "blows" to which man has been exposed in the last 500 years. Copernicus destroyed the idea that man stood at the center of the universe; Darwin tried to refute the idea that man was a special creation; and Freud attacked the idea that man even reigned over his own psyche.

According to Freud, the child enters the world driven by instinctual needs which he cannot gratify by himself. Very quickly and painfully he realizes his separateness from the rest of the world and yet his dependence on it.

He tries to get others to gratify his needs through a variety of blatant means, including intimidation and supplication. Continual frustration leads him to perfect more subtle mechanisms for gratifying his instincts.

As he grows, his psyche becomes increasingly complex. A part of his psyche—the id—remains the reservoir of his strong drives and urges. Another part—the ego—becomes his conscious planning center for finding outlets for his drives. And a third part—his super-ego—channels his instinctive drives into socially approved outlets to avoid the pain of guilt or shame.

The guilt or shame which man feels toward some of his urges—especially his sexual urges—causes him to repress them from his consciousness. Through such defense mechanisms as rationalization and sublimation, these urges are denied or become transmuted into socially approved expressions. Yet these urges are never eliminated or under perfect control; and they emerge, sometimes with a vengeance, in dreams, in slips-of-the-tongue, in neurotic and obsessional behavior, or ultimately in mental breakdown where the ego can no longer maintain the delicate balance between the impulsive power of the id and the oppressive power of the super-ego.

The individual's behavior, therefore, is never simple. His motivational wellsprings are not obvious to a casual observer nor deeply understood by the individual himself. If he is asked why he purchased an expensive foreign sports-car, he may reply that he likes its maneuverability and its looks. At a deeper level he may have purchased the car to impress others, or to feel young again. At a still deeper level, he may be purchasing the sports-car to achieve substitute gratification for unsatisfied sexual strivings.

Many refinements and changes in emphasis have occurred in this model since the time of Freud. The instinct concept has been replaced by a more careful delineation of basic drives; the three parts of the psyche are regarded now as theoretical concepts rather than actual entities; and the behavioral perspective has been extended to include cultural as well as biological mechanisms.

Instead of the role of the sexual urge in psychic development—Freud's discussion of oral, anal, and genital stages and possible fixations and traumas—Adler[13] emphasized the urge for power and how its thwarting manifests itself in superiority and inferiority complexes; Horney[14] emphasized cultural mechanisms; and Fromm[15] and Erickson[16] emphasized the role of existential crises in personality development. These philosophical divergencies, rather than debilitating the model, have enriched and extended its interpretative value to a wider range of behavioral phenomena.

MARKETING APPLICATIONS OF FREUDIAN MODEL

Perhaps the most important marketing implication of this model is that buyers are motivated by *symbolic* as well as *economic-functional* product concerns. The change of a bar of soap from a square to a round shape may be more important in its sexual than its functional connotations. A cake mix that is advertised as involving practically no labor may alienate housewives because the easy life may evoke a sense of guilt.

Motivational research has produced some interesting and occasionally some bizarre hypotheses about what may be in the buyer's mind regarding certain purchases. Thus, it has been suggested at one time or another that

[13] Alfred Adler, *The Science of Living* (New York: Greenberg, 1929).

[14] Karen Horney, *The Neurotic Personality of Our Time* (New York: W. W. Norton & Co., 1937).

[15] Erich Fromm, *Man For Himself* (New York: Holt, Rinehart & Winston, Inc., 1947).

[16] Erik Erikson, *Childhood and Society* (New York: W. W. Norton & Co., 1949).

Many a businessman doesn't fly because of a fear of posthumous guilt—if he crashed, his wife would think of him as stupid for not taking a train.

Men want their cigars to be odoriferous, in order to prove that they (the men) are masculine.

A woman is very serious when she bakes a cake, because unconsciously she is going through the symbolic act of giving birth.

A man buys a convertible as a substitute "mistress."

Consumers prefer vegetable shortening because animal fats stimulate a sense of sin.

Men who wear suspenders are reacting to an unresolved castration complex.

There are admitted difficulties of proving these assertions. Two prominent motivational researchers, Ernest Dichter and James Vicary, were employed independently by two separate groups in the prune industry to determine why so many people dislike prunes. Dichter found, among other things, that the prune aroused feelings of old age and insecurity in people, whereas Vicary's main finding was that Americans had an emotional block about prunes' laxative qualities.[17] Which is the more valid interpretation? Or if they are both operative, which motive is found with greater statistical frequency in the population?

Unfortunately the usual survey techniques—direct observation and interviewing—can be used to establish the representativeness of more superficial characteristics—age and family size, for example—but are not feasible for establishing the frequency of mental states which are presumed to be deeply "buried" within each individual.

Motivational researchers have to employ time-consuming projective techniques in the hope of throwing individual "egos" off guard. When carefully administered and interpreted, techniques such as word association, sentence completion, picture interpretation, and role-playing can provide some insights into the minds of the small group of examined individuals; but a "leap of faith" is sometimes necessary to generalize these findings to the population.

Nevertheless, motivation research can lead to useful insights and provide inspiration to creative men in the advertising and packaging world. Appeals aimed at the buyer's private world of hopes, dreams, and fears can often be as effective in stimulating purchase as more rationally-directed appeals.

[17] L. Edward Scriven, "Rationality and Irrationality in Motivation Research," in Robert Ferber and Hugh G. Wales, editors, *Motivation and Marketing Behavior* (Homewood, Illinois: Richard D. Irwin, Inc., 1958), pp. 69–70.

THE VEBLENIAN SOCIAL-PSYCHOLOGICAL MODEL

While most economists have been content to interpret buyer behavior in Marshallian terms, Thorstein Veblen struck out in different directions.

Veblen was trained as an orthodox economist, but evolved into a social thinker greatly influenced by the new science of social anthropology. He saw man as primarily a *social animal*—conforming to the general forms and norms of his larger culture and to the more specific standards of the subcultures and face-to-face groupings to which his life is bound. His wants and behavior are largely molded by his present group-memberships and his aspired group-memberships.

Veblen's best-known example of this is in his description of the leisure class.[18] His hypothesis is that much of economic consumption is motivated not by intrinsic needs or satisfaction so much as by prestige-seeking. He emphasized the strong emulative factors operating in the choice of conspicuous goods like clothes, cars, and houses.

Some of his points, however, seem overstated by today's perspective. The leisure class does not serve as everyone's reference group; many persons aspire to the social patterns of the class immediately above it. And important segments of the affluent class practice conspicuous underconsumption rather than overconsumption. There are many people in all classes who are more anxious to "fit in" than to "stand out." As an example, William H. Whyte found that many families avoided buying air conditioners and other appliances before their neighbors did.[19]

Veblen was not the first nor the only investigator to comment on social influences in behavior; but the incisive quality of his observations did much to stimulate further investigations. Another stimulus came from Karl Marx, who held that each man's world-view was determined largely by his relationship to the "means of production."[20] The early field-work in primitive societies by social anthropologists like Boas[21] and Malinowski[22] and the later field-work in urban societies by men like Park[23] and Thomas[24] contributed much to understanding the

[18] Thorstein Veblen, *The Theory of the Leisure Class* (New York: The Macmillan Company, 1899).

[19] William H. Whyte, Jr., "The Web of Word of Mouth," *Fortune*, Vol. 50 (November, 1954), pp. 140 ff.

[20] Karl Marx, *The Communist Manifesto*, 1848 (London: Martin Lawrence, Ltd., 1934).

[21] Franz Boas, *The Mind of Primitive Man* (New York: The Macmillan Company, 1922).

[22] Bronislaw Malinowski, *Sex and Repression in Savage Society* (New York: Meridian Books, 1955).

[23] Robert E. Park, *Human Communities* (Glencoe, Illinois: Free Press, 1952).

[24] William I. Thomas, *The Unadjusted Girl* (Boston: Little, Brown and Company, 1928).

influence of society and culture. The research of early Gestalt psychologists—men like Wertheimer,[25] Köhler,[26] and Koffka[27]—into the mechanisms of perception led eventually to investigations of small-group influence on perception.

MARKETING APPLICATIONS OF VEBLENIAN MODEL

The various streams of thought crystallized into the modern social sciences of sociology, cultural anthropology, and social psychology. Basic to them is the view that man's attitudes and behavior are influenced by several levels of society—culture, subcultures, social classes, reference groups, and face-to-face groups. The challenge to the marketer is to determine which of these social levels are the most important in influencing the demand for his product.

Culture. The most enduring influences are from culture. Man tends to assimilate his culture's mores and folkways, and to believe in their absolute rightness until deviants appear within his culture or until he confronts members of another culture.

Subculture. A culture tends to lose its homogeneity as its population increases. When people no longer are able to maintain face-to-face relationships with more than a small proportion of other members of a culture, smaller units or subcultures develop, which help to satisfy the individual's needs for more specific identity.

The subcultures are often regional entities, because the people of a region, as a result of more frequent interactions, tend to think and act alike. But subcultures also take the form of religions, nationalities, fraternal orders, and other institutional complexes which provide a broad identification for people who may otherwise be strangers. The subcultures of a person play a large role in his attitude formation and become another important predictor of certain values he is likely to hold.

Social Class. People become differentiated not only horizontally but also vertically through a division of labor. The society becomes stratified socially on the basis of wealth, skill, and power. Sometimes castes develop in which the members are reared for certain roles, or

[25] Max Wertheimer, *Productive Thinking* (New York: Harper & Brothers, 1945).
[26] Wolfgang Köhler, *Gestalt Psychology* (New York: Liveright Publishing Co., 1947).
[27] Kurt Koffka, *Principles of Gestalt Psychology* (New York: Harcourt, Brace and Co., 1935).

social classes develop in which the members feel empathy with others sharing similar values and economic circumstances.

Because social class involves different attitudinal configurations, it becomes a useful independent variable for segmenting markets and predicting reactions. Significant differences have been found among different social classes with respect to magazine readership, leisure activities, food imagery, fashion interests, and acceptance of innovations. A sampling of attitudinal differences in class is the following:

> Members of the *upper-middle* class place an emphasis on professional competence; indulge in expensive status symbols; and more often than not show a taste, real or otherwise, for theater and the arts. They want their children to show high achievement and precocity and develop into physicists, vice-presidents and judges. This class likes to deal in ideas and symbols.
>
> Members of the *lower-middle* class cherish respectability, savings, a college education, and good housekeeping. They want their children to show self-control and prepare for careers as accountants, lawyers, and engineers.
>
> Members of the *upper-lower* class try to keep up with the times, if not with the Joneses. They stay in older neighborhoods but buy new kitchen appliances. They spend proportionately less than the middle class on major clothing articles, buying a new suit mainly for an important ceremonial occasion. They also spend proportionately less on services, preferring to do their own plumbing and other work around the house. They tend to raise large families and their children generally enter manual occupations. This class also supplies many local businessmen, politicians, sports stars, and labor-union leaders.

Reference Groups.   There are groups in which the individual has no membership but with which he identifies and may aspire to—reference groups. Many young boys identify with big-league baseball players or astronauts, and many young girls identify with Hollywood stars. The activities of these popular heroes are carefully watched and frequently imitated. These reference figures become important transmitters of influence, although more along lines of taste and hobby than basic attitudes.

Face-to-face Groups.   Groups that have the most immediate influence on a person's tastes and opinions are face-to-face groups. This includes all the small "societies" with which he comes into frequent contact: his family, close friends, neighbors, fellow workers, fraternal associates, and so forth. His informal group memberships are influenced largely by his occupation, residence, and stage in the life cycle.

The powerful influence of small groups on individual attitudes has been demonstrated in a number of social psychological experiments.[28]

---

[28] See, for example, Solomon E. Asch, "Effects of Group Pressure Upon the Modification & Distortion of Judgments," in Dorwin Cartwright and Alvin Zander, *Group*

There is also evidence that this influence may be growing. David Riesman and his coauthors have pointed to signs which indicate a growing amount of *other-direction*, that is, a tendency for individuals to be increasingly influenced by their peers in the definition of their values rather than by their parents and elders.[29]

For the marketer, this means that brand choice may increasingly be influenced by one's peers. For such products as cigarettes and automobiles, the influence of peers is unmistakable.

The role of face-to-face groups has been recognized in recent industry campaigns attempting to change basic product attitudes. For years the milk industry has been trying to overcome the image of milk as a "sissified" drink by portraying its use in social and active situations. The men's-wear industry is trying to increase male interest in clothes by advertisements indicating that business associates judge a man by how well he dresses.

Of all face-to-face groups, the person's family undoubtedly plays the largest and most enduring role in basic attitude formation. From them he acquires a mental set not only toward religion and politics, but also toward thrift, chastity, food, human relations, and so forth. Although he often rebels against parental values in his teens, he often accepts these values eventually. Their formative influence on his eventual attitudes is undeniably great.

Family members differ in the types of product messages they carry to other family members. Most of what parents know about cereals, candy, and toys comes from their children. The wife stimulates family consideration of household appliances, furniture, and vacations. The husband tends to stimulate the fewest purchase ideas, with the exception of the automobile and perhaps the home.

The marketer must be alert to what attitudinal configurations dominate in different types of families, and also to how these change over time. For example, the parent's conception of the child's rights and privileges has undergone a radical shift in the last 30 years. The child has become the center of attention and orientation in a great number of households, leading some writers to label the modern family a "filiarchy." This has important implications not only for how to market to today's family, but also on how to market to tomorrow's family when the indulged child of today becomes the parent.

The Person. Social influences determine much but not all of the

---

Dynamics (Evanston, Illinois: Row, Peterson & Co., 1953), pp. 151–162; and Kurt Lewin, "Group Decision and Social Change," in Theodore M. Newcomb and Eugene L. Hartley, editors, *Readings in Social Psychology* (New York: Henry Holt Co., 1952).

[29] David Riesman, Reuel Denney, and Nathan Glazer, *The Lonely Crowd* (New Haven, Connecticut: Yale University Press, 1950).

behavioral variations in people. Two individuals subject to the same influences are not likely to have identical attitudes, although these attitudes will probably converge at more points than those of two strangers selected at random. Attitudes are really the product of social forces interacting with the individual's unique temperament and abilities.

Furthermore, attitudes do not automatically guarantee certain types of behavior. Attitudes are predispositions felt by buyers before they enter the buying process. The buying process itself is a learning experience and can lead to a change in attitudes.

Alfred Politz noted at one time that women stated a clear preference for G.E. refrigerators over Frigidaire, but that Frigidaire continued to outsell G.E.[30] The answer to this paradox was that preference was only one factor entering into behavior. When the consumer preferring G.E. actually undertook to purchase a new refrigerator, her curiosity led her to examine the other brands. Her perception was sensitized to refrigerator advertisements, sales arguments, and different product features. This led to learning and a change in attitudes.

THE HOBBESIAN ORGANIZATIONAL-FACTORS MODEL

The foregoing models throw light mainly on the behavior of family buyers.

But what of the large number of people who are organizational buyers? They are engaged in the purchase of goods not for the sake of consumption, but for further production or distribution. Their common denominator is the fact that they (1) are paid to make purchases for others and (2) operate within an organizational environment.

How do organizational buyers make their decisions? There seem to be two competing views. Many marketing writers have emphasized the predominance of rational motives in organizational buying.[31] Organizational buyers are represented as being most impressed by cost, quality, dependability, and service factors. They are portrayed as dedicated servants of the organization, seeking to secure the best terms. This view has led to an emphasis on performance and use characteristics in much industrial advertising.

Other writers have emphasized personal motives in organizational

30 Alfred Politz, "Motivation Research—Opportunity or Dilemma?", in Ferber and Wales, same reference as footnote 17, at pp. 57–58.

31 See Melvin T. Copeland, *Principles of Merchandising* (New York: McGraw-Hill Book Co., Inc., 1924).

buyer behavior. The purchasing agent's interest to do the best for his company is tempered by his interest to do the best for himself. He may be tempted to choose among salesmen according to the extent they entertain or offer gifts. He may choose a particular vendor because this will ingratiate him with certain company officers. He may short-cut his study of alternative suppliers to make his work day easier.

In truth, the buyer is guided by both personal and group goals; and this is the essential point. The political model of Thomas Hobbes comes closest of any model to suggesting the relationship between the two goals.[32] Hobbes held that man is "instinctively" oriented toward preserving and enhancing his own well-being. But this would produce a "war of every man against every man." This fear leads men to unite with others in a corporate body. The corporate man tries to steer a careful course between satisfying his own needs and those of the organization.

MARKETING APPLICATIONS OF HOBBESIAN MODEL

The import of the Hobbesian model is that organizational buyers can be appealed to on both personal and organizational grounds. The buyer has his private aims, and yet he tries to do a satisfactory job for his corporation. He will respond to persuasive salesmen and he will respond to rational product arguments. However, the best "mix" of the two is not a fixed quantity; it varies with the nature of the product, the type of organization, and the relative strength of the two drives in the particular buyer.

Where there is substantial similarity in what suppliers offer in the way of products, price, and service, the purchasing agent has less basis for rational choice. Since he can satisfy his organizational obligations with any one of a number of suppliers, he can be swayed by personal motives. On the other hand, where there are pronounced differences among the competing vendors' products, the purchasing agent is held more accountable for his choice and probably pays more attention to rational factors. Short-run personal gain becomes less motivating than the long-run gain which comes from serving the organization with distinction.

The marketing strategist must appreciate these goal conflicts of the organizational buyer. Behind all the ferment of purchasing agents to develop standards and employ value analysis lies their desire to avoid being thought of as order-clerks, and to develop better skills in reconciling personal and organizational objectives.[33]

[32] Thomas Hobbes, *Leviathan*, 1651 (London: G. Routledge and Sons, 1887).

[33] For an insightful account, see George Strauss, "Tactics of Lateral Relationship: The Purchasing Agent," *Administrative Science Quarterly*, Vol. 7 (September, 1962), pp. 161–186.

CONCLUSION

Think back over the five different behavioral models of how the buyer translates buying influences into purchasing responses.

Marshallian man is concerned chiefly with economic cues—prices and income—and makes a fresh utility calculation before each purchase.

Pavlovian man behaves in a largely habitual rather than thoughtful way; certain configurations of cues will set off the same behavior because of rewarded learning in the past.

Freudian man's choices are influenced strongly by motives and fantasies which take place deep within his private world.

Veblenian man acts in a way which is shaped largely by past and present social groups.

And finally, Hobbesian man seeks to reconcile individual gain with organizational gain.

Thus, it turns out that the "black box" of the buyer is not so black after all. Light is thrown in various corners by these models. Yet no one has succeeded in putting all these pieces of truth together into one coherent instrument for behavioral analysis. This, of course, is the goal of behavioral science.

RETROSPECTIVE COMMENT

Most of the writings on buyer behavior analysis before this article was written were addressed to single relationships that might exist between some aspect of buyer behavior and some demographic or psychological variable that might influence or explain it. A few writings were more systematic and comprehensive, leaning heavily on one school of thought about buyer behavior, such as learning theory or Freudian theory.

My purpose in this article was to suggest several competing *grand theories* for attempting to explain large ranges of observable buyer behavior. I identified five schools of thought and called them the Marshallian model, the Pavlovian model, the Freudian model, the Veblenian model, and the Hobbesian model. Each involved an interrelated and self-contained set of concepts that could throw theoretical and practical light on concrete buying situations. Subsequently, the field of consumer behavior began to experience a major boom in grand theory with efforts of such scholars as John A. Howard, Jagdish N. Sheth, Francesco M. Nicosia, Alan R. Andreasen, James F. Engel, David T. Kollat, and Roger D. Blackwell. Many of these models took their lead from stimulus-response learning theory or *gestalt* tradition and still neglect some of the factors suggested in my article. For example, the current buyer behavior models almost completely disregard Freudian psychological mechanisms and Hobbesian motivations.

The still unanswered questions is whether the field will ever be able to forge one model that answers all purposes of buyer behavior analysis or should attempt to create a repertoire of several self-contained models that are eminently suitable for analyzing particular problems in buyer behavior.—*Philip Kotler*

PART I. QUESTIONS FOR DISCUSSION

1. Develop a definition of "product" based on Levy's article.

2. What effect, if any, did previous purchases of instant coffee have on the respondents' descriptions of the instant coffee purchaser?

3. What shortcomings are present in orthodox economic theory in explaining consumer behavior? What contributions does economic theory make in the study of consumer behavior?

4. Contrast the Pavlovian learning model as described by Kotler with the Freudian psychoanalytic model.

5. Is the study of consumer behavior also applicable to organizational buying behavior? Defend your answer.

Part II.
Individual Factors in Consumer Behavior

A logical starting point in the search for an understanding of why the consumer behaves as he does is the examination of basic *individual* influences—motivation, perception, cognition, attitudes, learning, personality. Each of these influences are examined in one or more of the selections in Part II.

James A. Bayton's article serves as an introduction to this section by reviewing the basic behavioral determinants of motivation, cognition, and learning. Maslow's well-known discussion of the needs hierarchy is followed by Professor Raymond A. Bauer's treatment of perceived risk as a factor in buyer behavior. Grubb and Grathwohl discuss the importance of the concept of *self*, while Allison and Uhl describe their experiments in taste perception. Two selections by Katz and by Robert J. Lavidge and the late Gary A. Steiner are devoted to attitude and attitude change while the following selections by Tucker and Painter and Kassarjian analyze the influence of personality in consumer behavior. The final two selections in this section analyze the role of learning and the development of brand loyalty.

5. Motivation, Cognition, Learning— Basic Factors in Consumer Behavior

James A. Bayton

The analysis of consumer behavior presented here is derived from diverse concepts of several schools of psychology—from psychoanalysis to reinforcement theory.

Human behavior can be grouped into three categories—motivation, cognition, and learning. Motivation refers to the drives, urges, wishes, or desires which initiate the sequence of events known as "behavior." Cognition is the area in which all of the mental phenomena (perception, memory, judging, thinking, etc.) are grouped. Learning refers to those changes in behavior which occur through time relative to external stimulus conditions.

Each broad area is pertinent to particular problems of consumer behavior. All three together are pertinent to a comprehensive understanding of consumer behavior.

MOTIVATION

HUMAN NEEDS

Behavior is initiated through needs. Some psychologists claim that words such as "motives," "needs," "urges," "wishes," and "drives" should not be used as synonyms; others are content to use them interchangeably. There is one virtue in the term "drive" in that it carries the connotation of a force pushing the individual into action.

Motivation arises out of tension systems which create a state of disequilibrium for the individual. This triggers a sequence of psychological events directed toward the selection of a goal which the individual *anticipates* will bring about release from the tensions and the selection of patterns of action which he *anticipates* will bring him to the goal.

One problem in motivation theory is deriving a basic list of the human needs. Psychologists agree that needs fall into two general

Reprinted by permission of the author and publisher from the Journal of Marketing, *Vol. 22 (January 1958), pp. 282–289.*

categories—those arising from tension-systems physiological in nature (biogenic needs such as hunger, thirst, and sex), and those based upon tension-systems existing in the individual's subjective psychological state and in his relations with others (psychogenic needs).

Although there is not much disagreement as to the list of specific biogenic needs, there is considerable difference of opinion as to the list of specific psychogenic needs. However, the various lists of psychogenic needs can be grouped into three broad categories:

1. *Affectional needs*—the needs to form and maintain warm, harmonious, and emotionally satisfying relations with others.

2. *Ego-bolstering needs*—the needs to enhance or promote the personality; to achieve; to gain prestige and recognition; to satisfy the ego through domination of others.

3. *Ego-defensive needs*—the needs to protect the personality to avoid physical and psychological harm; to avoid ridicule and "loss of face"; to prevent loss of prestige; to avoid or to obtain relief from anxiety.

One pitfall in the analysis of motivation is the assumption that a particular situation involves just one specific need. In most instances the individual is driven by a combination of needs. It seems likely that "love" brings into play a combination of affectional, ego-bolstering, and ego-defensive needs as well as biogenic needs. Within the combination some needs will be relatively strong, others relatively weak. The strongest need within the combination can be called the "prepotent" need. A given consumer product can be defined in terms of the specific need-combination involved and the relative strengths of these needs.

Another pitfall is the assumption that identical behaviors have identical motivational backgrounds. This pitfall is present whether we are thinking of two different individuals or the same individual at two different points in time. John and Harry can be different in the motivational patterns leading to the purchase of their suits. Each could have one motivational pattern influencing such a purchase at age twenty and another at age forty.

EGO-INVOLVEMENT

One important dimension of motivation is the degree of ego-involvement. The various specific need-patterns are not equal in significance to the individual. Some are superficial in meaning; others represent (for the individual) tremendous challenges to the very essence of existence. There is some evidence that one of the positive correlates of degree of ego-involvement is the amount of cognitive activity (judging, thinking, etc.) involved. This means that consumer goods which tap low degrees of ego-involvement will be purchased with a relatively lower degree of conscious decision-making activity than goods which tap higher degrees of ego-involvement. Such a factor must be considered when decisions are made on advertising and marketing tactics.

At times the ego-involvement factor is a source of conflict between client and researcher. This can occur when research reveals that the product taps a low degree of ego-involvement within consumers. The result is difficult for a client to accept; because *he* is ego-involved and, therefore, cognitively active about his product, consumers must certainly be also. It is hard for such a client to believe that consumers simply do not engage in a great deal of cognitive activity when they make purchases within his product class. One way to ease this particular client-researcher conflict would be for the researcher to point out this implication of the ego-involvement dimension.

"TRUE" AND RATIONALIZED MOTIVES

A particular difficulty in the study of motivation is the possibility that there can be a difference between "true" motives and rationalized motives. Individuals sometimes are unaware of the exact nature of drives initiating their behavior patterns. When this occurs, they attempt to account for their behavior through "rationalization" by assigning motivations to their behavior which are acceptable to their personality structures. They may do this with no awareness that they are rationalizing. There can be other instances, however, in which individuals are keenly aware of their motivations, but feel it would be harmful or socially unacceptable to reveal them. When this is the case, they deliberately conceal their motivations.

These possibilities create a problem for the researcher. Must he assume that every behavior pattern is based upon unconscious motivation? If not, what criteria are to be used in deciding whether to be alert to unconscious motivation for this behavior pattern and not that one? What is the relative importance of unconscious motives, if present, and rationalized motives? Should rationalized motives be ignored? After all, rationalized motives have a certain validity for the individual—they are the "real" motives insofar as he is aware of the situation.

The situation is even more complicated than this—what about the dissembler? When the individual actually is dissembling, the researcher must attempt to determine the true motives. But, how shall we determine whether we are faced with a situation where the respondent is rationalizing or dissembling? In a given case, did a projective technique reveal an unconscious motive or the true motive of a dissembler? Conceptually, rationalized motives and dissembled motives are not equal in psychological implication; but it is rare, if ever, that one finds attempts to segregate the two in consumer research directed toward the analysis of motivation. This failure is understandable, to some extent, because of the lack of valid criteria upon which to base the distinction.

COGNITION

NEED-AROUSAL

Motivation, thus, refers to a state of need-arousal—a condition exerting "push" on the individual to engage in those activities which he anticipates will have the highest probability of bringing him gratification of a particular need-pattern. Whether gratification actually will be attained or not is a matter of future events. Central to the psychological activities which now must be considered in the sequence are the complex of "mental" operations and forces known as the cognitive processes. We can view these cognitive processes as being *purposive* in that they serve the individual in his attempts to achieve satisfaction of his needs. These cognitive processes are *regulatory* in that they determine in large measure the direction and particular steps taken in his attempt to attain satisfaction of the initiating needs.

THE EGO-SUPEREGO CONCEPT

The ego-superego concept is pertinent to a discussion of cognitive activities which have been triggered by needs. Discussions of the ego-superego concept usually come under the heading of motivation as an aspect of personality. It is our feeling that motivation and the consequences of motivation should be kept systematically "clean." In the broadest sense, ego and superego are mental entities in that they involve memory, perceiving, judging, and thinking.

The Ego. The ego is the "executive," determining how the individual shall seek satisfaction of his needs. Through perception, memory, judging, and thinking the ego attempts to integrate the needs, on the one hand, and the conditions of the external world, on the other, in such manner that needs can be satisfied without danger or harm to the individual. Often this means that gratification must be postponed until a situation has developed, or has been encountered, which does not contain harm or danger. The turnpike driver who does not exceed the speed limit because he sees signs saying there are radar checks is under the influence of the ego. So is the driver who sees no cars on a straight stretch and takes the opportunity to drive at excessive speed.

The Superego. The superego involves the ego-ideal and conscience. The ego-ideal represents the positive standards of ethical and moral conduct the individual has developed for himself. Conscience is, in a sense, the "judge," evaluating the ethics and morality of behavior and, through guilt-feelings, administering punishment when these are violated. If a driver obeys the speed limit because he would feel guilty in doing otherwise, he is under the influence of the superego. (The first driver above is under the influence of the ego because he is avoiding a fine, not guilt feelings.)

SPECIFIC EXAMPLES

Credit is a form of economic behavior based to some extent upon ego-superego considerations. It is generally felt that one cause of consumer-credit expansion has been a shift away from the superego's role in attitudes toward credit. The past ego-ideal was to build savings; debt was immoral—something to feel guilty about, to avoid, to hide. These two superego influences restrained the use of credit. For some cultural reason, credit and debt have shifted away from superego dominance and are now more under the control of the ego—the primary concern now seems to be how much of it can be used without risking financial danger.

The purchasing of specific consumer goods can be considered from the point of view of these two influences. Certain goods (necessities, perhaps) carry little superego influence, and the individual is psychologically free to try to maximize the probability of obtaining satisfaction of his needs while minimizing the probability of encountering harm in so doing. Other goods, however, tap the superego. When a product represents an aspect of the ego-ideal there is a strong positive force to possess it. Conversely, when a product involves violation of the conscience, a strong negative force is generated against its purchase.

Let us assume that, when the need-push asserts itself, a variety of goal-objects come into awareness as potential sources of gratification. In consumer behavior these goal-objects may be different brand names. The fact that a particular set of goal-objects come into awareness indicates the generic character of this stage in the cognitive process—a class of goal-objects is seen as containing the possible satisfier. What the class of goal-objects and the specific goal-objects within the class "promise" in terms of gratification are known as "expectations."

There are, then, two orders of expectation: generic expectancies, and object-expectancies. Suppose the needs were such that the individual "thought" of brands of frozen orange juice. Some of the generic expectations for frozen orange juice are a certain taste, quality, source of vitamin C, protection against colds, and ease of preparation. The particular brands carry expectations specifically associated with one brand as against another. The expectation might be that brand A has a more refreshing taste than brand B.

In many instances, cognitive competition occurs between two or more generic categories before it does between goal-objects within a generic category. Much consumer-behavior research is directed toward the investigation of generic categories—tires, automobiles, appliances, etc. But perhaps not enough attention has been given to the psychological analysis of cognitive competition between generic categories. An example of a problem being studied is the competition between television viewing, movie going, and magazine reading. For a particular producer, cognitive competition within the pertinent generic category is usually of more concern than cognitive competition between his generic category and others. The producer usually wants only an intensive analysis of consumer psychology with respect to the particular generic category of which his product is a member.

Let us now assume that under need-push four alternative goal-objects (brands A, B, C, and D) came into awareness. Why these particular brands and not others? Why are brands E and F absent? An obvious reason for brand E's absence might be that the individual had never been exposed to the fact that brand E exists. He had been exposed to brand F, however. Why is it absent? The problem here is one of memory—a key cognitive process. The producers of brands E and F obviously are faced with different problems.

Two sets of circumstances contain the independent variables that determine whether a given item will be remembered. One is the nature of the experience resulting from actual consumption or utilization of the goal-object. This will be discussed later when we come to the reinforcement theory of learning. The other is the circumstances present on what might be called vicarious exposures to the goal-object—vicarious in that at the time of exposure actual consumption or utilization of the goal-object does not occur. The most obvious example would be an advertisement of the goal-object. Of course, the essential purpose of an advertisement is to expose the individual to the goal-object in such a manner that at some subsequent time it will be remembered readily. The search for the most effective methods of doing this by manipulation of the physical aspects of the advertisement and the appeals used in it is a continuing effort in consumer-behavior research. Finally, for many consumers these two sets of circumstances will be jointly operative. Experiences with the goal-object and subsequent vicarious exposures can coalesce to heighten the memory potential for an item.

MAKING A CHOICE

With, say, four brands in awareness, the individual must now make a choice. What psychological factors underlie this choice? The four brands could be in awareness due to the memory factor because they are immediately present in the environment; or some because they are in the environment, and the others because of memory.

The first problem is the extent to which the items are differentiated. The various goal-objects have attributes which permit the individual to differentiate between them. The brand name is one attribute; package another; design still another. These differentiating attributes (from the point of view of the consumer's perceptions) can be called signs or cues. All such signs are not equally important in consumer decisions. Certain of them are depended upon much more than others. For example, in a study of how housewives select fresh oranges, the critical or key signs were thickness of skin, color of skin, firmness of the orange, and presence or absence of "spots" on the skin.

The signs have expectancies associated with them. Package (a sign) can carry the expectancy of quality. Thin-skin oranges carry the expectancy of juice; spots carry the expectancy of poor taste quality and insufficient amount of juice. Often sign-expectancies determined through consumer research are irrelevant or invalid. Signs are irrelevant when they do not represent a critical differentiating attribute of a goal-object. Certain discolorations on oranges have nothing to do with their intrinsic quality. Expectancies are invalid when they refer to qualities that do not in fact exist in association with a particular sign.

The different goal-objects in awareness can be assessed in terms of the extent to which they arouse similar expectancies. This phenomenon of similarity of expectations within a set of different goal-objects is known as generalization. One goal-object (brand A, perhaps), because of its associated expectancies, can be assumed to have maximum appeal within the set of alternative goal-objects. The alternates then can be ordered in terms of how their associated expectancies approximate those of brand A. Is this ordering and the psychological distances between the items of the nature of:

Brand A		Brand A
Brand B		
	or	Brand B
Brand C		Brand C

These differences in ordering and psychological distance are referred to as generalization gradients. In the first case, the expectancies associated with brand B are quite similar to those for brand A, but are not quite as powerful in appeal. Brand C has relatively little of this. In the second case, the generalization gradient is of a different form, showing that brand B offers relatively little psychological competition to brand A. (There will also be generalization gradients with respect to cognitive competition between generic categories.) In addition to the individual producer being concerned about the memory potential of his particular brand, he needs to determine the nature of the generalization gradient for his product and the products of his competitors. Mere ordering is not enough—the "psychological distances" between positions must be determined, also, and the factor determining these distances is similarity of expectancy.

The discussion above was concerned with cognitive processes as they relate to mental representation of goal-objects under the instigation of need-arousal. The items brought into awareness, the differentiating sign-expectancies, and the generalization gradient are the central factors in the particular cognitive field aroused under a given "need-push." One important dimension has not yet been mentioned—instrumental acts. These are acts necessary in obtaining the goal-object and the acts involved in consuming or utilizing it. Examples are: "going downtown" to get to a department store, squeezing the orange to get its juice, ease of entry into service stations, and the operations involved in do-it-yourself house painting.

Instrumental acts can have positive or negative value for the individual. One who makes fewer shopping trips to downtown stores because of traffic and parking conditions displays an instrumental act with negative value. Frozen foods are products for which much of the appeal lies in the area of instrumental acts. The development of automatic transmissions and of power-steering in automobiles are examples of product changes concerned with instrumental acts. The point is that concentration upon cognitive reactions to the goal-object, *per se*, could be masking critical aspects of the situation based upon cognitive reactions to the instrumental acts involved in obtaining or utlizing the goal-object.

LEARNING

GOAL-OBJECT

Starting with need-arousal, continuing under the influence of cognitive processes, and engaging in the necessary action, the individual arrives at consumption or utilization of a goal-object. Using our consumer-behavior illustration, let us say that the consumer bought brand A and is now in the process of consuming or utilizing it. We have now arrived at one of the most critical aspects of the entire psychological sequence. It is with use of the goal-object that degree of gratification of the initial needs will occur.

REINFORCEMENT

When consumption or utilization of the goal-object leads to gratification of the initiating needs there is "reinforcement." If at some later date the same needs are aroused, the individual will tend to repeat the process of selecting and getting to the same goal-object. If brand A yields a high degree of gratification, then at some subsequent time, when the same needs arise, the consumer will have an increased tendency to select brand A once again. Each succeeding time that brand A brings gratification, further reinforcement occurs, thus further increasing the likelihood that in the future, with the given needs, brand A will be selected.

This type of behavioral change—increasing likelihood that an act will be repeated—is learning; and reinforcement is necessary for learning to take place. Continued reinforcement will influence the cognitive processes. Memory of the goal-object will be increasingly enhanced; particular sign-expectancies will be more and more firmly established; and the generalization gradient will be changed in that the psychological distance on this gradient between brand A and the competing brands will be increased.

HABIT

One of the most important consequences of continued reinforcement is the influence this has on the extent to which cognitive processes enter the picture at the times of subsequent need-arousal. With continued reinforcement, the amount of cognitive activity decreases; the individual engages less and less in decision-making mental activities. This can continue until, upon need-arousal, the goal-obtaining activities are practically automatic. At this stage there is a habit.

Note this use of the term "habit." One frequently hears that a person does certain things by *force* of habit," that habit is an initiator of behavioral sequences. Actually habits are not initiating forces in themselves; habits are repeated response patterns accompanied by a minimum of cognitive activity. There must be some condition of need-arousal before the habit-type response occurs. This has serious implications in the field of consumer behavior. The promotional and marketing problems faced by a competitor of brand A will be of one type if purchase behavior for brand A is habitual, of another if this is not true. If the purchase is largely a habit, there is little cognitive activity available for the competitor to "work on."

Frequency of repeating a response is not a valid criterion for determining whether or not a habit exists. An act repeated once a week can be just as much a habit as one repeated several times a day. The frequency of a response is but an index of the frequency with which the particular need-patterns are aroused. Frequency of response also is often used as a measure of the *strength* of a habit. The test of the strength of a habit is the extent to which an individual will persist in an act after it has ceased providing need gratification. The greater this persistence, the stronger was the habit in the first place.

PROBLEM—CONCEPT—RESEARCH

The above views integrate concepts in contemporary psychology which seem necessary for a comprehensive explanation of human behavior, and apply these concepts to the analysis of consumer behavior. Each psychological process touched upon contains areas for further analysis and specification.

Some type of comprehensive theory of human behavior is necessary as a *working tool* to avoid a lack of discipline in attacking problems in consumer behavior. Too frequently a client with a practical problem approaches a researcher with an indication that all that is needed is a certain methodology—depth interviewing, scaling, or projective devices for example.

The first step should be to take the practical problem and translate it into its pertinent conceptual entities. This phase of the problem raises the question of motivations. Here is a question involving relevance and validity of sign-expectancies. There is a question dealing with a generalization gradient, etc. Once the pertinent conceptual entities have been identified, and only then, we arrive at the stage of hypothesis formulation. Within each conceptual entity, a relationship between independent and dependent variables is established as a hypothesis to be tested.

Often the relation between conceptual entities must be investigated. For example, what is the effect of continuing reinforcement on a specific generalization gradient? Within the same research project, one psychological entity can be a dependent variable at one phase of the research and an independent variable at another. At one time we might be concerned with establishing the factors associated with differential memory of sign-expectancies. At another time we could be concerned with the influence of remembered sign-expectancies upon subsequent purchase-behavior.

Discipline requires that one turn to methodology only when the pertinent conceptual entities have been identified and the relationships between independent and dependent variables have been expressed in the form of hypotheses. Fundamentally this sequence in the analysis of a problem serves to delimit the methodological possibilities. In any event, the methodologies demanded are those which will produce unambiguous tests of each particular hypothesis put forth. Finally, the results must be translated into the terms of the original practical problem.

We have used the term "discipline" in this phase of our discussion. The researcher must discipline himself to follow the above steps. Some find this a difficult thing to do and inevitably their data become ambiguous. They must resort to improvisation in order to make sense of the results *after* the project is completed. A research project is truly a work of art when the conceptual analysis, the determination of the hypotheses, and the methodologies have been developed in such an "air-tight" sequence that practically all that is necessary is to let the facts speak for themselves.

RETROSPECTIVE COMMENT

Since 1958 the component of the equation, motivation—cognition—learning, that appears to have received the greatest emphasis in consumer psychology has been cognition. This emphasis has paralleled theoretical and methodological developments, dealing with cognition, in experimental and social psychology. Of particular importance has been the application of some older and some newer statistical procedures. Much of this emphasis has been upon identifying cognitive structures that are involved in consumer responses. Factor analytic techniques have been used to identify independent cognitive patterns that are brought into play when consumers have occasion to think about products. There has been use of factor analysis to determine the cognitive structure involved in corporate images. Also, factor analysis has served in efforts to identify types of consumers who are similiar in their attitudes, beliefs and opinions with respect to products. In addition, the development of multi-dimensional scaling methods has opened new ways of attacking problems of how consumers' "minds" organize themselves in terms of dissimilarities and preferences. Finally, recent advances in multivariate statistics are stimulating intensive analysis of the cognitive and behavioral (learning) aspects of consumer behavior.
—*James A. Bayton*, Howard University

6. A Theory of Human Motivation

A. H. Maslow

THE "PHYSIOLOGICAL" NEEDS

The needs that are usually taken as the starting point for motivation theory are the so-called physiological drives. Two recent lines of research make it necessary to revise our customary notions about these needs: first, the development of the concept of homeostasis, and, second, the finding that appetites (preferential choices among foods) are a fairly efficient indication of actual needs or lacks in the body.

Homeostasis refers to the body's automatic efforts to maintain a constant, normal state of the blood stream. Cannon[1] has described this process for (1) the water content of the blood, (2) salt content, (3) sugar content, (4) protein content, (5) fat content, (6) calcium content, (7) oxygen content, (8) constant hydrogen-iron level (acid-base balance) and (9) constant temperature of the blood. Obviously this list can be extended to include other minerals, the hormones, vitamins, etc.

Young[2] has summarized the work on appetite in its relation to body needs. If the body lacks some chemical, the individual will tend to develop a specific appetite or partial hunger for that food element.

Thus it seems impossible as well as useless to make any list of fundamental physiological needs for they can come to almost any number one might wish, depending on the degree of specificity of description. We cannot identify all physiological needs as homeostatic. That sexual desire, sleepiness, sheer activity, and maternal behavior in animals are homeostatic, has not yet been demonstrated. Furthermore, this list would not include the various sensory pleasures (tastes, smells, tickling, stroking) which are probably physiological and which may become the goals of motivated behavior.

[1] W. B. Cannon, *Wisdom of the Body* (New York: Norton, 1932).
[2] P. T. Young, "The Experimental Analysis of Appetite," *Psychological Bulletin,* XXXVIII (1941), 129–64.

Abridged from "A Theory of Human Motivation," Psychological Review, *Vol. 50 (1943), pp. 370–396. Copyright 1943 by The American Psychological Association.*

In a previous paper[3] it has been pointed out that these physiological drives or needs are to be considered unusual rather than typical because they are isolable and because they are localizable somatically. That is to say, they are relatively independent of each other, of other motivations and of the organism as a whole, and, in many cases, it is possible to demonstrate a localized, underlying somatic base for the drive. This is true less generally than has been thought (exceptions are fatigue, sleepiness, maternal responses), but it is still true in the classic instances of hunger, sex, and thirst.

It should be pointed out again that any of the physiological needs and the consummatory behavior involved with them serve as channels for all sorts of other needs as well. The person who thinks he is hungry may actually be seeking more for comfort or dependence than for vitamins or proteins. Conversely, it is possible to satisfy the hunger need in part by other activities such as drinking water or smoking cigarettes. In other words, these physiological needs are only relatively isolable.

Undoubtedly these physiological needs are the most prepotent of all needs. What this means specifically is that, in the human being who is missing everything in life in an extreme fashion, it is most likely that the major motivation would be the physiological needs rather than any others. A person who is lacking food, safety, love and esteem would most probably hunger for food more strongly than for anything else.

If all the needs are unsatisfied, and the organism is then dominated by the physiological needs, all other needs may become simply non-existent or be pushed into the background. It is then fair to characterize the whole organism by saying simply that it is hungry, for consciousness is almost completely pre-empted by hunger. All capacities are put into the service of hunger-satisfaction, and the organization of these capacities is almost entirely determined by the one purpose of satisfying hunger. The receptors and effectors, the intelligence, memory, habits, all may now be defined simply as hunger-gratifying tools. Capacities that are not useful for this purpose lie dormant or are pushed into the background. The urge to write poetry, the desire to acquire an automobile, the interest in American history, the desire for a new pair of shoes are, in the extreme case, forgotten or become of secondary importance. For the man who is extremely and dangerously hungry, no other interests exist but food. He dreams food, he remembers food, he thinks about food, he emotes only about food, he perceives only food, and he wants only food. The more subtle determinants that ordinarily fuse with the physiological drives in organizing even feeding, drinking, or sexual behavior, may now be so completely overwhelmed as to allow us to

[3] A. H. Maslow, "A Preface to Motivation Theory," *Psychosomatic Medicine* (1943), 85–92.

speak at this time (but *only* at this time) of pure hunger drive and behavior, with the one unqualified aim of relief.

Another peculiar characteristic of the human organism when it is dominated by a certain need is that the whole philosophy of the future tends also to change. For our chronically and extremely hungry man, utopia can be defined very simply as a place where there is plenty of food. He tends to think that, if only he is guaranteed food for the rest of his life, he will be perfectly happy and will never want anything more. Life itself tends to be defined in terms of eating. Anything else will be defined as unimportant. Freedom, love, community feeling, respect, philosophy, may all be waved aside as fripperies which are useless, since they fail to fill the stomach. Such a man may fairly be said to live by bread alone.

It cannot possibly be denied that such things are true, but their *generality* can be denied. Emergency conditions are, almost by definition, rare in the normally functioning peaceful society. That this truism can be forgotten is due mainly to two reasons. First, rats have few motivations other than physiological ones, and since so much of the research upon motivation has been made with these animals, it is easy to carry the rat-picture over to the human being. Second, it is too often not realized that culture itself is an adaptive tool, one of whose main functions is to make the physiological emergencies come less and less often. In most of the known societies, chronic extreme hunger of the emergency type is rare rather than common. In any case, this is still true in the United States. The average American citizen is experiencing appetite rather than hunger when he says, "I am hungry." He is apt to experience sheer life-and-death hunger only by accident and then only a few times through his entire life.

Obviously a good way to obscure the "higher" motivations, and to get a lopsided view of human capacities and human nature, is to make the organism extremely and chronically hungry or thirsty. Anyone who attempts to make an emergency picture into a typical one and who will measure all of man's goals and desires by his behavior during extreme physiological deprivation is certainly being blind to many things. It is quite true that man lives by bread alone—when there is no bread. But what happens to man's desires when there is plenty of bread and when his belly is chronically filled?

At once other (and "higher") needs emerge and these, rather than physiological hungers, dominate the organism. And when these in turn are satisfied, again new (and still "higher") needs emerge and so on. This is what we mean by saying that the basic human needs are organized into a hierarchy of relative prepotency.

One main implication of this phrasing is that gratification becomes as important a concept as deprivation in motivation theory, for it releases the organism from the domination of a relatively more physiological need, permitting thereby the emergence of other more social goals. The physiological needs, along with their partial goals, when chronically gratified cease to exist as active determinants or organizers of behavior. They now exist only in a potential fashion in the sense that they may emerge again to dominate the organism if they are thwarted. But a want that is satisfied is no longer a want. The organism is dominated and its behavior organized only by unsatisfied needs. If hunger is satisfied, it becomes unimportant in the current dynamics of the individual.

This statement is somewhat qualified by a hypothesis to be discussed more fully later, namely, that it is precisely those individuals in whom a certain need has always been satisfied who are best equipped to tolerate deprivation of that need in the future; furthermore, those who have been deprived in the past will react to current satisfactions differently from the one who has never been deprived.

THE SAFETY NEEDS

If the physiological needs are relatively well gratified, there then emerges a new set of needs, which we may categorize roughly as the safety needs. All that has been said of the physiological needs are equally true, although in lesser degree, of these desires. The organism may equally well be wholly dominated by them. They may serve as the almost exclusive organizers of behavior, recruiting all the capacities of the organism in their service, and we may then fairly describe the whole organism as a safety-seeking mechanism. Again we may say of the receptors, the effectors, of the intellect and the other capacities that they are primarily safety-seeking tools. Again, as in the hungry man, we find that the dominating goal is a strong determinant not only of his current world-outlook and philosophy but also of his philosophy of the future. Practically everything looks less important than safety (even sometimes the physiological needs which being satisfied, are now underestimated). A man, in this state, if it is extreme enough and chronic enough, may be characterized as living almost for safety alone.

Although in this paper we are interested primarily in the needs of the adult, we can approach an understanding of his safety needs perhaps more efficiently by observation of infants and children, in whom these needs are much more simple and obvious. One reason for the clearer appearance of the threat or danger reaction in infants is that they do not inhibit this reaction at all, whereas adults in our society have been taught to inhibit it at all costs. Thus even when adults do feel their safety to be threatened, we may not be able to see this on the surface. Infants will react in a total fashion and as if they were endangered, if they are disturbed or dropped suddenly, startled by loud noises, flashing light, or other unusual sensory stimulation, by rough handling, by general loss of support in the mother's arms, or by inadequate support.[4]

In infants we can also see a much more direct reaction to bodily illnesses of various kinds. Sometimes these illnesses seem to be immediately and per se threatening and seem to make the child feel unsafe. For instance, vomiting, colic, or other sharp pains seem to make the child look at the whole world in a different way. At such a moment of pain, it may be postulated that, for the child, the appearance of the whole world suddenly changes from sunniness to darkness, so to speak, and becomes a place in which anything at all might happen, in which previously stable things have suddenly become unstable. Thus a child who because of some bad food is taken ill may, for a day or two, develop fear, nightmares, and a need for protection and reassurance never seen in him before his illness.

Another indication of the child's need for safety is his preference for some kind of undisrupted routine or rhythm. He seems to want a predictable, orderly world. For instance, injustice, unfairness, or inconsistency in the parents seems to make a child feel anxious and unsafe. This attitude may be not so much because of the injustice per se or any particular pains involved, but rather because this treatment threatens to make the world look unreliable or unsafe or unpredictable. Young children seem to thrive better under a system which has at least a skeletal outline of rigidity, in which there is a schedule of a kind, some sort of routine, something that can be counted upon, not only for the present, but also far into the future. Perhaps one could express this more accurately by saying that the child needs an organized world rather than an unorganized or unstructured one.

The central role of the parents and the normal family setup are indisputable. Quarreling, physical assault, separation, divorce, or death within the family may be particularly terrifying. Also parental outbursts of rage or threats of punishment directed to the child, calling him names, speaking to him harshly, shaking him, handling him roughly, or actual physical punishment sometimes elicit such total panic and terror in the child that we must assume more is involved than the physical pain alone. While it is true that in some children this terror may represent also a fear of loss of parental love, it can also occur in completely rejected children, who seem to cling to the hating parents more for sheer safety and protection than because of hope of love.

---

[4] As the child grows up, sheer knowledge and familiarity as well as better motor development make these "dangers" less and less dangerous and more and more manageable. Throughout life it may be said that one of the main conative functions of education is this neutralizing of apparent dangers through knowledge, e.g., I am not afraid of thunder because I know something about it.

Confronting the average child with new, unfamiliar, strange, unmanageable stimuli or situations will too frequently elicit the danger or terror reaction, as, for example, getting lost or even being separated from the parents for a short time, being confronted with new faces, new situations, or new tasks, the sight of strange, unfamiliar or uncontrollable objects, illness, or death. Particularly at such times, the child's frantic clinging to his parents is eloquent testimony to their role as protectors (quite apart from their roles as food-givers and love-givers).

From these and similar observations, we may generalize and say that the average child in our society usually prefers a safe, orderly, predictable, organized world which he can count on and in which unexpected, unmanageable, or other dangerous things do not happen and in which, in any case, he has all-powerful parents who protect and shield him from harm.

That these reactions may so easily be observed in children is in a way a proof of the fact that children in our society feel too unsafe (or, in a word, are badly brought up). Children who are reared in an unthreatening, loving family do *not* ordinarily react as we have described above.[5] In such children the danger reactions are apt to come mostly to objects or situations that adults too would consider dangerous.[6]

The healthy, normal, fortunate adult in our culture is largely satisfied in his safety needs. The peaceful, smoothly running, "good" society ordinarily makes its members feel safe enough from wild animals, extremes of temperature, criminals, assault and murder, tyranny, etc. Therefore, in a very real sense, they no longer have any safety needs as active motivators. Just as a sated man no longer feels hungry, a safe man no longer feels endangered. If we wish to see these needs directly and clearly we must turn to neurotic or near-neurotic individuals, and to the economic and social underdogs. In between these extremes, we can perceive the expressions of safety needs only in such phenomena as, for instance, the common preference for a job with tenure and protection, the desire for a savings account, and for insurance of various kinds (medical, dental, unemployment, disability, old age).

Other broader aspects of the attempt to seek safety and stability in the world are seen in the very common preference for familiar rather

[5] M. Shirley, "Children's Adjustments to a Strange Situation," *Journal of Abnormal and Social Psychology*, XXXVII (1942), 201–17.

[6] A "test battery" for safety might be confronting the child with a small exploding firecracker or with a bewhiskered face, having the mother leave the room, putting him upon a high ladder, giving him a hypodermic injection, having a mouse crawl up to him, etc. Of course I cannot seriously recommend the deliberate use of such "tests," for they might very well harm the child being tested. But these and similar situations come up by the score in the child's ordinary day-to-day living and may be observed. There is no reason why these stimuli should not be used with, for example, young chimpanzees.

than unfamiliar things, or for the known rather than the unknown. The tendency to have some religion or world-philosophy that organizes the universe and the men in it into some sort of satisfactorily coherent, meaningful whole is also in part motivated by safety-seeking. Here too we may list science and philosophy in general as partially motivated by the safety needs (we shall see later that there are also other motivations to scientific, philosophical, or religious endeavor).

Otherwise the need for safety is seen as an active and dominant mobilizer of the organism's resources only in emergencies, e.g., war, disease, natural catastrophes, crime waves, societal disorganization, neurosis, brain injury, chronically bad situation. . . .

THE LOVE NEEDS

If both the physiological and safety needs are fairly well gratified, then there will emerge the love and affection and belongingness needs, and the whole cycle already described will repeat itself with this new center. Now the person will feel keenly, as never before, the absence of friends or a sweetheart or a wife or children. He will hunger for affectionate relations with people in general, namely, for a place in his group, and he will strive with great intensity to achieve this goal. He will want to attain a place more than anything else in the world and may even forget that once, when he was hungry, he sneered at love.

In our society the thwarting of these needs is the most commonly found core in cases of maladjustments and more severe psychopathology. Love and affection, as well as their possible expression in sexuality, are generally looked upon with ambivalence and are customarily hedged about with many restrictions and inhibitions. Practically all theorists of psychopathology have stressed thwarting of the love needs as basic in the picture of maladjustment. Many clinical studies have therefore been made of this need and we know more about it perhaps than any of the other needs except the physiological ones.[7]

One thing that must be stressed at this point is that love is not synonymous with sex. Sex may be studied as a purely physiological need. Ordinarily sexual behavior is multi-determined, that is to say, determined not only by sexual but also by other needs, chief among which are the love and affection needs. Also not to be overlooked is the fact that the love needs involve both giving *and* receiving love.[8]

[7] Maslow and Mittelmann, *op. cit.*

[8] For further details see A. H. Maslow, "The Dynamics of Psychological Security-Insecurity," *Character and Personality*, X (1942), 331–44, and J. Plant, *Personality and the Cultural Pattern* (New York: Commonwealth Fund, 1937), chap. v.

THE ESTEEM NEEDS

All people in our society (with a few pathological exceptions) have a need or desire for a stable, firmly based, (usually) high evaluation of themselves, for self-respect, or self-esteem, and for the esteem of others. By firmly based self-esteem, we mean that which is soundly based upon real capacity, achievement, and respect from others. These needs may be classified into two subsidiary sets. These are, first, the desire for strength, for achievement, for adequacy, for confidence in the face of the world, and for independence and freedom.[9] Second, we have what we may call the desire for reputation or prestige (defining it as respect or esteem from other people), recognition, attention, importance, or appreciation.[10] These needs have been relatively stressed by Alfred Adler and his followers, and have been relatively neglected by Freud and the psychoanalysts. More and more today, however, there is appearing widespread appreciation of their central importance.

Satisfaction of the self-esteem need leads to feelings of self-confidence, worth, strength, capability, and adequacy, of being useful and necessary in the world. But thwarting of these needs produces feelings of inferiority, of weakness, and of helplessness. These feelings in turn give rise to either basic discouragement or else compensatory or neurotic trends. An appreciation of the necessity of basic self-confidence and an understanding of how helpless people are without it, can be easily gained from a study of severe traumatic neurosis.[11]

THE NEED FOR SELF-ACTUALIZATION

Even if all these needs are satisfied, we may still often (if not always) expect that a new discontent and restlessness will soon develop, unless

[9] Whether or not this particular desire is universal we do not know. The crucial question, especially important today, is, "Will men who are enslaved and dominated inevitably feel dissatisfied and rebellious?" We may assume on the basis of commonly known clinical data that a man who has known true freedom (not paid for by giving up safety and security but rather built on the basis of adequate safety and security) will not willingly or easily allow his freedom to be taken away from him. But we do not know that this is true for the person born into slavery. The events of the next decade should give us our answer. See discussion of this problem in E. Fromm, *Escape from Freedom* (New York: Farrar Rinehart, 1941), chap. v.

[10] Perhaps the desire for prestige and respect from others is subsidiary to the desire for self-esteem or confidence in one's self. Observation of children seems to indicate that this is so, but clinical data give no clear support of such a conclusion.

[11] A. Kardiner, *The Traumatic Neuroses of War* (New York: Hoeber, 1941). For more extensive discussion of normal self-esteem, as well as for reports of various researches, see A. H. Maslow, "Dominance, Personality, and Social Behavior in Women," *Journal of Social Psychology*, X (1939), 3–39.

the individual is doing what he is fitted for. A musician must make music, an artist must paint, a poet must write, if he is to be ultimately happy. What a man *can* be, he *must* be. This need we may call self-actualization.

This term, first coined by Kurt Goldstein, is being used in this paper in a much more specific and limited fashion. It refers to the desire for self-fulfillment, namely, to the tendency for one to be actualized in what one is potentially. This tendency might be phrased as the desire to become more and more what one is, to become everything that one is capable of becoming.

The specific form that these needs take will of course vary greatly from person to person. In one individual it may be expressed maternally, as the desire to be an ideal mother, in another athletically, in still another aesthetically, in the painting of pictures, and in another inventively in the creation of new contrivances. It is not necessarily a creative urge although in people who have any capabilities for creation it will take this form.

The clear emergence of these needs rests upon prior satisfaction of the physiological, safety, love and esteem needs. We shall call people who are satisfied in these needs, basically satisfied people, and it is from these that we may expect the fullest (and healthiest) creativeness.[12] Since, in our society, basically satisfied people are the exception, we do not know much about self-actualization, either experimentally or clinically. It remains a challenging problem for research.

THE PRECONDITIONS FOR THE BASIC NEED SATISFACTIONS

There are certain conditions which are immediate prerequisites for the basic need satisfactions. Danger to these is reacted to almost as if it were a direct danger to the basic needs themselves. Such conditions as freedom to speak, freedom to do what one wishes so long as no harm is done to others, freedom to express one's self, freedom to investigate and seek for information, freedom to defend one's self, justice, fairness, honesty, orderliness in the group are examples of such preconditions for basic need satisfactions. Thwarting in these freedoms will be re-

[12] Clearly creative behavior, like painting, is like any other behavior in having multiple determinants. It may be seen in "innately creative" people whether they are satisfied or not, happy or unhappy, hungry or sated. Also, it is clear that creative activity may be compensatory, ameliorative, or purely economic. It is my impression (as yet unconfirmed) that it is possible to distinguish the artistic and intellectual products of basically satisfied people from those of basically unsatisfied people by inspection alone. In any case, here too we must distinguish, in a dynamic fashion, the overt behavior itself from its various motivations or purposes.

acted to with a threat or emergency response. These conditions are not ends in themselves but they are *almost* so, since they are closely related to the basic needs, which are apparently the only ends in themselves. These conditions are defended because without them the basic satisfactions are quite impossible, or at least, very severely endangered.

If we remember that the cognitive capacities (perceptual, intellectual, learning) are a set of adjustive tools, which have, among other functions, that of satisfaction of our basic needs, then it is clear that any danger to them, any deprivation or blocking of their free use, must also be indirectly threatening to the basic needs themselves. Such a statement is a partial solution of the general problems of curiosity, the search for knowledge, truth, and wisdom, and the ever persistent urge to solve the cosmic mysteries.

We must therefore introduce another hypothesis and speak of degrees of closeness to the basic needs, for we have already pointed out that *any* conscious desires (partial goals) are more or less important as they are more or less close to the basic needs. The same statement may be made for various behavior acts. An act is psychologically important if it contributes directly to satisfaction of basic needs. The less directly it so contributes, or the weaker this contribution is, the less important this act must be conceived to be from the point of view of dynamic psychology. A similar statement may be made for the various defense or coping mechanisms. Some are very directly related to the protection or attainment of the basic needs, others are only weakly and distantly related. Indeed, if we wished, we could speak of more basic and less basic defense mechanisms and then affirm that danger to the more basic defenses is more threatening than danger to less basic defenses (always remembering that this is so only because of their relationship to the basic needs).

THE DESIRES TO KNOW AND TO UNDERSTAND

So far, we have mentioned the cognitive needs only in passing. Acquiring knowledge and systematizing the universe have been considered as, in part, techniques for the achievement of basic safety in the world, or, for the intelligent man, expressions of self-actualization. Also freedom of inquiry and expression have been discussed as preconditions of satisfactions of the basic needs. True though these formulations may be, they do not constitute definitive answers to the question as to the motivation role of curiosity, learning, philosophizing, experimenting, etc. They are, at best, no more than partial answers.

This question is especially difficult because we know so little about the facts. Curiosity, exploration, desire for the facts, desire to know may certainly be observed easily enough. The fact that they often are pursued even at great cost to the individual's safety is an earnest of the partial character of our previous discussion. In addition, the writer must admit that, though he has sufficient clinical evidence to postulate the desire to know as a very strong drive in intelligent people, no data are available for unintelligent people. It may then be largely a function of relatively high intelligence. Rather tentatively, then, and largely in the hope of stimulating discussion and research, we shall postulate a basic desire to know, to be aware of reality, to get the facts, to satisfy curiosity, or as Wertheimer phrases it, to see rather than to be blind.

This postulation, however, is not enough. Even after we know, we are impelled to know more and more minutely and microscopically, on the one hand, and, on the other, more and more extensively in the direction of a world philosophy, religion, etc. The facts that we acquire, if they are isolated or atomistic, inevitably get theorized about, and either analyzed or organized or both. This process has been phrased by some as the search for "meaning." We shall then postulate a desire to understand, to systematize, to organize, to analyze, to look for relations and meanings.

Once these desires are accepted for discussion, we see that they too form themselves into a small hierarchy in which the desire to know is prepotent over the desire to understand. All the characteristics of a hierarchy of prepotency that we have described above, seem to hold for this one as well.

We must guard ourselves against the too easy tendency to separate these desires from the basic needs we have discussed above, i.e., to make a sharp dichotomy between "cognitive" and "conative" needs. The desire to know and to understand are themselves conative, i.e., have a striving character, and are as much personality needs as the "basic needs" we have already discussed.[13]

CONCLUSION

There are at least five sets of goals which we may call basic needs. These are briefly physiological, safety, love, esteem, and self-actualization. In addition, we are motivated by the desire to achieve or maintain the various conditions upon which these basic satisfactions rest and by certain more intellectual desires.

These basic goals are related to one another, being arranged in a hierarchy of prepotency. This means that the most prepotent goal will monopolize consciousness and will tend of itself to organize the recruitment of the various capacities of the organism. The less prepotent needs

[13] M. Wertheimer, unpublished lectures at the New School for Social Research.

are minimized, even forgotten or denied. But when a need is fairly well satisfied, the next prepotent ("higher") need emerges, in turn to dominate the conscious life and to serve as the center of organization of behavior, since gratified needs are not active motivators.

Thus man is a perpetually wanting animal. Ordinarily the satisfaction of these wants is not altogether mutually exclusive but only tends to be. The average member of our society is most often partially satisfied and partially unsatisfied in all of his wants. The hierarchy principle is usually empirically observed in terms of increasing percentages of nonsatisfaction as we go up the hierarchy. Reversals of the average order of the hierarchy are sometimes observed. Also it has been observed that an individual may permanently lose the higher wants in the hierarchy under special conditions. There are not only ordinarily multiple motivations for usual behavior but, in addition, many determinants other than motives.

Any thwarting or possibility of thwarting of these basic human goals, or danger to the defenses which protect them or to the conditions upon which they rest, is considered to be a psychological threat. With a few exceptions, all psychopathology may be partially traced to such threats. A basically thwarted man may actually be defined as a "sick" man.

It is such basic threats which bring about the general emergency reactions. . . .

RETROSPECTIVE COMMENT

At one level, it appears presumptuous for one to attempt to "update" the classic theory of motivation originally postulated over thirty years ago by such a monumental figure in the discipline of psychology as Abraham Maslow. Fortunately, however, we have evidence available from Maslow himself as to where he stood relative to this theory right up to the date of his death in 1970. So in one sense, this is really Maslow's own footnote. We will deal here with just two questions: What would Maslow subtract from what he said in 1943? And what would he add?

The bulk of evidence must rest on the author's master work, *Motivation and Personality*. The first copy of the 1970 revision of that book arrived on his desk one day before his death. There is evidence that he considered the book a final statement of his theory. In a tape cassette to the editors of *Psychology Today*, he said that he had ". . . been doing the preface for months when it should have taken only a couple of days. In fact, I permitted myself to hold up everybody and to write and rewrite and fiddle with it."

Among a number of things Maslow says in that preface is that the second edition, unlike the first, is not a theory building on the classical psychologies, but is a new "humanistic" psychology, which repudiates experimental psychology and psychoanalysis. He had ". . . stressed the profoundly holistic nature of human nature in contradiction to the analytic-dissecting-atomistic-Newtonian approach of the behavorisms and of Freudian psychoanalysis." He recognizes that the theory cannot be put to a test in the laboratory. The only real test of the theory has been in the work of scholars such as Douglas McGregor ". . . who have applied the theory successfully in the industrial situation." Indeed, its test ". . . needs a life situation of the total human being in his social environment."

So if by 1970, Maslow considers the theory fully developed, how does it differ from the 1943 version reprinted here? The answer to the question of what he would subtract from what is here is, "practically nothing." Chapter 4 of *Motivation and Personality* (except for a few word and punctuation changes) is identical to the exposition of the theory here. Even the titles of the chapter and the article are identical. To update Maslow, then, we must turn to what has been added.

The original article begins with a series of twelve propositions which should (according to Maslow) be included in any theory of human motivation. These were based on his previous article, "A Preface to Motivation Theory" published in the same year. By the time of the article reprinted here, he had added the thirteenth, i.e., that motivation theory is not synonymous with behavior theory. Chapter 3 of the 1970 book is also titled "Preface to Motivation Theory." In that chapter, Maslow reiterates those same thirteen propositions (with, of course, much more detail and justification than appears in their abbreviated state in the article). What is important is that all thirteen retain their same thrust in his last work.

But, by 1970, Maslow had added three additional propositions which should be included in any theory of human motivation. The fourteenth proposition is labeled "Possibility of Attainment." Referencing Dewey and Thorndike, he argues that motives are strongly affected by man's realistic wishing, more realistic than the psychoanalysts, absorbed with unconscious wishes, would allow. "The average American yearns for automobiles, refrigerators, and television sets because they are real possibilities;" he does not wish for yachts or airplanes, probably not even unconsciously. This is crucial to understanding differences in motivations between classes within a culture, and motivations across cultures.

Maslow's fifteenth proposition, "Influence of Reality," was apparently still open to some question in his own mind. He quotes Freud's description of id impulses as having no intrinsic relatedness to anything else in the world ("chaos, a cauldron of seething excitement"). He contrasts this notion with Dewey's contention that in adult humans, all impulses are integrated with and affected by reality (or what Freud would call ego). "In a word, this is the equivalent of maintaining that there are no id impulses, or reading between the lines, if there are, that they are intrinsically pathological rather than intrinsically healthy." If the present author is also allowed to "read between the lines," it appears that Maslow would agree with Dewey rather than Freud (since he would on nearly all issues). While not flatly denying the existence of id impulses, he asks whether they are evidences of sickness or of health. If they *do* exist in all of us, ". . . then we must ask, When do they appear? Under what conditions? Are they necessarily the troublemakers that Freud assumed them to be? *Must* they be in opposition to reality?" He doesn't give us the answers.

The final proposition, "Knowledge of Healthy Motivation," is (and was by 1943) crucial to Maslow's humanistic psychology. He complains that most of what we know of human motivation comes not from psychologists but from psychotherapists, and that data from their patients is a great source of error. "Health is not just the absence of disease or the opposite of it." A complete theory of motivation must ". . . deal with the highest capacities of the healthy and strong man as well as with the defensive maneuvers of crippled spirits."

A number of other issues should be included in an "update" of Maslow's theory. He ends the 1943 article with a list of thirteen basic problems not dealt with at that time. Limitation of space prohibits our dealing here with all of them, but a few of the more important ones are worth mentioning.

One is the relationship between his theory and Allport's theory of functional autonomy. Allport postulates that *means* to an end may ultimately become the satisfactions themselves; they become wanted for their own sake, functionally autonomous from their origins. Maslow concludes that there is no contradiction in the two theories, rather that they complement each other. The strong, healthy autonomous person who is able to withstand the loss of love and popularity *got that way* by the early chronic gratification of safety, love and belongingness, and esteem needs. "Which is to say that these aspects of the person have become functionally autonomous, i.e., independent of the very gratifications that created them."

Another problem not dealt with was the role of *values* in motivation theory. In a sense, Maslow's entire life's work speaks to this issue. It is part of his total commitment to a humanistic psychology, seen often in his sometimes acid criticisms of psychoanalytic and behavioristic psychologies which are devoid of the consideration of man's values. "This is the equivalent of an accusation against psychology, that it offers little to the modern man whose most desperate need is a naturalistic or humanistic end or value system."

Two other problems he mentioned were the etiology (cause, source) of the basic needs, and the implications of his theory for hedonistic theory. He deals with these rather strongly. He argues that there is no evidence to indicate other than that all the basic needs, at all levels of the hierarchy, are instinctoid in nature. Even our needs for love, esteem and self-actualization are instinctive rather than learned. This is based on his position that, yes, man is an animal, but "we are very special animals." Therefore, there can be some instinctive needs associated *only* with man. The pessimistic view of many other psychologists would disagree strongly with him on this issue. His position leads to a need to recast hedonistic theory. If all levels of needs are instinctive, then what is selfish and what is unselfish? "If our instinctoid impulses, for instance, to love, arrange it so that we get more personal 'selfish' pleasure from watching our children eat a goody than from eating it ourselves, then how shall we define 'selfish' and how differentiate it from 'unselfish'?" This argues that a higher need hedonism might well replace the lower need hedonism. It also has major implications for our concepts of what is animal and nonanimal, what is rational and irrational, what is the rational life and the instinctive life.

Two other problems Maslow did not deal with in the 1943 article are the relations of his theory to the theories of interpersonal relations and of society. Maslow's position on the former is straight-forward and un-equivocal. Except for the lowest psysiological needs, gratification of all the basic needs at all levels of the hierarchy can only come from other people. "These cannot be satisfied by trees, mountains, or even dogs. Only from another human being can we get fully satisfying respect and protection and love, and it is only to other human beings that we can give these in the fullest measure." Maslow's views of perfecting society are optimistic, but above all realistic. He argues that society is much more open to improvement than most people think, as are most human beings. However, "Instant self-actualization, in a great moment of insight or awakening *does* happen, but it is extremely rare and should not be counted upon." By 1970, the more thoughtful leaders of T-groups, encounter groups, etc., were going through the painful process of giving up the "Big Bang" theory of self-actualization.

This realism did not prohibit Maslow from suggesting some dimensions of a psychological utopia, which he called "Eupsychia." While he admits that he is unsure of a number of aspects of such a society (particularly economic aspects), he says Eupsychia would be a society of freer choice, of loving relationships, of respect for all of other's needs. In such a society, people will not press upon others their own religion, fashion, tastes in food, clothing or women, and such a society will be more honest in all meanings of that word.

Abraham Maslow was 35 years old when he wrote the article reprinted here. He spent much of the rest of his life developing his humanistic psychology. A great deal of his effort was in studying self-actualizing people. His humanistic and optimistic approach is evident in his books with titles such as the *Farther Reaches of Human Nature* (1969), *Toward a Psychology of Being* (1968), and in what he said he would have liked to title his masterwork, *Higher Ceilings for Human Nature*. The latest statement of his theory of human motivation was for him a triumphant summary of his lifelong struggle to prove that ". . . wonderful people *can* and do exist—even though in short supply, and having feet of clay."—*Dr. Peter D. Bennett*, Professor of Marketing, Pennsylvania State University

7. Consumer Behavior as Risk Taking

Raymond A. Bauer

One of the fads in discussions of marketing research is to say that the field of marketing research has been marked by fads. Thus, we have become accustomed to the statement: "Last year it was Motivation Research; this year it's Operations Research; I wonder what it will be next year." Seldom is any such new emphasis a radical departure from the past. At least there is always a handful of protesting orthodox practitioners to exclaim: "-but we've been doing it all along." Operations Research, properly speaking, probably should be considered as concerned with simulation as much as with experimentation. But most of the operations research work I have seen in market research uses experimentation rather than simulation, and in this is continuous with traditional, albeit rare, well-executed experiments in marketing research. These new approaches are characterized by a distinctive concentration of attention on particular variables, concepts or techniques. After their potential has been pretty well explored and developed they get absorbed into the general body of research knowledge and technique, usually after having generated a few healthy antibodies.

I make these general remarks about fads in marketing research because I am about to make a modest effort to start a new one. However, if I am to be as modest as my effort I should also state that I have neither confidence nor anxiety that my proposal will cause any major stir. At most, it is to be hoped that it will attract the attention of a few researchers and practitioners and at least survive through infancy. The proposal is that we look at consumer behavior as an instance of risk taking.

We are accustomed to use the term "consumer decision making." Yet, there has been little concentration of research on the element of risk taking that is as characteristic of consumer behavior as it is of all decision-making. A conspicuous exception is the work of Katona and Mueller on prepurchase deliberation. They found, when buying durable goods, that middle-income people deliberated more than either lower-or upper-income people. When buying sport shirts, lower-income people deliberated most.

Reprinted by permission of the author and publisher from Robert Hancock (ed.), Dynamic Marketing for a Changing World, *published by the American Marketing Association (1960), pp. 389–398.*

Consumer behavior involves risk in the sense that any action of a consumer will produce consequences which he cannot anticipate with anything approximating certainty, and some of which at least are likely to be unpleasant. At the very least, any one purchase competes for the consumer's financial resources with a vast array of alternate uses of that money. The man who buys a pint of whiskey today does not know to what degree he prejudices his son's college education 20 years hence. But, he risks more than alternate purchases. Unfortunate consumer decisions have cost men frustration and blisters, their self-esteem and the esteem of others, their wives, their jobs, and even their lives. Nor is the problem of calculation of consequences a trivial one. It is inconceivable that the consumer can consider more than a few of the possible consequences of his actions, and it is seldom that he can anticipate even these few consequences with a high degree of certainty. When it comes to the purchase of large ticket items the perception of risk can become traumatic. Paul Lazarsfeld tells me that certain unpublished data show that the prospective automobile buyer often goes into a state of virtual panic as he reaches the point of decision, and rushes into his purchase as an escape from the enormity of the problem.

If I may now anticipate what is on your minds, I suspect that about at this point you are saying to yourselves that I have painted an unrealistic picture of the consumer. He simply does not in most instances stand about trying to calculate probabilities and consequences nor is he overtaken by anxiety. True, these things happen on occasion, and particularly on big ticket items, but only in rare instances does the consumer appear to tackle these problems as "risk taking."

If these objections are on your mind, I agree with them. The consumer who consistently tried to act like the classical "rational man" would quickly sink into inaction. This, in fact, is precisely what I would like to stress. Consumers characteristically develop decision strategies and ways of reducing risk that enable them to act with relative confidence and ease in situations where their information is inadequate and the consequences of their actions are in some meaningful sense incalculable. (When I say "in some meaningful sense incalculable," I mean that not only can the outcomes not be anticipated reliably, but the consequences may be drastic.)

Up to now, what I have to say has been abstract and general. Therefore, for the next few minutes I would like to move back to familiar ground and argue that many of the phenomena with which we habitually deal have a strong bearing on the problem of "risk taking." I am not going to contend that risk taking is the only thing involved in these phenomena, but rather that it is a common thread which runs through them and is worth pulling out for inspection.

One of our traditional problems is that of brand loyalty. Brand loyalty may involve a number of considerations. In recent years we have heard stressed the compatibility of the brand image with one's self-image, or with the norms of one's reference group. Brand loyalty is also seen as a means of economizing of decision effort by substituting habit for repeated, deliberate, decisions. Without for a moment minimizing such considerations, I would like to reintroduce the old-fashioned concept of "reliability." Much brand loyalty is a device for reducing the risks of consumer decisions. I am told that sugar is one product for which it has traditionally been difficult to develop brand loyalty. But my friend Edward Bursk tells me that when he was a salesman in Lancaster, Pennsylvania, there was a strong loyalty to a particular brand of sugar. The Pennsylvania Dutch housewives of that area are avid and proud bakers and there is more risk involved in making a cake than in sweetening a cup of coffee or a bowl of cereal. Suppose we were to limit ourselves to small ticket items, and to interview a sample of housewives as to the risks—that is a combination of uncertainty plus seriousness of outcome involved—associated with each category of product. I would predict a strong correlation between degree of risk and brand loyalty.

The recently popular phrase that advertising gives "added value" to a product also bears on the question of risk taking. The "added value" of advertising has usually been discussed in terms of the satisfaction of consumer motives that extend beyond the primary function of the product. It is perhaps worth recalling that one of the customer's motives is to have a feeling of confidence in the product he buys. Some, but not all, consumers are willing to pay added money for added confidence. Others prefer to read "Consumers Reports" in the hope that some obscure, unadvertised, low-priced brand will be rated a best buy. And, it is worth recalling, there are still other consumers in whom advertising does not generate confidence but rather the suspicion that it is added, worthless cost.

Now, relating the questions of brand loyalty and the "added value" of advertising to risk taking, or its reciprocal "confidence," is scarcely a radical departure from tradition. This must be the working assumption of every competent marketing practitioner. It is instructive, however, to note how little this relationship has been exploited as a research problem. We know that some people are inclined to favor advertised brands in some categories, and that other people will consistently buy the cheapest product in these same categories. This is about the level on which our knowledge rests. It is my suspicion that our recent concern with the prestige element of advertising and well known brands has deflected our attention from the problem of risk taking even when it was right under our nose.

Another recently popular area of concern where the problem of risk taking has been obscured is the phenomenon known as "personal influence." There are exceptions to what I am about to say, but *in general* discussions of personal influence on consumer behavior have been couched in terms that suggest only that opinion leaders are followed because they are style setters and that the follower wants to accrue to himself the prestige of behaving like the pace setters. Seldom is the fact made explicit that one of the very important functions of opinion leaders is to reduce the perceived risk of the behavior in question.

The work of Katz, Menzel, and Coleman on physicians' adoption of a new drug is very pertinent. They found that the doctors they studied tended to follow the lead of respected colleagues *early* in the life history of the drug when adequate information was lacking. Once the drug became sufficiently well established, personal influence no longer played a role. The period of risk was passed.

I have seen data on related products that reenforce the notion that the Katz, Menzel, Coleman findings are related to risk taking. We studied two types of products in the same general product category. We were interested in whether the probability of trial of a product and subsequent preference for that product, was influenced by preference for one or another of the companies, or by preference for the salesmen of the various companies. For these particular types of products we confirmed the findings of the drug studies. Both company and salesman preference were more strongly correlated with product trial and preference in the newer products in the general line. That is to say, apparently both company *and* salesmen preference had more influence when product was new and relatively unknown.

However, if I may be permitted some freedom of assumptions and inference, and a certain amount of liberty in filtering out the noise in the data, there were some findings that bore in a more interesting fashion on the problem of personal influence and risk taking. Let me start with some assumptions about the difference between company preference and salesman preference. Relative to each other, company preference is more associated with risk reduction, and salesman preference more with personal influence in the sense of "compliance," of one person "going along" with someone whom he likes. The company is a relatively impersonal entity, and the main function of its reputation is in this instance to guarantee the quality of the product. The salesman, to some extent, also guarantees quality. However, he also exploits his strictly personal relationships to the buyer. Thus we have personal influence operating in two ways, to produce compliance, and to reduce risk. Compliance is relatively more associated with salesman preference, and risk reduction with company preference.

If you accept the above assumptions as reasonable, then certain findings are quite interesting. You will remember that I said we studied two product types. These product types differed as to the degree of risk associated with them. Product type A was by common consent risky. Product type B was safe. In the case of product type A, the risky type of product, the relationship of company preference to product preference was twice as strong as the "effect" (in quotes) of salesman preference. In the case of product type B, the "effect" of company and salesman preference was just about equal. My interpretation of these findings is that when risk was high, the risk relevant factor of company image was the dominant source of influence, and that when risk was low, "personal influence" in the sense of compliance played a relatively more prominent role.

In addition to "personal influence" we have recently been concerned with the effect of "group influence" on consumer behavior. We have heard a great deal in the past few years about the fact that consumers judge their behavior by the standards of groups with whom they identify themselves, or—although this is seldom dealt with—from whom they dissociate themselves. This has been treated predominantly like the classical "keeping up with the Jones." The consumer looks to his reference groups for cues as to the type of consumption that is valued by people whose esteem he in turn values. "But, dahling, everybody, but everybody, knows Wente Brothers' chablis is the best California chablis!"

In his recent work, "Sociological Reflection on Business," Lazarsfeld suggests that group influence will be stronger in those instances in which the wisdom of one's decision is difficult to assess. Interpreted in one way, this suggestion could lead us to the popular notion that when the primary functions of a product are hard to assess, or when all products in a category work equally well, then "secondary attributes" such as group approval come to the fore. Under this interpretation the influence of the group is to get the consumer to pay attention to different attributes of the product. It is equally plausible that in many instances the function of group influence is to reduce perceived risk by confirming the wisdom of the choice. That is to say, the individual may already share the values of his group and agree on the desirability of a given type of purchase but look to the group for guidance as to what is a wise purchase. By a "wise" purchase, I mean one that is likely to satisfy the values for which it is made. In other words, we not only look to our reference groups for standards of values, but on occasion we also use the judgment of the people around us as an informal "Consumer Report." This is what the psychological student of cognition would call "consensual validation." Lacking any sound basis of judgment, we accept the judgment of others.

A final traditional problem worth considering in terms of risk taking is impulse buying, or perhaps we might prefer the label of "prepurchase deliberation." A simple economic approach to impulse buying would suggest that it should increase as a function of the discretionary funds available to the consumer. This would be consistent with Katona and Mueller's finding that the amount of deliberation involved in buying sport shirts was inverse to the consumer's income. Yet, a number of studies show that in many instances the middle-class consumer is more given to deliberation than is the lower-class consumer. When we compare the middle- and lower-class consumers something more than economics simply considered seems to be involved. We speak of the tendency of the middle-class person to plan over a longer period and of various other aspects of middle-class and lower-class culture. Not for a moment would I want to underplay the importance of such cultural factors. However, it is worth while to think of the fact that the middle-class person has both a greater possibility of planning and a greater reason to plan. He has more of an investment in career, reputation, and accumulated property to risk if he gets into serious financial difficulty. The lower-class person has less to risk in terms of such long-run investments. Perhaps more pertinently it is more difficult for him to calculate the consequences of his actions because among other things he is likely to have less information. He is also less likely to have time for deliberation, because, as Katona and Mueller found with respect to durable goods, people of lower income are more likely to make a purchase in a situation where the product to be replaced has already broken down.

So that I may not seem to be arguing against a cultural interpretation, let me say simply that the lower-class consumer seems more prone to a decision strategy based on the assumption that the consequences of one's behavior are essentially incalculable in any event, so one may as well take a plunge and do what seems immediately desirable.

My argument to this point has been that the issue of risk taking is readily seen as an integral part of many familiar phenomena of consumer behavior. This is by no means surprising, and is probably novel only in the degree that I have stressed the fact of risk taking. What will be of more interest will be to understand with more elaboration the devices through which consumers handle the problem of risk. In effect I have suggested mainly one device, namely reliance on some outside source for guidance, whether that outside source be the reputation of the manufacturer of product, an opinion leader or a reference group. This can scarcely exhaust the means that consumers employ to reduce perceived risk, nor does it tell us how the consumer decides where to place his confidence. The discussion of lower-*v.* middle-class deliberation in purchases of durable goods suggests an additional mechanism of reducing perceived risk, namely, to suppress the possible consequences from consciousness and rush through the process with rapidity. This is no more than a caricature of what we all do at times.

It should be noted that I have carefully said "perceived risk" whenever I referred to risk reduction. This is because the individual can respond to and deal with risk only as he perceives it subjectively. If risk exists in the "real world" and the individual does not perceive it, he cannot be influenced by it. On the other hand, he may reduce "perceived risk" by means which have no effect on affairs in the real world. Thus, if he reads advertisements favoring an automobile he has just bought, he may console himself on the wisdom of his action, but he does not reduce the objective probability of the muffler falling off.

Close study will probably reveal a wide range of decision rules which consumers invoke with regularity to reduce the perceived uncertainty involved in the outcome of their decisions. We are not totally oblivious to the existence of such rules. For example, there is a dying race of Americans who abide by the decision rule of not buying anything for which they cannot pay cash. A recent study shows that this is still a dominant decision rule for eating in restaurants. A majority of respondents thought it was improper to use credit cards for eating out, because "you should not eat out when you cannot afford it."[1] Other persons will buy products with plain and sensible design, fearing that surface aesthetics are designed to cover up bad workmanship and material. Some others will buy the most expensive product, and still others the cheapest product when both have equal amounts of money at their disposal. Such persons, for reasons about which we can only speculate, vary in the extent to which they are willing to pay money to minimize the risk of being disappointed in a product. There may be others who expect a certain rate of product failure as assurance that they are not wasting money on overly-engineered and constructed products. It is doubtful that they will be joyful over the failure of any individual product, but they may persist in patronizing an outlet that features low prices and poor service. The shabbyness of the store and the rudeness of sales personnel may give further reassurance that one is not paying too much for what he buys.

A long list of such decision rules could probably be produced by the reader. However, I suspect that as ingenious as we all are, it is still worth turning to actual consumers to find out from them what their operating decision rules are. We may be in for some surprises. It is of course difficult for a consumer to articulate a notion such as a "decision rule." In an effort to get at such difficult-to-articulate notions, Donald Cox, one of our doctoral students, interviewed two consumers at very great length —an hour or two a week for several months—on their shopping habits. Many of the decision rules reported by these respondents were ones familiar to us. The following two, I suspect, are not entirely familiar. One of the respondents favored shopping in small shops because she saw the proprietor or buyer as having reduced her range of decision by having reduced the number of brands among which he had to choose, and

[1] Study by Benson and Benson reported in *Wall Street Journal*, May 12, 1960.

also as having weeded out the least preferable lines. The same consumer would look about to see if a store carried advertised brands. She used this as a means of legitimizing *the store*. Once having satisfied herself on this score she was willing to buy off-brands from this same store. The novelty of individual decision rules is not so important as the fact that the decision rules of each of these subjects appeared to form coherent but contrasting strategies for stabilizing the uncertain world of shopping. Both of these young women could be characterized as highly conscious of the risk involved in shopping. But one regularly relied on external sources of reassurance, while the other was extremely energetic in seeking out information and attempting to achieve the guise of rationality. We plan to continue such exploratory work with consumers. But in the meantime the problem of decision-making has been tackled in other quarters.

There has been a good deal of research on decision-making under conditions of uncertainty, but not much of this work can at this point be translated into terms useful for students of consumer behavior. The students of statistical decision theory have concentrated on how decisions *ought* to be made. That is to say that the decision theorists have been concerned with the calculation of an optimum decision within the framework of an explicitly defined limited set of conditions, rather than with how people habitually *do* make decisions in the real world. Experimental psychological research on decision-making, on the other hand, has studied how people *do* make restricted types of decisions in a laboratory situation. Such research shows minimally that problems of risk and uncertainty are handled variously by different people and under different conditions. Even though it is doubtful that any of these findings are directly applicable in the field of marketing, they have an important general implication for us by demonstrating that people do in fact evolve preferred decision rules even in situations much less complicated than that faced by the consumer on a day-to-day basis.

One body of work deserves our attention. Most of it is reported in Leon Festinger's book called *A Theory of Cognitive Dissonance*. Festinger and his associates have concentrated on the ways in which people reduce perceived risk *after* decisions are made. People will seek out information that confirms the wisdom of their decisions. Thus, people who have just bought an automobile tend preferentially to read ads in favor of the automobile they have bought. People will also perceive information in a way to reenforce their decision; smokers are less likely than non-smokers to believe that cigarettes cause lung cancer, and this relationship holds even after those people who stopped smoking, because they believed in this relationship, were eliminated from the sample. People, finally, change their own attitudes to bolster their perception of the desirability of their actions. They have more favorable attitudes toward products after they have selected them than before they made the decision. Festinger has amassed considerable data to demonstrate that people do employ devices to reduce the perceived risk associated with consumer-type behavior.

Certain psychological research on problems of cognition also promises to be helpful. The book of Bruner, Goodnow, and Austin, *A Study of Thinking*, for example, deals with the way in which people develop decision strategies in handling situations of incomplete information.

The major reason for my remarks on the importance of the risk taking in consumer decision making is my conviction, frankly still in a somewhat less clear state than I would wish, that this is a fruitful area of research. It is my hope that others will suggest leads of which I am ignorant.

RETROSPECTIVE COMMENT

"Consumer Behavior as Risk Taking" represents my response to the forces converging on me in 1960. I had been trained in social psychology and therefore was receptive to the notion that consumers used goods and the buying act itself to bolster their egos and enhance their status relative to other people. Yet, I was also exposed to decision theorists and to rather practical, skeptical, old line marketers. Gradually I came to realize that we were dealing with two partial models of buying behavior. The notion that people defended their egos or enhanced their esteem in the eyes of others was not incompatible with the notion that they also engaged in a certain amount of problem solving. Happily, I had some data which, when appropriately analyzed, showed shifts in the relative dominance of these two models of response under sensible conditions.

I delivered this paper at a meeting of the American Marketing Association with a considerable amount of uncertainty and trepidation, which is reflected in the body of the article. Oddly, it was one of those ideas that took off like a shot. Apart from the fact that it may have offered a genuinely fresh insight, it also had the happy attribute of spawning a lot of researchable ideas and thereby being a bonanza for doctoral students who had theses to write and junior faculty who needed publications to facilitate their promotions. Readers of marketing journals of the past fifteen years will understand my point. We are now at a stage where review articles are beginning to pull the whole thing together.—*Raymond A. Bauer*, Professor, Harvard Business School

8. Consumer Self-Concept, Symbolism and Market Behavior: A Theoretical Approach

Edward L. Grubb and Harrison L. Grathwohl

Efforts to understand the totality of consumer behavior have taken researchers into related fields, with some of the most fruitful results in terms of both theory and practice coming from the behavioral sciences. Two conceptual areas within the behavioral sciences which promise to yield meaningful information about consumer behavior are self-theory and symbolism. A substantial amount of work has been done in these areas, primarily by psychologists, but marketing researchers and theorists do not seem to have developed the marketing potential of the available theory and substance.[1] Some products, brands, and stores have long been recognized as having psychic values to certain market segments, but little has been done to fabricate formal theories useful in predicting consumer behavior.

This article is an effort to develop a partial theory of consumer behavior by linking the psychological construct of an individual's self-concept with the symbolic value of goods purchased in the marketplace. The authors briefly examine previous research and lay theoretical footings from which a set of hypotheses and a qualitative model of consumer behavior are promulgated.

REVIEW OF RELATED RESEARCH

PERSONALITY AND CONSUMER BEHAVIOR

A number of researchers have attempted to relate purchases of product types or specific brands to personality traits of the purchasers. These researchers advanced the basic hypothesis that individuals who con-

[1] George A. Field, John Douglas, and Lawrence X. Tarpey, *Marketing Management: A Behavioral Systems Approach* (Columbus, Ohio: Charles E. Merrill Books, 1966), p. 106.

Reprinted by permission of the authors and publisher from the Journal of Marketing, *published by the American Marketing Association, Vol. 31 (October 1967), pp. 22–27.*

sume in a certain manner will also manifest certain common personality characteristics, leading to prediction of consumer behavior. Evans conducted empirical investigations to determine if choice of automobile brand reflects the personality of the owner.[2] Applying the Edwards' Personal Preference Schedule, he could find no important personality differences between a limited sample of Chevrolet and Ford owners and, therefore, could not show that psychological testing predicted consumer behavior more accurately than standard marketing research. However, Kuehn submitted the same data to further statistical analysis and concluded that prediction could indeed be based upon two of the measured personality characteristics (dominance and affiliation).[3]

Westfall experimented with automobile owners to determine if the personalities of owners of standard models, of compact models, and of convertible models varied.[4] Using the Thurstone Temperament Schedule as a personality measuring instrument, he found little difference between the owners of compact and standard models, but discovered that convertible owners are more active, vigorous, impulsive, dominant, and social, yet less stable and less reflective than the other two groups of owners.

The results of these and similar studies demonstrate the existence of some relationship between personalities of the consumers and the products they consume.[5] Yet the results indicate as well the limitations of our understanding of this relationship. Because of the limited results produced by these and similar studies, further refinements in the theoretical foundations may be necessary to provide useful insights.

PERSONALITY, PRODUCT IMAGE, AND THE CONSUMPTION OF GOODS

A further refinement in the attempt to relate personality and purchases was the advancement of the assumption that consumer buying behavior is determined by the interaction of the buyer's personality and the image of the purchased product. Pierre Martineau, a strong advocate of this position, argued that the product or brand image is a symbol of the buyer's personality.[6] In later work, Walter A. Woods

[2] Franklin B. Evans, "Psychological and Objective Factors in the Prediction of Brand Choice: Ford vs. Chevrolet," *Journal of Business*, Vol. XXXII (October, 1959), p. 340.

[3] Alfred A. Kuehn, "Demonstration of a Relationship between Psychological Factors and Brand Choice," *Journal of Business*, Vol. XXXVI (April, 1963), p. 237.

[4] Ralph Westfall, "Psychological Factors in Predicting Product Choice," *Journal of Marketing*, Vol. 26 (April, 1962), p. 34.

[5] For a bibliography of similar studies see: *Are There Consumer Types?* (New York: Advertising Research Foundation, 1964), p. 28.

[6] Pierre Martineau, *Motivation in Advertising* (New York: McGraw-Hill Book Company, 1957).

identified various types of consumers and the importance of the symbolic content of the product to the purchase. Woods asserted that where ego-involvement with the product is high, product image is important to the consumer.[7]

Along similar lines, Duesenberry advanced the idea that the act of consumption as symbolic behavior may be more important to the individual than the benefits provided by the functioning of the product purchased.[8] The relationship of product image and personality was further substantiated by a recent study that found a low, but statistically significant, correlation between the masculinity of cigarette smokers and the perceived masculinity of the brand they consumed.[9]

Though meaningful, the early work has not developed the theoretical relationships between the personality of the individual and the product image. To be useful as a guide to marketing decision-making and research, the variables of the buyer's personality and the image of the purchased products need to be organized into a conceptual totality that will allow relevant material to be systematized, classified, and interrelated. Further, the conceptual interrelationship of these variables should be arranged and developed in such a manner that the *why* of the interrelationship is explained. Exposure of all the elements of the theory to critical evaluation should encourage testing of hypotheses, followed by improvement (re-testing of theory) so that more informed judgments can be made relative to the marketing value of the approach.

SELF-THEORY AND CONSUMER BEHAVIOR

A more specific means of developing a theoretical approach to consumer behavior is to link the psychological construct of an individual's self-concept with the symbolic value of the goods purchased in the marketplace. The concept of the self is more restricted than personality, which facilitates measurement and centers on the critical element of how the individual perceives himself.[10] Further, use of self-theory allows

7 Walter A. Woods, "Psychological Dimensions of Consumer Decision," JOURNAL OF MARKETING, Vol. 24 (January, 1960), pp. 15–19.

8 James S. Duesenberry, *Income, Savings, and the Theory of Consumer Behavior* (Cambridge: Harvard University Press, 1949). For a discussion of the theory of consumption, see James S. Duesenberry, "A Theory of Consumption," *Marketing: The Firm's Viewpoint*, Schuyler F. Otteson, William Panschar, and James M. Patterson (editors) (New York: The Macmillan Co., 1964), pp. 125–133.

9 Paul C. Vitz and Donald Johnston, "Masculinity of Smokers and the Masculinity of Cigarette Images," *Journal of Applied Psychology*, Vol. XLIX (October, 1965), pp. 155–159.

10 E. Earl Baughman and George Schlager Welsh, *Personality: A Behavioral Science* (Englewood Cliffs: Prentice-Hall, Inc., 1962), p. 339.

application of the behavioral concept of symbolic interaction; this provides meaning to the association of an individual's buying behavior with his self-concept.

SELF-THEORY

Self-theory has been the subject of much psychological and sociological theorizing and empirical research with the accompanying development of a rather large body of assumptions and empirical data.[11] The available knowledge strongly supports the role of the self-concept as a partial determinant of human behavior and, therefore, represents a promising area for marketing research.

Current theory and research places emphasis on the concept of the self as an object which is perceived by the individual. The self is what one is aware of, one's attitudes, feelings, perceptions, and evaluations of oneself as an object.[12] The self represents a totality which becomes a principal value around which life revolves, something to be safeguarded and, if possible, to be made still more valuable.[13] An individual's evaluation of himself will greatly influence his behavior, and thus, the more valued the self, the more organized and consistent becomes his behavior.

THE SELF AND THE INTERACTION PROCESS

The self develops not as a personal, individual process, but it evolves through the process of social experience. From the reactions of others, man develops his self-perception. According to Rogers:

> A portion of the total perceptual field gradually becomes differentiated as the self . . . as a result of the interaction with the environment, and particularly as a result of evaluational interactions with others, the structure of the self is formed—an organized, fluid, but consistent conceptual pattern of perceptions of characteristics and relationships of the "I" or the "me" together with values attached to these concepts.[14]

Since the self-concept grows out of the reactions of parents, peers, teachers, and significant others, self-enhancement will depend upon

---

[11] See, for example, Ruth Wylie, *The Self-Concept* (Lincoln, Nebraska: The University of Nebraska Press, 1961).

[12] Calvin S. Hall and Gardner Lindsay, *Theories of Personality* (New York: John Wiley and Sons, Inc., 1957), pp. 469–475, or David Krech, Richard S. Crutchfield, and Egerton L. Ballachey, *Individual in Society* (New York: McGraw-Hill Book Company, 1962), pp. 495–496.

[13] Theodore M. Newcomb, *Social Psychology* (New York: The Dryden Press, 1956), p. 319.

[14] Hall and Lindsay, same reference as footnote 12, p. 483.

the reactions of these people. Recognition and reinforcing reactions from these persons will further strengthen the conception the individual has of himself. Thus, the individual will strive to direct his behavior to obtain a positive reaction from his significant references.

CONTEXT OF THE INTERACTION PROCESS

The interaction process does not take place in a vacuum; the individuals are affected both by the environmental setting and the "personal attire" of each involved individual. Therefore, the individual will strive to control these elements to facilitate proper interpretations of his performance.[15] Items of the environmental setting or the personal attire become the tools or a means of goal accomplishment for individuals in the interaction process.

GOODS AS SYMBOLS

A more meaningful way of understanding the role of goods as social tools is to regard them as symbols serving as a means of communication between the individual and his significant references. Defined as "things which stand for or express something else," symbols should be thought of as unitary characters composed of signs and their meanings.[16] If a symbol is to convey meaning it must be identified by a group with which the individual is associated whether the group consists of two people or an entire society, and the symbol must communicate similar meaning to all within the group. The nature of goods as symbols has been attested quite adequately by Veblen,[17] Duesenberry,[18] and Benedict.[19]

SYMBOLS AND BEHAVIOR

If a product is to serve as a symbolic communicative device it must achieve social recognition, and the meaning associated with the product must be clearly established and understood by related segments of society. This process is in reality a classification process where one object is placed in relation to other objects basic to society.

[15] Erving Goffman, *The Presentation of Self in Everyday Life* (Garden City, New York: Doubleday and Co., Inc., 1959), p. 22.

[16] Lloyd Warner, *The Living and the Dead* (New Haven: Yale University Press, 1959), p. 3.

[17] Thorstein Veblen, *The Theory of the Leisure Class* (New York: Mentor Books, 1953).

[18] Same reference as footnote 8.

[19] Ruth Benedict, *Patterns of Culture* (New York: Mentor Books, 1934).

The necessity for any group to develop a common or shared terminology leads to an important consideration; the direction of activity depends upon the particular way that objects are classified.[20]

Classification systems are society's means of organizing and directing their activities in an orderly and sensible manner.

A prime example of symbolic classification and consumer behavior is fashion. If a particular style becomes popular, behavior of a segment of society will be directed toward the purchase and use of items manifesting this style. As the fashion declines in popularity, the group will discontinue purchase of these items and may reject the use of the remaining portion of previous purchases. Thus, an act of classification not only directs action, but also arouses a set of expectations toward the object classified. Individuals purchase the fashion item because of their feelings about what the item will do for them. The *essence* of the object resides not in the object but in the relation between the object and the individuals classifying the object.

Classification and symbolism become means of communication and of directing or influencing behavior. If a common symbol exists for two or more people, then the symbol should bring forth a similar response in each, and therefore members of a group can use the symbol in their behavior pattern. Further, the symbolic social classification of a good allows the consumer to relate himself directly to it, matching his self-concept with the meaning of the good. In this way self-support and self-enhancement can take place through association with goods which have a desirable social meaning and from the favorable reaction of significant references in the social interaction process.

GOODS AND SELF-ENHANCEMENT

The purchase and consumption of goods can be self-enhancing in two ways. First, the self-concept of an individual will be sustained and buoyed if he believes the good he has purchased is recognized publicly and classified in a manner that supports and matches his self-concept. While self-enhancement results from a personal, internal, intra-action process, the effect on the individual is ultimately dependent upon the product's being a publicly-recognized symbol. Because of their recognized meaning, public symbols elicit a reaction from the individual that supports his original self-feelings. Self-enhancement can occur as well in the interaction process. Goods as symbols serve the individual, becoming means to cause desired reactions from other individuals.

These two means of self-enhancement are represented in diagrammatic form in Figure 1.

[20] Anselm Strauss, *Mirrors and Masks: The Search for Identity* (Glencoe, Illinois: The Free Press of Glencoe, 1959), p. 9.

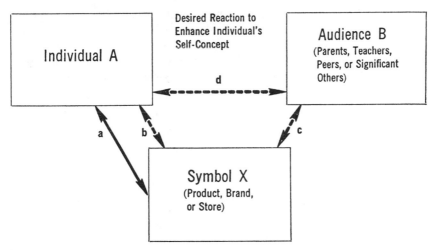

Figure 8.1. RELATIONSHIP OF THE CONSUMPTION OF GOODS AS SYMBOLS TO THE SELF-CONCEPT.

Individual A purchases and uses symbol X which has intrinsic and extrinsic value as a means of self-enhancement. (Symbol X could include a purchase of a certain product type such as a swimming pool; purchase of a specific brand such as a Pontiac GTO; or a purchase from a specific store or distributive outlet.) The intrinsic value is indicated by the double-headed arrow a, while the extrinsic values are indicated by the arrows b, c, and d. By the use of symbol X, an individual is communicating with himself; he is transferring the socially attributed meanings of symbol X to himself. This internal, personal communication process with symbol X becomes a means of enhancing his valued self-concept. An example of this situation is the individual who owns and uses a standard 1300 series Volkswagen. He may perceive himself as being thrifty, economical, and practical; and by using the Volkswagen, which has a strong image of being thrifty, economical, and practical, the individual achieves internal self-enhancement. This private and individual symbolic interpretation is largely dependent on one's understanding of the meaning associated with the product. Though the individual may treat this process in a private manner, he has learned the symbolic meaning from public sources.

By presenting Symbol X to Audience B, which may consist of one or more individuals from parents, peers, teachers, or significant others, the individual is communicating with them. Double-headed arrows b and c indicate that in presenting Symbol X to Audience B, Individual A is attributing meaning to it, and that in interpreting Symbol X, the relevant references in Audience B are also attributing meaning to the symbol. If Symbol X has a commonly-understood meaning between Individual A and the references of Audience B, then the desired communication can take place and the interaction process will develop as desired by A. This means the behavior of the significant references will be the desired reaction to Individual A (as shown by arrow d) and, therefore, self-enhancement will take place.

A MODEL OF CONSUMING BEHAVIOR

The following qualitative model is proposed to clarify the systematic relationship between self-theory and goods as symbols in terms of consumer behavior.

Consumption of Symbols: A Means to Self-Enhancement

    1. An individual does have a self-concept of himself.

    2. The self-concept is of value to him.

    3. Because this self-concept is of value to him, an individual's behavior will be directed toward the furtherance and enhancement of his self-concept.

    4. An individual's self-concept is formed through the interaction process with parents, peers, teachers, and significant others.

    5. Goods serve as social symbols and, therefore, are communication devices for the individual.

    6. The use of these good-symbols communicates meaning to the individual himself and to others, causing an impact on the intra-action and/or the interaction processes and, therefore, an effect on the individual's self-concept.

Prediction of the model:

    7. Therefore, the consuming behavior of an individual will be directed toward the furthering and enhancing of his self-concept through the consumption of goods as symbols.

This model becomes the theoretical base for a conceptual means to understand consumer behavior. The self-conception approach to understanding consumer behavior is not all-inclusive but does provide a meaningful conceptual framework for the systematic ordering and comprehension of consumer behavior. Of further importance is that this model, although general, can be an aid to the marketing decision-maker and a guide for future research.

SELF-CONCEPT THEORY OF BEHAVIOR AND MARKETING RESEARCH

This theoretical model can and should be used as a guide for further research. As Myers and Reynolds state, "We need to know a good deal more about the matching process and the conditions under which it does and does not occur."[21] Opportunity and need exist for both theoretical and applied research.

Further research is needed in terms of specific consumer decision situations to determine to what extent self-enhancement involves a conformity concept or an ideal self-image concept. For example, are consumers, through their consuming behavior and the interaction process, seeking support for their self-concept as they now perceive themselves, or are they seeking reactions that will promote the attainment of a more ideal self? For the average person, self-concept and self-ideal overlap to a large extent, although in specific circumstances one or the other could be the chief motivator of behavior.[22] This information is of central importance to help management evolve promotional efforts that either support the self-concepts of consumers as they now are *or* as they would like to be.

Useful results will be obtained from well-designed research pertaining to the present and desired symbolic content of products, brands, or stores, and how these symbolic meanings can be related to the self-concepts of present and potential users. Success or failure of a product often depends upon the social classification given to the product. Therefore, it is vital that the firm identify those specific products where the symbolic meaning of the product and its relation to the self-concept of the purchaser are active influences in the consumer decision process.

SELF-CONCEPT THEORY OF BEHAVIOR AND MARKETING MANAGEMENT

Firms can and should identify and/or segment their markets in terms of differentiated self-concepts. Recent research has indicated significant differences in self-concepts of different consuming groups both for product classes and for different brands.[23] Identification of self-concept segments may be a key element in the determination of marketing strategy and how, where, and to whom the exact tactics should be directed to achieve the desired goals.

Of real importance to the success of a brand of product is the development of a commonly understood symbolic meaning for the product. This means that management of a firm should carefully control the marketing of a product so that the relevant segments of the market properly classify the product and, therefore, behave toward the product

[21] James H. Myers and William H. Reynolds, *Consumer Behavior and Marketing Management* (New York: Houghton Mifflin Co., 1967), p. 204.

[22] Same reference as footnote 10, p. 348.

[23] Edward L. Grubb, "Consumer Perception of 'Self-Concept' and Its Relationship to Brand Choice of Selected Product Types," unpublished D.B.A. dissertation, University of Washington, 1965, pp. 120–124.

in the manner desired by the marketer. Through product design, pricing, promotion, and distribution the firm must communicate to the market the desired clues for consumer interpretation and, therefore, develop the desired symbolic meaning for the brand.

CONCLUSION

From a review of the literature of the behavioral sciences, the authors have developed a more complete theory of consumer behavior based upon self-theory and symbolism. This theory can serve as a theoretical foundation for understanding and predicting consumer market behavior, with particular emphasis on its role as the guide for research and decision-making.

The hypothesis presented by the authors stresses the role of the image an individual has of himself as a motivator of human behavior in the marketplace. Because the self-concept is of value and of central importance to the individual, he will direct his behavior to maintain and enhance his self-concept. The self-concept is formed in the interaction process between the individual and others; therefore, the individual will strive for self-enhancement in the interaction process. Of prime importance is the fact that the interaction process will be affected by the "tools" used by individuals and their significant references. Many of these tools are consumer goods, serving as symbolic communication devices. By carefully using goods as symbols, the individual communicates meaning about himself to his references, which causes a desired response and has an impact on the interaction process, thus reenforcing and enhancing his self-concept.

Enhancement of the self-concept can occur through an intra-action process whereby an individual communicates with himself through the medium of goods-symbols, thus supporting his self-concept. This is an internal process which takes place without specific response from others regarding a particular act. However, intra-action self-enhancement is possible only through group classification systems which bestow symbolic value upon certain goods or "tools."

The model of consuming behavior presented here is still in a theoretical state and, therefore, in need of research to refine and further substantiate its predictive value. Research is needed to determine whether and in what circumstances the motivating force is the presently held self-concept or the ideal self-concept. Basic research also is needed to determine what products have symbolic value and how this meaning is related to the consumers' self-concepts.

The advanced hypothesis is an activist theory having real value as a guide for present marketing decision-making. Marketers should consider segmenting their markets on the basis of consumer self-concepts as well as on demographic factors. Further, they must develop and direct their marketing strategy to meet the needs of these specific self-concept segments. Management would be wise to recognize that the success or failure of a product may depend upon the symbolic meaning established for that product. Significant marketing effort should be employed to ensure that the relevant segments of the market properly classify the product which in turn will tend to bring about desired consumer behavior.

RETROSPECTIVE COMMENT

A return to this subject a decade after publication of the original article has been interesting and rewarding. The proposed model applying self-theory to consuming behavior has been empirically tested and conceptually analyzed by a number of researchers and theoreticians. These efforts have led to developing a body of knowledge which generally supports the model, yet better defines its parameters and the issues associated with its use.

Research since 1967 has indicated that consumers of specific products, i.e. cars, beer, cigarettes, tooth paste and bar soap, perceive those products to have specific symbolic meaning and that these symbolic meanings are congruent with their self-concepts, but significantly different than the self-concepts and symbolic meanings associated with users of competing brands. Recent research has indicated that, as the model would predict, there exists also a congruent relationship between self-concept and images of preferred stores. Empirical data have been generated which indicate that consumers and their significant others perceive a like stereotype of the generalized user of the consumer's brand and, therefore, supports the model's prediction of enhancement for the consumer's perceived self-concept through interaction with significant others.

Additional research has been undertaken to explore the question of the ideal self versus the perceived self. The results have indicated that under certain circumstances the ideal self-image may be the better predictor, nevertheless the process as proposed by the original model would still be the same. The theory has been tested also with pre-purchase intentions. The results generally support the correlation of either self or ideal self prior to, as well as after, the purchase.

The essential theory of the model has been tested and supported. The resulting body of knowledge (empirical data, theoretical relationships, and research methods) is more complex. Questions have been raised which will require further research; research which is more sophisticated and more specific to generate the needed results for the second generation of testing the basic relationships of self theory to consuming behavior.—*Edward L. Grubb* and *Harrison L. Grathwohl*

9. Impact of Beer Brand Identification on Taste Perception

Ralph I. Allison and Kenneth P. Uhl

As a company tries to find the factors accounting for strong and weak markets, typical consumer explanations for both tend to be about the physical attributes of the product. That is, the product quality often becomes both the hero and the culprit, like Dr. Jekyll and Mr. Hyde, but with the hideous reversal coming not by night but by market. The experiment presented in this paper was also designed to give rough measurements of the magnitude of the marketing influences. Unidentified and then labeled bottles of beer were delivered to homes of taste testing participants on successive weeks. The drinkers' taste test ratings provided the data for the study.

THE EXPERIMENTAL DESIGN[1]

The principal hypothesis subjected to testing through experimentation was this: "Beer drinkers cannot distinguish among major brands of unlabeled beer either on an overall basis or on selected characteristics." Beer drinkers were identified as males who drank beer at least three times a week.

The test group was composed of 326 drinkers who were randomly selected, agreed to participate in the study, and provided necessary classification data. Each participant in the experiment was given a six-pack of unlabeled beer, identified only by tags bearing the letters A, B, C, D, E, F, G, H, I, or J. The labels had been completely soaked off and the crowns had been wire brushed to remove all brand identification from the 12-ounce deposit brown bottles. Each six-pack contained three

---

[1] The experimental design and the findings outlined are from one market area. However, similar experiments were conducted and similar results were obtained in several other markets.

Reprinted by permission of the authors and publisher from the Journal of Marketing Research, *published by the American Marketing Association, Vol. 1 (August 1964), pp. 36–39.*

brands of beer with individual bottles randomly placed in the pack so no one lettered tag predominated in any one position.[2] There were six different pairs placed among the 326 participants. An effort was made to give each participant a six-pack that contained the brand of beer he said he most often drank. The groups and numbers were placed as follows:

		Placed
Group 1 (AB, CD, EF)		53
Group 2 (AB, CD, IJ)		55
Group 3 (AB, CD, GH)		55
Group 4 (AB, EF, IJ)		55
Group 5 (AB, GH, IJ)		54
Group 6 (AB, EF, GH)		54
		326

A and B represented one of the company's beer brands; C and D represented one major regional beer brand; and E and F were one other major brand of regional beer. G and H were one national brand; and I and J were the fifth well-known beer brand used in the experiment. Among these five brands there were some taste differences discernible to expert taste testers.

The lettered tags (one around the collar of each bottle in the six-pack) carried a general rating scale from "1" (poor) through "10" (excellent) on the one side and a list of nine specific characteristics on the reverse side (see Exhibit #1). The specific characteristics, which included after-taste, aroma, bitterness, body, carbonation, foam, lightness, strength, and sweetness, could each be rated as "too much," "just enough," or "not enough." These nine specific characteristics were selected from a much larger field. Their selection was based on both greater agreement on meaning among beer drinkers and on the ability of beer drinkers, in general, to identify and rate them.

One week after the distribution of the unlabeled beer, the empties, nude except for the rating tags, were picked up and new six-packs left behind. This time, however, the bottles were properly labeled with each six-pack containing six different brands of beer (the same five brands plus a sixth brand that was added for the labeled test). In addition, each deposit bottle was tagged (as shown in Exhibit #1), but these tags were identified by the letters K through P. A week after the second placement the empties and rating tags were picked up.

---

[2] Pretesting gave no evidence of a positional or letter bias; *i.e.*, for participants to drink or rate the beer in any particular alphabetical or spatial order.

Exhibit 1
RATING TAGS

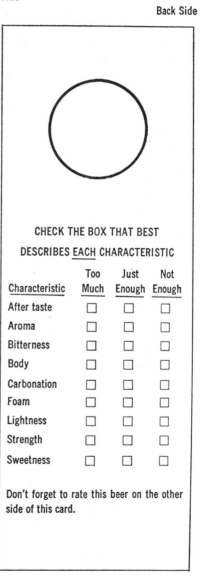

Exhibit 1
RATING TAGS

Front Side

TEST BEER "F"

Don't forget to give us your opinion about this beer by placing a cross (X) in the ONE block of the Rating Scale that best expresses your opinion about it.

RATING SCALE
EXCELLENT

☐
☐
☐
☐
☐
☐
☐
☐
☐
☐

VERY POOR

Don't forget to rate this beer on the other side of this card.

Back Side

CHECK THE BOX THAT BEST

DESCRIBES EACH CHARACTERISTIC

Characteristic	Too Much	Just Enough	Not Enough
After taste	☐	☐	☐
Aroma	☐	☐	☐
Bitterness	☐	☐	☐
Body	☐	☐	☐
Carbonation	☐	☐	☐
Foam	☐	☐	☐
Lightness	☐	☐	☐
Strength	☐	☐	☐
Sweetness	☐	☐	☐

Don't forget to rate this beer on the other side of this card.

THE FINDINGS

The experiment produced a number of useful findings. More specifically, evidence was available to answer these questions:

1. Could beer drinkers, in general, distinguish among various beers in a blind test?
2. Could beer drinkers identify "their" brands in a blind test?
3. What influence would brand identification have on consumers' evaluations of various beer brands?
4. What influence would brand identification have on consumers' evaluations of specified beer characteristics?

TASTE DIFFERENCES IN A BLIND TEST

The data produced by the experiment indicated that the beer drinkers, as a group, could not distinguish the taste differences among the brands on an overall basis. Table 1 contains the evidence on these ratings.

Table 9.1. BLIND OVERALL TASTE TEST—ALL PARTICIPANTS

Beer brand	Overall rating	Significantly different from other brands[a]
AB	65.0	No
CD	64.1	No
EF	63.3	No
GH	63.4	No
IJ	63.3	No

[a]At the .05 level.
Source: Carling Brewing Company.

Basically, there appeared to be no significant difference among the various brands at the .05 level.

Beer drinkers when asked to rate the nine characteristics listed in Table 2 as "not enough," "just enough," and "too much," indicated a difference that was significant in "just enough" votes for one characteristic on one beer (carbonation of brand CD). Other than the one case, the reported differences among brands were so minor as to be not significant. A second analysis of the data, in which the "just enough" category was treated as a neutral or a zero and the "too much" and "not enough" positions as +1 and −1 respectively, in general, substantiated the percentage findings.[3] In addition, this analysis indicated that four of the characteristics—aroma, body, foam, and strength—were rated rather uniformly among the brands as "not enough" and one characteristic—bitterness—received a clear "too much" rating. Based on the overall taste test and the specified characteristics test, the conclusion was that beer drinkers could *not* distinguish taste differences among the beer brands presented in unlabeled bottles.

Table 9.2. BLIND TASTE TEST—SPECIFIC CHARACTERISTICS (ALL PARTICIPANTS)

Characteristic	Per cent indicating "just right" by beer brands					Significant difference among brands[a]
	AB	CD	EF	GH	IJ	
After-taste	59	52	57	55	55	No
Aroma	64	63	63	62	62	No
Bitterness	53	54	53	54	54	No
Body	53	53	60	53	57	No
Carbonation	64	70	62	62	65	Only CD
Foam	62	66	63	59	66	No
Lightness	68	63	69	64	69	No
Strength	50	51	56	50	53	No
Sweetness	64	61	59	62	66	No

[a]At the .05 level.
Source: Carling Brewing Company.

COULD DRINKERS IDENTIFY "THEIR" BRANDS?

The labeled test clearly indicated that beer drinkers would assign "their" brands superior ratings and, accordingly, it was assumed that if participants could identify "their" brands in the blind test that they would respond to them with superior ratings. The general ratings in the nude bottle test, by brand drunk most often, indicated that *none* of the brand groups rated the taste of "their" brand beer superior over all of the other beers (see Table 3). For example, regular drinkers of brand AB, indicated via their ratings that they preferred "their" brand over EF and CD, but they gave virtually similar ratings to brands IJ and GH as they gave to their own brand. Drinkers of the other brands did not rate "their" brands as favorably in the blind comparison tests as did AB drinkers. Drinkers of brand EF rated beer CD significantly above "their"

[3] This three-place neutral center scale is in need of further testing and comparison with four- and five-position scales to help determine the amount of bias it induces.

Table 9.3. USERS LOYALTY TO "THEIR" BRAND (BLIND TEST)

Brand drunk most often	Taste test ratings by brand rated					Own brand rated significantly higher than all others[a]
	AB	CD	EF	GH	IJ	
AB	67.0	62.4*	57.7*	65.0	65.8	No
CD	64.9	65.6	65.4	63.2	63.9	No
EF	68.8	74.5*	65.0	62.5	61.4	No
GH	55.4	59.2	68.7*	60.0	71.4*	No
IJ	68.4	60.5*	69.2	62.0	65.6	No

[a]At the .05 level.
*Brands significantly different from user's own brand.
Source: Carling Brewing Company.

brand. Users of IJ rated all of the comparison brands except CD as equal and CD was rated as poorer tasting. Drinkers of brand GH must not have drunk the brand because they preferred its flavor—they rated two of the four comparison brands as superior in flavor and the other two as no less than equal to "their" brand. And based on the overall taste ratings, the regular drinkers of brand CD could just as well have drunk any of the other comparison brands—there were no significant differences among the assigned ratings.

INFLUENCE OF BRAND IDENTIFICATION ON OVERALL RATINGS

A number of important findings arose out of comparisons of the data from the nude bottle phase with the labeled bottle phase. The overall ratings for all of the brands increased considerably with brand identifications. However, there was also much variation in the amount of increase registered among the various brands. And when beer drinkers were categorized according to the brand most frequently drunk, they consistently rated "their" beer higher than comparison beers in this positive identification taste test. Also, there was much variation in the amounts of increase—some brands received much higher ratings (*i.e.,* overall ratings) from their regular users than did other brands from their regular users. The differences in the ratings were assumed to be due to the presence of labels—the only altered conditions of the experiment.

The data that give rise to the several statements about the effects of brand identification are examined in more detail below. In the *blind* test, none of the five brands received overall ratings that were sufficiently different from all of the others to be considered statistically significant. However, in the labeled test the differences in all but two of the overall ratings were significant (the ratings assigned to brands EF and IJ were relatively the same). Looking at some of the other figures, brand GH was rated significantly higher than all of the other brands and CD was rated higher than all brands but GH. Other differences that were judged statistically significant can be noted in Table 4. And as can be seen in this table, all five brands in the labeled test were rated significantly higher than the same brands in the blind test. Remember, these were the same brands of beer used in the nude test, but in the labeled test the participants could clearly identify each beer brand.

Table 9.4. COMPARISON TASTE TEST—BLIND VS. LABELED (OVERALL RATINGS)

Beer brand	Blind test	Labeled test	Significant difference between blind and labeled test[a]
AB	65.0	70.6	Yes
CD	64.1	72.9	Yes
EF	63.3	67.8	Yes
GH	63.4	76.9	Yes
IJ	63.3	67.0	Yes
Significant differences between brands	None	Yes[b]	

[a]At the .05 level.
[b]All brands were significantly different from all others at the .05 level except EF and IJ relative to each other.
Source: Carling Brewing Company.

The loyalty of the participants toward "their" brands increased when positive brand identification was possible (see Table 5). All of the labeled ratings assigned by regular users were significantly higher than the blind test ratings. In the blind test, participants indicated, at best, very little ability to pick "their" beers and set them off with relatively high overall ratings. For example, the regular drinkers of brand CD in the blind test awarded all of the brands about the same overall rating. However, in the labeled test, the CD drinkers awarded their beer brand an overall rating of 83.6, an 18 point increase over the blind test rating. This change was sufficiently above their overall ratings of all comparison brands to be statistically significant.

The gains in ratings were not uniform from one group to another. In the labeled test, brands GH, CD, and EF picked up more sizable gains

Table 9.5. USERS LOYALTY TO "THEIR" BRAND (LABEL TEST)

Brand drunk most often	Taste test ratings by brand rated					Own brand rated significantly higher[a]	Blind test ratings for own brand
	AB	CD	EF	GH	IJ		
AB	(77.3)	61.1	62.8	73.4	63.1	Yes	(67.0)
CD	66.3	(83.6)	67.4	78.3	63.1	Yes	(65.6)
EF	67.3	71.5	(82.3)	71.9	71.5	Yes	(65.0)
GH	73.1	72.5	77.5	(80.0)	67.5	Only over IJ	(60.0)
IJ	70.3	69.3	67.2	76.7	(73.5)	Only over EF	(65.6)

[a]At the .05 level.
Source: Carling Brewing Company.

than did AB and IJ. Comparison of the data in Table 5 with that in Table 3 will indicate other important rating changes from the blind to the label test.

INFLUENCE OF BRAND IDENTIFICATION ON SPECIFIED CHARACTERISTICS

The labeled test also produced some changes in ratings of specified characteristics of beer brands. In the blind test with the "just enough" category assigned a zero value, the participants tended to rate all of the beers as not having enough aroma, body, foam, and strength. All but one of the beers were rated on bitterness as "too much," and accordingly, not sweet enough. In the labeled ratings, "aroma" was greatly improved as was "body," "foam," and "strength." However, the ratings on "bitterness" and "sweetness" remained virtually the same as recorded in the nude test.

CONCLUSION

Participants, in general, did not appear to be able to discern the taste differences among the various beer brands, but apparently labels, and their associations, did influence their evaluations. In other words, product distinctions or differences, in the minds of the participants, arose primarily through their receptiveness to the various firms' marketing efforts rather than through perceived physical product differences. Such a finding suggested that the physical product differences had little to do with the various brands' relative success or failure in the market (assuming the various physical products had been relatively constant). Furthermore, this elimination of the product variable focused attention on the various firms' marketing efforts, and, more specifically, on the resulting brand images.

This experiment also has helped the Company measure and rank its brand image relative to competitive brand images and has offered base comparison marks for similar experiments, both in the same and other markets at later dates. Such information has helped in Company evaluation and competitive marketing efforts. And to the extent that product images, and their changes, are believed to be a result of advertising (*i.e.*, as other variables can be accounted for or held to be homogeneous among the competitive firms), the ability of firms' advertising programs to influence product images can be more thoroughly examined.

RETROSPECTIVE COMMENT

Taste testing procedures and experimental designs used by business organizations have undergone considerable improvement since this study was completed. A triangle taste test with subjects sampling from only three containers, two of which contain identical beverages, offers a much better procedure and resulting data set for most taste perception situations. Such a procedure is designed principally for use in laboratory settings, but certainly could be adapted to field situations even though there would be less control.

The design of the field experiment (reported in the study) nicely supported what many researchers have generalized about experimental designs. Namely, external validity—inference beyond the specific subjects—is normally bought through more natural settings, but at the cost of loss of internal validity—valid explanation within the subject set. The question with field experiments was and typically remains, can a more comfortable level of internal validity be secured without skyrocketing costs or giving up the questions that management needs answered?

Finally, the central conclusion from the study has held up well over the years. ". . . product distinctions or differences, in the minds of the participants, arose primarily through their receptiveness to the various firms' marketing efforts rather than through perceived product differences." In this perspective commentary, I hasten to add more explicitly, "among brands that were basically undifferentiated." The study involved five brands of beer that professional taste testers could distinguish among. However, the five beers were purposely similar because of the belief that the other four brands, because of their similarities, provided the main competition. Consequently, please do *not* use the study to generalize that beer drinkers cannot detect differences among beers. That is not a valid conclusion from the study.—*Ralph I. Allison* and *Kenneth P. Uhl*

10. The Functional Approach to the Study of Attitudes

Daniel Katz

The study of opinion formation and attitude change is basic to an understanding of the public opinion process even though it should not be equated with this process. The public opinion process is one phase of the influencing of collective decisions, and its investigation involves knowledge of channels of communication, of the power structures of a society, of the character of mass media, of the relation between elites, factions and masses, of the role of formal and informal leaders, of the institutionalized access to officials. But the raw material out of which public opinion develops is to be found in the attitudes of individuals, whether they be followers or leaders and whether these attitudes be at the general level of tendencies to conform to legitimate authority or majority opinion or at the specific level of favoring or opposing the particular aspects of the issue under consideration. The nature of the organization of attitudes within the personality and the processes which account for attitude change are thus critical areas for the understanding of the collective product known as public opinion.

EARLY APPROACHES TO THE STUDY OF ATTITUDE AND OPINION

There have been two main streams of thinking with respect to the determination of man's attitudes. The one tradition assumes an irrational model of man: specifically it holds that men have very limited powers of reason and reflection, weak capacity to discriminate, only the most primitive self-insight, and very short memories. Whatever mental capacities people do possess are easily overwhelmed by emotional forces and appeals to self-interest and vanity. The early books on the psychology of advertising, with their emphasis on the doctrine of suggestion, exemplify this approach. One expression of this philosophy is in the propagandist's concern with tricks and traps to manipu-

Reprinted by special permission from Public Opinion Quarterly, *Vol. 24 (Summer 1960).*

late the public. A modern form of it appears in *The Hidden Persuaders,* or the use of subliminal and marginal suggestion, or the devices supposedly employed by "the Madison Avenue boys." Experiments to support this line of thinking started with laboratory demonstrations of the power of hypnotic suggestion and were soon extended to show that people would change their attitudes in an uncritical manner under the influence of the prestige of authority and numbers. For example, individuals would accept or reject the same idea depending upon whether it came from a positive or a negative prestige source.[1]

The second approach is that of the ideologist who invokes a rational model of man. It assumes that the human being has a cerebral cortex, that he seeks understanding, that he consistently attempts to make sense of the world about him, that he possesses discriminating and reasoning powers which will assert themselves over time, and that he is capable of self-criticism and self-insight. It relies heavily upon getting adequate information to people. Our educational system is based upon this rational model. The present emphasis upon the improvement of communication, upon developing more adequate channels of two-way communication, of conferences and institutes, upon bringing people together to interchange ideas, are all indications of the belief in the importance of intelligence and comprehension in the formation and change of men's opinions.

Now either school of thought can point to evidence which supports its assumptions, and can make fairly damaging criticisms of its opponent. Solomon Asch and his colleagues, in attacking the irrational model, have called attention to the biased character of the old experiments on prestige suggestion which gave the subject little opportunity to demonstrate critical thinking.[2] And further exploration of subjects in these stupid situations does indicate that they try to make sense of a nonsensical matter as far as possible. Though the same statement is presented by the experimenter to two groups, the first time as coming from a positive source and the second time as coming from a negative source, it is given a different meaning dependent upon the context in which it appears.[3] Thus the experimental subject does his best to give some rational meaning to the problem. On the other hand, a large body of experimental work indicates that there are many limitations in the rational approach in that people see their world in terms of their

[1] Muzafer Sherif, *The Psychology of Social Norms,* New York, Harper, 1936.

[2] Solomon E. Asch, *Social Psychology,* New York, Prentice-Hall, 1952.

[3] *Ibid.,* pp. 426–427. The following statement was attributed to its rightful author, John Adams, for some subjects and to Karl Marx for others: "those who hold and those who are without property have ever formed distinct interests in society." When the statement was attributed to Marx, this type of comment appeared: "Marx is stressing the need for a redistribution of wealth." When it was attributed to Adams, this comment appeared: "This social division is innate in mankind."

own needs, remember what they want to remember, and interpret information on the basis of wishful thinking. H. H. Hyman and P. Sheatsley have demonstrated that these experimental results have direct relevance to information campaigns directed at influencing public opinion.[4] These authors assembled facts about such campaigns and showed conclusively that increasing the flow of information to people does not necessarily increase the knowledge absorbed or produce the attitude changes desired.

The major difficulty with these conflicting approaches is their lack of specification of the conditions under which men do act as the theory would predict. For the facts are that people do act at times as if they had been decorticated and at times with intelligence and comprehension. And people themselves do recognize that on occasion they have behaved blindly, impulsively, and thoughtlessly. A second major difficulty is that the rationality-irrationality dimension is not clearly defined. At the extremes it is easy to point to examples, as in the case of the acceptance of stupid suggestions under emotional stress on the one hand, or brilliant problem solving on the other; but this does not provide adequate guidance for the many cases in the middle of the scale where one attempts to discriminate between rationalization and reason.

RECONCILIATION OF THE CONFLICT IN A FUNCTIONAL APPROACH

The conflict between the rationality and irrationality models was saved from becoming a worthless debate because of the experimentation and research suggested by these models. The findings of this research pointed toward the elements of truth in each approach and gave some indication of the conditions under which each model could make fairly accurate predictions. In general the irrational approach was at its best where the situation imposed heavy restrictions upon search behavior and response alternatives. Where individuals must give quick responses without adequate opportunities to explore the nature of the problem, where there are very few response alternatives available to them, where their own deep emotional needs are aroused, they will in general react much as does the unthinking subject under hypnosis. On the other hand, where the individual can have more adequate commerce with the relevant environmental setting, where he has time to obtain more feedback from his reality testing, and where he has a number of realistic

4 Herbert H. Hyman and Paul B. Sheatsley, "Some Reasons Why Information Campaigns Fail," *Public Opinion Quarterly*, Vol. 11, 1947, pp. 413-423.

choices, his behavior will reflect the use of his rational faculties.[5] The child will often respond to the directive of the parent not by implicit obedience but by testing out whether or not the parent really meant what he said.

Many of the papers in this issue, which describe research and theory concerning consistency and consonance, represent one outcome of the rationality model. The theory of psychological consonance, or cognitive balance, assumes that man attempts to reduce discrepancies in his beliefs, attitudes, and behavior by appropriate changes in these processes. While the emphasis here is upon consistency or logicality, the theory deals with all dissonances, no matter how produced. Thus they could result from irrational factors of distorted perception and wishful thinking as well as from rational factors of realistic appraisal of a problem and an accurate estimate of its consequences. Moreover, the theory would predict only that the individual will move to reduce dissonance, whether such movement is a good adjustment to the world or leads to the delusional systems of the paranoiac. In a sense, then, this theory would avoid the conflict between the old approaches of the rational and the irrational man by not dealing with the specific antecedent causes of behavior or with the particular ways in which the individual solves his problems.

In addition to the present preoccupation with the development of formal models concerned with cognitive balance and consonance, there is a growing interest in a more comprehensive framework for dealing with the complex variables and for bringing order within the field. The thoughtful system of Ulf Himmelstrand, presented in the following pages, is one such attempt. Another point of departure is represented by two groups of workers who have organized their theories around the functions which attitudes perform for the personality. Sarnoff, Katz, and McClintock, in taking this functional approach, have given primary attention to the motivational bases of attitudes and the processes of attitude change.[6] The basic assumption of this group is that both attitude formation and attitude change must be understood in terms of the needs they serve and that, as these motivational processes differ, so too will the conditions and techniques for attitude change. Smith, Bruner, and White have also analyzed the different functions

[5] William A. Scott points out that in the area of international relations the incompleteness and remoteness of the information and the lack of pressures on the individual to defend his views results in inconsistencies. Inconsistent elements with respect to a system of international beliefs may, however, be consistent with the larger system of the personality. "Rationality and Non-rationality of International Attitudes," *Journal of Conflict Resolution*, Vol. 2, 1958, pp. 9–16.

[6] Irving Sarnoff and Daniel Katz, "The Motivational Bases of Attitude Change," *Journal of Abnormal and Social Psychology*, Vol. 49, 1954, pp. 115–124.

which attitudes perform for the personality.[7] Both groups present essentially the same functions, but Smith, Bruner, and White give more attention to perceptual and cognitive processes and Sarnoff, Katz, and McClintock to the specific conditions of attitude change.

The importance of the functional approach is threefold.

1. Many previous studies of attitude change have dealt with factors which are not genuine psychological variables, for example, the effect on group prejudice of contact between two groups, or the exposure of a group of subjects to a communication in the mass media. Now contact serves different psychological functions for the individual and merely knowing that people have seen a movie or watched a television program tells us nothing about the personal values engaged or not engaged by such a presentation. If, however, we can gear our research to the functions attitudes perform, we can develop some generalizations about human behavior. Dealing with nonfunctional variables makes such generalization difficult, if not impossible.

2. By concerning ourselves with the different functions attitudes can perform we can avoid the great error of oversimplification—the error of attributing a single cause to given types of attitude. It was once popular to ascribe radicalism in economic and political matters to the psychopathology of the insecure and to attribute conservatism to the rigidity of the mentally aged. At the present time it is common practice to see in attitudes of group prejudice the repressed hostilities stemming from childhood frustrations, though Hyman and Sheatsley have pointed out that prejudiced attitudes can serve a normative function of gaining acceptance in one's own group as readily as releasing unconscious hatred.[8] In short, not only are there a number of motivational forces to take into account in considering attitudes and behavior, but the same attitude can have a different motivational basis in different people.

3. Finally, recognition of the complex motivational sources of behavior can help to remedy the neglect in general theories which lack specification of conditions under which given types of attitude will change. Gestalt theory tells us, for example, that attitudes will change to give better cognitive organization to the psychological field. This theoretical generalization is suggestive, but to carry out significant re-

[7] M. Brewster Smith, Jerome S. Bruner, and Robert W. White, *Opinions and Personality*, New York, Wiley, 1956.

[8] Herbert H. Hyman and Paul B. Sheatsley, "The Authoritarian Personality: A Methodological Critique," in Richard Christie and Marie Jahoda, editors, *Studies in the Scope and Method of the Authoritarian Personality*, Glencoe, Ill., Free Press, 1954, pp. 50–122.

search we need some middle-level concepts to bridge the gap between a high level of abstraction and particularistic or phenotypical events. We need concepts that will point toward the types of motive and methods of motive satisfaction which are operative in bringing about cognitive reorganization.

Before we attempt a detailed analysis of the four major functions which attitudes can serve, it is appropriate to consider the nature of attitudes, their dimensions, and their relations to other psychological structures and processes.

NATURE OF ATTITUDES: THEIR DIMENSIONS

Attitude is the predisposition of the individual to evaluate some symbol or object or aspect of his world in a favorable or unfavorable manner. Opinion is the verbal expression of an attitude, but attitudes can also be expressed in nonverbal behavior. Attitudes include both the affective, or feeling core of liking or disliking, and the cognitive, or belief, elements which describe the object of the attitude, its characteristics, and its relations to other objects. All attitudes thus include beliefs, but not all beliefs are attitudes. When specific attitudes are organized into a hierarchical structure, they comprise *value systems.* Thus a person may not only hold specific attitudes against deficit spending and unbalanced budgets but may also have a systematic organization of such beliefs and attitudes in the form of a value system of economic conservatism.

The dimensions of attitudes can be stated more precisely if the above distinctions between beliefs and feelings and attitudes and value systems are kept in mind. The *intensity* of an attitude refers to the strength of the *affective* component. In fact, rating scales and even Thurstone scales deal primarily with the intensity of feeling of the individual for or against some social object. The cognitive, or belief, component suggests two additional dimensions, the *specificity* or *generality* of the attitude and the *degree of differentiation* of the beliefs. Differentiation refers to the number of beliefs or cognitive items contained in the attitude, and the general assumption is that the simpler the attitude in cognitive structure the easier it is to change.[9] For simple structures there is no defense in depth, and once a single item of belief has been changed the attitude will change. A rather different dimension of attitude is the *number and strength of its linkages to a related value system.* If an attitude favoring budget balancing by the Federal government is

[9] David Krech and Richard S. Crutchfield, *Theory and Problems of Social Psychology*, New York, McGraw-Hill, 1948, pp. 160–163.

tied in strongly with a value system of economic conservatism, it will be more difficult to change than if it were a fairly isolated attitude of the person. Finally, the relation of the value system to the personality is a consideration of first importance. If an attitude is tied to a value system which is closely related to, or which consists of, the individual's conception of himself, then the appropriate change procedures become more complex. The *centrality* of an attitude refers to its role as part of a value system which is closely related to the individual's self-concept.

An additional aspect of attitudes is not clearly described in most theories, namely, their relation to action or overt behavior. Though behavior related to the attitude has other determinants than the attitude itself, it is also true that some attitudes in themselves have more of what Cartwright calls an action structure than do others.[10] Brewster Smith refers to this dimension as policy orientation[11] and Katz and Stotland speak of it as the action component.[12] For example, while many people have attitudes of approval toward one or the other of the two political parties, these attitudes will differ in their structure with respect to relevant action. One man may be prepared to vote on election day and will know where and when he should vote and will go to the polls no matter what the weather or how great the inconvenience. Another man will only vote if a party worker calls for him in a car. Himmelstrand's work is concerned with all aspects of the relationship between attitude and behavior, but he deals with the action structure of the attitude itself by distinguishing between attitudes where the affect is tied to verbal expression and attitudes where the affect is tied to behavior concerned with more objective referents of the attitude.[13] In the first case an individual derives satisfaction from talking about a problem; in the second case he derives satisfaction from taking some form of concrete action.

Attempts to change attitudes can be directed primarily at the belief component or at the feeling, or affective, component. Rosenberg theorizes that an effective change in one component will result in changes in the other component and presents experimental evidence to confirm this hypothesis.[14] For example, a political candidate will often attempt to win people by making them like him and dislike his opponent, and thus communicate affect rather than ideas. If he is successful, people

[10] Dorwin Cartwright, "Some Principles of Mass Persuasion," *Human Relations*, Vol. 2, 1949, pp. 253–267.

[11] M. Brewster Smith, "The Personal Setting of Public Opinions: A Study of Attitudes toward Russia," *Public Opinion Quarterly*, Vol. 11, 1947, pp. 507–523.

[12] Daniel Katz and Ezra Stotland, "A Preliminary Statement to a Theory of Attitude Structure and Change," in Sigmund Koch, editor, *Psychology: A Study of a Science*, Vol. 3, New York, McGraw-Hill, 1959, pp. 423–475.

[13] See pages 224–250 of this issue of the *Quarterly*.

[14] See pages 319–340 of this issue of the *Quarterly*.

will not only like him but entertain favorable beliefs about him. Another candidate may deal primarily with ideas and hope that, if he can change people's beliefs about an issue, their feelings will also change.

FOUR FUNCTIONS WHICH ATTITUDES PERFORM FOR THE INDIVIDUAL

The major functions which attitudes perform for the personality can be grouped according to their motivational basis as follows:

The instrumental, adjustive, or utilitarian function upon which Jeremy Bentham and the utilitarians constructed their model of man. A modern expression of this approach can be found in behavioristic learning theory.

The ego-defensive function in which the person protects himself from acknowledging the basic truths about himself or the harsh realities in his external world. Freudian psychology and neo-Freudian thinking have been preoccupied with this type of motivation and its outcomes.

The value-expressive function in which the individual derives satisfactions from expressing attitudes appropriate to his personal values and to his concept of himself. This function is central to doctrines of ego psychology which stress the importance of self-expression, self-development, and self-realization.

The knowledge function based upon the individual's need to give adequate structure to his universe. The search for meaning, the need to understand, the trend toward better organization of perceptions and beliefs to provide clarity and consistency for the individual, are other descriptions of this function. The development of principles about perceptual and cognitive structure have been the contribution of Gestalt psychology.

Stated simply, the functional approach is the attempt to understand the reasons people hold the attitudes they do. The reasons, however, are at the level of psychological motivations and not of the accidents of external events and circumstances. Unless we know the psychological need which is met by the holding of an attitude we are in a poor position to predict when and how it will change. Moreover, the same attitude expressed toward a political candidate may not perform the same function for all the people who express it. And while many attitudes are predominantly in the service of a single type of motivational process, as described above, other attitudes may serve more than one purpose for the individual. A fuller discussion of how attitudes serve the above four functions is in order.

THE ADJUSTMENT FUNCTION

Essentially this function is a recognition of the fact that people strive to maximize the rewards in their external environment and to minimize the penalties. The child develops favorable attitudes toward the objects in his world which are associated with the satisfactions of his needs and unfavorable attitudes toward objects which thwart him or punish him. Attitudes acquired in the service of the adjustment function are either the means for reaching the desired goal or avoiding the undesirable one, or are affective associations based upon experiences in attaining motive satisfactions.[15] The attitudes of the worker favoring a political party which will advance his economic lot are an example of the first type of utilitarian attitude. The pleasant image one has of one's favorite food is an example of the second type of utilitarian attitude.

In general, then, the dynamics of attitude formation with respect to the adjustment function are dependent upon present or past perceptions of the utility of the attitudinal object for the individual. The clarity, consistency, and nearness of rewards and punishments, as they relate to the individual's activities and goals, are important factors in the acquisition of such attitudes. Both attitudes and habits are formed toward specific objects, people, and symbols as they satisfy specific needs. The closer these objects are to actual need satisfaction and the more they are clearly perceived as relevant to need satisfaction, the greater are the probabilities of positive attitude formation. These principles of attitude formation are often observed in the breach rather than the compliance. In industry, management frequently expects to create favorable attitudes toward job performance through programs for making the company more attractive to the worker, such as providing recreational facilities and fringe benefits. Such programs, however, are much more likely to produce favorable attitudes toward the company as a desirable place to work than toward performance on the job. The company benefits and advantages are applied across the board to all employees and are not specifically relevant to increased effort in task performance by the individual worker.

Consistency of reward and punishment also contributes to the clarity of the instrumental object for goal attainment. If a political party bestows recognition and favors on party workers in an unpredictable and inconsistent fashion, it will destroy the favorable evaluation of the importance of working hard for the party among those whose motivation is of the utilitarian sort. But, curiously, while consistency of reward needs to be observed, 100 per cent consistency is not as effective as a pattern which is usually consistent but in which there are some lapses.

[15] Katz and Stotland, *op. cit.*, pp. 434-443.

When animal or human subjects are invariably rewarded for a correct performance, they do not retain their learned responses as well as when the reward is sometimes skipped.[16]

THE EGO-DEFENSIVE FUNCTION

People not only seek to make the most of their external world and what it offers, but they also expend a great deal of their energy on living with themselves. The mechanisms by which the individual protects his ego from his own unacceptable impulses and from the knowledge of threatening forces from without, and the methods by which he reduces his anxieties created by such problems, are known as mechanisms of ego defense. A more complete account of their origin and nature will be found in Sarnoff's article in this issue.[17] They include the devices by which the individual avoids facing either the inner reality of the kind of person he is, or the outer reality of the dangers the world holds for him. They stem basically from internal conflict with its resulting insecurities. In one sense the mechanisms of defense are adaptive in temporarily removing the sharp edges of conflict and in saving the individual from complete disaster. In another sense they are not adaptive in that they handicap the individual in his social adjustments and in obtaining the maximum satisfactions available to him from the world in which he lives. The worker who persistently quarrels with his boss and with his fellow workers, because he is acting out some of his own internal conflicts, may in this manner relieve himself of some of the emotional tensions which beset him. He is not, however, solving his problem of adjusting to his work situation and thus may deprive himself of advancement or even of steady employment.

Defense mechanisms, Miller and Swanson point out, may be classified into two families on the basis of the more or less primitive nature of the devices employed.[18] The first family, more primitive in nature, are more socially handicapping and consist of denial and complete avoidance. The individual in such cases obliterates through withdrawal and denial the realities which confront him. The exaggerated case of such primitive mechanisms is the fantasy world of the paranoiac. The second type of defense is less handicapping and makes for distortion rather than denial. It includes rationalization, projection, and displacement.

Many of our attitudes have the function of defending our self-image.

16 William O. Jenkins and Julian C. Stanley, "Partial Reinforcement: A Review and Critique," *Psychological Bulletin*, Vol. 47, 1950, pp. 193–234.

17 See pp. 251–279.

18 Daniel R. Miller and Guy E. Swanson, *Inner Conflict and Defense*, New York, Holt, 1960, pp. 194–288.

When we cannot admit to ourselves that we have deep feelings of in-feriority we may project those feelings onto some convenient minority group and bolster our egos by attitudes of superiority toward this un-derprivileged group. The formation of such defensive attitudes differs in essential ways from the formation of attitudes which serve the ad-justment function. They proceed from within the person, and the ob-jects and situation to which they are attached are merely convenient outlets for their expression. Not all targets are equally satisfactory for a given defense mechanism, but the point is that the attitude is not created by the target but by the individual's emotional conflicts. And when no convenient target exists the individual will create one. Utili-tarian attitudes, on the other hand, are formed with specific reference to the nature of the attitudinal object. They are thus appropriate to the nature of the social world to which they are geared. The high school student who values high grades because he wants to be admitted to a good college has a utilitarian attitude appropriate to the situation to which it is related.

All people employ defense mechanisms, but they differ with respect to the extent that they use them and some of their attitudes may be more defensive in function than others. It follows that the techniques and conditions for attitude change will not be the same for ego-defensive as for utilitarian attitudes.

Moreover, though people are ordinarily unaware of their defense mechanisms, especially at the time of employing them, they differ with respect to the amount of insight they may show at some later time about their use of defenses. In some cases they recognize that they have been protecting their egos without knowing the reason why. In other cases they may not even be aware of the devices they have been using to delude themselves.

THE VALUE-EXPRESSIVE FUNCTION

While many attitudes have the function of preventing the individual from revealing to himself and others his true nature, other attitudes have the function of giving positive expression to his central values and to the type of person he conceives himself to be. A man may con-sider himself to be an enlightened conservative or an internationalist or a liberal, and will hold attitudes which are the appropriate indication of his central values. Thus we need to take account of the fact that not all behavior has the negative function of reducing the tensions of bio-logical drives or of internal conflicts. Satisfactions also accrue to the person from the expression of attitudes which reflect his cherished be-liefs and his self-image. The reward to the person in these instances is not so much a matter of gaining social recognition or monetary rewards as of establishing his self-identity and confirming his notion of the sort of person he sees himself to be. The gratifications obtained from value expression may go beyond the confirmation of self-identity. Just as we find satisfaction in the exercise of our talents and abilities, so we find reward in the expression of any attributes associated with our egos.

Value-expressive attitudes not only give clarity to the self-image but also mold that self-image closer to the heart's desire. The teenager who by dress and speech establishes his identity as similar to his own peer group may appear to the outsider a weakling and a craven conformer. To himself he is asserting his independence of the adult world to which he has rendered childlike subservience and conformity all his life. Very early in the development of the personality the need for clarity of self-image is important—the need to know "who I am." Later it may be even more important to know that in some measure I am the type of person I want to be. Even as adults, however, the clarity and stability of the self-image is of primary significance. Just as the kind, considerate person will cover over his acts of selfishness, so too will the ruthless individualist become confused and embarrassed by his acts of sympathetic compassion. One reason it is difficult to change the character of the adult is that he is not comfortable with the new "me." Group support for such personality change is almost a necessity, as in Alcoholics Anonymous, so that the individual is aware of approval of his new self by people who are like him.

The socialization process during the formative years sets the basic outlines for the individual's self-concept. Parents constantly hold up before the child the model of the good character they want him to be. A good boy eats his spinach, does not hit girls, etc. The candy and the stick are less in evidence in training the child than the constant appeal to his notion of his own character. It is small wonder, then, that children reflect the acceptance of this model by inquiring about the characters of the actors in every drama, whether it be a television play, a political contest, or a war, wanting to know who are the "good guys" and who are the "bad guys." Even as adults we persist in labeling others in the terms of such character images. Joe McCarthy and his cause collapsed in fantastic fashion when the telecast of the Army hearings showed him in the role of the villain attacking the gentle, good man represented by Joseph Welch.

A related but somewhat different process from childhood socialization takes place when individuals enter a new group or organization. The individual will often take over and internalize the values of the group. What accounts, however, for the fact that sometimes this occurs and sometimes it does not? Four factors are probably operative, and some combination of them may be necessary for internalization. (1) The values of the new group may be highly consistent with existing values central to the personality. The girl who enters the nursing profession finds it congenial to consider herself a good nurse because of previous values of the importance of contributing to the welfare of others. (2) The new group may in its ideology have a clear model of what the good group member should be like and may persistently indoctrinate group members in these terms. One of the reasons for the code of conduct for members of the armed forces, devised after the revelations about the conduct of American prisoners in the Korean War, was to attempt to establish a model for what a good soldier does and does not do. (3) The activities of the group in moving toward its goal permit the individual genuine opportunity for participation. To become ego-involved so that he can internalize group values, the new member must find one of two conditions. The group activity open to him must tap his talents and abilities so that his chance to show what he is worth can be tied into the group effort. Or else the activities of the group must give him an inactive voice in group decisions. His particular talents and abilities may not be tapped but he does have the opportunity to enter into group decisions, and thus his need for self-determination is satisfied. He then identifies with the group in which such opportunities for ego-involvement are available. It is not necessary that opportunities for self-expression and self-determination be of great magnitude in an objective sense, so long as they are important for the psychological economy of the individuals themselves. (4) Finally, the individual may come to see himself as a group member if he can share in the rewards of group activity which includes his own efforts. The worker may not play much of a part in building a ship or make any decisions in the process of building it. Nevertheless, if he and his fellow workers are given a share in every boat they build and a return on the proceeds from the earnings of the ship, they may soon come to identify with the ship-building company and see themselves as builders of ships.

THE KNOWLEDGE FUNCTION

Individuals not only acquire beliefs in the interest of satisfying various specific needs, they also seek knowledge to give meaning to what would otherwise be an unorganized chaotic universe. People need standards or frames of reference for understanding their world, and attitudes help to supply such standards. The problem of understanding, as John Dewey made clear years ago, is one "of introducing (1) *definiteness* and *distinction* and (2) *consistency* and *stability* of meaning into what is otherwise vague and wavering."[19] The definiteness and stability are

[19] John Dewey, *How We Think*, New York, Macmillan, 1910.

provided in good measure by the norms of our culture, which give the otherwise perplexed individual ready-made attitudes for comprehending his universe. Walter Lippmann's classical contribution to the study of opinions and attitudes was his description of stereotypes and the way they provided order and clarity for a bewildering set of complexities.[20] The most interesting finding in Herzog's familiar study of the gratifications obtained by housewives in listening to daytime serials was the unsuspected role of information and advice.[21] The stories were liked "because they explained things to the inarticulate listener."

The need to know does not of course imply that people are driven by a thirst for universal knowledge. The American public's appalling lack of political information has been documented many times. In 1956, for example, only 13 per cent of the people in Detroit could correctly name the two United States Senators from the state of Michigan and only 18 per cent knew the name of their own Congressman. People are not avid seekers after knowledge as judged by what the educator or social reformer would desire. But they do want to understand the events which impinge directly on their own life. Moreover, many of the attitudes they have already acquired give them sufficient basis for interpreting much of what they perceive to be important for them. Our already existing stereotypes, in Lippmann's language, "are an ordered, more or less consistent picture of the world, to which our habits, our tastes, our capacities, our comforts and our hopes have adjusted themselves. They may not be a complete picture of the world, but they are a picture of a possible world to which we are adapted." It follows that new information will not modify old attitudes unless there is some inadequacy or incompleteness or inconsistency in the existing attitudinal structure as it relates to the perceptions of new situations.

RETROSPECTIVE COMMENT

The functional approach to the study of attitude formation and change has had an interesting history since its formulation in the writings of Smith, Bruner and White (1947 and 1956) and myself and my colleagues Sarnoff, McClintock, and Stotland at Michigan (1954, 1959). On the one hand, people outside the field of experimental psychology have found the functional approach useful in their analysis of problems and suggestive in their research. On the other hand, this widespread

20 Walter Lippmann, *Public Opinion*, New York, Macmillan, 1922.
21 Herta Herzog, "What Do We Really Know about Daytime Serial Listeners?" in Paul F. Lazarsfeld and Frank N. Stanton, editors, *Radio Research 1942–1943*, New York, Duell, Sloan & Pearce, 1944, pp. 3–33.

interest in functional concepts in the social sciences has not been paralleled by the generation of research in the experimental laboratory with the exception of the work of the Michigan group (Culbertson 1957, McClintock 1958, Wagman 1955, Stotland, 1959).

The reasons for this two-sided reception are not hard to find. The functional approach with its recognition of several motives is essentially a way of dealing with multiple variables in complex social settings. Social scientists and practitioners need to go beyond a single process to take account of the variance in the real social world. Experimental social psychology as a young discipline has seen a narrowing of focus and has concentrated in good part upon the testing of single concept theories. Dissonance theory and other consistency notions, for example, have generated hundreds of experimental investigations. It is much easier to utilize the laboratory to demonstrate the effect of a single variable than for the study of multi-dimension social interactions. Moreover, the move toward simplification has gone so far that even group experimentation, the reason for the existence of experimental social psychology, has been replaced in fair measure by work on the cognitive psychology of the individual. This emphasis upon cognitive processes incidentally is another reason for the slighting of the functional approach which is directed mainly at motivational processes (Katz, 1968).

There are some straws in the wind, however, which indicate that experimental social psychologists are again becoming more interested in analyzing the complex dimensions of problems. An early indication was the experimentation of Herbert Kelman and Reuben Baron (1974) based upon the functional assumption that dissonance produced by attitude-discrepant behavior needs to be examined in relation to the motivational implications of the discrepant action. Their findings demonstrated that moral dissonance, or violation of a moral precept, leads to different outcomes than hedonic dissonance based upon the unpleasantness of the task undertaken. And Messick and McClintock (1968) have broken out of the cage of the traditional Prisoner's Dilemma game to demonstrate the varied motives in gaming studies and have successfully decomposed motives of cooperation, competition, and utilitarian gain. A number of experimenters now are bringing problems from the real social world into the laboratory which means less reliance upon single factors or principles.

The functional approach, however, has seen its greatest usefulness outside the laboratory in political science and sociology. In Denmark Peter Hansen and his colleagues have applied functional concepts to studies of attitudes toward foreign policies. They report that utilitarian and pragmatic considerations were more significant than value expressive and ego defensive attitudes for Danish voters in their stand on entering the European Common Market. The author and his colleagues have utilized concepts adapted from the functional approach in a series of studies on nationalism in the U. S. (DeLamater, Katz and Kelman, 1969), Greece (Katz, Kelman, and Vassiliou, 1969), and Yugoslavia (DeLamater, 1969 and Katz, DeLamater and Stojic, 1974). Wallace Loh (1975) has supplemented this work with an investigation of nationalism among the Wallonians in Belgium and the French Canadians in Quebec. This line of research shows that nationalism is not of one piece, that its differential motivational base results in different outcomes with respect to hostility toward out-groups and tolerance of non-conformity in the in-group.

The functional approach has also been used to break down the blanket concept of political party identification. Earlier Gabriel Almond (1948) had distinguished between pragmatic parties, ideological parties and symbolic or traditional parties. Ole Borre and the author (1973) examined these distinctions as they applied to individual party members in a nationwide study of the Danish electorate. The evidence was clear that, even within one party, identification could be based upon different motivational patterns. Moreover, the motivational patterns revealed more about the character of political behavior (such as political activism) than did the one dimension of strength of party identification.

Finally, the promise of the functional approach requires considerable methodological research for its full realization. It is not too difficult to contrive a laboratory technology for the study of single variables which can then be used by a number of investigators. To develop measures of motivational patterns is a formidable task. McClelland, Atkinson and Veroff have shown that this can be done and have been brilliant innovators in their attack upon the measurement of the needs for achievement, affiliation and power. What is needed at the present time is improvement in the techniques for assessing the motivational patterns underlying attitudes so that investigators can have some common core of standardized instruments at their disposal. Technology should not be the main source of scientific progress but the facts are that without it we walk along when we might run.—*Daniel Katz*

REFERENCES

ALMOND, GABRIEL A. and Coleman, James S. (eds.). *The Politics of Developing Areas.* Princeton: University Press, 1948. p. 47.

BORRE, OLE and Katz, Daniel. Party Identification and Its Motivational Base in a Multiparty System: A Study of the Danish General Election of 1971. Oslo, Norway: *Scandinavian Political Studies,* Vol. 8, 1973, 69–111.

CULBERTSON, FRANCES M. Modification of an Emotionally Held Attitude Through Role Playing. *Journal of Abnormal and Social Psychology*, 1957, 54, 230–233.

DELAMATER, JOHN. *Commitment to the Political System in a Multi-National State.* Doctoral Dissertation, Univ. of Michigan, June, 1969.

DELAMATER, JOHN, Katz, Daniel and Kelman, Herbert. On the Nature of National Involvement: A Preliminary Study. *Journal of Conflict Resolution,* 13, Sept. 1969, 320–357.

HANSEN, PETER, Petersen, Nikalai and Redder, K. *Foreign Policy Attitudes in Denmark.* Manuscript in preparation.

KATZ, DANIEL. Consistency for What? The Functional Approach. *Theories of Cognitive Consistency: a Sourcebook,* edited by Abelson, Robert et al. New York: Rand McNally, 1968, 179–191.

KATZ, DANIEL and Stotland, Ezra. A Preliminary Statement to a Theory of Attitude Structure and Change in Koch, Sigmund (ed.). *Psychology: a Study of a Science.* New York: McGraw-Hill, 1959, pp. 423–475.

KATZ, DANIEL, Sarnoff, Irving, and McClintock, Charles. Ego-Defense and Attitude Change, *Human Relations,* 1956, 9, 27–45.

KATZ, DANIEL, Kelman, Herbert, and Vassiliou, Vasso. A Comparative Approach to the Study of Nationalism. *Peace Research Society Papers,* XIV, 1969, The Ann Arbor Conference.

KATZ, DANIEL, DeLamater, John and Stojic, Ljuba. Nacionalismo en el Estado Multinacional de Yugoslavia (I). *Revista de Estudios Sociales,* 1974, 10–11, 11–39.

KELMAN, HERBERT C. and Baron, Reuben M. Moral and Hedonic Dissonance: A Functional Analysis of the Relationship between Discrepant Action and Attitude Change. pp. 558–575 in Himmelfarb, Samuel and Eagly, Alice H. *Readings in Attitude Change.* New York: Wiley, 1974.

LOH, WALLACE D. A Social-Psychological Study of Political Commitment in Quebec and Belgium. *Journal of Conflict Resolution,* June 1975, Vol. XIX, No. 2.

McCLINTOCK, CHARLES G. Personality Syndromes and Attitude Change. *Journal of Personality* 1958, 26, 479–593.

MESSICK, DAVID M. and McClintock, Charles G. Motivational Bases of Choice in Experimental Games. *Journal of Experimental Social Psych.* 1968, 4, 1–25.

SARNOFF, IRVING and Katz, Daniel. The Motivational Bases of Attitude Change. *Journal of Abnormal and Social Psychology,* 1954, 49, 115–124.

SMITH, BREWSTER, M. The Personal Setting of Public Opinion: a Study of Attitudes Toward Russia. *Public Opinion Quarterly,* 1947, 11, 507–523.

SMITH, BREWSTER M., Bruner, Jerome S., and White, Robert W. *Opinions and Personality:* New York: Wiley, 1956.

STOTLAND, EZRA, Katz, Daniel and Patchen, Martin. The Reduction of Prejudice through the Arousal of Self-Insight. *Journal of Personality,* 1959, 27, No. 4, 507–531.

WAGMAN, MORTON. Attitude Change and the Authoritarian Personality. *Journal of Psychology,* 1955, 40, 3–24.

11. A Model for Predictive Measurements of Advertising Effectiveness

Robert J. Lavidge and Gary A. Steiner

What are the functions of advertising? Obviously the ultimate function is to help produce sales. But all advertising is not, should not, and cannot be designed to produce immediate purchases on the part of all who are exposed to it. *Immediate* sales results (even if measurable) are, at best, an incomplete criterion of advertising effectiveness.

In other words, the effects of much advertising are "long-term." This is sometimes taken to imply that all one can really do is wait and see—ultimately the campaign will or will not produce.

However, if something is to happen in the long run, *something* must be happening in the short run, something that will ultimately lead to eventual sales results. And this process must be measured in order to provide anything approaching a comprehensive evaluation of the effectiveness of the advertising.

Ultimate consumers normally do not switch from disinterested individuals to convinced purchasers in one instantaneous step. Rather, they approach the ultimate purchase through a process or series of steps in which the actual purchase is but the final threshold.

SEVEN STEPS

Advertising may be thought of as a force, which must move people up a series of steps:

1. Near the bottom of the steps stand potential purchasers who are completely *unaware of the existence* of the product or service in question.

2. Closer to purchasing, but still a long way from the cash register, are those who are merely *aware of its existence.*

3. Up a step are prospects who *know what the product has to offer.*

4. Still closer to purchasing are those who have favorable attitudes toward the product—those who *like the product.*

Reprinted by permission of Robert J. Lavidge and the publisher from the Journal of Marketing, *published by the American Marketing Association, Vol. 25 (October 1961), pp. 59–62.*

5. Those whose favorable attitudes have developed to the point of *preference* over all other possibilities are up still another step.

6. Even closer to purchasing are consumers who couple preference with a desire to buy and the *conviction* that the purchase would be wise.

7. Finally, of course, is the step which translates this attitude into actual *purchase*.

Research to evaluate the effectiveness of advertisements can be designed to provide measures of movement on such a flight of steps.

The various steps are not necessarily equidistant. In some instance the "distance" from awareness to preference may be very slight, while the distance from preference to purchase is extremely large. In other cases, the reverse may be true. Furthermore, a potential purchaser sometimes may move up several steps simultaneously.

Consider the following hypotheses. The greater the psychological and/or economic commitment involved in the purchase of a particular product, the longer it will take to bring consumers up these steps, and the more important the individual steps will be. Contrariwise, the less serious the commitment, the more likely it is that some consumers will go almost "immediately" to the top of the steps.

An impulse purchase might be consummated with no previous awareness, knowledge, liking, or conviction with respect to the product. On the other hand, an industrial good or an important consumer product ordinarily will not be purchased in such a manner.

DIFFERENT OBJECTIVES

Products differ markedly in terms of the role of advertising as related to the various positions on the steps. A great deal of advertising is designed to move people up the final steps toward purchase. At an extreme is the "Buy Now" ad, designed to stimulate immediate overt action. Contrast this with industrial advertising, much of which is not intended to stimulate immediate purchase in and of itself. Instead, it is designed to help pave the way for the salesman by making the prospects aware of his company and products, thus giving them knowledge and favorable attitudes about the ways in which those products or services might be of value. This, of course, involves movement up the lower and intermediate steps.

Even within a particular product category, or with a specific product, different advertisements or campaigns may be aimed primarily at different steps in the purchase process—and rightly so. For example, advertising for new automobiles is likely to place considerable emphasis on the lower steps when new models are first brought out. The advertiser recognizes that his first job is to make the potential customer aware of the new product, and to give him knowledge and favorable attitudes about the product. As the year progresses, advertising emphasis tends to move up the steps. Finally, at the end of the "model year" much emphasis is placed on the final step—the attempt to stimulate immediate purchase among prospects who are assumed, by then, to have information about the car.

The simple model assumes that potential purchasers all "start from scratch." However, some may have developed negative attitudes about the product, which place them even further from purchasing the product than those completely unaware of it. The first job, then, is to get them off the negative steps—before they can move up the additional steps which lead to purchase.

THREE FUNCTIONS OF ADVERTISING

The six steps outlined, beginning with "aware," indicate three major functions of advertising. (1) The first two, awareness and knowledge, relate to *information or ideas*. (2) The second two steps, liking and preference, have to do with favorable *attitudes or feelings* toward the product. (3) The final two steps, conviction and purchase, are to produce *action*—the acquisition of the product.

These three advertising functions are directly related to a classic psychological model which divides behavior into three components or dimensions:

1. The cognitive component—the intellectual, mental, or "rational" states.

2. The effective component—the "emotional" or "feeling" states.

3. The conative or motivational component—the "striving" states, relating to the tendency to treat objects as positive or negative goals.

This is more than a semantic issue, because the actions that need to be taken to stimulate or channel motivation may be quite different from those that produce knowledge. And these, in turn, may differ from actions designed to produce favorable *attitudes* toward something.

FUNCTIONS OF ADVERTISING RESEARCH

Among the first problems in any advertising evaluation program are to:

1. Determine what steps are most critical in a particular case, that is, what the steps leading to purchase are for most consumers.

2. Determine how many people are, at the moment, on which steps.

3. Determine which people on which steps it is most important to reach.

Advertising research can *then* be designed to evaluate the extent to which the advertising succeeds in moving the specified "target" audience(s) up the critical purchase steps.

Table 1 summarizes the stair-step model, and illustrates how several common advertising and research approaches may be organized according to their various "functions."

OVER-ALL AND COMPONENT MEASUREMENTS

With regard to most any product there are an infinite number of additional "subflights" which can be helpful in moving a prospect up the main steps. For example, awareness, knowledge, and development of favorable attitudes toward a *specific product feature* may be helpful in building a preference for the *line* of products. This leads to the concept of other steps, subdividing or "feeding" into the purchase steps, but concerned solely with more specific product features or attitudes.

Advertising effectiveness measurements may, then, be categorized into:

1. Over-all or "global" measurements, concerned with measuring the results—the consumers' positions and movement on the purchase steps.

2. Segment or component measurements, concerned with measuring the relative effectiveness of various *means* of moving people up the purchase steps—the consumers' positions on ancillary flights of steps, and the relative importance of these flights.

MEASURING MOVEMENT ON THE STEPS

Many common measurements of advertising effectiveness have been concerned with movement up either the *first* steps or the *final* step on the primary purchase flight. Examples include surveys to determine the extent of brand awareness and information and measures of purchase and repeat purchase among "exposed" versus "unexposed" groups.

Self-administered instruments, such as adaptations of the "semantic differential" and adjective check lists, are particularly helpful in providing the desired measurements of movement up or down the middle steps. The semantic differential provides a means of scaling attitudes with regard to a number of different issues in a manner which facilitates gathering the information on an efficient quantitative basis. Adjective lists, used in various ways, serve the same general purpose.

Table 11.1. ADVERTISING AND ADVERTISING RESEARCH RELATED TO THE MODEL

Related behavioral dimensions	Movement toward purchase	Examples of types of promotion or advertising relevant to various steps	Examples of research approaches related to steps of greatest applicability
	PURCHASE		
CONATIVE —the realm of motives. Ads stimulate or direct desires.	↑	Point-of-purchase Retail store ads Deals "Last-chance" offers Price appeals Testimonials	Market or sales tests Split-run tests Intention to purchase Projective techniques
	CONVICTION		
	↑		
	PREFERENCE		Rank order of preference for brands
AFFECTIVE —the realm of emotions. Ads change attitudes and feelings.	↑	Competitive ads Argumentative copy "Image" ads Status, glamor appeals	Rating scales Image measurements, including check lists and semantic differentials Projective techniques
	LIKING ↑		
	KNOWLEDGE	Announcements	Information questions
COGNITIVE —the realm of thoughts. Ads provide information and facts.	↑	Descriptive copy Classified ads Slogans Jingles Sky writing	Play-back analyses Brand awareness surveys
	AWARENESS	Teaser campaigns	Aided recall

Such devices can provide relatively spontaneous, rather than "considered," responses. They are also quickly administered and can contain enough elements to make recall of specific responses by the test participant difficult, especially if the order of items is changed. This helps in minimizing "consistency" biases in various comparative uses of such measurement tools.

Efficiency of these self-administered devices makes it practical to obtain responses to large numbers of items. This facilitates measurement of elements or components differing only slightly, though importantly, from each other.

Carefully constructed adjective check lists, for example, have shown remarkable discrimination between terms differing only in subtle shades of meaning. One product may be seen as "rich," "plush," and "expensive," while another one is "plush," "gaudy," and "cheap."

Such instruments make it possible to secure simultaneous measurements of both *global* attitudes and *specific* image components. These can be correlated with each other and directly related to the content of the advertising messages tested.

Does the advertising change the thinking of the respondents with regard to specific product attributes, characteristics or features, including not only physical characteristics but also various image elements such as "status"? Are these changes commercially significant?

The measuring instruments mentioned are helpful in answering these questions. *They provide a means for correlating changes in specific attitudes concerning image components with changes in global attitudes or position on the primary purchase steps.*

TESTING THE MODEL

When groups of consumers are studied over time, do those who show more movement on the measured steps eventually purchase the product in greater proportions or quantities? Accumulation of data utilizing the stair-step model provides an opportunity to test the assumptions underlying the model by answering this question.

THREE CONCEPTS

This approach to the measurement of advertising has evolved from three concepts:

1. Realistic measurements of advertising effectiveness must be related to an understanding of the functions of advertising. It is helpful to think in terms of a model where advertising is likened to a force which, if successful, moves people up a series of steps toward purchase.

2. Measurements of the effectiveness of the advertising should provide measurements of changes at *all* levels on these steps—not just at the levels of the development of produce or feature awareness and the stimulation of actual purchase.

3. Changes in attitudes as to specific image components can be evaluated together with changes in over-all images, to determine the extent to which changes in the image components are related to movement on the primary purchase steps.

RETROSPECTIVE COMMENT

"A Model for Predictive Measurements of Advertising Effectiveness" was published in 1961. Prior to that date, it was used for approximately a decade in planning research projects and in teaching. It now is more than a quarter-century old and despite its years, continues to give evidence of vitality.

Several questions have been raised about the validity of the basic assumption underlying the model. This was addressed in the article as follows:

> Ultimate consumers normally do not switch from disinterested individuals to convinced purchasers in one instantaneous step. Rather, they approach the ultimate purchase through a process or series of steps in which the actual purchase is but the final threshold.

Several writers have stated that not *all* purchasers will have passed through the stages described in the model before making their purchases. There is no argument with this. The model was not designed to fit, and should not be construed as fitting *all* purchase behavior and decision-making. As noted in the article: "An impulse purchase might be consummated with no previous awareness, knowledge, liking, or conviction with respect to the product." For example, I have observed and have interviewed consumers purchasing new flavors of cookies in supermarkets. Several of them exhibited classic impulse purchasing behavior. Prior to the time when they saw the new cookies on the store shelves, they did not know of their existence. They certainly had not developed favorable attitudes toward them nor a conviction that they should purchase them. It might be argued that they developed awareness, favorable attitudes and conviction during the seconds immediately prior to purchase. However, such impulse purchasing clearly does not fit a model designed to be used in evaluating the effectiveness of advertising.

The term "hierarchy of effects" has been used in referring to the model. It has been stated that the "hierarchical hypothesis" has not been proven. That, also, was pointed out in the article along with comments about testing the model and its underlying assumptions. However, since 1961, the body of evidence in support of the "hierarchical hypothesis" has grown. For example, during the past few years, several simulated test marketing procedures have been used to predict the sales of new products prior to their introduction into the marketplace. The procedures used are based upon the assumption that purchase behavior with respect to new products will be related to awareness of the product, attitudes toward it and purchase intentions as well as immediate purchase behavior. Hundreds of cases involving the use of these procedures have been reported with an astonishing incidence of success in predicting the subsequent behavior of the new products in the marketplace.

On the other hand, evidence has been presented to show that increases in the level of awareness of a product and/or attitudes toward it have not always coincided with increases in sales. Other, more sophisticated analyses involving lagged data, have indicated that measurable sales increases sometimes have not *followed* increases in levels of awareness and/or attitudes. However, the model does *not* assume that individuals who are made aware of the product or those who develop favorable attitudes toward it, necessarily will buy it. Rather, it assumes that those who know about it are better prospects than those who. do not. Those who have favorable attitudes toward it are better prospects than those who do not. It is quite possible that a given advertising campaign will do an excellent job of building awareness of a product, or, perhaps, building more favorable attitudes toward it but do a poor job of stimulating purchasing. Conversely, as pointed out in the article, a "buy now" campaign may be very effective in stimulating purchasing among people who have favorable attitudes toward a product but do little or nothing to build favorable attitudes among others. If all of the effort in a campaign is expended on one level in the "hierarchy" inverse correlation between improvements with respect to that level and improvements with respect to other levels, including the final purchase level, should not be a surprise.

It has been argued on numerous occasions that sales results are *the* measure. However, as pointed out in the article: ". . . all advertising is not, should not, and cannot be designed to produce immediate purchases on the part of all who are exposed to it. *Immediate* sales results (even if measurable) are, at best, an incomplete criterion of advertising effectiveness." Attention to the model certainly does not obviate the need for measures of sales. It suggests, rather, that sales measures are necessary but, normally, are not sufficient.

The model set forth in the article does not, as such, give attention to repeat purchasing of a product or service. However, the model has been used with success in predicting repeat purchasing: In such cases, attention has been focused on attitudes, purchase convictions and purchase behavior, that is, on the affective and conative dimensions rather than on the cognitive dimensions concerned with awareness and knowledge of the product.

The article notes that: ". . . some [potential purchasers] may have developed negative attitudes about the product, which place them even further from purchasing the product than those completely unaware of it." This must be borne in mind with respect to evaluations of the likelihood of repeat purchasing among people who have had experience with a product. Those who have tried a product and disliked it may be much poorer prospects than others who never have heard of the product. It also has been noted that the process described in the model involving an evolution from lack of awareness of a product through the development of knowledge, favorable attitudes and conviction to purchase of it, is more likely to be a continuum, or an incline than a set of steps. That certainly is true. The steps should be thought of only as a convenient way to think about the process, a way that has been useful in describing it, in planning and executing research and in developing advertising plans.

What proportion of the people in a target audience are unaware of the existence of our product? How many of them do not yet know of its attributes and of the benefits it offers them? How many of them have developed favorable attitudes toward the product in comparison with competitive alternatives but have not yet developed a conviction that they should buy? How many have developed such conviction but have failed to act upon it? What are the characteristics of the people within each of these categories? How can they best be reached? What messages should be addressed to them? These questions suggest the usefulness of the model in developing advertising strategy and tactics as well as in designing and analyzing advertising effectiveness studies.

Despite its usefulness, a persistent problem in using the model "for predictive measurements of advertising effectiveness" remains. This relates to the difficulty frequently experienced in measuring the changes, if any, which take place as a result of exposure to an advertisement, a commercial or a campaign. This is especially true when the advertising is concerned with products that already are widely known and with which a large share of the potential purchasers have had experience. Significant advertising expenditures may lead to very little "movement" on the steps. As a result, measurements among very large numbers of potential purchasers may be needed to detect the little movement that does occur. This is complicated by the conditioning effect of interviewing. Questioning people before exposure to advertising may have more effect upon them than the advertising. As a result, the traditional before-and-after measures sometimes are inappropriate. When that is the case, large "matched samples" may be needed to evaluate differences between people who are exposed and others who are unexposed to the advertising. This might require research which would be too costly to be justified. It also could lead to results that are ambiguous when consideration is given to sampling errors.

The "Model for Predictive Measurements of Advertising Effectiveness" appears to have stood the test of time remarkably well. However, it was not, and is not, without limitations.—*Robert J. Lavidge*

12. Personality and Product Use

W. T. Tucker and John J. Painter

Perhaps no subject in marketing has received greater attention in the past few years than the relationship between personality and purchasing behavior. All of the furor over motivation research is clearly predicated on the premise that such a relationship exists, although some reporters seem to assume that all persons are, at base, alike. Yet even here, the factors referred to as common to all persons are most often those which personality studies have shown to be variables rather than constants. For instance, the importance of fear of the father image, which is reputed to militate against the use of banking services, must be conceived of as varying with some personality characteristic such as ego strength or emotional maturity if it is not to influence all persons in a highly similar way.

Talk about the importance of personality as a marketing variable has become common at advertising clubs and at marketing association meetings. The recent book by Pierre Martineau (1957) contains a chapter entitled "An Automobile for Every Personality." Charles Cannell (Ferber & Wales, 1958) says: "It may be that the determination of airplane travel has something to do with basic personality characteristics such as personal feelings of security or insecurity" (p. 10). And Ernest Dichter (Ferber & Wales) says confidently: "What we are searching for are psychological and personality elements which may have a dynamic effect on consumers' attitudes toward a product" (p. 26). Newman (1957) views personality as one of the major factors determining marketing behavior.

In the light of such points of view it may seem surprising that few efforts have been made to demonstrate that personality characteristics actually do influence product use. But the dearth of evidence on this point can be explained in part by supposition. First, the concept of personality itself has not been very clearly formulated. Second, the instruments available for the ready classification of personality types are few and generally suspect. Third, most self-respecting psychologists

W. T. Tucker and John J. Painter, "Personality and Product Use," Journal of Applied Psychology, Vol. 45 (October 1961), pp. 325–329. Copyright 1961 by the American Psychological Association, and reproduced by permission.

are apparently convinced that marketing behavior, pervasive as it may be, is of interest for commercial purposes only. Fourth, marketers probably have little understanding of the need for experimental evidence of their assumptions.

Yet it would seem that there is much to be learned about both person ality and a large segment of human behavior by such studies. Scott's (1957) study of motion picture preferences is perhaps of less interest to the movie producer than it is to the individual who wants a clearer understanding of the personality factors isolated by the Minnesota Multiphasic Index. That these factors are less than completely clear is indicated by Scott's inability to provide a rationale for all of the significant correlations. And Eysenck's (Eysenck, Tarrant, Woolf, & England, 1960) recent findings that rigidity and extraversion relate to the number of cigarettes smoked by an individual may be as important to the understanding of those characteristics as they are as a possible explanation of lung cancer in heavy smokers.

The present study was undertaken to test the hypothesis that marketing behavior is related to personality traits. At the same time, it was expected that the location of significant relationships would throw additional light on the meaning of personality characteristics studied.

METHOD

The Gordon Personal Profile was administered to 133 students of marketing along with a so-called Sales and Marketing Personality Index which included questions on the use of headache remedies, cigarettes, chewing gum, deodorants, mouthwash, and other items commonly purchased by college students. Blind questions were interspersed to give the index the appearance of a personality or interest test. Results were then compared to determine the difference in personality trait scores for groups that professed to different rates of product use or interest. That the subjects accepted the index was indicated by the large number of students who asked after completing the forms if they could find out whether they would make good salesmen, advertisers, etc.

SUBJECTS

The subjects were all students of the first course in marketing at the University of Texas. The great majority were juniors; a few were in the last semester of their sophomore year, and others were in the beginning of their senior year. Since the Gordon Personal Profile has different norms for male and female students, and, since the frequency of use of a number of products was clearly related to sex, the 31 responses by females are not included in this report. Also, one subject was eliminated because he failed to fill out the Gordon Personal Profile completely. While this group of subjects can hardly be characterized as representative of even such a limited universe as college juniors, for purposes of this study their only necessary characteristic was that of providing a diverse group of scores on the Gordon Personal Profile and reasonable diversity in response to questions about products.

TEST MATERIALS

The Gordon Personal Profile was selected as the personality test to use since it measures four characteristics which seem intuitively meaningful as components of the "normal" personality and since it is based on college student norms. The profile rates persons on the variables of ascendency, responsibility, emotional stability, and sociability.

The form used to determine use of products or other marketing characteristics included nine questions relevant to the experiments and seven blind questions. Most of the experimental questions referred to frequency of use of a particular product, as in the following:

How frequently do you experience a headache that requires a headache remedy (aspirin, Bufferin, Anacin, etc.)
  a. Never
  b. Once or twice a year
  c. About once a month
  d. More often than once a month, but less than once a week
  e. Once a week or more

Questions of this sort were asked about the use of headache remedies, vitamins, chewing gum, tobacco, mouthwash, alcoholic beverages, and deodorants. Two other questions related to the readiness with which the individual accepted new styles or fashions and preference in automobiles.

Blind questions were rather similar to those asked on interest tests:

Which of the following positions in an organization would you prefer to hold?
  a. Secretary-Treasurer
  b. Program chairman
  c. President
  d. Membership chairman
  e. Ordinary member, no office

The list of 16 questions was pretested in order to insure their clearness and to make sure that multiple choice answers would elicit a reasonable spread of response. As a result of this pretesting, multiple choice answers were altered to fit the normal variations in frequency of use of various products. For instance, the most frequent use of headache remedies indicated by answers was "once a week or more," while the most frequent use of deodorants was described as "more than once a day," since the pretest demonstrated these to be common frequencies for heavy users.

PROCEDURE

Subjects filled out both forms at a single sitting of about 20 minutes, answering the Gordon Personal Profile first and the Sales and Marketing Personality Index second. While subjects were asked to fill in their sex, age, marital status, and year in school on the Gordon Personal Profile, names were not taken in order to encourage the greatest frankness in response. Each pair of tests handed out was numbered in advance.

INSTRUCTIONS TO SUBJECTS

Students in each class tested were given the following instructions:

As you all know, one of the difficult problems in business is the determination of an individual's interests, or what kind of job he can do best. Attempts to solve such problems have led to the development of a number of written tests—some of which take an hour or more to complete. You have in front of you two rather new tests that try to accomplish this for certain marketing jobs in just a few minutes. We know that one of these is moderately successful. We are interested in whether scores on the other are different or much the same. Do these tests really meaure the same things?

To determine this, we need your help. We are not interested in your score as an individual but in the relationship of your score on one test with your score on the other.

For that reason, we do not want your name on the paper; we merely want you to answer the questions honestly and conscientiously. Instructions for each test appear at the top of the test.

First, make sure the red number on each of your tests is the same. Then fill in your age, sex, marital status, and year in school on Test #1, the Gordon Personal Profile. Then read the instructions on that test and answer the questions. When you are finished, go directly to the second test, read the instructions, then answer the questions.

You will find that on both tests there are some questions where none of the answers seem just right for you. Just pick the one that seem closest and do not worry about exact wording. Remember to read the test instructions carefully, since you have to answer each test in a somewhat different way.

ANALYTIC METHOD

Results were analyzed by comparing the difference in mean scores on one personality characteristic for groups with different product use patterns.

Table 12.1. MEAN RESPONSIBILITY SCORES FOR GROUPS WITH DIFFERENT PATTERNS OF USE OF MOUTHWASH

Response	*Mean Score*	*Number of Cases*
Never use mouthwash	7.26	31
Quite infrequently	5.00	40
Once or twice a week	4.50	16
Once a day	3.90	10
More than once a day	6.50	4

Table 1 shows the mean scores on responsibility for groups which answered the mouthwash question in each of the possible ways.

While responsibility seems to be inversely related to frequency of use of mouthwash, despite relatively high scores for the four persons who use mouthwash more than once a day, the number of cases in some of the cells is too small for analysis of variance to show a significant relationship. For this reason, the last four groups were combined and compared using the *t* test with those who reported never using mouthwash. The resulting *t* of 2.12 is significant at the .05 level. The *F* test for homogeneity of variance was not significant.

This same method of analysis was used for each of the products on each of the personality characteristics, with the point for division into two groups being determined on the basis of scores and the number of subjects remaining in each of the groups.

It is entirely proper to question whether five-point scales of the sort used here should be dichotomized *after* observing the means of each of the categories. Such dichotomization obviously makes it possible to maximize the number of "significant" relationships. Where possible, it should therefore be avoided and some independent method should be used for dichotomization.

Since there is no apparent rationale for predicting relationships between personality characteristics and product use, it seems foolhardy to develop a purely arbitrary dichotomization method in the present case. Such a method could easily minimize relationships if it were only extremes of product use that related to personality measures and the cutting point closest to the median were arbitrarily used, for instance. It happens that dichotomizing the data shown in Table 1 by combining the top two categories and the bottom three does not lead to a significant *t*. The resulting quandary is more philosophical than statistical. It seems to the authors that refusing to locate the cutting point that leads to statistically significant differences is the more serious error when dealing with the kind of problem discussed here.

RESULTS AND DISCUSSION

A total of 36 comparisons (9 product categories × 4 personality characteristics) included 13 significant relationships. As might be expected, some products were associated with no personality trait; others were associated with one or more; and one product, vitamins, was associated with all four of the personality traits.

Table 2 shows those relationships indicating the significance level. In addition it shows correlation ratios in parentheses to indicate the approximate strength of the relationships.

The results clearly indicate that there is a relationship between product use and personality traits. This relationship apparently may include both frequency of use of a particular product and preference among different brands of a single product, since preference in automobiles is significantly related to scores on responsibility. At the same time, some

Table 12.2. SIGNIFICANT PERSONALITY TRAITS IN THE USE OR PREFERENCE FOR SOME CONSUMER PRODUCTS

	Ascendency	Responsi- bility	Emotional Stability	Sociability
Headache remedies	−.05 (.464)ᶜ	—	−.05 (.320)ᶜ	—
Acceptance of new fashions	.01 (.331)ᶜ	—	—	.01 (.566)ᶜ
Vitamins	−.05 (.332)ᶜ	−.01 (.297)ᶜ	−.01 (.091)ᶜ	−.05 (.272)ᶜ
Cigarettes	—	—	—	—
Mouthwash	—	−.05 (.224)ᶜ	—	—
Alcoholic drinks	—	−.01 (.362)ᶜ	—	—
Deodorants	—	—	—	—
Automobilesᵃ	—	.01 (.281)ᶜ	—	—
Chewing gumᵇ	—	.05 (.295)ᶜ	.01 (.331)ᶜ	—

Note.—In all cases except for the last two products, the sign indicates the nature of the relationship. High ascendancy is related to infrequent use of headache remedies, for instance, but with rapid acceptance of new fashions.

ᵃSubjects who preferred the more popular makes of car such as Buick, Dodge, Mercury, Ford, Chevrolet, and Plymouth rated higher on the responsibility scale than those who stated a preference for such sports cars as the Corvette or Thunderbird.

ᵇWhile there is no significant difference in personality trait scores and the amount of gum chewed, those who chew gum *only when offered it by someone else*, are significantly lower than others in responsibility and emotional stability.

ᶜCorrelation ratios.

products are used frequently or infrequently without relationship to any of the personality traits tested. Each personality trait seems to bear a relationship to the use of some products, each of the four traits scored by the Gordon Personal Profile relating to the use of at least two of the products considered in the present experiment.

It should be pointed out, however, that the relationships located between product use and personality are not particularly strong, certainly less strong than popular marketing concepts of the day suggest.

An obvious corollary to the conclusion that personality traits and product use are related is that the Gordon Personal Profile does isolate personality traits related to behavioral differences. Further, an examination of the pattern of significant relationships shown in Table 2 is persuasive that the four traits, ascendency, responsibility, emotional stability, and sociability, have considerable independence. The manual for the test indicates that the intercorrelations are generally low except for those between ascendency and sociability (.43) and between emotional stability and responsibility (.46). Those correlations were considerably higher in the present experiment as shown in Table 3. The remaining correlations are quite low. It must be concluded that the Gordon Personal Profile does not measure four independent characteristics but two independent sets of related characteristics. However, it seems that one of a set of related characteristics can still prove to have enough relative independence to be conceptually valuable.

Most of the significant relationships between product use and character traits located are intuitively acceptable. One would expect that high ascendency and high sociability would be related to the rapid acceptance of new fashions, especially since ascendency is described largely as social leadership. On the other hand there seems to be no particular reason for expecting all personality characteristics to be associated with the frequency of use of vitamins, unless one conceives that personality traits are most likely to affect behavior that society neither rewards nor punishes.

The results cast some possible light on the nature of responsibility as a character trait. It is related to avoidance of vitamins and mouthwash, preference for popular cars and moderate drinking or abstinence. Since

Table 12.3. INTERCORRELATIONS AMONG PERSONALITY TRAITS

Traits	Ascendency	Responsibility	Emotional Stability
Responsibility	.058		
Emotional Stability	.035	.695	
Sociability	.708	.035	.086

these are all modal characteristics of the group being tested, a reasonably strong case might be made for the fact that responsibility is closely related to the acceptance of group norms.

A comparison of the present results with those of Eysenck (1960) suggests that sociability on the Gordon Personal Profile is considerably different from extroversion, with which it might seem related. Eysenck's results showed a strong, significant correlation between extroversion and heavy cigarette smoking, while the present experiment did not even hint at such a relationship between sociability and heavy smoking. It is possible that the difference in age (Eysenck's subjects were considerably older) or difference in nationality (Eysenck's subjects were British) might explain this apparent contradiction.

CONCLUSION

The answers to the Gordon Personal Profile and a disguised product use questionnaire by 101 college of business students demonstrate that personality traits are often related to product use. Thirteen of a possible 36 such relations were significant at the .05 level or above.

A corollary conclusion is that the Gordon Personal Profile distinguishes personality traits related to behavioral differences, although the four traits are not "independent."

RETROSPECTIVE COMMENT

"Personality and Product Use," is now a rather ancient article, looser in methodology than one might wish and just as inconclusive as it seemed at the time. Its inclusion in this volume reflects a continuing interest in locating the nature of the theoretically important relationship between personality and behavior as well as the general failure of numerous subsequent experiments to find stronger relationship than those discovered fifteen years ago.

No study of which I am aware suggests that more than some 5–8 percent of the variance in consumer behavior can be attributed to personality variables that we are capable of measuring. The warning is clear: human behavior (even such relatively simple choices as those observed in the market) is far more complex and richer in its diversity and meaning than rudimentary psychological theory suggests. Strictly implied is a degree of consumer freedom from internal pressures and market manipulation that is either discouraging or gratifying, depending on one's viewpoint. Frankly, I am gratified.

Were I now studying the same set of relationships, I believe that I would attempt to locate those personality types which are most effective in dealing with the market—that is, those who have learned to make choices that lead to personal growth and maturation as well as joy. For it seems to me that, if there are such types and their nature is understood, their numbers might flourish. Then the market would have a king.—*W. T. Tucker*

REFERENCES

EYSENCK, H. J., Tarrant, Mollie, Woolf, Myra, & England, L. Smoking and personality. *Brit. med.* J., 1960, 5184, 1456–1460.

FERBER, R., & Wales, H. *Motivation and marketing behavior.* Homewood, Ill.: Irwin, 1958.

MARTINEAU, P. *Motivation in advertising.* New York: McGraw-Hill, 1957.

NEWMAN, J. W. *Motivation research and marketing management.* Boston: Harvard Univer. Press, 1957.

SCOTT, E. M. Personality and movie preference. *Psychol. Rep.*, 1957, 3, 17–18.

13. Personality and Consumer Behavior: A Review

Harold H. Kassarjian

INTRODUCTION

The past two decades, especially the last five years, have been exciting times in the field of consumer behavior. New data, theories, relationships, and models have been received with such enthusiasm that, in fact, a new field of scientific inquiry has developed. Studies such as consumer economics, rural sociology, social and mathematical psychology, social anthropology, and political science have been so churned and milled that from their amorphous mass the study of consumer behavior has become a relatively well delineated scientific discipline.

One of the more engrossing concepts in the study of consumer behavior is that of personality. Purchasing behavior, media choice, innovation, segmentation, fear, social influence, product choice, opinion leadership, risk taking, attitude change, and almost anything else one can think of have been linked to personality. The purpose of this article is to review the literature of consumer behavior and organize its contributions around the theoretical stems from which it grows.

Unfortunately, analysts do not agree on any general definition of the term "personality,"[1] except to somehow tie it to the concept of consistent responses to the world of stimuli surrounding the individual. Man does tend to be consistent in coping with his environment. This consistency of response allows us to type politicians as charismatic or

[1] Hall and Lindzey, in attempting to deal with the dozens of approaches that exist in the literature, frustratingly submit that *personality is defined by the particular concepts which are part of the theory of personality employed by the observer.* Because this article reviews marketing literature rather than psychological literature, the various theories are not described in detail. For a very brief description of several theories and a bibliographic listing of primary sources and references, as well as examples of about a dozen well known volumes on the general topic, see [43, 46].

Reprinted by permission of the author and publisher from the Journal of Marketing Research, *published by the American Marketing Association, Vol. 8 (November 1971), pp. 409–419.*

Harold H. Kassarjian is Professor of Business Administration, University of California, Los Angeles. Appreciation is expressed to Jacob Jacoby for his invaluable role in the preparation of this article.

obnoxious, students as aggressive or submissive, and colleagues as charming or "blah." Since individuals do react fairly consistently in a variety of environmental situations, these generalized patterns of response or modes of coping with the world can be called personality.

Personality, or better yet, the inferred hypothetical constructs relating to certain persistent qualities in human behavior, have fascinated both laymen and scholars for many centuries. The study of the relationship between behavior and personality has a most impressive history, ranging back to the earliest writings of the Chinese and Egyptians, Hippocrates, and some of the great European philosophers. In the fields of marketing and consumer behavior, the work in personality dates from Sigmund Freud and his popularizers in the commercial world, and the motivation researchers of the post-World War II era.

PSYCHOANALYTIC THEORY

The psychoanalytic theories and philosophies of Freud have influenced not only psychology but also literature, social science, and medicine, as well as marketing. Freud stressed the unconscious nature of personality and motivation and said that much, if not all, behavior is related to the stresses within the personality system. The personality's three interacting sets of forces, the id, ego, and superego, interact to produce behavior.

According to Freudian theory, the id is the source of all driving psychic energy, but its unrestrained impulses cannot be expressed without running afoul of society's values. The superego is the internal representative of the traditional values and can be conceptualized as the moral arm of personality. The manner in which the ego guides the libidinal energies of the id and the moralistic demands of the superego accounts for the rich variety of personalities, interests, motives, attitudes, and behavior patterns of people. It accounts for the purchase of a four-door sedan rather than a racy sports car, the adoption of a miniskirt, and the use of Ultra-Brite toothpaste (with its promise of sex appeal) as a substitute for the rental of a motel room. The tools of the ego are defenses such as rationalization, projection, identification, and repression; its goals are integrated action.

Freud further believed that the child passes through various stages of development—the oral, anal, phallic, and genital periods—that determine the dynamics of his personality. The degree of tension, frustration, and love at these stages leads to his adult personality and behavior.

The influence of Freud and psychoanalytic theory cannot be overestimated. Most of the greatest names in psychiatry and psychology have been followers, disciples, or critics of Freud, much as many good marketing research studies have been criticisms of motivation researchers or experiments applying scientific procedures to motivation research. The work of Sidney Levy, Burleigh Gardner and Lee Rainwater, some of the projects of Martineau, and the proprietary studies of Social Research, Inc., are in the latter tradition. Although today the critics of psychoanalytic applications to consumer behavior far outweigh the adherents, Freud and his critics have contributed much to advances in marketing theory.

SOCIAL THEORISTS

In his lifetime, several members of Freud's inner ring became disillusioned with his insistence on the biological basis of personality and began to develop their own views and their own followers. Alfred Adler, for example, felt that the basic drive of man is not the channelization of the libido, but rather a striving for superiority. The basic aim of life, he reasoned, is to overcome feelings of inferiority imposed during childhood. Occupations and spouses are selected, homes purchased, and automobiles owned in the effort to perfect the self and feel less inferior to others.

Erich Fromm stressed man's loneliness in society and his seeking of love, brotherliness, and security. The search for satisfying human relationships is of central focus to behavior and motivations.

Karen Horney, also one of the neo-Freudian social theorists, reacted against theories of the biological libido, as did Adler, but felt that childhood insecurities stemming from parent-child relationships create basic anxieties and that the personality is developed as the individual learns to cope with his anxieties.

Although these and other neo-Freudians have influenced the work of motivation researchers, they have had minimal impact on research on consumer behavior. However, much of their theorizing can be seen in advertising today, which exploits the striving for superiority and the needs for love, security, and escape from loneliness to sell toothpaste, deodorants, cigarettes, and even detergents.

The only research in consumer behavior based directly on a neo-Freudian approach is Cohen's psychological test that purports to measure Horney's three basic orientations toward coping with anxiety—the compliant, aggressive, and detached types. Cohen found that compliant types prefer brand names and use more mouthwash and toilet soaps; aggressive types tend to use a razor rather than an electric shaver, use more cologne and after-shave lotion, and buy Old Spice deodorant and Van Heusen shirts; and detached types seem to be least aware of brands. Cohen, however, admitted to picking and choosing from his data, and although the published results are by no means conclusive, his work does indicate that the Horney typology may have some relevance to marketing. Several follow-up studies using his instruments are unpublished to date.

STIMULUS-RESPONSE THEORIES

The stimulus-response or learning theory approach to personality presents perhaps the most elegant view, with a respected history of research and laboratory experimentation supporting it. Its origins are in the work of Pavlov, Thorndike, Skinner, Spence, Hull, and the Institute of Human Relations at Yale University. Although the various theorists differ among themselves, there is agreement that the link between stimulus and response is persistent and relatively stable. Personality is seen as a conglomerate of habitual responses acquired over time to specific and generalized cues. The bulk of theorizing and empirical research has been concerned with specifying conditions under which habits are formed, changed, replaced, or broken.

A drive leads to a response to a particular stimulus, and if the response is reinforced or rewarded, a particular habit is learned. Unrewarded and inappropriate responses are extinguished or eliminated. Complex behavior such as consumer decision processes is learned in a similar manner.

According to Dollard and Miller, a drive is a stimulus strong enough to impel activity; it energizes behavior but, by itself, does not direct it. Any stimulus may become a drive if it reaches sufficient intensity. Some stimuli are linked to the physiological processes necessary for the survival of the individual, others are secondary or acquired. With the concepts of cues, drives, responses, and reinforcement, complex motives such as the need for achievement or self-esteem are learned in the same manner as brand preference, racism, attitudes towards big business, purchasing habits, or dislike of canned spinach.

Marketing is replete with examples of the influence of learning theory, ranging from Krugman's work to the Yale studies on attitudes and attitude change, from lightweight discussions on the influence of repetition and reinforcement in advertising texts to Howard and Sheth's buyer behavior theory and the work in mathematical models. However, very few personality studies have used this theoretical orientation.

The reason for the lack of impact is probably that personality tests and measuring instruments using this theoretical base do not exist. Typically, clinical psychologists have developed measuring instruments, but until this past decade clinicians were not trained directly in learning theory. Recently, however, behavior modification based on the work of Skinner has become a psychotherapeutic technique. Many clinical psychologists are turning to learning theory for guidelines in the treatment of abnormality. Unfortunately, they do not seem to be predisposed to create psychological tests to measure personality in line with their definitions, but are more concerned with behavioral change. Until such instruments are developed there will be little use of these theories in relating consumer behavior to personality, irrespective of their completeness and extreme relevance.

TRAIT AND FACTOR THEORIES

As learning theory approaches to personality have evolved from the tough-minded empirical experimentation of the animal laboratories, factor theories have evolved from the quantitative sophistication of statistical techniques and computer technology. The core of these theories is that personality is composed of a set of traits or factors, some general and others specific to a particular situation or test. In constructing a personality instrument, the theorist typically begins with a wide array of behavioral measures, mostly responses to test items, and with statistical techniques distills factors which are then defined as the personality variables.

For one large group of personality instruments the researcher begins with the intent to measure certain variables, for example, need for achievement or aggressiveness. Large samples of subjects predetermined as aggressive or not aggressive (say, by ratings from teachers and employers) are given the instrument. Each item is statistically analyzed to see if it discriminates aggressive from nonaggressive subjects. By a series of such distilling measures and additional validation and reliability studies, an instrument is produced which measures traits the researcher originally was attempting to gauge. Several of these variables are often embodied in, for example, a single 200-item instrument.

A second type of personality instrument is created not with theoretically predetermined variables in mind, but rather to identify a few items (by factor analysis) which account for a significant portion of the variance. Subjects are given questionnaires, ratings, or tests on a wide variety of topics, and test items are grouped in the factor analysis by how well they measure the same statistical factor. The meaning of a particular factor is thus empirically determined and a label arbitrarily attached to it that hopefully best describes what the researcher presumes the particular subset of items measures. Further reliability and validation measures lead to creation of a test instrument with several variables that supposedly account for the diversity and complexity of behavior. The theoretical structure is statistical and the variables are empirically determined and creatively named or labeled.

The concept of traits, factors, or variables that can be quantitatively measured has led to virtually hundreds of personality scales and dozens of studies in consumer behavior. Instruments of this type are discussed below.

GORDON PERSONAL PROFILE

This instrument purports to measure ascendency, responsibility, emotional stability, and sociability. Tucker and Painter found significant correlations between use of headache remedies, vitamins, mouthwash, alcoholic drinks, automobiles, chewing gum, and the acceptance of new fashions and one or more of these four personality variables. The correlations ranged from .27 to .46, accounting for perhaps 10% of the variance.

Kernan used decision theory in an empirical test of the relationship between decision behavior and personality. He added the Gordon Personal Inventory to measure cautiousness, original thinking, personal relations, and vigor. Pearsonian and multiple correlations indicated few significant relationships, but canonical correlation between sets of personality variables and decision behavior gave a coefficient of association of .77, significant at the .10 level. Cluster analysis then showed that behavior is consistent with personality profiles within clusters. Kernan's results, like those of Tucker and Painter, show interesting relationships but are by no means startling.

EDWARDS PERSONAL PREFERENCE SCHEDULE

The EPPS has been used in about two dozen studies or rebuttals in consumer behavior from a trait and factor theory approach. The purpose of the instrument was to develop a factor-analyzed, paper-and-pencil, objective instrument to measure the psychoanalytically-oriented needs or themes developed by Henry Murray. Its popularity in consumer behavior can be traced to Evans' landmark study, in which he could find no differences between Ford and Chevrolet owners to an extent that would allow for prediction. He was, however, able to account for about 10% of the variance. Criticism of Evans' study and conclusions came from many fronts and on many grounds. Rejoinders were written, and finally Evans replicated the study. Using Evans' original data, Kuehn then concluded that predictive ability can be improved if one computes a discriminant function based on the two needs displaying the largest initial predictive ability. Kuehn improved Evans' results by using dominance scores minus affiliation scores. However, the psychological significance of dominance minus affiliation has escaped me for five years. Nevertheless, the controversy over Evans' study is in the very finest tradition of the physical and social sciences, with argument and counterargument, rejoinder and replication, until the facts begin to emerge, something very seldom seen in marketing and consumer behavior research. The final conclusion that seems to trickle through is that personality does account for some variance but not enough to give much solace to personality researchers in marketing.

Along other lines, Koponen used the EPPS scale with data collected on 9,000 persons in the J. Walter Thompson panel. His results indicate that cigarette smoking is positively related to sex dominance, aggression, and achievement needs among males and negatively related to order and compliance needs. Further, he found differences between filter and nonfilter smokers and found that these differences were made more pronounced by heavy smoking. In addition, there seems to be a relationship between personality variables and readership of three unnamed magazines.

Massy, Frank, and Lodahl used the same data in a study of the purchase of coffee, tea, and beer. Their conclusion was that personality accounted for a very small percentage of the variance. In fact, personality plus socioeconomic variables accounted for only 5% to 10% of the variance in purchases.

In a sophisticated study, Claycamp presented the EPPS to 174 subjects who held savings accounts in banks or savings and loan associations. His results indicate that personality variables predict better than demographic variables whether an individual is a customer of a bank or a savings and loan association. These results contradict those of Evans, who concluded that socioeconomic variables are more effective than personality as measured by the same instrument. Using personality variables alone, Claycamp correctly classified 72% of the subjects.

Brody and Cunningham reanalyzed Koponen's data employing techniques like those of Claycamp and Massy, Frank, and Lodahl with similar results, accounting for about 3% of the variance. Further, these results are similar to those from the Advertising Research Foundation's study on toilet paper in which 5% to 10% of the variance was accounted for by personality and other variables. Brody and Cunningham argued that the weak relationships may have been caused by an inadequate theoretical framework. Theirs consisted of three categories: perceived performance risk—the extent different brands perform differently in important ways; specific self-confidence—how certain the consumer is that a brand performs as he expects; and perceived social risk—the extent he thinks he will be judged on the basis of his brand decision. The authors concluded that, "when trying to discriminate the brand choice of people most likely to have perceived-high performance risk and to have high specific self-confidence, personality variables were very useful." For people who were 100% brand loyal, 8 personality variables explained 32% of the variance. As the minimum purchase of the favorite brand dropped from 100% to 40%, the explained variance fell to 13%.

THURSTONE TEMPERAMENT SCHEDULE

This is another factor-analyzed instrument. Westfall, in a well known study that is often interpreted as a replication of Evans' study, compared personalities of automobile owners and could find no difference between brands. He further found no difference between compact and standard car owners on the Thurstone variables. However, personality characteristics did differ between owners of convertibles and standard models.

Using the same instrument, Kamen showed a relationship between the number of people who had no opinion on foods to be rated and the number of items they left unanswered on the Thurstone scale. Using a specially created questionnaire, he concluded that the dimension of "no opinion" is not related to food preference. Proneness to have an opinion does not seem to be a general trait, but rather is dependent on the content area.

CALIFORNIA PERSONALITY INVENTORY

This is the newest paper-and-pencil test to be used extensively. Robertson and Myers, and Bruce and Witt developed measures for innovativeness and opinion leadership in the areas of food, clothing, and appliances. A multiple stepwise regression with 18 traits on the CPI indicated poor R^2's; the portion of variance accounted for was 4% for clothing, 5% for food, and 23% for appliances. The study tends to support the several dozen previous studies on innovation and opinion leadership that show a minimal relationship between personality variables and behavior toward new products. Several studies indicate that gregariousness and venturesomeness are relevant to opinion leadership. Two studies using personality inventories have found a relationship between innovation and personality, while three others could find none. Other traits, such as informal and formal social participation, cosmopolitanism, and perceived risk, are related to innovative behavior in about half a dozen studies, while an additional half a dozen studies show no differences.

A very recent study by Boone attempted to relate the variables on the California Personality Inventory to the consumer innovator on the topic of a community antenna television system. His results indicate significant differences between innovators and followers on 10 of 18 scales. Unfortunately, the statistical techniques were quite different from those employed by Robertson and Myers, so it is not possible to determine whether or not the two studies are in basic agreement.

Finally, Vitz and Johnston, using the masculinity scale of both the CPI and the Minnesota Multiphasic Personality Inventory, hypothesized that the more masculine a smoker's personality, the more masculine the image of his regular brand of cigarettes. The correlations were low but statistically significant, and the authors concluded that the results moderately support product preference as a predictable interaction between the consumer's personality and the product's image.

THEORIES OF SELF AND SELF-CONCEPT

Relationships of product image and self-image have been studied quite thoroughly by the motivation researchers and, particularly Levy and Gardner. The theoretical base for this work, I presume, rests in the writings and philosophies of Carl Rogers, William James, and Abraham Maslow and the symbolic interactionism proposed by Susan Langer and others.

The core of these views is that the individual has a real- and an ideal-self. This *me* or *self* is "the sum total of all that a man can call his—his body, traits, and abilities; his material possessions; his family, friends, and enemies; his vocations and avocations and much else." It includes evaluations and definitions of one's self and may be reflected in much of his actions, including his evaluations and purchase of products and services. The belief is that individuals perceive products that they own, would like to own, or do not want to own in terms of symbolic meaning to themselves and to others. Congruence between the symbolic image of a product (e.g., a .38 caliber is aggressive and masculine, a Lincoln automobile is extravagant and wealthy) and a consumer's self-image implies greater probability of positive evaluation, preference, or ownership of that product or brand. For example, Jacobson and Kossoff studied self-perception and attitudes toward small cars. Individuals who perceived themselves as "cautious conservatives" were more likely to favor small cars as a practical and economic convenience. Another self-classified group of "confident explorers" preferred large cars, which they saw as a means of expressing their ability to control the environment.

Birdwell, using the semantic differential, tested the hypotheses that: (1) an automobile owner's perception of his car is essentially congruent with his perception of himself and (2) the average perception of a specific car type and brand is different for owners of different sorts of cars. The hypotheses were confirmed with varying degrees of strength. However, this does not imply that products have personalities and that a consumer purchases those brands whose images are congruent with his self-concept; Birdwell's study did not test causality. It could very well be that only after a product is purchased does the owner begin to perceive it as an extension of his own personality.

Grubb and Grathwohl found that consumers' different self-perceptions are associated with varying patterns of consumer behavior. They claimed that self-concept is a meaningful mode of market segmentation. Grubb found that beer drinkers perceived themselves as more confident, social, extroverted, forward, sophisticated, impulsive, and temperamental than their non-beer-drinking brethren. However, the comparison of self-concept and beer brand profiles revealed inconclusive results: drinkers and nondrinkers perceived brands similarly.

In a follow-up study of Pontiac and Volkswagen owners, Grubb and Hupp indicated that owners of one brand of automobile perceive themselves as similar to others who own the same brand and significantly different from owners of the other brand. Sommers indicated by the use of a Q-sort of products that subjects are reliably able to describe themselves and others by products rather than adjectives, say on a semantic differential or adjective checklist. That is, individuals are able to answer the questions, "What kind of a person am I?" and "What kind of a person is he?" by Q-sorting products.

Dolich further tested the congruence relationship between self-images and product brands and concluded that there is a greater similarity between one's self-concept and images of his most preferred brands than images of least preferred brands. Dolich claimed that favored brands are consistent with and reinforce self-concept.

Finally, Hamm and Cundiff related product perception to what they call self-actualization, that is, the discrepancy between the self and ideal-self. Those with a small discrepancy were called low self-actualizers, a definition which does not seem consistent with Maslow's work on the hierarchy of needs. High self-actualizers describe themselves in terms of products differently from low self-actualizers, and in turn perceive products differently. For both groups, some products such as house, dress, automatic dishwasher, and art prints tend to represent an ideal-self, wife, or mother, while others such as cigarettes, TV dinners, or a mop do not.

LIFE STYLE

An integration of the richness of motivation research studies and the tough-mindedness and statistical sophistication of computer technology has led to another type of research involving personality, variously called psychographic or life-style research. The life-style concept is based on distinctive or characteristic modes of living of segments of a society. The technique divides the total market into segments based on interests, values, opinions, personality characteristics, attitudes, and demographic variables using techniques of cluster analysis, factor analysis, and canonical correlation. Wells dubbed the methodology "backward segmentation" because it groups people by behavioral characteristics before seeking correlates. Pessemier and Tigert reported that some preliminary relationships were found between the factor-analyzed clusters of people and market behavior.

Generally, the relationship of the attitude-interest-personality clusters, when correlated with actual buyer behavior, indicates once again that 10% or less of the variance is accounted for. Yet quite properly the proponents of the technique claim that very rich data are available in the analyses for the researcher and practitioner interested in consumer behavior.

MISCELLANEOUS OTHER APPROACHES

The overall results of other studies with other points of view are quite similar. Some researchers interpret their results as insignificant while others interpret similarly minimal relationships as significant, depending on the degree of statistical sophistication and the statistical tools used. A hodgepodge of other studies indicates that heavy and light users of several product classes do not differ on the McClosky Personality Inventory or Dunnette Adjective Checklist. Axelrod found a predictable relationship between the mood produced by viewing a movie—*The Nuremburg Trial*—and attitudes toward consumer products such as savings bonds, sewing machines, typewriters, and daiquiris. Eysenck, Tarrant, Woolf, and England indicated that smoking is related to genotypic personality differences. Summers found a minimal relationship between characteristics of opinion leaders and the Borgatta personality variables. Pennington and Peterson have shown that product preferences are related to vocational interests as measured on the Strong Vocational Interest Blank. Finally, Jacoby has demonstrated that Rokeach's concepts of open and closed mindedness are relevant to consumer behavior and found that low dogmatics tend to be more prone to innovation. The correlation between innovation and dogmatism was $-.32$, the explained variance about 10%. Myers, in a study of private brand attitudes, found that Cattell's 16-Personality Factor Inventory explained about 5% of the variance. Once again, the results are in the same order—5% to 10% of the variance accounted for.

SOCIAL CHARACTER

In the usual pattern of applying psychological and sociological concepts to marketing and consumer behavior, several researchers have turned their attention to Riesman's theories, which group human beings into three types of social character: tradition-directed, inner-directed, and other-directed. A society manifests one type predominantly, according to its particular phase of development.

Riesman by no means intended his typology to be interpreted as a personality schema, yet in the consumer behavior literature social character has been grouped with personality, and hence the material is included in this review.

A society of tradition-directed people, seldom encountered in the United States today, is characterized by general slowness of change, a dependence on kin, low social mobility, and a tight web of values. Inner-directed people are most often found in a rapidly changing, industrialized society with division of labor, high social mobility, and less security; these persons must turn to inner values for guidance. In contrast, other-directed persons depend upon those around them to give direction to their actions. The other-directed society is industrialized to the point that its orientation shifts from production to consumption. Thus success in the other-directed society is not through production and hard work but rather through one's ability to be liked by others, develop charm or "personality," and manipulate other people. The contemporary United States is considered by Riesman to be almost exclusively populated by the latter two social character types and is rapidly moving towards an other-directed orientation.

Dornbusch and Hickman content analyzed consumer goods advertising over the past decades and noted a clear trend from inner- to other-direction. Kassarjian and Centers have shown that youth is significantly more other-directed and that those foreign born or reared in small towns tend to be inner-directed.

Gruen found no relationship between preference for new or old products and inner-other-direction. Arndt and Barban, Sandage, Kassarjian, and Kassarjian could find little relationship between innovation and social character; Donnelly, however, has shown a relationship between housewives' acceptance of innovations and social character, with the inner-directed being slightly more innovative. Linton and Graham indicated that inner-directed persons are less easily persuaded than other-directed persons. Centers and Horowitz found that other-directed individuals were more susceptible to social influence in an experimental setting than were inner-directed subjects. Kassarjian found that subjects expressed a preference for appeals based on their particular social character type. There was minimal evidence for differential exposure to various mass media between the two Riesman types.

In a similar study, Woodside found no relationship between consumer products and social character, although he did find a minimal relationship between advertising appeals and inner-other-direction.

Finally, Kassarjian and Kassarjian found a relationship between social character and Allport's scale of values as well as vocational interests but could find no relationship between inner-other-direction and personality variables as measured by the MMPI. Once again, the results follow the same pattern: a few studies find and a few do not find meaningful relationships between consumer behavior and other measures.

PERSONALITY AND PERSUASIBILITY

To complete a review on the relationship between personality and consumer behavior, the wide body of research findings relating personality to persuasibility and attitude change must be included. In addition to the dozens of studies carried out under Carl Hovland, there are many relating personality characteristics to conformity, attitude change, fear appeals, and opinions on various topics. The consumer behavior literature studies by Cox and Bauer, Bell, Carey, and Barach tied self-confidence to persuasibility in the purchase of goods. These studies indicated a curvilinear relationship between generalized self-confidence and persuasibility and between specific self-confidence and persuasibility. Venkatesan's results, however, throw some doubt on these findings. In recent reanalysis and review of much of this literature, Schuchman and Perry found contradictory data and felt these were inconsequential. The authors claim that neither generalized nor specific self-confidence appears to be an important determinant of persuasibility in marketing. Bauer, in turn, has found fault with the Schuchman and Perry reanalysis.

CONCLUSION

A review of these dozens of studies and papers can be summarized in the single word, *equivocal*. A few studies indicate a strong relationship between personality and aspects of consumer behavior, a few indicate no relationship, and the great majority indicate that if correlations do exist they are so weak as to be questionable or perhaps meaningless. Several reasons can be postulated to account for these discrepancies. Perhaps the major one is based on the validity of the particular personality measuring instruments used: a typically "good" instrument has a test-retest reliability of about .80 and a split-half reliability of about .90. Validity coefficients range at most from .40 to about .70; that is, when correlated against a criterion variable, the instrument typically accounts for about 20% to 40% of the variance. Too often the marketing researcher is just plain disinterested in reliability and validity criteria. *Tests validated for specific uses on specific populations, such as college students, or as part of mental hospital intake batteries are applied to available subjects in the general population.* The results may indicate that 10% of the variance is accounted for; this is then interpreted as a weak relationship and personality is rejected as a determinant of purchase. The consumer researcher too often expects more from an instrument than it was originally intended to furnish.

An additional problem for the marketing researcher is the conditions under which the test instrument is given. As Wells has pointed out the instrument is often presented in the classroom or on the doorstep, rather than in the office of a psychometrician, psychotherapist, or vocational counselor.

> The measurements we take may come from some housewife sitting in a bathrobe at her kitchen table, trying to figure out what it is she is supposed to say in answering a questionnaire. Too often, she is not telling us about herself as she really is, but instead is telling us about herself as she thinks she is or wants us to think she is.

To compound the error, consumer researchers often forget that the strength of a correlation is limited by the reliability of the measures being correlated. Not only the personality test but also the criterion itself may be unreliable under these conditions, as Wells has pointed out. Often the criterion used in these studies is the consumer's own account of her purchasing behavior. More often than not, these data are far more unreliable than we may wish to admit.

ADAPTATION OF INSTRUMENTS

Much too often, in order to adjust test items to fit specific demands, changes are made in the instrument. Items are taken out of context of the total instrument, words are changed, items are arbitrarily discarded, and the test is often shortened drastically. This adjustment would undoubtedly horrify the original developer of the instrument, and the disregard for the validity of the modified instrument should horrify the rest of us. Just how much damage is done when a measure of self-confidence or extroversion is adapted, revised, and restructured is simply not known, but it would not be a serious exaggeration to claim it is considerable. And, most unfortunately, from time to time even the name of the variable is changed to fit the needs of the researcher. For example, Cohen has pointed out that in the Koponen study male smokers scored higher than average on self-depreciation and association, variables not included in the Edwards instrument. The researcher was apparently using the abasement and affiliation scales. Such changes may or may not be proper, and although they may not necessarily violate scientific canons, they certainly do not help reduce the confusion in attempting to sort out what little we know about the relationships of personality to consumer behavior.

PSYCHOLOGICAL INSTRUMENTS IN MARKETING RESEARCH

A second reason for discrepancies in the literature is that instruments originally intended to measure gross personality characteristics such as sociability, emotional stability, introversion, or neuroticism have been used to make predictions of the chosen brand of toothpaste or cigarettes. The variables that lead to the assassination of a president, confinement in a mental hospital, or suicide may not be identical to those that lead to the purchase of a washing machine, a pair of shoes, or chewing gum. *Clearly, if unequivocal results are to emerge, consumer behavior researchers must develop their own definitions and design their own instruments to measure the personality variables that go into the purchase decision rather than using tools designed as part of a medical model to measure schizophrenia or mental stability.*

Development of definitions and instruments can perhaps be handled in two ways. One will require some brilliant theorizing as to what variables do relate to the consumer decision process. If neuroticism and sociability are not the relevant personality variables, then perhaps new terms such as risk aversion, status seeking, and conspicuous consumption will emerge. Personality variables that in fact are relevant to the consumer model need to be theorized and tests developed and validated.

Another approach to developing such instruments might be that of the factor theorists. Dozens of items measuring behavior, opinions, purchases, feelings, or attitudes can be factor analyzed in the search for general and specific factors that in turn can be validated against the marketing behavior of the individual. The research group at Purdue and the recent work of Wells and Wilkie, have made refreshingly new attempts at personality measurement and come very close to the research techniques developed by the factor theorists. Whether or not these attempts will succeed in producing a new approach to personality research is yet to be proved; the studies to date are encouraging.

Only with marketing-oriented instruments will we be able to determine just what part personality variables play in the consumer decision process and, further, if they can be generalized across product and service classes or must be product-specific instruments. At that stage, questions of the relevancy of these criteria for market segmentation, shifting demand curves, or creating and sustaining promotional and advertising campaigns can be asked.

A third reason for the lackluster results in the personality and consumer behavior literature is that *many studies have been conducted by a shotgun approach with no specific hypotheses or theoretical justification*. Typically a convenient, available, easily scored, and easy-to-administer personality inventory is selected and administered along with questionnaires on purchase data and preferences. The lack of proper scientific method and hypotheses generation is supposedly justified by the often-used disclaimer that the study is exploratory. As Jacoby has pointed out:

> Careful examination reveals that, in most cases, no a priori thought is directed to *how*, or especially *why*, personality should or should not be related to that aspect of consumer behavior being studied. Moreover, the few studies which do report statistically significant findings usually do so on the basis of post-hoc "picking and choosing" out of large data arrays.

Statistical techniques are applied and anything that turns up looking halfway interesting furnishes the basis for the discussion section.

An excellent example of the shotgun approach to science, albeit a more sophisticated one than most, is Evans' original study examining personality differences between Ford and Chevrolet owners. Jacoby, in an excellent and most thoughtful paper, noted that Evans began his study with specific hypotheses culled from the literature and folklore pertaining to personality differences to be expected between Ford and Chevrolet owners. He then presented the EPPS to subjects, measuring 11 variables, 5 of which seemed to be measuring the variables in question; the remaining 6 were irrelevant to the hypotheses with no a priori basis for expecting differences. If predictions were to have been made on these six scales, Jacoby says, they should have been ones of *no* difference. Using one-tailed tests of significance, since the directions also should have been hypothesized, 3 of the 5 key variables were significant at the .05 level and none of the remaining 6 were significant. In short, Evans' data could have been interpreted such that 9 of the 11 scales were "significant" according to prediction. Jacoby's interpretation leads to a conclusion quite different from Evans', that there are no personality differences between Ford and Chevrolet owners. Also, with a priori predictions, Jacoby did not have to pick and choose from his data, as

Kuehn was forced to do in showing a relationship between "dominance minus affiliation" scores and car ownership.

Finally, personality researchers and researchers in other aspects of marketing seem to need simple variables which can be somehow applied in the marketplace. We seem to feel that the only function of science and research is to predict rather than to understand, to persuade rather than to appreciate. Social scientists can fully accept that personality variables are related to suicide or crime, to assassinations, racial prejudice, attitudes toward the USSR, or the selection of a spouse. They do not get upset that personality is not the only relevant variable or that the portion of the explained variance is merely 20% or 10% or 5%. Yet personality researchers in consumer behavior much too often ignore the many interrelated influences on the consumer decision process, ranging from price and packaging to availability, advertising, group influences, learned responses, and preferences of family members, in addition to personality. *To expect the influence of personality variables to account for a large portion of the variance is most certainly asking too much.* What is amazing is not that there are many studies that show no correlation between consumer behavior and personality, but rather that there are any studies at all with positive results. That 5% or 10% or any portion of the variance can be accounted for by personality variables measured on ill-chosen and inadequate instruments is most remarkable, indeed!

RETROSPECTIVE COMMENT[1]

By late 1969 some one hundred studies were available in the marketing literature relating personality variables to consumer behavior. A review of these studies can be summarized by the single word, "equivocal." The purpose of this paper is to enumerate what has happened to the field in the ensuing half decade. The previous quarter century had produced some one hundred studies. The outpouring of recent research has accumulated an additional one hudred studies in the last five years, not including working papers, privately distributed pre-prints and unpublished proprietary studies.

No major obvious changes have been discernible although some new fads in researchable variables have emerged. For example, one no

1 This retrospective comment originally appeared as Harold H. Kassarjian and Mary Jane Sheffet, "Personality and Consumer Behavior: One More Time," Edward M. Mazze (editor), *Marketing: The Challenges and the Opportunities*, published by the American Marketing Association. Reprinted by permission of the author and publisher.

longer finds the topic of motivation research from a psychoanalytic point of view in the literature. The only true attempt to use a projective technique to be found in the published literature is a replication of the classic Mason Haire Shopping List study by Webster and Von Pechmann which interestingly, yielded significantly different results from the original paper. Instant coffee users are no longer perceived as psychologically different from drip grind users. The only other attempts at the use of projective techniques are studies by David Gardner and Hughes in which McClelland's TAT type picture were used to measure need for achievement. Landon measured the same variable but by using Merabian's paper and pencil test avoided the interpretation problems of a projective tool.

The use of the traditionally available paper and pencil psychological inventories is still quite popular. The Edwards Personal Preference Schedule, originally used by Evans in his landmark Ford-Chevrolet study, was used in studies by Alpert, Peterson and Bither and Dolich. Horton, in a penetrating article, attacked the use of this and similar paper-and-pencil tools on procedural grounds. The Thurstone Temperament Schedule appears in a study by Wiseman using linear discriminant analysis while the Gordon instrument was utilized in two studies. Cohen's CAD test of Horney's classification scheme is reported in three papers. One by Kernan concerning message advocacy, group influence, fashions, brand loyalty, and new product information produced significant results with the conclusion that the instrument "works." The second by Cohen and Goldberg again produced positive results and a third by Nicely found correlations between CAD, Eysenck's introversion-extroversion variable and Kassarjian's inner-and-other-direction variables. Donnelly and Ivancevich in turn found a weak but positive relationship between inner-other-direction and innovator characteristics. Perry tied in anxiety, the Eysenck variables, and heredity to product choice concluding that consumption was genetically influenced. He claimed that this genetic relationship has application to primary demand but not product choice.

Rokeach's dogmatism as a variable appeared in some half a dozen studies correlating the variable to risk, innovation and adoption, generally with weak but significant results. Openmindedness seems to be positively related to risk taking and willingness to innovate.

Several new instruments appeared for the first time in consumer type studies. Morris and Cundiff and Vavra and Winn turned their attention to anxiety and the Taylor Manifest Anxiety Scale, and Hawkins used the State-Trait Anxiety Inventory. The mixed results generally indicate that low anxiety is related to acceptance of more threatening material such as males' acceptance of feminine products. Peters and Ford used the California Test of Personality and could find no personality difference between women who buy and do not buy from door-to-door salesmen. Hughes compared the CPI and Rotter's Locus of Control to bargaining behavior. Webster aimed the CPI at Social responsibility concluding that the better socially and psychologically integrated consumer displays greater social consciousness.

The most widely used instrument new to consumer behavior is the Jackson Personality Research Form. Wilson, et. al., correlated these scores with segmentation variables, Fry and Ahmed with cigarette smoking, Kinnear and Taylor with ecological products, Worthing, et al., with a variety of consumer products, and Matthews, et al., with perceived risk.

Studies using intolerance of ambiguity and Rotter's internal and external control have appeared using available instruments. Additional new instruments appeared in the literature as Paul and Enis, Goldberg Kirchner, Kegerreis and Engel, Baumgarten, and Feldman and Armstrong developed their own tools to measure venturesomeness, Murray's needs, ordinal birth position, personal competence and so on.

Self-confidence had been heavily examined prior to 1969. Its fascination to researchers has not diminished. Studies by Bither and Wright, Barach and Ostlund have since appeared. Work in self-concept continues to appear in some eleven studies in the struggle to explain purchase behavior by measuring the ideal self and actual self concept.

Perhaps the most dramatic change in the field has been the influence of studies using life style, AIO, or psychographics as they are alternatively termed. These factor analyzed scales have been applied to media exposure, credit card usage, advertising, creativity, opinion leadership and innovation, and market segmentation. Discussion articles of The Methodology as well as reliability and validity studies are now available among many others. These two dozen articles, however, merely scratch the surface. The book by King and Tigert, *Life Style and Psychographics* by Bill Wells and the AMA Attitude Research Proceedings contribute still more papers to this field. In addition, no topic in our memory has produced as many unpublished papers, university working papers, and private pre-prints as has life style research. Interestingly, the impact has not been as great as the sheer weight of publications might suggest, although psychographics certainly has become a buzz word in industry.

On overview, the conclusions from published research studies over the past five years remains quite similar to those drawn in 1969. The additional studies have generally made little contribution to the depth of our knowledge, although its breadth has certainly been expanded. The correlation or relationship between personality test scores and consumer behavior variables such as product choice, media exposure, innovation, segmentation, etc., are weak at best and thus of little value in prediction. The reasons for such poor predictions have been discussed by Jacoby, Wells and Beard and Kassarjian, and all agree that personality is a critical variable in the explanation of the purchasing process. The critical question is why do we insist on considering personality, by itself, a salient variable when the data are at best equivocal?

Nakanishi, in a most insightful paper presented at the 1972 meetings of the Association For Consumer Research, has suggested that the low explanatory power of personality characteristics may have stemmed, in part, from naive conceptualizations of the relationship between personality and consumer behavior often held by researchers in the field. It is obvious that simple linear statistics such as variance analysis, chi square and t-tests are insufficient. For example, canonical correlations have been used by Sparks and Tucker, Bither and Dolich, Alpert and Darden and Reynolds with more complex results and somewhat more variance statistically explained. Unfortunately, this adding of additional variables still involves a static view of the consumer. Personality is perhaps better conceived of as a dynamic concept which is not constant over a variety of situations. Rather, personality is a consistency in the manner the individual adjusts to change over time and over situations. Nakanishi writes it is perhaps, "more correct to conceive of personality as a moderator variable whose function is to moderate the effects of environmental change in the individual's behavior. This dynamic concept of personality has not been taken seriously in personality research."

Nakanishi seems to be suggesting that what we need is data somewhat analogous to a combination of cross-sectional and times series analysis. The studies conducted to date are of the cross-sectional variety correlating test inventory variables with consumption variables over subjects. And yet, as Wells points out, a single personality trait may lead to a variety of behaviors. For instance compulsiveness can lead to extremely orderly behavior or expulsive disorderly behavior depending on the situation. On the other hand, several personality traits may lead to a single response, again depending on the situation. Correlating a single trait with a single behavior is bound to be frustrating.

Hence, according to Nakanishi, the relevant variables include personality traits, response and behavior patterns, moderator variables, situations and individuals. Furthermore, for some of these variables it is essential that measurements be taken over time. That is, as we sample individuals, traits and responses, we should also take samplings of situations over time.

If one turns to other concepts in consumer research, an overview of the results again appears to be frustrating at times. For example, static research and linear statistics on the relationship between attitudes, values, or beliefs and the behavior of the individual are weak at best.

Research on repetition and learning, perceived risk, motivation, level of involvement, group influence, reference groups, personal influence, class, and cultural influence have produced similar conclusions. The data indicate sufficient relationships between the concept and behavior to be enticing and to encourage even further research, but quite insufficient to satisfy a statistician attempting to validate a simple mathematical model or the marketer seeking explanations of the variance in consumer behavior that are not so small as to be meaningless.

If one can generalize from Nakanishi, the low explanatory power of each of these variables stems from naive conceptualizations of the relationships between the variable and the actions of the consumer in the marketplace.

Trained as we have been, by psychoanalytic logic, simplistic beliefs emerging from stimulus-response psychology, and basic Aristotelian modes of thought, we insist on retaining the belief that, "The stimulus possesses an adhesion with certain reactions." This adhesion is regarded as the cause of the event, and somehow, there are mechanically rigid connections or associations between a stimulus and a response. The purchase of canned peas is somehow related to a specific personality variable, a specific type of perceived risk, or to a set of attributions. The belief is that once the mathematical relationship of this mechanically rigid connection is uncovered, the variance will be accounted for and a statistical error term will no longer exist. Hence, if the Edwards schedule does not account for the variance, perhaps the Jackson Inventory will, and if not, there are still Fishbein attitude models, reference groups, and measures of the level of involvement upon which to fall back.

The conception that the individual must be perceived as a dynamic whole, has not yet been internalized by the modern-day consumer researcher. We ought not to be concerned with rigid connections, but rather with temporally extended whole individuals. In short, further traditional research attempting to connect the purchase of canned peas with a personality variable using cross sectional data is bound to fail. What is missing are the interaction effects of that personality variable with other personality characteristics as well as the interaction effects accounted for by needs, motives, moods, memories, attitudes, beliefs, opinions, perceptions, values, etc. in addition to the situation or field. As Tucker has already suggested, our theories must begin with the study of the whole individual in a purchase act, at a point in time. In short, every specific instance of behavior must be viewed as the result of the interaction and integration of a variety of influences or forces impinging upon the person. The description of behavior cannot concentrate exclusively on one or another of the variables involved. Only after the analysis examines the situation as a whole, is it possible to turn to the specific elements and the interactions among the elements. Unfortunately a simple methodology for research of this sort has not yet emerged. We do not necessarily advocate a return to the extensive study of a single individual such as the psychoanalytic methodology employed by Freud, or the environmental probability of Egon Brunswick. But, greater awareness of views espoused by Tolman, Freud, Brunswick, Lewin, and other great minds in the social sciences and philosophy might help point out the location of the light at the end of the tunnel.

Only when we can explain the behavior of a single individual in a variety of situations over time, can we grasp the idea that there are, in fact, interactions between personality, attitudes, perceived risk, and the psychological field or situation. Once the concept of an interaction effect has been internalized, we can turn from an examination of the whole to analyses of the parts. The proper question then would be, "All other things being equal, what is the relationship between a specific personality variable and a specific act?" The problem with the literature as it exists today is that "all other things are not equal" and yet we continue to express dismay, surprise, or pleasure that personality measures, or attitude measures, or what have you, only account for 5% of the variance. As has already been expressed, "What is amazing is not that there are many studies that show no correlation between consumer behavior and personality, but rather that there are any studies at all with positive results. That 5% or 10% or any portion of the variance can be accounted for by personality variables (taken out of context and studied independently of other cognitive or physical variables) . . . is most remarkable, indeed!"—*Harold H. Kassarjian* and *Mary Jane Sheffet*

REFERENCES TO RETROSPECTIVE COMMENT

AHMED, S. A. "Prediction of Cigarette Consumption Level with Personality and Socioeconomic Variables," *Journal of Applied Psychology*, 56 (October 1972), 437–438.

ALPERT, LEWIS and Ronald Gatty. "Product Positioning by Behavioral Life Styles," *Journal of Marketing*, 33 (April 1969), 65–69.

ALPERT, MARK I. "A Canonical Analysis of Personality and the Determinants of Automobile Choice," *Combined Proceedings*, American Marketing Association, 1971, 312–316.

ALPERT, MARK I. "Personality and The Determinants of Product Choice," *Journal of Marketing Research*, 5 (February 1972), 89–92.

AMERICAN MARKET RESEARCH BUREAU. "Measuring Self-Concept," Unpublished Working Paper, May 1972.

AMERICAN MARKETING ASSOCIATION. *Attitude Research Reaches New Heights*, Chicago: American Marketing Association, 1971.

ANDERSON, W. T. and William H. Cunningham, "Gauging Foreign Product Promotion," *Journal of Advertising Research*, 12 (February 1972), 29–44.

BARACH, JEFFREY A. "Self-Confidence, Risk Handling, and Mass Communications," *Proceedings*, Fall Conference, American Marketing Association, 1969, 323–329.

BARACH, JEFFREY A. "Self Confidence and Four Types of Persuasive Situations," *Combined Proceedings*, American Marketing Association, 1972, 418–422.

BASS, FRANK M., Edgar A. Pessemier, and Douglas J. Tigert. "A Taxonomy of Magazine Readership Applied to Problems in Marketing Strategy and Media Selection," *Journal of Business*, 42 (July 1969), 337–363.

BAUMGARTEN, STEVEN A. "The Innovative Communicator in The Diffusion Process," *Journal of Marketing Research*, 12 (February 1975), 12–18.

BITHER, STEWART W. and Ira J. Dolich. "Personality as a Determinant Factor in Store Choice," *Proceedings*, Association For Consumer Research, 1972, 9–19.

BITHER, STEWART W. and Peter L. Wright. "The Self Confidence-Advertising Response Relationship A Function of Situational Distraction," *Journal of Marketing Research*, 10 (May 1973), 146–152.

BLAKE, BRIAN, Robert Perloff, and Richard Heslin. "Dogmatism and Acceptance of New Products," *Journal of Marketing Research* 7 (November 1970), 483–486.

BLAKE, BRIAN, Robert Perloff, Robert Zenhausern, and Richard Heslin. "The Effect of Intolerance of Ambiguity Upon Product Perceptions," *Journal of Applied Psychology*, 58 (October 1973), 239–243.

BRUNO, ALBERT V. and Edgar A. Pessemier. "An Empirical Investigation of The Validity of Selected Attitude and Activity Measures," *Proceedings*, Association for Consumer Research, 1972, 456–473.

BUSHMAN, F. ANTHONY. "Market Segmentation Via Attitudes and Life Style," *Combined Proceedings*, American Marketing Association, 1971, 594–599.

CARMAN, JAMES M. "Correlates of Brand Loyalty: Some Positive Results," *Journal of Marketing Research*, 7 (February 1970), 67–76.

COHEN, JOEL B. and Ellen Golden. "Informational Social Influence and Product Evaluation," *Journal of Applied Psychology*, 50 (February 1972), 54–59.

CONEY, KENNETH A. "Dogmatism and Innovation: A Replication," *Journal of Marketing Research*, 9 (November 1972), 453–455.

DARDEN, WILLIAM R. and Fred D. Reynolds. "Predicting Opinion Leadership For Men's Apparel Fashions," *Journal of Marketing Research*, 9 (August 1972), 324–328.

DARDEN, WILLIAM R. and Fred D. Reynolds. "Backward Profiling of Male Innovators," Journal of Marketing Research, 11 (February 1974), 79–85.

DOLICH, IRA J. and Neb Shilling. "A Critical Evaluation of 'The Problem of Self-Concept in Store Image Studies,'" *Journal of Marketing*, 35 (January 1971), 71–73.

DONNELLY, JAMES H., JR. and John M. Ivancevich. "A Methodology for Identifying Innovator Characteristics of New Brand Purchasers," *Journal of Marketing Research*, 11 (August 1974), 331–334.

ENGEL, JAMES F., David T. Kollat, and Roger D. Blackwell. "Personality Measures and Market Segmentation," *Business Horizons*, 12 (June 1969), 61–70.

FELDMAN, LAURENCE P. and Gary M. Armstrong. "Identifying Buyers of a Major Automobile Innovation," *Journal of Marketing*, 39 (January 1975), 47–53.

FRENCH, WARREN A. and Alan B. Flaschner. "Levels of Actualization as Matched

Against Life Style Evaluation of Products," *Combined Proceedings*, American Marketing Association, 1971, 358–362.

FRY, JOSEPH N. "Personality Variables and Cigarette Brand Choice," *Journal of Marketing Research*, 8 (August 1971), 298–304.

GARDNER, DAVID M. "An Exploratory Investigation of Achievement Motivation Effects on Consumer Behavior," *Proceedings*, Association For Consumer Research, 1972, 20–33.

GOBLE, ROSS LAWRENCE. "New Psychometric Measurements For Consumer Credit Behavior," *Proceedings*, Fall Conference, American Marketing Association, 1969, 368–376.

GOLDBERG, MARVIN E. "A Cognitive Model of Innovative Behavior: The Interaction of Product and Self-Attitudes," *Proceedings*, Association For Consumer Research, 1971, 313–330.

GREEN, PAUL E., Arun Maheshwari and V. R. Rao. "Self Concept and Brand Preference: An Empirical Application of Multidimensional Scaling," *Journal of the Marketing Research Society*, 11 (1969), 343–360.

GREENO, DANIEL W., Montrose S. Sommers, and Jerome B. Kernan. "Personality and Implicit Behavior Patterns," *Journal of Marketing Research*, 10 (February 1973), 63–69.

GRUBB, EDWARD L. and Bruce L. Stern. "Self-Concept and Significant Others," *Journal of Marketing Research*, 8 (August 1971), 382–385.

HAWKINS, DEL I. "Reported Cognitive Dissonance and Anxiety: Some Additional Findings," *Journal of Marketing*, 36 (July 1972), 63–66.

HORTON, RAYMOND L. "The Edwards Personal Preference Schedule and Consumer Personality Research," *Journal of Marketing Research*, 11 (August 1974), 333–337.

HUGHES, G. DAVID and Jose L. Guerrero, "Automobile Self-Congruity Models Reexamined," *Journal of Marketing Research*, 8 (February 1971), 125–127.

HUGHES, G. DAVID, Joseph B. Juhasz, and Bruno Contino. "The Influence of Personality on The Bargaining Process," *The Journal of Business of The University of Chicago*, 46 (October 1973), 593–603.

HUSTAD, THOMAS P. and Edgar A. Pessemier. "Industry's Use of Life Style Analysis: Segmenting Consumer Market with Activity and Attitude Measures," *Combined Proceedings*, American Marketing Association, 1971 a, 296–301.

HUSTAD, THOMAS P. and Edgar A. Pessemier. "Segmenting Consumer Markets with Activity and Attitude Measures," Unpublished Working Paper, Purdue University, 1971.

JACOBY, JACOB. "Multiple-Indicant Approach for Studying New Product Adopters," *Journal of Applied Psychology*, 55 (1971), 384–388.

JOYCE, TIMOTHY. "Personality Classification of Consumers," Unpublished paper presented at 1972 Annual Meetings, American Psychological Association.

KASSARJIAN, HAROLD H. "Personality and Consumer Behavior: A Review," *Journal of Marketing Research*, 8 (November 1971), 409–418.

KASSARJIAN, HAROLD H. "Field Theory in Consumer Behavior," in Scott Ward and Thomas S. Robertson (eds.), *Consumer Behavior: Theoretical Sources*, Englewood Cliffs: Prentice Hall, Inc. 1973, 118–140.

KEGERREIS, ROBERT J. and James F. Engel. "The Innovative Consumer: Characteristics of the Earliest Adopters of a New Automotive Service," *Proceedings*, American Marketing Association, 1969, 357–361.

KERNAN, JEROME B. "The CAD Instrument in Behavioral Diagnosis," *Proceedings*, Association For Consumer Research, 1971, 301–312.

KING, CHARLES W. and John O. Summers, "Attitudes and Media Exposure," *Journal of Advertising Research*, 11 (February 1971), 26–32.

KING, CHARLES W. and Douglas J. Tigert (eds.), *Attitude Research Reaches New Heights*. Chicago: American Marketing Association, 1971.

KINNEAR, THOMAS C., James R. Taylor, and Sadrudin A. Ahmed. "Socioeconomic and Personality Characteristics as They Relate To Ecologically Constructive Purchasing Behavior," *Proceedings*, Association For Consumer Research, 1972, 34–60.

KINNEAR, THOMAS C., James R. Taylor, and Sadrudin A. Ahmed. "Ecologically Concerned Consumers: Who are They?," *Journal of Marketing*, 38 (April 1974), 20–24.

KIRCHNER, DONALD F. "Personal Influence, Ordinal Position and Purchasing Behavior," *Proceedings*, Association For Consumer Research, 1971, 82–98.

LANDON, E. LAIRD, JR. "A Sex-Role Explanation of Purchase Intention Differences of Consumers Who Are High and Low in Need Achievement," *Proceedings*, Association For Consumer Research, 1972, 1–8.

LANDON, E. LAIRD, JR. "Self Concept, Ideal Self Concept, and Consumer Purchase Intentions," *Journal of Consumer Research*, 1 (September 1974), 44–51.

LEWIN, KURT. *A Dynamic Theory of Personality*, New York: McGraw-Hill, 1935, 43–65.

MARTIN, WARREN S. *Personality and Product Symbolism*. Austin, Texas: Bureau of Business Research, Graduate School of Business, University of Texas, 1973.

MASON, JOSEPH BARRY and Morris L. Mayer. "The Problem of The Self-Concept in Store Image Studies," *Journal of Marketing*, 34 (April 1970), 67–69.

MATHEWS, H. LEE, John W. Slocum, Jr., and Arch G. Woodside. "Perceived Risk, Individual Differences, and Shopping Orientations," *Proceedings*, Association For Consumer Research, 1971, 299–306.

MAZIS, MICHAEL B. and Timothy W. Sweeney. "Novelty and Personality with Risk as a Moderating Variable," *Combined Proceedings*, American Marketing Association, 1972, 406–411.

MICHAELS, PETER W. "Life Style and Magazine Exposure," *Combined Proceedings*, American Marketing Association, 1972, 324–331.

MICHMAN, RONALD D. "Market Segmentation Strategies: Pitfalls and Potentials," *Combined Proceedings*, American Marketing Association, 1971, 322–326.

MORRIS, GEORGE P. and Edward W. Cundiff. "Acceptance by Males of Feminine Products," *Journal of Marketing Research*, 8 (August 1971), 372–374.

MORRISON, BRUCE JOHN and Richard C. Sherman. "Who Responds to Sex in Advertising," *Journal of Advertising Research*, 12 (April 1972), 15–19.

NAKANISHI, MASAO. "Personality and Consumer Behavior: Extentions," *Proceedings*, Association For Consumer Research, 1972, 61–65.

NICELY, ROY E. "E, I–O and CAD Correlations," Unpublished Working Paper, Virginia Polytechnic Institute & State University, 1972.

OSTLUND, LYMAN E. "The Role of Product Perceptions in Innovative Behavior," *Proceedings*, Fall Conference, American Marketing Association, 1969, 259–266.

OSTLUND, LYMAN E. "The Interaction of Self Confidence Variables in the Context of Innovative Behavior," *Proceedings*, Association For Consumer Research, 1971, 351–357.

OSTLUND, LYMAN E. "Identifying Early Buyers," *Journal of Advertising Research*, 12 (April 1972), 25–30.

PAUL, GORDON W. and Ben M. Enis. "Psychological and Socioeconomic Atypicality of Consumer Panel Members," *Proceedings*, Fall Conference, American Marketing Association, 1969, 387–391.

PERRY, ARNON. "Heredity, Personality Traits, Product Attitude and Product Consumption-An Exploratory Study," *Journal of Marketing Research*, 10 (November 1973), 376–379.

PESSEMIER, EDGAR A. and T. P. Hustad. "Segmenting Consumer Markets with Activity and Attitude Measures," Unpublished Paper, Marketing Science Institute, 1971.

PETERS, MICHAEL P. and M. Venkatesan. "Exploration of Variables Inherent in Adopting an Industrial Product," *Journal of Marketing Research*, 10 (August 1973), 312–315.

PETERS, WILLIAM H. and Neil M. Ford. "A Profile of Urban Inhome Shoppers: The Other Half," *Journal of Marketing*, 36 (January 1972), 62–64.

PETERSON, ROBERT A. "Psychographics and Media Exposure," *Journal of Advertising Research*, 12 (June 1972), 17–20.

PLUMMER, JOSEPH T. "Life Style and Advertising: Case Studies," *Combined Proceedings*, American Marketing Association, 1971 a, 290–295.

PLUMMER, JOSEPH T. "Life Style Patterns and Commercial Bank Credit Card Usage," *Journal of Marketing*, 35 (April 1971 b), 35–41.

REYNOLDS, FRED D. and William R. Darden. "An Operational Construction of Life Style," *Proceedings*, Association For Consumer Research, 1972, 475–489.

ROSS, IVAN, "Self Concept and Brand Preference," *The Journal of Business of The University of Chicago*, 44 (January 1971), 38–50.

SPARKS, DAVID L. and W. T. Tucker. "A Multivariate Analysis of Personality and Product Use," *Journal of Marketing Research*, 8 (February 1971), 67–70.

SWAN, JOHN E. and Frederick E. May. "Comments on Personality and Persuasibility in Consumer Decision Making," *Journal of Advertising Research*, 10 (June 1970), 1–27.

TIGERT, DOUGLAS J. "Psychographics: A Test-Retest Reliability Analysis," *Proceedings*, Fall Conference, American Marketing Association, 1969, 310–315.

TIGERT, DOUGLAS J. and Stephen J. Arnold. "Profiling Self-Designated Opinion Leaders and Self-Designated Innovators Through Life Style Research," *Proceedings*, Association For Consumer Research, 1971, 425–445.

TUCKER, WILLIAM T. *Foundations for a Theory of Consumer Behavior*. New York: Holt, Rinehart and Winston, Inc., 1967.

VAVRA, TERRY G. and Paul R. Winn. "Fear Appeals in Advertising: An Investigation of The Influence of Order, Anxiety and Involvement," *Combined Proceedings*, American Marketing Association, 1971, 444–449.

VENKATESAN, M. "Personality and Persuasibility in Consumer Decision Making: A Reply," *Journal of Advertising Research*, 10 (June 1970), 1–12.

WEBSTER, FREDRICK E., JR. and Fredrick Von Pechmann. "A Replication of The 'Shopping List' Study," *Journal of Marketing*, 34 (April 1970), 61–63.

WEBSTER, FREDERICK E. "Determining The Characteristics of The Socially Conscious Consumer," Unpublished Paper, 1975.

WELLS, WILLIAM D. "Seven Questions About Lifestyle and Psychographics," *Combined Proceedings*, American Marketing Association, 1972, 462–465.

WELLS, WILLIAM D. (ed.). *Life Style and Psychographics*. Chicago: American Marketing Association, 1974.

WELLS, WILLIAM D. and Arthur D. Beard. "Personality and Consumer Behavior," in Scott Ward and Thomas S. Robertson (eds.), *Consumer Behavior: Theoretical Sources*. Englewood Cliffs: Prentice-Hall, 1973, 141–199.

WHEATLEY, J. J. and S. Oshikawa. "The Relationship Between Anxiety and Positive and Negative Advertising Appeals," *Journal of Marketing Research*, 7 (1970), 85–89.

WILSON, DAVID T., H. Lee Mathews and Timothy W. Sweeney. "Industrial Buyer Segmentation: A Psychographic Approach," *Combined Proceedings*, American Marketing Association, 1971, 327–331.

WIND, JERRY. "Life Style Analysis: A New Approach," *Combined Proceedings*, American Marketing Association, 1971, 302–305.

WINTER, EDWARD and John T. Russell. "Psychographics and Creativity," *Journal of Advertising*, 2 (1937), 32–35.

WISEMAN, FREDERICK. "A Segmentation Analysis on Automobile Buyers During The New Model Year Transition Period," *Journal of Marketing*, 35 (April 1971), 42–49.

WOODSIDE, ARCH G. "Effects of Prior Decision Making, Demographics and Psychographics on Marital Roles For Purchasing Durables," *Proceedings*, Association For Consumer Research, 1974, 81–91.

WORTHING, PARKER M., M. Vengatesan, and Steve Smith. "A Modified Approach to The Exploration of Personality and Product Use," *Combined Proceedings*, American Marketing Association, 1971, 363–367.

WORTHING, PARKER M., M. Venkatesan, and Steve Smith. "Personality and Product Use Revisited: An Exploration with the Personality Research Form," *Journal of Applied Psychology*, 57 (April 1973), 179–183.

ZIFF, RUTH. "Psychographics for Market Segmentation," *Journal of Advertising Research*, 11 (April 1971), 3–9.

ZIFF, RUTH. "Closing The Consumer-Advertising Gap Through Psychographics," *Combined Proceedings*, American Marketing Association, 1972, ·457–461.

REFERENCES

Are There Consumer Types? New York: Advertising Research Foundation, 1964.

ARNDT, JOHAN. "Role of Product-Related Conversations in the Diffusion of a New Product," *Journal of Marketing Research*, 4 (August 1967), 291–5.

———. "Profiling Consumer Innovators," in Johan Arndt, ed., *Insights Into Consumer Behavior*. Boston: Allyn and Bacon, 1968, 71–83.

AXELROD, JOEL N. "Induced Mood and Attitudes Towards Products," *Journal of Advertising Research*, 3 (June 1963), 19–24.

BARACH, JEFFREY A. "Self-Confidence and Reactions to Television Commercials," in Donald F. Cox, ed., *Risk Taking and Information Handling in Consumer Behavior*. Boston: Division of Research, Graduate School of Business, Harvard University, 1967, 428–41.

———. "Advertising Effectiveness and Risk in the Consumer Decision Process," *Journal of Marketing Research*, 6 (August 1969), 314–20.

BARBAN, ARNOLD N., C. H. Sandage, Waltraud M. Kassarjian, and Harold H.

Kassarjian. "A Study of Riesman's Inner-Other-Directedness Among Farmers," *Rural Sociology*, 35 (June 1970), 232–43.
BASS, KRANK M., Douglas J. Tigert, and Ronald T. Lonsdale. "Market Segmentation: Group Versus Individual Behavior," *Journal of Marketing Research*, 5 (August 1968), 264–70.
BAUER, RAYMOND A. "Self-Confidence and Persuasibility: One More Time," *Journal of Marketing Research*, 7 (May 1970), 256–8.
BELL, GERALD D. "Persuasibility and Buyer Remorse Among Automobile Purchasers," in Montrose S. Sommers and Jerome B. Kernan, eds., *Consumer Behavior*. Austin: Bureau of Business Research, The University of Texas, 1968, 77–102.
———. "Self-Confidence and Persuasion in Car Buying," *Journal of Marketing Research*, 4 (February 1967), 46–52.
BIRDWELL, AL E. "Influence of Image Congruence on Consumer Choice," *Proceedings*. Winter Conference, American Marketing Association, 1964, 290–303.
———. "A Study of the Influence of Image Congruence on Consumer Choice," *Journal of Business*, 41 (January 1968), 76–88.
———. "Automobiles and Self Imagery: Reply," *Journal of Business*, 41 (October 1968), 486–7.
BOONE, LOUIS E. "The Search for the Consumer Innovator," *Journal of Business*, 43 (April 1970), 135–40.
BRODY, ROBERT P. and Scott M. Cunningham. "Personality Variables and the Consumer Decision Process," *Journal of Marketing Research*, 5 (February 1968), 50–7.
BRUCE, GRADY D. and Robert E. Witt. "Personality Correlates of Innovative Buying Behavior," *Journal of Marketing Research*, 7 (May 1970), 259–60.
CAREY, JAMES W. "Personality Correlates of Persuasibility," *Proceedings*. Winter Conference, American Marketing Association, 1963, 30–43.
CENTERS, RICHARD. "An Examination of the Riesman Social Character Typology: A Metropolitan Survey," *Sociometry*, 25 (September 1962), 231–40.
——— and Miriam Horowitz. "Social Character and Conformity," *Journal of Social Psychology*, 60 (August 1963), 343–9.
CLAYCAMP, HENRY J. "Characteristics of Owners of Thrift Deposits in Commercial Banks and Savings and Loan Associations," *Journal of Marketing Research*, 2 (May 1965), 163–70.
COHEN, JOEL B. "An Interpersonal Orientation to the Study of Consumer Behavior," *Journal of Marketing Research*, 4 (August 1967), 270–8.
———. "Toward an Interpersonal Theory of Consumer Behavior," *California Management Review*, 10 (Spring 1968), 73–80.
COX, DONALD F. and Raymond A. Bauer. "Self-Confidence and Persuasibility in Women," *Public Opinion Quarterly*, 28 (Fall 1964), 453–66.
DICHTER, ERNEST. *The Strategy of Desire*. New York: Doubleday, 1960.
———. *Handbook of Consumer Motivations*. New York: McGraw-Hill, 1964.
DOLICH, IRA J. "Congruence Relationships Between Self Images and Product Brands," *Journal of Marketing Research*, 6 (February 1969), 80–4.
DONNELLY, JAMES H., JR. "Social Character and Acceptance of New Products," *Journal of Marketing Research*, 7 (February 1970), 111–3.
DORNBUSCH, SANFORD M. and Lauren C. Hickman. "Other-Directedness in Consumer Goods Advertising: A Test of Riesman's Historical Theory," *Social Forces*, 38 (December 1959), 99–102.

EVANS, FRANKLIN B. "Psychological and Objective Factors in the Prediction of Brand Choice," *Journal of Business*, 32 (October 1959), 340–69.

————. "Reply: You Still Can't Tell a Ford Owner From a Chevrolet Owner," *Journal of Buiness*, 34 (January 1961), 67–73.

————. "Correlates of Automobile Shopping Behavior," *Journal of Marketing*, 26 (October 1962), 74–7.

————. "True Correlates of Automobile Shopping Behavior," *Journal of Marketing*, 28 (January 1964), 65–6.

————. "Ford Versus Chevrolet: Park Forest Revisited," *Journal of Business*, 41 (October 1968), 445–59.

————. "Automobiles and Self-Imagery: Comment," *Journal of Business*, 41 (October 1968), 484–5.

———— and Harry V. Roberts. "Fords, Chevrolets, and the Problem of Discrimination," *Journal of Business*, 36 (April 1963), 242–9.

EYSENCK, H. J., Mollie Tarrant, Myra Woolf, and L. England. "Smoking and Personality," *British Medical Journal*, 1 (May 1960), 1456–60.

GARDNER, BURLEIGH B. and Sidney J. Levy. "The Product and the Brand," *Harvard Business Review*, 33 (March–April 1955), 33–9.

GRUBB, EDWARD L. "Consumer Perception of 'Self Concept' and Its Relationship to Brand Choice of Selected Product Types," *Proceedings*. Winter Conference, American Marketing Association, 1965, 419–22.

———— and Harrison L. Grathwohl. "Consumer Self-Concept, Symbolism and Market Behavior: A Theoretical Approach," *Journal of Marketing*, 31 (October 1967), 22–7.

GRUBB, EDWARD L. and Gregg Hupp. "Perception of Self, Generalized Stereotypes, and Brand Selection," *Journal of Marketing Research*, 5 (February 1968), 58–63.

GRUEN, WALTER. "Preference for New Products and Its Relationship to Different Measures of Conformity," *Journal of Applied Psychology*, 44 (December 1960), 361–6.

HALL, CALVIN S. and Gardner Lindzey. *Theories of Personality*. New York: John Wiley & Sons, 1957 (first edition), 1969 (second edition).

HAMM, B. CURTIS. "A Study of the Differences Between Self-Actualizing Scores and Product Perceptions Among Female Consumers," *Proceedings*. Winter Conference, American Marketing Association, 1967, 275–6.

———— and Edward W. Cundiff. "Self-Actualization and Product Perception," *Journal of Marketing Research*, 6 (November 1969), 470–2.

HILGARD, ERNEST R. and Gordon H. Bower. *Theories of Learning*, third edition. New York: Appleton-Century-Crofts, 1966.

HOVLAND, CARL I. and Irving L. Janis, eds. *Personality and Persuasibility*. New Haven, Conn.: Yale University Press, 1959.

JACOBSON, EUGENE and Jerome Kossoff. "Self-Percept and Consumer Attitudes Toward Small Cars," *Journal of Applied Psychology*, 47 (August 1963), 242–5.

JACOBY, JACOB. "Personality and Consumer Behavior: How Not to Find Relationships," Purdue Papers in Consumer Psychology, N. 102, Purdue University, 1969.

————. "A Multiple Indicant Approach for Studying Innovators," Purdue Papers in Consumer Psychology, No. 108, Purdue University, 1970.

————. "Personality and Innovation Proneness," *Journal of Marketing Research*, 8 (May 1971), 244–7.

KAMEN, JOSEPH M. "Personality and Food Preferences," *Journal of Advertising Research*, 4 (September 1964), 29–32.

KASSARJIAN, HAROLD H. "Social Character and Differential Preference for Mass Communication," *Journal of Marketing Research*, 2 (May 1965), 146–53.

———— and Waltraud M. Kassarjian. "Personality Correlates of Inner- and Other-Direction," *Journal of Social Psychology*, 70 (June 1966), 281–5.

KASSARJIAN, WALTRAUD M. "A Study of Riesman's Theory of Social Character," *Sociometry*, 25 (September 1962), 213–30.

———— and Harold H. Kassarjian. "Occupational Interests, Social Values and Social Character," *Journal of Counseling Psychology*, 12 (January 1966), 48–54.

KERNAN, JEROME. "Choice Criteria, Decision Behavior, and Personality," *Journal of Marketing Research*, 5 (May 1968), 155–64.

KOPONEN, ARTHUR. "Personality Characteristics of Purchasers," *Journal of Advertising Research*, 1 (September 1960), 6–12.

KUEHN, ALFRED A. "Demonstration of a Relationship Between Psychological Factors and Brand Choice," *Journal of Business*, 36 (April 1963), 237–41.

LAZER, WILLIAM. "Life Style Concepts and Marketing," *Proceedings*. Winter Conference, American Marketing Association, 1963, 130–9.

LEHMANN, STANLEY. "Personality and Compliance: A Study of Anxiety and Self-Esteem in Opinion and Behavior Change," *Journal of Personality and Social Psychology*, 15 (May 1970), 76–86.

LESSIG, V. PARKER and John O. Tollefson. "Market Segmentation Through Numerical Taxonomy," *Journal of Marketing Research*, 8 (November 1971), 480–7.

LEVY, SIDNEY J. "Symbols for Sale," *Harvard Business Review*, 37 (July–August 1959), 117–24.

LINTON, HARRIET and Elaine Graham. "Personality Correlates of Persuasibility," in Carl I. Hovland and Irving L. Janis, eds., *Personality and Persuasibility*. New Haven: Yale University Press, 1959, 69–101.

MARCUS, ALAN S. "Obtaining Group Measures from Personality Test Scores: Auto Brand Choice Predicted from the Edwards Personal Preference Schedule," *Psychological Reports*, 17 (October 1965), 523–31.

MARTINEAU, PIERRE. *Motivation in Advertising*. New York: McGraw-Hill, 1957.

————. "Letter to the Editor," *Advertising Age*, 30 (December 21, 1959), 76.

MASSY, WILLIAM F., Ronald E. Frank, and Thomas M. Lodahl. *Purchasing Behavior and Personal Attributes*. Philadelphia: University of Pennsylvania Press, 1968.

MURPHY, JOSEPH R. "Questionable Correlates of Automobile Shopping Behavior," *Journal of Marketing*, 27 (October 1963), 71–2.

MYERS, JOHN G. "Determination of Private Brand Attitudes," *Journal of Marketing Research*, 4 (February 1967), 73–81.

————. *Consumer Image and Attitude*. Berkeley: Institute of Business and Economic Research, University of California, 1968.

PENNINGTON, ALLAN A. and Robert A. Peterson. "Interest Patterns and Product Preferences: An Exploratory Analysis," *Journal of Marketing Research*, 6 (August 1969), 284–90.

PESSEMIER, EDGAR A. and Douglas J. Tigert. "Personality, Activity and Attitude Predictors of Consumer Behavior," *Proceedings*. World Congress, American Marketing Association, 1966, 332–347.

————. "Socio-Economic Status of the Family and Housewife Personality, Life

Style and Opinion Factors," Paper No. 197, Institute For Research on the Behavioral, Economic and Management Sciences, Purdue University, 1967.

PETERSON, ROBERT A. and Allan L. Pennington. "SVIB Interests and Product Preference," *Journal of Applied Psychology*, 53 (August 1969), 304–8.

ROBERTSON, THOMAS S. *Innovation and the Consumer*. New York: Holt, Rinehart and Winston, 1971.

———— and James H. Myers. "Personality Correlates of Opinion Leadership and Innovative Buying Behavior," *Journal of Marketing Research*, 6 (May 1969), 164–8.

————. "Personality Correlates of Innovative Buying Behavior: A Reply," *Journal of Marketing Research*, 7 (May 1970), 260–1.

RUCH, DUDLEY M. "Limitations of Current Approaches to Understanding Brand Buying Behavior," in Joseph W. Newman, ed., *On Knowing the Consumer*. New York: John Wiley & Sons, 1966, 173–86.

SHUCHMAN, ABE and Michael Perry. "Self-Confidence and Persuasibility in Marketing: A Reappraisal," *Journal of Marketing Research*, 6 (May 1969), 146–54.

SOMMERS, MONTROSE S. "Product Symbolism and the Perception of Social Strata," *Proceedings*. Winter Conference, American Marketing Association, 1963, 200–16.

————. "The Use of Product Symbolism to Differentiate Social Strata," *University of Houston Business Review*, 11 (Fall 1964), 1–102.

STEINER, GARY A. "Notes on Franklin B. Evans' 'Psychological and Objective Factors in the Prediction of Brand Choice,'" *Journal of Business*, 34 (January 1961), 57–60.

SUMMERS, JOHN O. "The Identity of Women's Clothing Fashion Opinion Leaders," *Journal of Marketing Research*, 7 (May 1970), 178–85.

TIGERT, DOUGLAS J. "A Psychological Profile of Magazine Audiences: An Investigation of a Media's Climate," paper presented at the American Marketing Association Consumer Behavior Workshop, 1969.

TUCKER, WILLIAM T. and John Painter. "Personality and Product Use," *Journal of Applied Psychology*, 45 (October 1961), 325–9.

VENKATESAN, M. "Personality and Persuasibility in Consumer Decision Making," *Journal of Advertising Research*, 8 (March 1968), 39–45.

VITZ, PAUL C. and Donald Johnston. "Masculinity of Smokers and the Masculinity of Cigarette Images," *Journal of Applied Psychology*, 49 (June 1965), 155–9.

WELLS, WILLIAM D. "General Personality Tests and Consumer Behavior," in Joseph Newman, ed., *On Knowing the Consumer*. New York: John Wiley & Sons, 1966, 187–9.

————. "Backward Segmentation," in Johan Arndt, ed., *Insights into Consumer Behavior*. Boston, Allyn and Bacon, 1968, 85–100.

———— and Douglas J. Tigert. "Activities, Interests and Opinions," *Journal of Advertising Research*, in press.

WESTFALL, RALPH. "Psychological Factors in Predicting Product Choice," *Journal of Marketing*, 26 (April 1962), 34–40.

WILKIE, WILLIAM. "Psychological Descriptors," paper presented at the Fall Conference, American Marketing Association, 1970.

WILSON, CLARK L. "Homemaker Living Patterns and Marketplace Behavior—A Psychometric Approach," *Proceedings*. World Congress, American Marketing Association, 1966, 305–31.

WINICK, CHARLES. "The Relationship Among Personality Needs, Objective Factors, and Brand Choice: A Re-examination," *Journal of Business*, 34 (January 1961), 61–6.

WOODSIDE, ARCH G. "Social Character, Product Use and Advertising Appeal," *Journal of Advertising Research*, 8 (December 1969), 31–5.

14. Consumer Brand Choice— A Learning Process?

Alfred A. Kuehn

The phenomenon of consumer brand shifting is a central element underlying the dynamics of the marketplace. To understand and describe market trends adequately, we must first establish the nature of the influences on consumer choice with respect to products and brands. Research directed at establishing the conditions under which consumers will shift from one brand to another offers hope of providing a framework within which to evaluate the influence of price, advertising, distribution and shelf space, and various types of sales promotion.

What do we know about brand choice? What behavioral mechanisms appear to underlie this phenomenon? Is such a behavior habitual? Is learning involved? Does repeated purchasing of a brand reinforce the brand choice response? What is the relationship between consumer purchase frequencies and brand shifting behavior? These questions will be discussed in the light of available empirical data and a model which appears to describe them.

A MODEL OF CONSUMER BRAND SHIFTING

A model equivalent to a generalized form of the Estes[1] and Bush-Mosteller[2] stochastic (probabilistic) learning models appear to describe consumer brand shifting quite well. To illustrate how this brand shifting model describes changes in the consumer's probability of purchasing any given brand as a result of his purchases of that brand (for example, Brand A) and competing brands (for example, Brand X), let us examine the effect of the four-purchase sequence XAAX upon a consumer with initial probability P_{A1} by referring to Figure 1.

[1] William K. Estes, "Individual Behavior in Uncertain Situations: An Interpretation in Terms of Statistical Association Theory," in Thrall, R. M., C. H. Coombs, and R. L. Davis (eds.), *Decision Processes* (New York: John Wiley & Sons, Inc., 1954).

[2] Robert R. Bush and Frederick Mosteller, *Stochastic Models for Learning* (New York: John Wiley & Sons, Inc., 1955).

Reprinted from the Journal of Advertising Research. © *Copyright (1962), by the Advertising Research Foundation.*

The model is described or defined in terms of four parameters, namely the intercepts and slopes of the two lines referred to in Figure 1 as the Purchase Operator and the Rejection Operator. If the brand in question is purchased by the consumer on a given buying occasion, the consumer's probability of again buying the same brand the next time that type product is purchased is read from the Purchase Operator. If the brand is rejected by the consumer on a given buying occasion, the consumer's probability of buying that brand when he next buys that type product is read from the Rejection Operator. Thus, note in Figure 1 that our hypothetical consumer begins on trial 1 with the probability $P_{A,1}$ of buying Brand A. The consumer chooses some other brand (X) on trial 1, however, and thus his probability of buying Brand A on trial 2 ($P_{A,2}$) is obtained from the Rejection Operator, resulting in a slight reduction in the probability of purchasing A on the next trial. On trial 2, however, the consumer does purchase Brand A and thus increases the likelihood of his again buying the brand on the next occasion (trial 3) to $P_{A,3}$. Continuing in this fashion, the consumer again buys A on trial 3, thereby increasing his probability of purchasing Brand A on trial 4 to $P_{A,4}$. He again rejects A on trial 4, however, decreasing his probability of buying A on trial 5 to $P_{A,5}$.

Two characteristics of the model should be noted: (1) The probability $P_{A,t}$ approaches but never exceeds the upper limit U_A with repeated purchasing of the brand, and (2) the probability $P_{A,t}$ approaches but

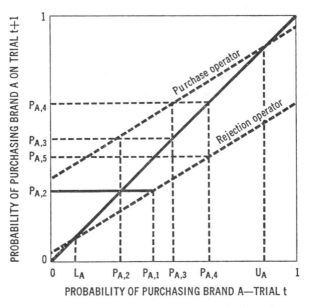

Figure 14.1. STOCHASTIC (PROBABILISTIC) BRAND SHIFTING MODEL.

never drops below the lower limit L_A with continued rejection of the brand. Using Bush and Mosteller's terminology, this would be referred to as an incomplete learning, incomplete extinction model insofar as U_A is less than 1 and L_A is greater than 0. This is equivalent to saying that consumers will generally not develop such strong brand loyalties (or buying habits) as to insure either the rejection or purchase of a given brand.

It should also be pointed out that the Purchase and Rejection Operators are functions of the time elapsed between the consumer's t^{th} and $t + 1^{st}$ purchases and the merchandising activities of competitors. The time effect can be illustrated by three sets of operators shown for high, medium, and very low frequency purchases of a rapidly consumed, nondurable consumer product (see Figure 2). Note that the slopes of the Purchase and Rejection Operators decrease and that the upper and lower limits approach each other as the time between purchases increases.

At the one limit ($\triangle$ time between purchases approaching 0) the Purchase and Rejection Operators approach the diagonal, L approaches 0, and U approaches 1. At the other limit ($\triangle$ time between purchases approaching ∞), L and U approach each other and the Purchase and Rejection Operators approach a slope equal to 0.

The main problem that remains in making use of the model is then the estimation of the four parameters defining the Purchase and Rejection Operators as a function of the time between purchases. If this could be done a priori, the model might be of value to marketing management for use in forecasting. At present, however, the model's primary use is in evaluating the effects of past and current competitive marketing activity. Thus, the parameters of the model are estimated for short time periods and related to the actions of all competitors in the market. Since the path of aggregate consumer purchasing behavior could be established for any given set of parameter values, it follows that the parameter estimates obtained from fitting the model can provide a means for evaluating the influence of the market conditions prevailing during the period in which the sequential purchase data are collected.

An efficient method has been developed to estimate these brand shifting parameters (maximum likelihood estimates) on the basis of sequences of two to four purchases. This makes it feasible to relate this model to consumer purchasing behavior observed during relatively short periods of time. This is a must if the technique is to be useful, since merchandising conditions do not remain constant for long periods of time—products are modified, advertising themes and budgets are altered, special promotions are generally temporary in nature, and price levels may change from time to time. The technique used to estimate the brand shifting parameters will be outlined in the near future as a working paper in

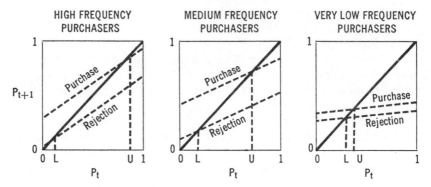

Figure 14.2. EFFECT OF TIME BETWEEN PURCHASES UPON PURCHASE AND REJECTION OPERATORS.

the Carnegie Tech (GSIA) Research in Marketing Project series. The Bush-Mosteller approach to estimating the parameters of their stochastic learning model cannot, in its current state of development, be applied to the brand shifting model since (1) techniques have not been developed to estimate simultaneously the four basic parameters of the model, and (2) the methods outlined require a long history or records of trials (and, therefore, data collected over a long period of time during which there is stability in merchandising activity) from which to develop parameter estimates.

EMPIRICAL BRAND SHIFTING RESEARCH

What evidence is there in support of the model? Three types of empirical studies have led to the formulation and continued development of the above model: [3]

    1. Analysis of 3, 4, 5, and 6 purchase sequences of consumer brand purchases.

    2. Analysis of effects of time between consumer purchases upon a consumer's probability of purchasing individual brands of product.

    3. Simulation of consumer brand choice behavior.

Each of these three studies is discussed briefly below.

    [3] The first two of the following three studies are reported in detail in Alfred A. Kuehn, "An Analysis of the Dynamics of Consumer Behavior and Its Implications for Marketing Management" (unpublished Ph.D. dissertation, Graduate School of Industrial Administration, Carnegie Institute of Technology, 1958).

ANALYSIS OF BRAND PURCHASE SEQUENCES

Sequential purchase data can provide some insight into consumer brand switching. The data analyzed below represent the frozen orange juice purchases of approximately 600 Chicago families in the three years 1950 to 1952. More than 15,000 individual purchases of frozen orange juice were collected in monthly diaries by the *Chicago Tribune* Consumer Panel during this period. Data were analyzed as sequences of five purchases by means of a factorial analysis to determine the influence of the consumer's first four brand choices within each sequence upon his choice of a brand on the next (fifth in the sequence) buying occasion. The data and analysis prepared for the Snow Crop brand are summarized in Table 1.

In column 1, the letter "S" is used to represent a purchase of the Snow Crop brand, the letter "O" to represent the purchase of any brand of frozen orange juice *other* than Snow Crop. Thus the sequence SSSS indicates a sequence of four purchases of Snow Crop. The sequences OSSS represents one purchase of some brand other than Snow Crop followed by three purchases of Snow Crop.

Column 2 tabulates the sample sizes from which the observed and predicted probabilities of purchasing Snow Crop on the subsequent buying occasion (fifth purchase in the sequence) were calculated.

Column 3 is computed on the basis of the observed frequencies of the five-purchase sequences. Thus, there were 296 sequences exhibiting the pattern SSSO in the first four positions of the sequence. Snow Crop was purchased on the fifth buying occasion in 144 of these sequences. The best estimate of the observed probability of buying Snow Crop given the past purchase record of SSSO is therefore $144/296 = 0.486$.

The predicted column is based upon the results of the previously referred to factorial analysis of past purchase effects. Each of the four past brand purchases were examined with respect to their individual (primary) effects and the effects of their interactions with each other. The individual effects of the past four purchase positions were highly significant but the interaction effects were not significantly different from 0 to 5 percent level at the significance (that is, there was greater than 5 percent probability of results as extreme as those observed arising by chance if there were in fact no interaction effects).

There is close agreement between the observed and predicted probabilities in view of the limited sample size. There appear, however, to be systematic deviations on the high side when Snow Crop is purchased either one or three times (also predictions are generally low given two purchases) during the last four buying occasions. Subsequent analysis indicated that these systematic deviations were reduced or eliminated

Table 14.1. COMPARISON OF OBSERVED AND PREDICTED PROBABILITY OF PURCHAS-
ING SNOW CROP GIVEN THE FOUR PREVIOUS BRAND PURCHASES

Previous Purchase *Pattern* (1)	*Sample* *Size* (2)	*Observed* *Probability* *of Purchase* (3)	*Predicted* *Probability* *of Purchase* (4)	*Deviation* *of* *Predictions* (5)
SSSS	1,047	0.806	0.832	+0.026
OSSS	277	0.690	0.691	+0.001
SOSS	206	0.665	0.705	+0.040
SSOS	222	0.595	0.634	+0.039
SSSO	296	0.486	0.511	+0.025
OOSS	248	0.552	0.564	+0.012
SOOS	138	0.565	0.507	−0.058
OSOS	149	0.497	0.493	−0.004
SOSO	163	0.405	0.384	−0.021
OSSO	181	0.414	0.370	−0.044
SSOO	256	0.305	0.313	+0.008
OOOS	500	0.330	0.366	+0.033
OOSO	404	0.191	0.243	+0.052
OSOO	433	0.129	0.172	+0.043
SOOO	557	0.154	0.186	+0.032
OOOO	8,442	0.048	0.045	−0.003

when a record of the fifth past brand purchase was included in the analysis.

Casual inspection of Table 1 suggests that the most recent purchase of the consumer is not the only one influencing his brand choice. This finding raises some question about the uses currently being made of purchase-to-purchase Markov Chain Analyses which assume that only the most recent purchase of the consumer is influential. The analysis of "primary" effects referred to above showed that the purchase of Snow Crop on the most recent buying occasion added 0.321 to the probability of the consumer buying Snow Crop on his next purchase. Similarly, the second most recent purchase added 0.198, the third 0.127 and the fourth 0.141.[4]

Note that the first three purchase effects decline roughly exponentially. That is, the ratio of the importance of the first purchase to that of the second is approximately equal to the ratio of the second to the third. The fourth, however, increases rather than decreases! This reversal has been traced to the fact that past purchases beyond the fourth

[4] To illustrate the computation of the predicted probabilities in column 4, Table 1, the probability of a Snow Crop purchase given the history SOOO is 0.045 (the probability of purchase given OOOO) plus 0.141 or 0.186, the probability given SOOS is 0.045 + 0.141 + 0.321 = 0.507 and the predicted probability given OSSS is 0.045 + 0.127 + 0.198 + 0.321 = 0.691.

most recent purchase were excluded from the analysis. The increased importance attached to the fourth most recent purchase for purposes of prediction reflects its high correlation with the fifth and earlier past purchases not incorporated in the study. When these same data were re-analyzed using six-purchase sequences, the exponential relationship of declining primary purchase effects fit the first through fourth past purchases. As would be expected, however, the fifth past purchase effect was larger than the fourth because of its higher correlation with the consumer's sixth and even earlier past purchases.

Observation of the exponentially declining effects of past purchases led to the testing of the brand shifting model outlined in Figure 1 since that model has the characteristic of weighting the influence of past brand choices exponentially when the slopes of the Purchase and Rejection operators are identical. Subsequent research with products other than frozen orange juice has tended to confirm the exponential weighting of past brand purchases by consumers for predictive purposes. The exponential weights vary substantially, however, among product classes. Products such as toilet soap, cereals, and toothpaste were found to have substantially lower rates of decline in weights as one goes back into the purchase history as a result of the tendency of purchasing families to use some mix of brands on a routine basis to satisfy different uses, desires for variety, and differences in preference of individual family members. To be sure, this brand-mix effect is operative even in the case of frozen orange juice but for quite a different reason. Many families use a mix of brands of frozen orange juice because of the lack of availability of individual brands of product in all of the stores among which the consumer shifts in the course of his week-to-week shopping trips.

EFFECT OF CONSUMER PURCHASE FREQUENCIES

Let us consider the effect of time between purchases upon the consumer's probability of repurchasing the same brand. In Figure 3 we observe the probability of a consumer's buying the same brand on two consecutive purchases of the product decreasing to the share of market of the brand as time between purchases increases. Whenever a great amount of time has elapsed since the consumer's last purchase of the product, the brand he last bought has little influence upon his choice of a brand—the probability of his buying any given brand in this case is approximately equal to the share of market of that brand. It should be noted that the probability of repurchase decreases at a constant rate with the passing of time; this characteristic, which we shall refer to as the "time rate of decay of purchase probability," is significant since it provides a simple framework within which to incorporate the effects of time into a procedure for forecasting consumer purchase probabilities.

Let us now expand our view of the effects of time upon repurchase probability in terms of the time period required for the consumer to make N individual purchases of frozen orange juice concentrate. Note that the curve in Figure 4 labeled $N = 1$ is the same curve as in Figure 3.

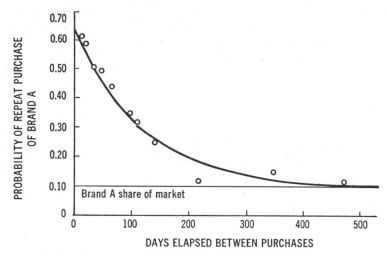

Figure 14.3. THE PROBABILITY OF A CONSUMER'S BUYING THE SAME BRAND ON TWO CONSECUTIVE PURCHASES OF FROZEN ORANGE JUICE DECREASES EXPONENTIALLY WITH AN INCREASE IN TIME BETWEEN THOSE PURCHASES.

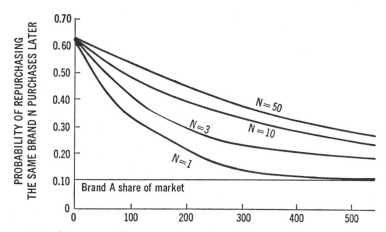

Figure 14.4. CONSUMERS BUYING FROZEN ORANGE JUICE WITH GREATEST FREQUENCY HAVE THE HIGHEST PROBABILITY OF CONTINUING TO BUY THE SAME BRAND.

Observe also that the probability of repurchasing the same brand at any given time in the future, without regard to the brands chosen in the interim, increases as we go up from $N = 1$ to $N = 3$, $N = 10$, and $N = 50$. Thus, on the average, a consumer who makes his fiftieth purchase of frozen orange juice 300 days after some arbitrary purchase of a given brand has a much higher probability of again choosing that brand than does the consumer who makes only 1, 3, or 10 purchases in that interval of time.

Figure 5 illustrates the relationship between the rates of decay of purchase probability associated with the curves in Figure 4 and the average time elapsed between purchases. The rate of decay of $N = 1$ in Figure 4 is 0.01298 per day. The rate of decay of $N = 50$ is 0.00282. Here again we find a relationship which, because of its simplicity, can after some manipulation be conveniently incorporated into a model forecasting consumer brand choice probabilities. The rate of decay increases linearly with an increase in the average time between purchases. The data points plotted in Figure 5 represent the rates of decay computed for 10 values of N, four of which were illustrated by the curves in Figure 4.

SIMULATION OF CONSUMER BRAND CHOICE

The brand shifting model outlined in Figure 1 earlier in this paper has been tested by computing the predicted purchase probabilities of consumers on each of approximately 13,000 occasions of purchase of frozen orange juice and comparing aggregates of these predictions with recorded brand purchases. The procedure followed was to first divide the probability space, zero to one, into 76 probability ranges. Then, whenever the computer programmed model predicted a certain probability for a given family buying a given brand on a given buying occasion, the results of that purchase were recorded in the computer storage location representing the corresponding probability range. Thus, it was possible to compare within each of the 76 probability cells the average predicted probability of purchasing individual brands with the observed proportion of trials on which the brand was in fact purchased. The predicted and observed probabilities and numbers of purchases were then compared individually and simultaneously for all 76 cells with respect to the binomial and χ^2 distributions that would be expected if the model were perfect. The 76 normal deviates, referred to here by "t," computed for the individual cells with respect to the Snow Crop predictions were approximately normally distributed, 50 lying within 1 standard deviation, 71 lying within 2 standard deviations, and 76 falling within 3 standard deviations. The χ^2 value indicated no significant

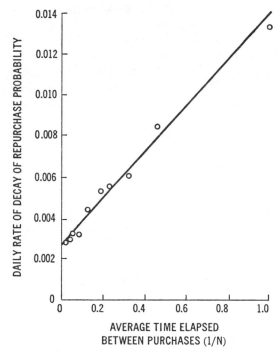

Figure 14.5. RELATIONSHIP OF DECAY RATES TO TIME BETWEEN PURCHASES.

deviation at the 10 percent level. Similar results were obtained in an analysis of predictions for the Minute Maid brand, 53 "t" values lying within one standard deviation, 70 lying within two standard deviations and all 76 cases falling within three standard deviations.

The above results suggest that the model offers promise for use in describing consumer behavior in probabilistic terms. The model was not tested with respect to individual families, the number of purchases being made by most individual families being considered as providing too small a sample to yield a reasonably powerful test of the predictions of the model. In other words, since rejection is unlikely given a small sample size per family, acceptance does not carry much weight with respect to an evaluation of the model. In the aggregate, the model stood up surprisingly well given the over-all test sample size of approximately 13,000 purchase predictions. (Interestingly enough, when the lower limit L was held at zero in certain tests designed to determine its importance in the model, the "t" values associated with certain low probability cells ranged from 40 to 65 standard deviations.) Of course, if the

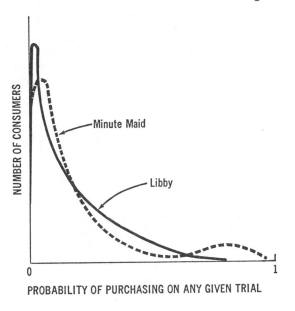

PROBABILITY OF PURCHASING ON ANY GIVEN TRIAL

Figure 14.6.

sample size were to be increased substantially, significant deviations would have been obtained since the model is not a perfect representation of the brand purchase sequences of consumers.

The predictions of the model were also used to obtain a frequency distribution of consumers throughout the three-year time period according to their probability of buying specific brands of product. Figure 6 provides a comparison of the profiles (smoothed) for Libby and Minute Maid frozen orange juice. As might be expected, most consumers have a low probability of buying any specific brand. Those consumers who have a high probability of buying one brand must necessarily have a low probability of buying several other brands. Minute Maid was in the enviable position of having a small group of customers with a very high probability of buying the brand. Libby did not have such a following. The fact that Minute Maid developed frozen orange juice and was the first brand available to consumers probably helped the firm develop the group of loyal (or habitual) customers, a sizable portion of which it had been able to retain in the face of growing competition. As the innovator of frozen orange juice, Minute Maid also developed a preeminent market position in terms of retail availability, a factor which undoubtedly helped the firm maintain a sales advantage relative to competition.

ADAPTIVE BEHAVIOR OR SPURIOUS RESULTS?

In a paper titled "Brand Choice as a Probability Process,"[5] Ronald Frank reports that certain results he has observed with respect to repeat purchase probabilities as a function of a brand's run length are similar in appearance to what would be expected with associative learning under conditions of reward. He then notes, in a footnote, that my data also seem to suggest this interpretation, a point on which there is agreement.[6] The balance of Frank's article is then directed at demonstrating that:

1. Purchase sequence data generated by families for a given brand using a Monte Carlo approach on the assumption that each family's probability of purchasing the brand remained constant throughout the time period produced repeat purchase probabilities as a function of run length which closely approximated in the aggregate the actual observed empirical probabilities.

2. The number of runs observed for *most* families is consistent with what might be expected under the assumption that each family's probability of purchasing any given brand remained constant throughout the time period.

As a result of his success in generating a relationship in (1) above that has the appearance of actual data. Frank states, "These results cast suspicion on the use of a 'learning' model to describe the observations." In view of this statement, which bears directly upon the work I have outlined earlier in this paper, in my thesis, and elsewhere, some defense appears to be in order.

Frank's observations in no way invalidate the findings outlined earlier in this paper. He has shown that it is inappropriate to attribute to learning *all* of the increase in repeat purchase probability associated with increases in run length, an error which has probably been made by more than a few researchers. This is not, however, the approach outlined here or in my thesis. As a matter of fact, the approach used in my thesis could be applied to Frank's coffee data to test whether the probabilities are in fact constant and, if this is not the case, to estimate the appropriate weightings. If consumers were to have a constant probability of brand choice from trial to trial, the most recent purchase positions would not have a greater primary effect on the predicted purchase probabilities than that of any other purchase position—all of the pri-

5 Ronald E. Frank, "Brand Choice as a Probability Process," *Journal of Business*, Vol. XXXV (January, 1962), pp. 43–56.

6 Alfred A. Kuehn, "A Model for Budgeting Advertising," in Bass, *et al.* (ed.), *Mathematical Models and Methods in Marketing* (Homewood, Ill.: Richard D. Irwin, Inc., 1961).

mary effects would be identical except for sampling variations. Similarly, if the probabilities of brand choice were constant from trial to trial, the Purchase and Rejection Operators in the adaptive brand shifting model outlined at the beginning of this paper would be superimposed on the diagonal (see Figure 1). In other words, the special case considered by Frank can be treated successfully by both of the analytic techniques used in my studies and discussed in this paper. Frank is correct when he states that much of what might appear to be a learning effect on the basis of repeat purchase probabilities as a function of run length is due to the aggregation of consumers having different probabilities (at the start of the run)—this is, however, no problem when one takes into account the effect of all past purchases which have a significant impact upon the consumer's purchase probability, since such an approach does not disregard the information contained in purchases prior to the current run, an important consideration when the run is very short. Since past purchases will, except in highly unusual cases, have decreasing effects (as one goes back in time) upon the consumer's subsequent purchase probability, taking into account all significant past purchases does not generally require the availability of an unduly long record of the consumer's purchase history.

The second point that Frank makes—namely, that most consumers behave as though they had constant purchase probabilities—would appear to represent a misinterpretation of statistical results. Frank sets up his hypothesis, tests it at some level of significance for each of a large number of cases (families), and then interprets the results as though all cases not shown to deviate statistically on an individual basis are consistent with the hypothesis. Actually, the hypothesis was that consumers have a constant probability of purchase, and the results indicated that a larger number of the individual cases tested lay outside the confidence limits than is consistent with the hypothesis, thereby rejecting the hypothesis *in toto!*

To be sure, the hypothesis of constant probability is, in effect, a straw man. It is generally recognized that consumers do change their buying behavior over time. Whether such behavior is called adjustment, adaptation, or learning is unimportant. It should be noted, however, that even though the over-all market for coffee was quite stable in the period studied by Frank, and the sample sizes were limited to 14 months of purchase by each family, the hypothesis was in fact rejected on an overall basis, the only appropriate way in which to interpret the results of the test. Perhaps, as Frank suggests, some consumers do have constant probabilities of choosing individual brands during certain periods of time. Such a hypothesis cannot be tested, however, unless a procedure independent of the test is available for identifying these consumers and the relevant time periods.

CONCLUSION

A model describing brand shifting behavior as a probabilistic process and incorporating the effects of past purchases and time elapsed between purchases had been outlined. A defense of this approach to the study of mechanisms underlying consumer brand choice has also been presented. What has not been discussed is the way in which such merchandising factors as price, advertising, product characteristics, retail availability, and promotions (price off, coupons, merchandise packs and so on) influence the parameters of the model and the extensions of the model that might be required to incorporate such effects. Some earlier results of research on the influence of these variables have been incorporated into an aggregate "expected value" form of the model presented here. Much work, however, remains to be done.

RETROSPECTIVE COMMENT

In his original article, Kuehn hypothesized that a stochastic learning process model partially explains aggregated brand repeat purchase patterns of family panel members. Since then the learning process hypothesis has been subjected to extensive testing by 1) analysis of individual rather than aggregated data; 2) experimental observation of the development of brand loyalty; and 3) comparison to other possible models that may explain the generation of brand repeat purchase sequences. These tests tend to confirm the validity of the learning process hypothesis as an important factor in generating brand purchase sequences. However, the effect of purchase frequencies (inter-purchase time) observed by Kuehn, has not been confirmed when individual consumer behavior rather than aggregate market behavior is examined.

Although other models explaining the generation of brand purchase sequences can not be excluded by tests of "goodness of fit," the learning process explanation is more satisfying from a psychological rather than a mathematical-statistical point of view. In updating the article one may want to take account of population heterogeneity, and deal with the possibility that some consumers may regularly accept several brands in a product category. Kuehn might also add that the model has been tested extensively on many other branded packaged grocery and drug items, and found to be useful in analyzing brand switching among competing brands, the effects of advertising and other marketing factors, and the relative size of advertising budgets.—*Dr. Frederick E. May*, Professor of Marketing, University of Missouri-St. Louis

15. The Development of Brand Loyalty

W. T. Tucker

Most studies of brand loyalty have involved the measurement and description of loyalties to existing brands of merchandise. From these studies it can be safely concluded that there are rather wide variations in loyalty among individuals and that brand loyalty is at least in part a function of the frequency and regularity with which a brand has been selected in the past and in part a function of the type of product involved. Rather sophisticated analyses have suggested that some sort of Markov process best describes the growth of brand loyalty. One of the primary characteristics of the relevant research is its reliance on maximum realism and the minimal distortion of the context of consumer behavior. Even efforts such as Pessemier's study measuring the strength of brand loyalty are ingenious in their efforts to maintain the semblance of realism under difficult circumstances.

Valuable as such methodological techniques are, they cannot be brought to bear on some critical aspects of brand loyalty. In order to discuss these meaningfully, it is necessary to define brand loyalty, despite the apparent simplicity of the terms. For purposes of this paper, brand loyalty is conceived to be simply biased choice behavior with respect to branded merchandise. If there are two cola drinks offered to a person a number of times, his degree of brand loyalty can be stated in terms of the relative frequency with which he chooses one brand rather than the other. If he selects Pepsi Cola rather than Coca Cola (and both are equally available) enough of the time to persuade the statistically sophisticated observer that the difference in frequency is not due to chance, he may be said to be brand loyal. No consideration should be given to what the subject thinks or what goes on in his central nervous system; his behavior is the full statement of what brand loyalty is.

It is always dangerous to fragment molar behavior into theoretical sub-systems, but the obviously complex character of brand loyalty demands some further analysis if it is to be fully useful either theoretically or to practical marketers. The loyalty may be to some subset of charac-

Reprinted by permission of the author and publisher from the Journal of Marketing Research, *published by the American Marketing Association, Vol. 1 (August 1964), pp. 32–35.*

teristics: the shape of the bottle, the sweetness of the drink, the colors on the cap, the brand name, or whatever. Now imagine that the loyalty to Pepsi Cola described above existed during that time when Pepsi was marketed in 12 oz. export beer bottles and the only bottled Coca Cola contained 6 oz. Imagine further that a single change was made: a new 12 oz. bottle of Coca Cola (there was such an experimental size at one time) was available to him as an alternative to the 12 oz. Pepsi. This might change his choice so that he would subsequently choose Coca Cola more frequently than Pepsi.

It is tempting to suggest that the individual was never really brand loyal to Pepsi at all, but merely preferred a larger drink. But chaos lies in this direction. Suppose for instance that the Pepsi Cola formula or drink is next placed in the Coca Cola bottle capped with the red, white and blue Pepsi Cola cap and the Coca Cola is placed in the old export beer bottle with a Coca Cola cap—and that the individual shifts back to the Pepsi. What becomes of brand loyalty? In fact brand loyalty is always a biased response to some combination of characteristics, not all of which are critical stimuli. This way of looking at brand loyalty may not be congenial, but something much like it (the gestalt approach suggests variations) seems required either for research on the nature of brand loyalty or practical questions regarding changes in product, packaging, or advertising.

One of the hypotheses that the experiment reported here undertakes to support is the notion that brand loyalty will grow in an almost completely infertile field, that biased choices will develop even when products are virtually identical and brand names are close to meaningless. Clearly, this hypothesis is an outgrowth of the preceding view of brand loyalty. It also stems from a confirmed belief that the stochastic learning model is not wholly satisfactory as a description of brand choice.

The stochastic learning model is based on an historical sequence of psychological experiments in which there were always right (rewarded or unpunished) responses and wrong (unrewarded or punished) responses. (Those few experiments not of this nature seem to have received little independent attention until recent years.) There seem to be two underlying problems in the learning model: (1) it assumes that a reinforced (usually a rewarded) response will have an increased probability of recurring; (2) it seems to imply that reinforcement, or differentials in level of reinforcement, from the sole basis of choice. It is possible that a rewarded choice (say the selection of a brand of shaving cream by the first-time user at age 15) may in fact decrease the likelihood of a repeat purchase if the individual is interested in finding out more about different kinds of creams or soaps. This could be referred to as search behavior. And, further, it seems possible that this boy could become brand loyal even if he could perceive no advantage whatsoever in any particular preparation, since such behavior would at least decrease the effort of decision making. More positive influences may be in the connotative meanings and associations that naturally grow around objects one uses, the activities he engages in, and people with whom he interacts. It is too easy an assumption to declare that brand loyalties established in this fashion would be fragile or transient. Psychological theory, if not learning theory, suggests that one may learn to like what he chooses as readily as he may learn to choose what he likes. Such possibilities seem worth investigating.

The present experiment differs from most of the previous work in that it suffers the disabilities of obvious artificiality at the same time that it gains the capacity to examine some of the above aspects of brand loyalty not open to observation in the "real" world. The experiment consisted simply of twelve successive consumer choices of bread from among four previously unknown brands. Forty-two women participated in the experiment. They were selected by two-stage random sampling from a single census tract in order to minimize delivery problems. Each woman was told that the study was designed to find out how women went about purchasing when they moved to a new location and were faced with unfamiliar brands. She was then asked to select one of four loaves of bread marked "L," "M," "P," and "H." Packaging was otherwise identical. Letter designations were chosen for ease of memory. And, although all are consonants from the middle of the alphabet and have approximately the same frequency of use in the English language, it is not assumed that they are "neutral" symbols. In fact, it seems probable that no set of symbols which are discriminable can be neutral or equally pleasing or have common meanings for all individuals.

The position of the brands on the tray was varied in Latin square design so that no brand was in the same position two times in a row and so that each brand occurred in each position with equal frequency. The bread used for all brands was identical, sandwich-loaf, thin-sliced bread, taken from a single oven on the morning of delivery.

In order to determine the strength of any brand loyalties formed during the experiment, once a panel member chose the same bread three times in succession, a premium was placed on another brand. The brand selected for the premium was that brand most seldom selected previously. Where two or more brands satisfied this requirement a random selection among them of the brand for the premium was made. The premium used was a new penny fixed to the brand label. If the woman did not select the brand with the premium on the first trial, the premium was increased by one penny per trial for each subsequent trial until the panel member selected the desired brand or the experiment ended.

It was anticipated that the experiment would begin with a period of search or exploratory behavior, during which the selection of any brand would decrease the probability that the same brand would be selected again. Following this period, it was believed that the selection of any brand would increase the likelihood that the same brand would be selected on the following trial. It was further anticipated that brand loyalty would be established despite homogeneity of product and that the degree of loyalty indicated by three successive choices of the same brand might be measurable in terms of the number of cents required to cause a change in selection.

THE PERIOD OF SEARCH

The evidence for a period of search or exploratory consumer behavior is clear. During the first several choices, the sequence of two choices of the same brand was far below that expected by chance. Twenty-nine of the forty-two women systematically tried each of the brands in order during their first four selections. Of course, it should be remembered that the nature of the experiment seems to suggest that a complete exploration is the sensible thing to do. Several of the panel members indicated in advance that they had already made the decision to try each of the four brands.

There is no clear indication when the period of search ends for an individual. Some of the housewives completed 12 successive choices without ever selecting the same brand twice in succession. Such behavior could equally well be described as extended search or indifference. At the same time, patterns for the entire group suggest that the first four choices were qualitatively different from the remaining selections. Table 1 shows the relative frequency of repeating a choice on each of the 12 trials. Included in the data are only those persons who have not become brand loyal and who have a brand run length of one.

Clearly something happens after the fourth choice in terms of willingness to repeat the selection of any given brand. The indication is not, however, that search activity has ended for all participants. The relative frequency of repeating the fourth choice on the fifth trial (given no earlier repeat of the third choice on the fourth trial) remains below the expected value of .25, although not significantly so. (The relative frequency of a repeated choice of this sort up to the fourth trial is significant far above the .10 level, is in fact about 31 standard errors *below* the expected.)

The tailing off in the relative frequency of a repeated selection during the later trials is in part the consequence of growth in brand loyalty. Women who had become brand loyal no longer have brand run lengths of one except under the influence of premiums. Therefore, persons who had become brand loyal (had selected the same brand three times in a

Table 15.1. RELATIVE FREQUENCY OF SELECTING X BRAND, GIVEN THE PRECEDING
SELECTION OF X, BUT NOT XX

Trial number	Relative frequency
2	.048
3	.050
4	.026
5	.210
6	.300
7	.346
8	.288
9	.240
10	.136
11	.261
12	.105

row) were eliminated from the data shown in Table 1 for all trials subsequent to the establishment of brand loyalty.

THE EMERGENCE OF BRAND LOYALTY

Exactly half of the women engaged in the experiment reached the criterion of brand loyalty by the end of twelve trials. These loyalties
emerged at every possible point. Table 2 shows the frequency with which
brand loyalty emerged on the various trials.

It can undoubtedly be presumed that additional women would have
reached the criterion of brand loyalty with further trials. Two of the
women not previously brand loyal selected the same brand on trials
eleven and twelve. The probability of selecting a brand the third time

Table 15.2. THE TRIALS ON WHICH WOMEN COMPLETED THEIR THIRD
CONSECUTIVE SELECTION OF ANY BRAND

Trial number	Number of women
3	1
4	2
5	1
6	3
7	1
8	3
9	3
10	2
11	1
12	4

given two consecutive selections throughout the experiment was .396, significantly above chance at the .05 level.

While it is impossible to state conclusively the stage of brand loyalty reached by those women who had not selected any brand on three consecutive trials, there were suggestions that some women had established a relative loyalty to two of the brands (ending trials of M, H, M, H, M and P, H, P, H) and that some had essentially eliminated one of the brands from further consideration (six of the non-loyal women selected one of the brands only once in the twelve trials).

The extremes in non-loyalty to brand were provided by four women who developed position loyalties of considerable duration. Position loyalties were not simple to judge, since participants could perform exploratory behavior among brands by the simple expedient of selecting from the same tray position for consecutive trials. Where continuous selection from a single position continued for a long period or where it emerged as an apparent solution to the decision process during the later trials, there seems rather conclusive evidence for stating that position loyalties did emerge. (It should be pointed out that all position loyalties were for the tray position at the participant's extreme left.)

A conclusion that seems almost inescapable is that women vary greatly in their susceptibility to brand loyalty. In some, the sort of behavior referred to as brand loyalty seems to have become functionally autonomous and may be a preferred form of behavior in any applicable situation.[1] At the other extreme there appear to be those (suggested here by the position-loyal participants) to whom brand differences unaccompanied by product differentiation are inconsequential. This variation among women in susceptibility to brand loyalty may be one of the major consumer variables which face the marketer of certain kinds of products.

THE STRENGTH OF LOYALTIES

There is a strong temptation to believe that when a woman encounters a preferred brand and another brand at a reduced price (simulated in this experiment by the addition of one or more pennies to a competing brand) her choice is somehow limited to those alternatives. Of course, behavior in the marketplace constantly demonstrates that this is not the case. In the present experiment, six of the women who switched from the brand to which they had become loyal, switched first to a brand that did not contain the premium of one or more pennies. Four of these switched to a non-premium brand when the first penny was placed on the premium brand. One switched after two cents was applied, one after

---

[1] Cunningham's position that no important number of shoppers is prone to brand loyalty is based on quite different data [1] and does not really contradict this position.

three cents. Undoubtedly a gestalt psychologist would suggest that the addition of a premium to any brand restructured the entire situation. As one woman who changed, but not to the premium brand, said, "No wonder you put the special on brand 'P.' It's the worst one of all." To her the premium apparently was a signal to do something, but anything rather than the encouraged action.

Six of the brand-loyal women switched to the premium brand for premiums varying from 2-7 cents. The average value of these accepted premiums was 3½ cents. Eight women were still selecting their favorite brand when the experiment ended. Premiums that they refused on the last opportunity varied from 1-7 cents. Their average was 3½ cents.

Even the women who had established position loyalties showed resistance to change. Three of these women were offered premiums. Two who were offered premiums on a different position after five consecutive choices from the same position switched to the premium position for premiums of one cent and two cents. The third woman, for whom premiums were begun after eight successive selections from the same position, shifted to a choice from another location when the premium reached three cents. She did not select a loaf from the premium position at any time, although a total of five cents was placed on the brand in that position at the time of her last choice.

Obviously because of the variation in response to premiums and the small number of women involved, it is impossible to draw any general conclusions about the average strength of brand or position loyalties that developed during the experiment. At the same time, it is clear that such loyalties are more than trivial, even though they are based on what may seem trivial distinctions.

OTHER FINDINGS

While there is no satisfactory evidence that the order of choice affects the likelihood that a particular brand will be the one to which a woman becomes loyal, Table 3 shows the relevant distributions.

Table 15.3. ORDER OF TRIAL OF BRANDS TO WHICH PARTICIPANTS BECAME BRAND-LOYAL

Rank order in which brand was chosen	Number of women who became loyal
First	8
Second	6
Third	2
Fourth	5

CONCLUSION

An exploratory experiment such as the one reported here is more often suggestive than conclusive. The following conclusions are, therefore, tentative: some consumers will become brand loyal even when there is no discriminable difference between brands other than the brand itself.

The brand loyalty established under such conditions is not trivial, although it may be based on what are apparently trivial and superficial differences.

Consumers vary greatly in their susceptibility to brand loyalty.

Brand loyalty and preference for particular product characteristics are quite different considerations that together make up what is normally referred to as brand loyalty.

While it is difficult to identify exploratory consumer behavior, it seems clear that some consumer selections are largely exploratory in nature and may indicate that a repeat purchase is highly unlikely.

RETROSPECTIVE COMMENT

It is not often that one rereads an article done years in the past without thinking of better research techniques or improved modes of presentation. But here, I would change nothing. There is, of course, a question of whether the letters used to designate different "brands" of bread are sufficiently "neutral" for the conclusions that are drawn. But, after long discussion with colleagues heavily involved in similar experimentation, I am persuaded that any set of discriminable symbols lacks inter-item equivalence.

The personal impact of the study may be of interest. Some researchers, of course, believe themselves to be different from and superior to the subjects of their research; I always assume that I may be as irrational and insensitive as anyone in the sample. Therefore, I tested a few of my own brand loyalties with the standard blindfold technique to see whether they were as poorly based as a strong preference for brand "M" bread. Those in beer, bourbon and stereo equipment turned out to be unrelated to activity of my palate and ears! Over the years, my savings on bourbon alone have been several hundred dollars.—*W. T. Tucker.*

REFERENCES

CUNNINGHAM, Ross M. "Brand Loyalty—What, Where, How Much?" *Harvard Business Review*, 34 (1956), 116.

FRANK, RONALD E. "Brand Choice as a Probability Process," *Journal of Business*, 35 (1962), 43.

HARRY, FRANK and Benjamin Lipstein. "The Dynamics of Brand Loyalty: A Markovian Approach," *Operations Research*, 10 (1962), 17.

HERTINER, JEROME D. and John F. Magee. "Customer Behavior as a Markov Process," *Operations Research*, 9 (1961), 105.

KUEHN, ALFRED A. "Consumer Brand Choice—A Learning Process" in Ronald E. Frank, Alfred A. Kuehn and William F. Massey, *Quantitative Techniques in Marketing Analysis*, Homewood, Ill.: Richard D. Irwin, 1962.

PECKHAM, JAMES O. "The Consumer Speaks," *Journal of Marketing*, 27 (1963), 21.

PESSEMIER, EDGAR A. "A New Way to Determine Buying Decisions," *Journal of Marketing*, 23 (1959), 41.

PART II. QUESTIONS FOR DISCUSSION

1. What are the two most important conclusions that can be drawn from Maslow's need hierarchy?

2. Relate the concept of consumer behavior as risk taking with the self concept.

3. What insights could a brewer gain from reading the Allison and Uhl article?

4. Briefly explain the four major functions performed by attitudes.

5. Relate the behavioral dimensions of attitudes to stages in the consumer adoption process.

6. Explain the failure of personality to adequately explain consumer behavior.

7. What determines the strength of brand loyalty?

Part III.

Environmental Influences in Consumer Behavior

Consumer behavior is determined through an interaction of such *individual* predispositions as needs, attitudes, perceptions, and personality and also by the influence of *others*. The environmental influences include cultural factors, reference groups, social class, and family influences. The decision to purchase certain brands or product classes or to patronize a particular store results from the interaction of these individual and group influences.

Reference group influence is the subject of the first three selections, while family roles are treated in the selection by Davis. The concept of social class and its role in influencing consumption patterns is analyzed in the selections by Coleman, Martineau, and Rich and Jain. Culture and its impact on marketing is the subject of the selection by Hall and the Black subculture is analyzed in the final selection in Part III.

16. Group Influence in Marketing

Francis S. Bourne

On the common sense level the concept of reference group influence says in effect that man's behavior is influenced in different ways and in varying degrees by other people. Comparing one's own success with that of others is a frequent source of satisfaction or disappointment. Similarly, before making a decision one often considers what such and such a person or such and such a group (whose opinion one has *some* reason to follow) would do in these circumstances, or what they would think of one for making a certain decision rather than another. Put in these ways, of course, reference group influence represents an unanalyzed truism which has long been recognized. The problem to which social scientists have been addressing themselves intensively only for the last two deades, however, concerns the refinement of this common sense notion to the end that it might be applied meaningfully to concrete situations.

The real problems are to determine which kinds of groups are likely to be referred to by which kinds of individuals under which kinds of circumstances in the process of making which decisions, and to measure the extent of this reference group influence. Towards this end empirical researches have been conducted in recent years which have at least made a start in the process of refining the reference group concept.

Reference group theory as it has developed has become broad enough to cover a wide range of social phenomena, both with respect to the relation of the individual to the group and with respect to the type of influence exerted upon the individual by the group in question.

KINDS OF REFERENCE GROUPS

Reference groups against which an individual evaluates his own status and behavior may be of several kinds.

They may be *membership* groups to which a person actually belongs. There can be small face-to-face groups in which actual association is the

Reprinted by permission from the Foundation for Research on Human Behavior, Group Influence in Marketing and Public Relations *(1956), pp. 1–12.*

rule, such as families or organizations, whether business, social, religious, or political. On the other hand, there can be groups in which actual membership is held but in which personal association is absent. (For example, membership in a political party, none of whose meetings are personally attended.)

Reference groups may be *categories* to which a person automatically belongs by virtue of age, sex, education, marital status and so on. This sort of reference group relationship involves the concept of role. For example, before taking a certain action an individual might consider whether this action would be regarded as appropriate in his role as a man or husband or educated person or older person or a combination of all of these roles. What is involved here is an individual's perception of what society, in general or that part of it with which he has any contact, expects people of his age, or sex, or education or marital status to do under given circumstances.

They may be *anticipatory* rather than actual membership groups. Thus a person who aspires to membership in a group to which he does *not* belong may be more likely to refer to it or compare himself with its standards when making a decision than he is to refer to the standards of the group in which he actually belongs but would like to leave. This involves the concept of upward mobility. When such upward mobility is sought in the social or business world it is ordinarily accompanied by a sensitivity to the attitudes of those in the groups to which one aspires, whether it involves the attitudes of country club members in the eyes of the aspiring non-member or the attitudes of management in the eyes of the ambitious wage earner or junior executive.

There are also negative, *dissociative* reference groups. These constitute the opposite side of the coin from the anticipatory membership groups. Thus an individual sometimes avoids a certain action because it is associated with a group (to which the individual may or may not in fact belong) from which he would like to dissociate himself.

INFLUENCE ON INDIVIDUAL BEHAVIOR

Reference groups influence behavior in two major ways. First, they influence *aspiration levels* and thus play a part in producing satisfaction or frustration. If the other members of one's reference group (for example, the neighbors) are wealthier, more famous, better gardeners, etc., one may be dissatisfied with one's own achievements and may strive to do as well as the others.

Second, reference groups influence *kinds* of behavior. They establish approved patterns of using one's wealth, of wearing one's fame, of designing one's garden. They set tabus too, and may have the power to apply actual sanctions (for example, exclusion from the group). They thus produce *conformity* as well as *contentment* (or discontentment).

These two kinds of influence have, however, a good deal in common. Both imply certain perceptions on the part of the individual, who attributes characteristics to the reference group which it may or may not actually have. Both involve psychological rewards and punishment.

RELATIVE DEPRIVATION—AN EXAMPLE OF REFERENCE GROUP INFLUENCE

As already indicated, one of the chief problems in the field of reference group theory is to identify which of several groups that might serve as a frame or reference under given circumstances actually is invoked by an individual.

This is sometimes difficult to get at directly, as individuals are not always *aware* of which reference groups they are evaluating their behavior against, or may not be anxious to reveal them where they are conscious of such groups.

During World War II the Research Branch of the United States Army was concerned with morale of troops under different circumstances, and the morale often seemed not to reflect objective conditions. Thus, for example, soldiers in the Military Police who had received fewer promotions than their opposite numbers in the Air Force were nevertheless more satisfied with their rank than were the average Air Force men. Many similar phenomena were noted in which the men who were apparently suffering greater hardship on an absolute basis were more satisfied than others apparently suffering less hardship on an absolute basis. In an effort to explain these *apparent* inconsistencies the concept of "relative deprivation" was introduced. It was found that in each case there existed a reference group with which the individual soldier tended to compare his own lot. Only if he felt deprived *relative to this group* did his morale suffer. Two examples should suffice.

Army Promotions. The fact that Military Police were often more satisfied with their progress than were the more rapidly promoted Air Force Men was explained as follows: Absolute achieved status evidently was not the key to their feelings but rather the relation of the soldier's status to that of others he regarded as his standard of comparison. Thus the Private First Class in the Military Police may have been more satisfied than the Corporal in the Air Force, because in the Military Police virtually no enlisted man expected to get higher than Private First Class, while in the Air Force soldiers saw sergeants and better all around them.

Negro Troops.   It was found that the morale of Northern Negroes in southern army camps was higher than that of Northern Negroes in northern camps located in the areas where presumably Negroes in general were accorded better treatment. This apparent incongruity was again explained by identifying the reference group against which the Northern Negro compared himself in each instance. The reference group which turned this apparent inconsistency into a plausible reaction in this case was the Negro civilians whom the soldiers encountered while on pass in neighboring towns. The Negro soldier's pay was the same in the North as it was in the South, but in the North he found Negro civilians making so much money in defense plants that his pay appeared small by comparison. On the other hand, relative to most Negro civilians he saw in southern towns, the Negro soldier had a position of comparative wealth and dignity. Thus the psychological values of Army life to the Negro soldier in the South relative to the Southern Negro civilian greatly exceeded the psychological values of Army life to the Negro soldier in the North relative to the Northern Negro civilian.

THE PRACTICAL VALUE OF THE REFERENCE GROUP
CONCEPT IN MARKETING AND PUBLIC RELATIONS

In applying the reference group concept to practical problems in marketing and public relations three basic questions arise:

1. Reference group relevance. How do you determine whether and to what extent reference group influence is operating in a given situation? The reference group is after all just one of many influences in decision making, varying greatly in prominence from situation to situation.

2. Reference group identification. How do you identify the particular reference group or groups or individuals who are most relevant in influencing decisions under given circumstances? This is perhaps the most difficult question to answer in many cases, particularly where multiple reference groups are involved.

3. Reference group identification and effective communication. Once having identified the nature of the group influence operating in a given situation, how do you then make use of this knowledge in achieving the most effective *communication* with the groups or individuals?

The payoff is of course in this area, since the answers to the first two questions are of value only to the extent that they can be translated into more pertinent and effective communications, designed to influence purchasing behavior or the attitudes of various publics towards an organization.

Experimental evidence is now available which sheds light on each of these three questions. From this evidence as well as from the general advancement in the methodology of social research in recent years there have emerged some generalizations, very tentative in nature. These can be applied only with the most careful attention to the special circumstances operating in individual instances, and serve more as guides to fruitful ways of examining problems as they arise than as simple answers to problems.

In marketing, it is rarely practical to utilize information about individual differences because products must be designed and advertised with large groups in mind.[1] In public relations, on the other hand, individual difference may be very important. In this area the *general* attention level with respect to a particular issue is often low. Under these circumstances the relevant public may be largely confined to a few individuals, and in such cases knowledge of the relation between these individuals and potential reference groups would certainly be to the point.

INDIVIDUAL DIFFERENCES AND REFERENCE GROUP INFLUENCE

THE RELATION OF SECURITY LEVEL AND CONFORMITY TO REFERENCE GROUP INFLUENCE

A tentative generalization which has emerged in this area and which has been supported by some experimental evidence is this:

Individuals enjoying the greatest amount of security by virtue of their prestige and status within a group will generally conform (both publicly and privately) to the standards of that group, but are also freest to deviate from the group norms on occasions when, to their minds, particular circumstances seem to justify such deviations. On the other hand those with lowest feelings of security and least status in a group are most likely *publicly* to conform to its norms on all occasions even though harboring private opposition and resentment. The latter holds, of course, only if there are penalties associated with loss of membership in the particular group. Conformity then serves the purpose of maintaining membership in that group.

The following experiment conducted under laboratory conditions at Yale University lent support to this hypothesis.

Eighteen groups, each composed of six Yale freshmen, were formed for the experiment. They were motivated to cooperate by being told that

[1] An exception to this generalization may be found in the case of personal selling, where knowledge of the individual's specific relation to and perception of certain groups would be highly relevant.

they would meet for several sessions to work on certain problems and that the best group would win a prize. To promote group cohesion without sacrificing cooperation, each group was told that it would stop from time to time to evaluate its own members and expel any who were seriously interfering with the progress of the group. It was pointed out, however, that such expulsion was not to be taken lightly, as it would carry a considerable stigma and hence was only to be considered under very serious circumstances. The groups were given several problems on which they were asked to come to some agreement. One of these problems was in the area of juvenile delinquency. Each of the 18 groups was presented with some information about two gangs of juvenile delinquents, and asked to decide which of these gangs most deserved help from a social worker. The information was structured in such a way as to make Gang A appear to be the logical candidate for aid from the social worker. As planned by the researchers, the various units deliberated and came to the jointly-arrived-at decision that Gang A most deserved aid. After these group decisions were made, artificial images were set up in the mind of each individual as to how highly he was regarded by the group to which he belonged. This was accomplished by having the group members rate each other, in writing; however, the experiment leader did not use this information but gave each student fictitious information on how he was regarded by other members of his six man group. One person in each group was told that he was very highly regarded, two were told that they had been given an average rating, another two that the group's regard for them was quite low, and finally one member of each group was told that he was on the verge of rejection.

After these varying images of esteem by the particular group had been established (designed to set up feelings ranging all the way from very high to very low sense of security) a new item of information about the juvenile gangs was introduced. This item introduced some counter evidence pointing rather clearly in favor of Gang B as being the logical choice for aid.

After the new evidence was introduced, private and public expressions of conformity to the originally announced judgments of the group were obtained from those of very low, average and high prestige (as artificially manipulated for experimental purposes) with the following results:

1. Men with lowest prestige and security in relation to their group—those who believed they were on the verge of expulsion—were, when queried privately, most willing to deviate from the originally established norm of their group. However, when placed in the position of having to take a public stand these same people were most likely to conform to the originally announced norms of the groups, and least likely to deviate even though their own private

inclination on the basis of the facts at hand was to do so.

2. Men with average status and security exhibited considerable conformity, even in their private opinions.

3. Men with highest status and security were found, when queried privately, to be quite willing to differ from the original group decision and felt the greatest freedom to express their non-conformity publicly.

These relationships may be expressed graphically as follows:

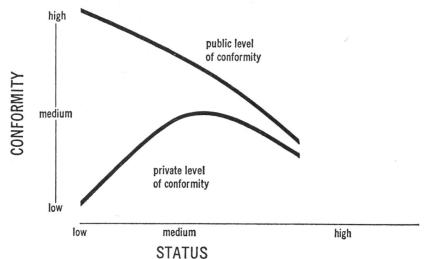

Figure 16.1. STATUS DETERMINES THE CONSISTENCY BETWEEN PUBLIC AND PRIVATE CONFORMITY.

Source: Department of Psychology, Yale University.

PRACTICAL IMPLICATIONS

If a person has high status and feels very secure relative to a group, he can be appealed to directly on the merits of the case and is in the best position to take the lead in deviating should he so desire, with least risk of losing status with the group he prizes. Seeking to influence such people through reference group appeals, when the merits of the case are inconsistent with the appeals, may have little success.

On the other hand, as suggested by the data just reviewed, those with lesser status in their group and less feeling of security are most likely to be influenced in public or visible actions by appeals involving their reference group. They are more likely to observe the norms of the group than others, even if they privately disagree with its specific position, since they require acceptance from the group for their own security. However, if the reference group influence conflicts with their own judgement or works against their own best interests, they are likely to develop an underlying resistance to the idea. Such resistance may find expression in other ways.

A practical example of the operation of this principle in the field of public relations and specifically in the area of influencing legislation may be drawn from experience in Washington. Particularly on issues where mass public attention and interest is low, considerable effort is concentrated on the most crucial of all publics, Congress itself. A Congressman of course has several reference groups, prominent among which are his constituents and the remainder of Congress. Naturally he greatly values the esteem of both of these groups. His very existence in Congress depends on the former and his self-esteem as well as the degree of cooperation he can depend upon getting for his own projects depends upon the high regard of the latter. The Congressman's status and security with regard to his constituents may be measured by such items as the size of his pluralities and the length of his service. Within Congress his status may be measured by, among other things, such items as seniority and cooperation by other members in the past.

Suppose a group was interested in changing a long standing piece of legislation which appeared to have represented the majority views of Congress for a considerable period of time. Suppose also that there was considerable merit in the proposed change, but that the public was relatively little concerned with this legislation. The Congressman's primary reference groups with respect to this issue is likely, therefore, to be his colleagues in the House. A freshman Congressman with little security and status would not, even though he privately favored this new legislation, be likely to oppose publicly the prevailing reference group position, by introducing the legislation or placing his name on an initial list of sponsors, while a Congressman with security and status might be more willing to do so.

For those outside of Congress interested in seeing the measure passed, winning the support of so-called bellwethers within Congress for this would be a primary objective. Such Congressmen, by virtue of their secure position in Congress, are most free to deviate and take the lead on occasions, where the case merits it. Though they generally show considerable respect for the norms of their "club" they are also in the best position to ignore this reference group when the right occasion arises.

THE INDIVIDUAL'S PERCEPTION OF NORMS OF POTENTIAL REFERENCE GROUP

Perhaps one of the more obvious limitations on the relevance of a potential reference group in influencing a decision is an individual's lack of knowledge or incorrect perception of the group's actual position on an issue, even where he values the group's views or at least its acceptance of him. Thus, for example, the American Legion may be an effective reference group for a substantial number of veterans with respect to veterans' legislation. It may be much less so, however, in connection with views on international affairs. The Legion has a position on such matters, but the average veteran is much less likely to know just what that position is. Along this line, a study[2] conducted for a Church Council found issues on which the Church's national policy was not followed by a considerable portion of the Church's members. The study revealed that these differences between Church policy and the opinions of its individual members were not necessarily conscious nonconformity with group norms, but rather in many cases reflected ignorance of what those norms were.

One practical implication from these studies is that the effective influence of a reference group, even one known to command a substantial following, may be increased by giving special publicity to the position of the group on a specific issue.

INDEPENDENT KNOWLEDGE ABOUT THE MATTER TO BE DECIDED

Experimental evidence has indicated that reference group influence is particularly potent in an informational vacuum. Where the individual has little if any knowledge about the attributes of a product or the issues involved in a public relations campaign, reference group influence is maximized. On the other hand, where the individual has personal knowledge and experience, the reference group influence is likely to be *less* relevant, other things being equal. Thus, for example, in the same study of a Church and its parishioners alluded to above, it was found that uninformed parishioners tended to have the same attitudes on secular issues as did their clergymen, but among those parishioners who were politically informed and had other sources of information on these issues there was a tendency more often to ignore the positions taken by their clergymen.

DIFFERENT KINDS OF DECISIONS AND REFERENCE GROUP INFLUENCE

MARKETING AND REFERENCE GROUP RELIANCE

As has already been suggested, the reference group constitutes just one of the many influences in buying decisions, and this influence varies from product to product. How then does one determine whether reference group influence is likely to be a factor in buying behavior in connection with a given product or brand? Research has been conducted

2 Source: Bureau of Applied Social Research, Columbia University.

on the various factors that influence buying behavior with reference to several products, and out of this have emerged some general ideas about how reference group influences may enter into purchasing.

Buying may be a completely individualistic kind of activity or it may be very much socially conditioned. Consumers are often influenced by what others buy, especially those persons with whom they compare themselves, or use as reference groups.

The conspicuousness of a product is perhaps the most general attribute bearing on its susceptibility to reference group influence. There are two aspects to conspicuousness in this particular context that help to determine reference group influence. First the article must be conspicuous in the most obvious sense that it can be seen and identified by others. Secondly it must be conspicuous in the sense of standing out and being noticed. In other words, no matter how visible a product is, if virtually everyone owns it, it is not conspicuous in the second sense of the word. This leads to a further distinction: reference groups may influence either (a) the purchase of a product, or (b) the choice of a particular brand or type, or (c) both.

The possible susceptibility of various product and brand buying to reference group influence is suggested in the following figure:

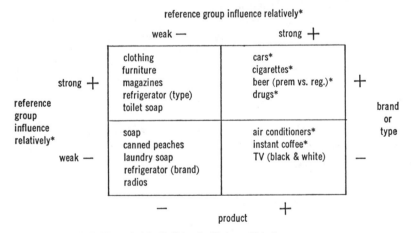

Source. Bureau of Applied Research, Columbia University (Glock, unpublished).

Figure 16.2. PRODUCTS AND BRANDS OF CONSUMER GOODS MAY BE CLASSIFIED BY EXTENT TO WHICH REFERENCE GROUPS INFLUENCE THEIR PURCHASE.

Source: Bureau of Applied Social Research, Columbia University (Glock, unpublished).

*The classification of all starred products is based on actual experimental evidence. Other products in this table are classified speculatively on the basis of generalizations derived from the sum of research in this area and confirmed by the judgment of seminar participants.

According to this classification a particular item might be susceptible to reference group influence in its purchase in three different ways, corresponding to three of the four cells in the above figure. Reference group influence may operate with respect to product alone (Brand + Product −) as in the upper left cell, or it may operate both with respect to brand and product (Brand + Product +) as in the upper right cell, or it may operate with respect to product but not brand (Brand − Product +) as in the lower right cell.

Only the "minus-minus" items of the kind illustrated (Brand − Product −) in the lower left cell are not likely to involve any significant reference group influence in their purchase *at the present time.*

What are some of the characteristics that place an item in a given category, and what significance do such placements have for marketing and advertising policy?

"Product—plus, brand-plus" items. Autos constitute an article where both the product and the brand are socially conspicuous. Whether or not a person buys a car, and also what particular brand he buys, is likely to be influenced by what others do. This also holds true for cigarettes, for drugs (decisions made by M.D.'s as to what to prescribe) and for beer with respect to type (premium vs. regular) as opposed to brand. Cigarettes and drugs, however, qualify as "plus-plus" items in a manner different from cars.

For example, while the car belongs to a class of products where brand differentiation is based at least substantially on real differences in attributes, the cigarette belongs to a class of product in which it is difficult to differentiate one brand from another by attributes: hence attributes are ascribed largely through reference group appeal built up by advertising. Popular images of the kinds of people who smoke various brands have been created at great cost, and in some cases additional images are being created to broaden a particular brand's market. In the case of drugs, it was found that the reference group influencing *whether* the product was used was different from that influencing the particular *brand* selected. Reference group influence was found to be prominent in determining whether or not beer was purchased at all, and also in determining whether regular or premium beer was selected. It did not appear to influence strongly choice of a particular brand.

"Product plus, brand minus" items. Instant Coffee is one of the best examples of this class of items. Whether it is served in a household depends in considerable part on whether the housewife, in view of her own reference groups and the image she has of their attitudes towards this product, considers it appropriate to serve it. The brand itself in this instance is not conspicuous or socially important and is a matter

largely for individual choice. In the case of air conditioners, it was found that little prestige attached to the particular brand used, and reference group influence related largely to the idea of purchasing the product itself. Analysis in one city revealed that the purchase of this often "visible from the outside" product was concentrated in small neighborhood areas. Clusters of conditioners were frequently located in certain rows and blocks. In many cases clusters did not even cross streets. Immediate neighbors apparently served as a powerfully influential group in the purchase of these appliances. In this general class may also be found the black and white TV set, with its antenna often visible on the outside of the house. As the saturation point in black and white TV set ownership rapidly approaches, however, the influence of reference groups may soon become minor, and the product can then be put in the "brand minus, product minus" quadrant, along with refrigerators. Color TV may remain in the "brand plus, product minus" quadrant, with type (color) rather than brand per se the element which is strongly related to reference groups.

"Product minus, brand plus" items. This group is made up essentially of products that all people or at least a very high proportion of people use, although differing as to type or brand.

Perhaps the leading example in this field is clothing. There could hardly be a more socially visible product than this, but the fact that everyone in our society wears clothing takes the *product* out of the area of reference group influence. The *type* of clothing purchased is, however, very heavily influenced by reference groups, with each subculture in the population (teenagers, zootsuiters, Ivy League collegians, western collegians, workers, bankers, advertising men, etc.) setting its own standards and often prescribing within fairly narrow limits what those who feel related to these groups can wear. Similarly, though not quite as dramatically, articles like furniture, magazines, refrigerators and toilet soap are seen in almost all homes, causing their purchase in general to fall outside of the orbit of reference group influence. The visibility of these items, however, coupled with the wide variety of styles and types among them make the selection of particular kinds highly susceptible to reference group influence.

"Product minus, brand minus," items Purchasing behavior in this class of items is governed largely by product attributes rather than by the nature of the presumed users. In this group neither the products nor the brands tend to be socially conspicuous. This is not to say that personal influence cannot operate with respect to purchasing the kind of items included in this group. As with all products, some people tend to exert personal influence and others tend to be inffuenced by individual

persons. Reference groups as such, however, exert relatively little influence on buying behavior in this class of items. Examples of items in this category are salt, canned peaches, laundry soap and radios. It is apparent that placement in this category is not *necessarily* inherent in the product itself and hence is not a static placement. Items can move in and out of this category.

While it is true that items which are essential socially inconspicuous, like salt and laundry soap, are natural candidates for this category, it is not entirely out of the realm of possibility that through considerable large scale advertising and other promotional efforts images of the kind of people who use certain brands of salt or laundry soap could be built up so as to bring reference group influence into play on such items, much as has been the case with cigarettes. The task here would be more difficult, however, since the cigarette is already socially visible. On the other hand, items such as radios and refrigerators which are conspicuously visible and whose purchase was once subject to considerable reference group influence have now slipped into this category through near saturation in ownership.

IMPLICATIONS OF STRONG AND WEAK REFERENCE GROUP INFLUENCE FOR ADVERTISING AND MARKETING

It should be stressed again that this scheme of analysis is introduced to show how reference group influence might enter into purchasing behavior in certain cases. It cannot be regarded as generally applicable to marketing problems on all levels. There is still a need to know more precisely where many different products or brands fit into this scheme. Attempts to fit products and brands into the classification above suggest research that needs to be done to obtain more relevant information about each product.

Assuming, however, that a product or brand has been correctly placed with respect to the part played by reference groups in influencing its purchase, how can this help in marketing the product in question?

Where neither product nor brand appear to be associated strongly with reference group influence, advertising should emphasize the product's attributes, intrinsic qualities, price, and advantages over competing products.

Where reference group influence is operative, the advertiser should stress the kinds of people who buy the product, reinforcing and broadening where possible the existing stereotypes of users. This involves learning what the stereotypes are and what specific reference groups enter into the picture, so that appeals can be "tailored" to each major group reached by the different media employed.

Although it is important to see that the "right" kind of people use a product, a crucial problem is to make sure that the popular image of the product's users is as broad as possible without alienating any important part of the product's present or potential market in the process. Creating or reinforcing a stereotype of consumers which is too small and exclusive for a mass-produced item may exclude a significant portion of the potential market. On the other hand, some attempts to appeal to new groups through advertising in mass media have resulted in the loss of existing groups of purchasers whose previous (favorable) image of the product-user was adversely affected. One possible means for increasing the base of the market for a product by enlarging the image of its users is to use separate advertising media through which a new group can be reached without reducing the product's appeal to the original group of users. Another method might be to appeal to a new group through cooperative advertising by a number of companies producing the product, possibly through a trade association. This would minimize the risk to an individual producer who, trying to reach a new group of users through his own advertising (women as opposed to men or wealthy as opposed to average people, for example), might antagonize people who had a strong need to identify with the *original* image of the product's kind of user.

PRODUCT ATTRIBUTES VERSUS REFERENCE GROUP INFLUENCE

A technique which could serve to assess the relative influence of reference groups, as compared with product attributes, on the purchase of any given product was employed in research on a food product which will be referred to as product "X".

A cross-section of "X" users was asked several questions relating to particular attributes of "X", such as whether it was more harmful or beneficial for one's health, whether or not it was considered fattening, whether it was considered extravagant or economical, whether or not it tasted good, and so on. These same people were also asked a reference group-oriented question about "X", to determine whether or not "X" was popular with most of their friends. It was found that there was usually more "X" eating among people who reacted negatively to "X"'s attributes but admitted to its popularity among most of their friends, than among those who reacted positively to "X"'s attributes but indicated that it was not popular with their friends.

These relationships are shown in Table 1. In this table, the scores in parentheses are those of people whose replies showed both attribute influence and reference group influence exerting pressure in the same direction.

Special attention should be directed towards the other scores. These represent situations in which people are under cross-pressures. For each of the four attributes considered, the reference group influence is stronger than the attribute influence, in the use of "X". This is brought out by the arrows, which point toward the cross-pressure situations where the reference group influence is adverse. In all of these, consumption frequency is less than where attribute influence alone is negative. Or, put another way, positive perception of reference group behavior with respect to the food product ("X" is very popular) coupled with negative perception of its actual attribute value ("X" does more harm than good, is fattening, etc.) leads to more consumption than negative perception of reference group behavior ("X" not very popular) coupled with positive perception of actual attribute value ("X" does more good than harm, not fattening, economical).

As can be seen from the comparisons indicated by the arrows, reference group influence is markedly stronger than attribute influence for three of the four attributes, only for "taste" does the attribute influence come close to competing with reference group influence in determining consumption of "X".

One implication of this finding would be that advertising by the "X" industry might stress the variables that are related to the products' *social* utility for its consumers, rather than base its advertising solely on the *physical* attributes of the product.

In a study of a beverage, it was found that, of those who drank the beverage in question, 95% claimed that their friends also drank it, while of those who did not drink this beverage 85% also claimed that their friends did *not* drink it.

Some products, then, must be sold to whole social groups rather than to individuals.

RETROSPECTIVE COMMENT

At a time that scientific knowledge is increasing exponentially, developments over a twenty year period may change completely the nature of a discipline. Francies S. Bourne wrote "Group Influence in Marketing and Public Relations" some twenty years ago. The twenty years have witnessed the introduction of the *Journal of Marketing Research* and *Journal of Advertising Research* to mention only a few of the U.S. professional marketing journals. At the same time, most other management journals have increased considerably their coverage of marketing and consumer behavior topics.

A new discipline of Consumer Behavior has emerged with University courses, professional journal (*Journal of Consumer Research*) and professional association (Association for Consumer Research). Thousands

Table 16.1. RELATION BETWEEN REFERENCE GROUP AND ATTRIBUTE
INFLUENCE IN USE OF FOOD PRODUCT "X"

$+$ *Reference Group* $-$

With most of respondent's friends "X" is:
Product Attribute   *Very Popular   Not Very Popular*

Effects of "X" on health   Index of Frequency of Eating "X" . *

$+$ more good than harm   (.41) $\longrightarrow$ $-$.01
$-$ more harm than good   .80 $\longrightarrow$ ($-$.51)

$+$ do not avoid fattening food   (.30) $-$.21
   and/or feel "X" is not really
   or a little fattening
$-$ try to avoid fattening food and   .14 $\nearrow$ ($-$.29)
   feel "X" is really or a little
   fattening

Economic Value Judgment
$+$ fairly economical   (.29) $\longrightarrow$ $-$.20
$-$ sort of an extravagance   .11 $\longrightarrow$ ($-$.33)

     (.42)
$+$ tastes good $\longrightarrow$ .05
$-$ no reference to good taste**   .09 $\longrightarrow$ ($-$.38)

*All scores in the above table constitute an index of the frequency of "X" eating
among respondents falling into the given cell. The scoring procedure used was:

    Frequent "X" users—score $-$1
    Medium "X" users—score 0
    Occasional "X" users—score $-$1

The final score is derived by subtracting the number of occasional "X" users in
a given cell from the number of frequent users and dividing the remainder by the
total number of respondents in the cell.

For example, the index score .41 was obtained as follows:

329 respondents felt that a moderate amount of "X" does more good than harm
AND report that "X" is very popular with most of their friends.

Of these 329 respondents 178 are frequent "X" users, 97 are medium "X" users,
and 43 are occasional "X" users.

    The score: 178 $-$43 $=$ 135   The Index value: 135/329 $=$ $-$.41

**"Tastes Good" represents the selection of this phrase from a word list of various
attributes that might be applied to "X". "No Reference to Good Taste" refers to
those respondents who did not select "Tastes Good" from the word list.

Source: Bureau of Applied Social Research, Columbia University

of Ph.D. dissertations on consumer behavior and marketing have been written during these years and dozens of consumer behavior texts have been introduced. Consumer and marketing research occupy today a much more prominent role as inputs to corporate marketing decisions, and, in some embryonic way, also public policy decisions.

Given these changes, and parallel changes in the behavioral sciences from which we in marketing tend to borrow both concepts and methodology, the obvious question that arises after reading Bourne's article is: "to what extent are the ideas presented in the article still relevent today?" In attempting to answer this question I do not intend to provide an up-to-date review of the reference group literature since this has been done elsewhere (e.g., Engel, Kollat, and Blackwell, 1973, Ostlund, 1973) but rather to highlight (a) the ideas presented by Bourne[3] which I feel are of lasting value, and (b) given the benefit of hindsight and our current state of knowledge to suggest some of the limitations of the concepts and findings presented by Bourne and his colleagues.

THE MAJOR CONTRIBUTIONS

Bourne's article suggests a number of ideas and approaches which are as relevant today as they were in 1957 and which most likely will be relevant in the years to come. These include:[4]

1. *A practical approach to the application of a behavioral science concept to marketing.*

In discussing the concept of reference group influence Bourne did not remain at the abstract level of suggested relevance, but rather did recognize that in applying the reference group concept to practical problems in marketing three basic questions should be answered:

Reference group relevance—How to determine whether and to what extent reference group influence is operating in a given situation?

Reference group identification—How to identify the particular reference group or groups, or individuals, who are most relevant in influencing decisions under given circumstances?

Reference group identification and effective communication—

---

3 Bourne summarized in this article not only his own ideas and research findings, but also those of other social psychologists and sociologists who participated in two seminars on *Group Influence*. These included Charles Y. Glock, Harold H. Kelley, Rensis Likert, Ithiel de Sola Pool, Everett M. Rogers, Samuel A. Stouffer, and Samuel P. Hayes, Jr.

4 The order in which the items are presented does not reflect any order of importance.

Having identified the nature of the group influence operating in a given situation, how to most effectively *communicate* with the groups or individuals you desire to influence?

These and similar questions can and should be asked with respect to any behavioral science concept one attempts to apply to practical problems in marketing. Unfortunately, too many of the behavioral science applications in marketing do not bother with such basic questions.

2. *Recognizing the diversity of available research approaches.*
Refreshingly to a behavioral science application in marketing article, Bourne does present a variety of research designs and data collection approaches to the identification of reference group influence. These include direct questioning, associative-projective techniques, check on actual homogeneity of attitudes within a group, check on the differences in attitudes between old and new members of a group, comparison of the attitudes of prestigeful, accepted members of an organization with those of peripheral members, sociometric techniques and direct observations.

Implicitly underlying the discussion of these diverse research approaches is the recognition that most behavioral concepts (and marketing phenomena) should be studied using more than a single approach. Applying this concept (which is consistent with Campbell and Fiske, 1959, philosophy) to consumer and marketing research would assure a higher quality research.

3. *Presenting an alternative approach to the classification of goods.*
The marketing literature has followed and accepted with only minor modifications Copeland's (1925) classification of goods theory into convenience shopping and speciality goods. Whereas, overwhelming acceptance of any concept tend quite often to stifle creativity in the given area, Bourne and his colleagues did not follow the trend of others and did suggest a refreshingly new approach to product classification; a classification scheme based on the extent to which reference groups influence the purchase of products and brands. Whether one accepts this classification system or not is immaterial. The major contribution of the article is by looking at a phenomena from a new and different point of view and suggesting an alternative approach.

4. *Recognizing the role of research in classifying products and brands.*
In developing the product and brand classification system, Bourne and his colleagues based some of their examples on actual empirical evidence. They further recognized the role of research stating

"Attempts to fit products and brands into the preceding classification suggest that research needs to be done in order to obtain more relevant information about each product." The recognition that classification of goods should be based on actual consumer research is at the heart of the current approach to product classification which avoids a generalized classification system and focuses on identifying a product's perceived positioning (Wind, 1975).

Bourne's recognition of the *role of research* is even more striking in the context of the utilization of a behavioral science concept (reference group) as guideline for marketing action. To some extent, Bourne resisted the temptation to suggest direct managerial implications and stated, "The strategy of the advertiser should involve *learning* what the stereotypes are and what specific reference groups enter into the picture." This approach to the utilization of behavioral science concepts in marketing (by suggesting hypotheses for study and *not* specific decisions) seem to be the more prudent and valuable one. Bourne did not follow this approach in all cases and did try his hand in some direct policy recommendations, yet, he started moving in the right direction.

5. *Explicitly distinguishing between products and brands.*
Despite the importance of this distinction, many of the consumer behavior studies do not distinguish explicitly between products and brands. Bourne and his colleagues did recognize the importance of this distinction and used it as a major dimension of their product classification framework.

6. *Recognizing the need for a strategy of market segmentation.*
Although the product classification matrix implies no segmentation and assumes that the market is homogeneous in its evaluation of the importance of reference group influence on the purchase of a product and brands, Bourne did recognize the possible heterogeneity with respect to the specific reference group involved. Hence he suggests that reference group appeals should be "tailored to each main group reached by the different media employed." Today, this *partial* acceptance of the market segmentation concept would not be acceptable. The importance of reference group to the purchase decision could serve either as a *basis* for segmentation or as a *descriptor* of other segments (based on some other desired bases such as usage pattern).

Yet, in an historical perspective Bourne and his colleagues did recognize the concept of segmentation (although only partially). Furthermore, he was aware of the possible risks of segmentation— "The possibility of alienating any important part of the product's present or potential market in the process (of using a segmented approach)."

7. *Recognizing the need to measure the importance of product attributes (benefits).*

Consistent with his empirical orientation Bourne suggested a measurement technique to assess the relative influence of reference groups, as compared with product attributes. One may argue with the specific measurement technique proposed by Bourne (subtracting the number of occasional product uses from the number of frequent users and dividing the remainder by the total number of respondents in the cell—all those who indicated that the product attribute or attributes are important). Yet, one should recall that most of the advances in attribute measurement techniques did occur in the last decade. Today, to assess the relative importance of reference group influence vis à vis other product attributes one may use a variety of measurement approaches ranging from the commonly used multiple regression model to the newer application of conjoint measurement.[5] These approaches can be used not only at the aggregate (total market) level but also at the segment level.

8. *Recognizing the importance of situational factors.*

In discussing the possible effect of reference group influence, Bourne did recognize the influence determinants which vary primarily according to the individual making the decision (customer characteristics) and those influence determinants which vary primarily according to the matter to be decided (situation specific characteristics). The recognition that the study of consumer behavior should include both of these aspects is generally accepted today and is consistent with the applied social research of the fifties (e.g., Lazarsfeld). Yet, it did present a welcome departure from many of the marketing research practices of the early fifties which focused primarily on general customer characteristics.

9. *Recognizing the dynamics and changing nature of the market place.*

In discussing the "Product Minus, Brand Minus" category, Bourne recognized that "placement in this category is not *necessarily* inherent in the product itself and hence is not a static placement. Items can move in and out of this category. The reader should extend this concept of *change* to the other three categories and, to that matter, to any product classification scheme." Hence, suggesting

[5] For a discussion of this approach see, for example, Green and Wind, 1975.

the need for continuous research to monitor the changes in the "position" (classification) of any product or brand over time.

10. *Relating one behavioral science concept to others.*

In his complete discussion of reference group influence two sections, which are often omitted (from reprints of the article),[6] focus on the relationship between reference group influence and the adoption of new products and the audience as a reference group. This attempt to relate one behavioral science concept (reference group) to other behavioral science concepts and findings is of great importance and should serve as a useful example to current researchers in the field.

11. *Recognizing that the effect of reference group influence is not limited to consumers and applies also to industrial buyers.*

Most of the efforts at applying behavioral science concepts to marketing have been limited to the explanation and prediction of the behavior of consumers (as individuals). Little attention has been given to the applicability to these concepts to the explanation of the behavior of organizational buyers. Bourne, and the group of social scientists who participated in the 1956 seminars on group influence, did recognize the potential applicability of the reference group concept to industrial marketing and devoted a whole section to it.[7]

Given the importance of understanding organizational buying behavior, it is hoped that reading Bourne's example will stimulate new efforts to apply group influence and other behavioral concepts to the study of organizational buying behavior.

SOME LIMITATIONS

In retrospect, Bourne and his colleagues did recognize at least implicitly many of the major concepts which constitute the body of marketing knowledge as of 1975. The major weakness of the reported concepts and

---

6 Most of the reading books that include the Bourne article reproduce only selected sections from the original article. Bliss (1967), for example, reproduced two sections, "Marketing and Reference Group Relevance" and "Product Attributes vs. Reference Group Influence," while Kassarjian and Robertson (1968) reproduce only the first of these, deleted the second and added a previous section on "Individual Differences and Reference Group Influence." Most of the reproductions of Bourne's article delete the sections on "The Concept of Reference Group Influence," "Methods of Identification (of Influence Groups)," "Examples of Identifying relevant Reference Groups," and "The Audience as a Reference Group."

7 Oddly enough this is also one of the frequently omitted sections of the Bourne article.

findings was in not carrying these ideas further and applying them to the areas of interest—the influence of reference group. The view of consumer behavior is *over-simplistic* and not always consistent with the concepts discussed earlier. Consider, for example, the following:

> In discussing the buying process Bourne identifies two decisions, the product and brand. At the least, the decision *where* to buy the product or brand should also be considered (especially when considering social influence). Given that the same brand can be bought at a luxury department store *and* a discount house, the *social* image of a store becomes of great importance. More specific treatment of the buying decision process can be undertaken following the process suggested in the Davis article and in some of the consumer behavior literature of the last decade.

> Despite the recognition of market segmentation and the reporting on one of the Yale studies on the relation between status and conformity, the most often cited section of the Bourne article (that dealing with his product and brand classification) is quite misleading since it does not recognize the existence of *individual differences* with respect to the magnitude and nature of influence exerted by reference groups. This is most likely the most serious limitation of the article, since even in the fifties social scientists did recognize the fact that individuals do differ in their susceptibility to social influence. Consider, for example, Bourne's own earlier discussion and Riesman's distinction between inner and other directed persons.

> Recognizing the need to *apply* behavioral science concepts to marketing, Bourne could not resist the temptation to propose a number of generalizations, ignoring the need to base such conclusions on empirical evidence and specific answers to the question he posed at the beginning of the article, concerning the determination of "which kinds of groups are likely to be referred to by which kinds of individuals under which kinds of circumstances in the process of making which decisions." Hence, the conclusions concerning the "product plus, brand plus," "product plus, brand minus" and "product minus, brand plus" might be quite misleading. The more cautious, research oriented approach, taken by Bourne for the "product minus, brand minus" cell is more reasonable and defensible.

Whereas these shortcomings can be overcome quite easily (once they are recognized), the key question facing the reader of the Bourne article is with respect to the value of the *reference group concept*, i.e., to what extent does reference group influence exist and what is its impact on consumers' behavior?

Bourne presents an insightful discussion of the concept of reference group influence and its importance. The conceptual discussion is supplemented with a number of empirical studies. In summarizing the findings of one of these studies, he concluded: ". . . Reference group influence is markedly stronger than (product) attribute influence for three of the four attributes. Only for 'taste' does the attribute influence come close to competing with reference-group influence in determining consumption of 'X' (a food product)."

Bourne's conclusion is widely accepted. Most consumer behavior texts quote some of Bourne's findings and conclusions and most consumer behavior models do include reference group influence as one of the determinants of consumer behavior. Yet, when one examines the empirical consumer behavior literature and in particular the commercially sponsored consumer and marketing studies, one is surprised to find almost no mention of reference group influence. Occasionally, if a large life style/psychographic battery is included in a study, few of the statements may relate to the respondent's perception of the influence of his reference group. Yet, most studies simply do not include this construct. Is this phenomena a result of oversight and negligence on the part of the researchers who "forget" to include this important factor in their studies? Or is it a reflection of the researchers' conscious decision to exclude the concept due to their belief that the concept of reference group is not very useful?

Although no conclusive evidence exists today to determine the value of the reference group concept, some of the conceptual and operational issues of the concept tend to suggest that it is of limited value to our understanding of consumer behavior. Some of the major questions to which we do not have very good answers are: Conceptually, how is reference group influence to be defined? What is its relationship to other forms of social and personal influence of groups (family, social class, etc.) and individuals (reference leaders, opinion leader, etc.)? What is the influence process and pattern involved in the influence of reference groups (is "referent power" normative or comparative in nature?) and how is it related to concepts such as "role perceptions" and "self concept"? Furthermore, how are positive and negative reference groups to be determined? Does reference group (or individuals) require face to face interaction among the group members or can it be psychological in nature (group to which the persons aspires to belong)? Does the group have general influence over a large class of behaviors or does it, like opinion leadership, vary with the subject involved? How does an individual select a reference group or person? Under what conditions are reference groups or individuals likely to influence a person's purchase behavior? What is the advantage of dealing with the concept of reference group as opposed to focusing on the mechanisms through which it might affect behavior (e.g., socialization and conformity) and how do consumers resolve conflicts between their personal preferences and their perceptions of the preferences of members of their reference group?

Whereas these and similar conceptual problems have been recognized in the sociological, social psychological, and consumer behavior literature, they have not been resolved. Furthermore, the major limitation of the concept of reference group is in its *operationalization*. Operational definitions of reference group influence vary widely from one researcher to another. This restricts our ability to isolate the impact of reference group influence as a special form of social influence and to compare and contrast the results of the few empirical marketing studies that attempt to study the effect of reference group and other social influence on consumer purchase behavior.

Advances in mathematical psychology provide today the measurement concepts and techniques necessary to measure rigorously the nature and magnitude of the influence of relevant others on individual purchase behavior. Yet, only very few studies have taken advantage of these methodological developments.[8] It is hoped that further reading of Bourne's article, while keeping in mind the recent methodological developments which can be employed in the study of influence, would encourage further work on both the conceptual and operational study of reference group influence (and other forms of social influence) on consumer behavior.

CONCLUSION

"Group Influence in Marketing" is one of the early attempts to suggest the applicability of behavioral science concepts to marketing. Despite some of its shortcomings, the article does serve as an extremely useful example for a *creative* approach in marketing—departing from the traditional classification of goods theories and suggesting a new basis for classification based on the importance of reference group influence in the purchase of products and brands.

Bourne's article is also one of the early attempts to suggest specific marketing applications of a sociological/social psychological concept. These applications, if viewed as hypotheses to be tested empirically in a specific marketing context, are still valuable.

Despite the tremendous methodological and conceptual advances that occurred in marketing since the publication of Bourne's article, the insightful ideas of Bourne and his colleagues suggest that not all relevant marketing knowledge was generated in the last decade. Insights into consumer behavior and encouragement for a more *creative* ap-

[8] For some initial efforts in this direction, see Wind, 1975.

proach to the study of consumer behavior and marketing phenomena can be gained by a careful study of the early writings in the field of consumer behavior (and the behavioral sciences).—*Yoram Wind,* Professor of Marketing, Wharton School, University of Pennsylvania

REFERENCES

BLISS, PERRY (ed.). *Marketing and the Behavioral Sciences.* Boston: Allyn and Bacon, 2nd ed., 1967.

BOURNE, FRANCES S. "Group Influence in Marketing and Public Relations." *Some Applications of Behavioral Science Research,* in Rensis Likert and Samuel P. Hayes, Jr. (eds.). Paris: UNESCO, 1957.

CAMPBELL, DONALD T. and D. W. Fiske. "Convergent and Discriminant Validation by a Multitrait-Multimethod Matrix." *Psychological Bulletin* 56 (1959), pp. 81–105.

COPELAND, MELVIN T. *Principles of Merchandising.* Chicago: A. W. Shaw Corp., 1925.

ENGEL, JAMES F., David T. Kollat, and Roger D. Blackwell. *Consumer Behavior.* New York: Holt, Rinehart & Winston, 2nd ed., 1973.

GREEN, PAUL E. and Yoram Wind. "New Way to Measure Consumers' Judgment." *Harvard Business Review* 53 (July–August, 1975), pp. 107–117.

KASSARJIAN, HAROLD H. and Thomas S. Robertson. *Perspectives in Consumer Behavior.* Glenview, Illinois: Scott, Foresman & Co., 1968.

OSTLUND, LYMAN E. "Role Theory and Group Dynamics." *Consumer Beravior: Theoretical Sources,* Scott Ward and Thomas S. Robertson (eds.). Englewood Cliffs, N.J.: Prentice-Hall, 1973.

WIND, YORAM. "Multiperson Influence and Usage Occasions as Determinants of Brand Choice. Paper presented at the August 1975 AMA Conference.

———. "The Perception of the Firm's Competitive Position." *Behavioral Models for Market Analysis: Foundations for Marketing Action,* F. Nicosia and Y. Wind (eds.). Hinsdale, Illinois: The Dryden Press, 1976.

17. Reference Groups as Perspectives

Tamotsu Shibutani

Although Hyman coined the term scarcely more than a decade ago, the concept of reference group has become one of the central analytic tools in social psychology, being used in the construction of hypotheses concerning a variety of social phenomena. The inconsistency in behavior as a person moves from one social context to another is accounted for in terms of a change in reference groups; the exploits of juvenile delinquents, especially in interstitial areas, are being explained by the expectations of peer-group gangs; modifications in social attitudes are found to be related to changes in associations. The concept has been particularly useful in accounting for the choices made among apparent alternatives, particularly where the selections seem to be contrary to the "best interests" of the actor. Status problems—aspirations of social climbers, conflicts in group loyalty, the dilemmas of marginal men—have also been analyzed in terms of reference groups, as have the differential sensitivity and reaction of various segments of an audience to mass communication. It is recognized that the same generic processes are involved in these phenomenally diverse events, and the increasing popularity of the concept attests to its utility in analysis.

As might be expected during the exploratory phases in any field of inquiry, however, there is some confusion involved in the use of this concept, arising largely from vagueness of signification. The available formal definitions are inconsistent, and sometimes formal definitions are contradicted in usage. The fact that social psychologists can understand one another in spite of these ambiguities, however, implies an intuitive recognition of some central meaning, and an explicit statement of this will enhance the utility of the concept as an analytic tool. The literature reveals that all discussions of reference groups involve some identifiable grouping to which an actor is related in some manner and the norms and values shared in that group. However, the relationship between these three terms is not always clear. Our initial task,

Tamotsu Shibutani, "Reference Groups as Perspectives," American Journal of Sociology, Vol. 60 (May 1955), pp. 562–569. Copyright © 1955 by the University of Chicago Press. Reprinted by permission.

then, is to examine the conceptions of reference group implicit in actual usage, irrespective of formal definitions.

One common usage of the concept is in the designation of that group which serves as the point of reference in making comparisons or contrasts, especially in forming judgments about one's self. In the original use of the concept Hyman spoke of reference groups as points of comparison in evaluating one's own status, and he found that the estimates varied according to the group with which the respondent compared himself. Merton and Kitt, in their reformulation of Stouffer's theory of relative deprivation, also use the concept in this manner; the judgments of rear-echelon soldiers overseas concerning their fate varied, depending upon whether they compared themselves to soldiers who were still at home or men in combat. They also propose concrete research operations in which respondents are to be asked to compare themselves with various groups. The study of aspiration levels by Chapman and Volkmann, frequently cited in discussions of reference-group theory, also involves variations in judgment arising from a comparison of one's own group with others.[1] In this mode of application, then, a reference group is a standard or check point which an actor uses in forming his estimate of the situation, particularly his own position within it. Logically, then, *any* group with which an actor is familiar may become a reference group.

A second referent of the concept is that group in which the actor aspires to gain or maintain acceptance: hence, a group whose claims are paramount in situations requiring choice. The reference group of the socially ambitious is said to consist of people of higher strata whose status symbols are imitated. Merton and Kitt interpret the expressions of willingness and felt readiness for combat on the part of inexperienced troops, as opposed to the humility of battle-hardened veterans, as the efforts of newcomers to identify themselves with veterans to whom they had mistakenly imputed certain values.[2] Thus, the concept is used to point to an association of human beings among whom one seeks to gain, maintain, or enhance his status; a reference group is that group in which one desires to participate.

In a third usage the concept signifies that group whose perspective constitutes the frame of reference of the actor. Thus, Sherif speaks of reference groups as groups whose norms are used an anchoring points

[1] H. H. Hyman, "The Psychology of Status," *Archives of Psychology*, XXXVIII (1942), 15; R. K. Merton and A. Kitt, "Contributions to the Theory of Reference Group Behavior," in R. K. Merton and P. F. Lazarsfeld (eds.), *Studies in the Scope and Method of "The American Soldier"* (Glencoe, Ill.: Free Press, 1950), pp. 42–53, 69; D. W. Chapman and J. Volkmann, "A Social Determinant of the Level of Aspiration," *Journal of Abnormal and Social Psychology*, XXXIV (1939), 225–38.

[2] *Op. cit.*, pp. 75–76.

in structuring the perceptual field,[3] and Merton and Kitt speak of a "social frame of reference" for interpretations.[4] Through direct or vicarious participation in a group one comes to perceive the world from its standpoint. Yet this group need not be one in which he aspires for acceptance; a member of some minority group may despise it but still see the world largely through its eyes. When used in this manner, the concept of reference group points more to a psychological phenomenon than to an objectively existing group of men; it refers to an organization of the actor's experience. That is to say, it is a structuring of his perceptual field. In this usage a reference group becomes any collectivity, real or imagined, envied or despised, whose perspective is assumed by the actor.

Thus, an examination of current usage discloses three distinct referents for a single concept: (1) groups which serve as comparison points; (2) groups to which men aspire and (3) groups whose perspectives are assumed by the actor. Although these terms may be related, treating together what should be clearly delineated as generically different can lead only to further confusion. It is the contention of this paper that the restriction of the concept of reference group to the third alternative —that group whose perspective constitutes the frame of reference of the actor—will increase its usefulness in research. Any group or object may be used for comparisons, and one need not assume the role of those with whom he compares his fate; hence, the first usage serves a quite different purpose and may be eliminated from further consideration. Under some circumstances, however, group loyalties and aspirations are related to perspectives assumed, and the character of this relationship calls for further exploration. Such a discussion necessitates a restatement of the familiar, but, in view of the difficulties in some of the work on reference groups, repetition may not be entirely out of order. In spite of the enthusiasm of some proponents there is actually nothing new in reference-group theory.

CULTURE AND PERSONAL CONTROLS

Thomas pointed out many years ago that what a man does depends largely upon his definition of the situation. One may add that the manner in which one consistently defines a succession of situations depends upon his organized perspective. A perspective is an ordered view of one's world—what is taken for granted about the attributes of various

[3] M. Sherif, "The Concept of Reference Groups in Human Relations," in M. Sherif and M. O. Wilson (eds.), *Group Relations at the Crossroads* (New York: Harper & Bros., 1953), pp. 203–31.

[4] *Op. cit.*, pp. 49–50.

objects, events, and human nature. It is an order of things remembered and expected as well as things actually perceived, an organized conception of what is plausible and what is possible; it constitutes the matrix through which one perceives his environment. The fact that men have such ordered perspectives enables them to conceive of their ever changing world as relatively stable, orderly, and predictable. As Riezler puts it, one's perspective is an outline scheme which, running ahead of experience, defines and guides it.

There is abundant experimental evidence to show that perception is selective; that the organization of perceptual experience depends in part upon what is anticipated and what is taken for granted. Judgments rest upon perspectives, and people with different outlooks define identical situations differently, responding selectively to the environment. Thus, a prostitute and a social worker walking through a slum area notice different things; a sociologist should perceive relationships that others fail to observe. Any change of perspectives—becoming a parent for the first time, learning that one will die in a few months, or suffering the failure of well-laid plans—leads one to notice things previously overlooked and to see the familiar world in a different light. As Goethe contended, history is continually rewritten, not so much because of the discovery of new documentary evidence, but because the changing perspectives of historians lead to new selections from the data.

Culture, as the concept is used by Redfield, refers to a perspective that is shared by those in a particular group; it consists of those "conventional understandings, manifest in act and artifact, that characterize societies."[5] Since these conventional understandings are the premises of action, those who share a common culture engage in common modes of action. Culture is not a static entity but a continuing process; norms are creatively reaffirmed from day to day in social interaction. Those taking part in collective transactions approach one another with set expectations, and the realization of what is anticipated successively confirms and reinforces their perspectives. In this way, people in each cultural group are continuously supporting one another's perspectives, each by responding to the others in expected ways. In this sense culture is a product of communication.

In his discussion of endopsychic social control Mead spoke of men "taking the role of the generalized other," meaning by that that each person approaches his world from the standpoint of the culture of his group. Each perceives, thinks, forms judgments, and controls himself

[5] R. Redfield, *The Folk Culture of Yucatan* (Chicago: University of Chicago Press, 1941), p. 132. For a more explicit presentation of a behavioristic theory of culture see *The Selected Writings of Eduard Sapir in Language, Culture and Personality*, ed. D. G. Mandelbaum (Berkeley: University of California Press, 1949), pp. 104–9, 308–31, 544–59.

according to the frame of reference of the group in which he is participating. Since he defines objects, other people, the world, and himself from the perspective that he shares with others, he can visualize his proposed line of action from this generalized standpoint, anticipate the reactions of others, inhibit undesirable impulses, and thus guide his conduct. The socialized person is a society in miniature; he sets the same standards of conduct for himself as he sets for others, and he judges himself in the same terms. He can define situations properly and meet his obligations, even in the absence of other people, because, as already noted, his perspective always takes into account the expectations of others. Thus, it is the ability to define situations from the same standpoint as others that makes personal controls possible.[6] When Mead spoke of assuming the role of the generalized other, he was not referring to people but to perspectives shared with others in a transaction.

The consistency in the behavior of a man in a wide variety of social contexts is to be accounted for, then, in terms of his organized perspective. Once one has incorporated a particular outlook from his group, it becomes his orientation toward the world, and he brings this frame of reference to bear on all new situations. Thus, immigrants and tourists often misinterpret the strange things they see, and a disciplined Communist would define each situation differently from the non-Communist. Although reference-group behavior is generally studied in situations where choices seem possible, the actor himself is often unaware that there are alternatives.

The proposition that men think, feel, and see things from a standpoint peculiar to the group in which they participate is an old one, repeatedly emphasized by students of anthropology and of the sociology of knowledge. Why, then, the sudden concern with reference-group theory during the past decade? The concept of reference group actually introduces a minor refinement in the long familiar theory, made necessary by the special characteristics of modern mass societies. First of all, in modern societies special problems arise from the fact that men sometimes use the standards of groups in which they are *not* recognized members, sometimes of groups in which they have never participated directly, and sometimes of groups that do not exist at all. Second, in our mass society, characterized as it is by cultural pluralism, each person internalizes several perspectives, and this occasionally gives rise to embarrassing dilemmas which call for systematic study. Finally, the development of reference-group theory has been facilitated by the increasing interest

6 G. H. Mead, "The Genesis of the Self and Social Control," *International Journal of Ethics*, XXXV (1925), 251–77, and *Mind, Self and Society* (Chicago: University of Chicago Press, 1934), pp. 152–64. Cf. T. Parsons, "The Superego and the Theory of Social Systems," *Psychiatry*, XV (1952), 15–25.

in social psychology and the subjective aspects of group life, a shift from a predominant concern with objective social structures to an interest in the experiences of the participants whose regularized activities make such structures discernible.

A reference group, then, is that group whose outlook is used by the actor as the frame of reference in the organization of his perceptual field. All kinds of groupings, with great variations in size, composition, and structure, may become reference groups. Of greatest importance for most people are those groups in which they participate directly—what have been called membership groups—especially those containing a number of persons with whom one stands in a primary relationship. But in some transactions one may assume the perspective attributed to some social category—a social class, an ethnic group, those in a given community, or those concerned with some special interest. On the other hand, reference groups may be imaginary, as in the case of artists who are "born ahead of their times," scientists who work for "humanity," or philanthropists who give for "posterity." Such persons estimate their endeavors from a postulated perspective imputed to people who have not yet been born. There are others who live for a distant past, idealizing some period in history and longing for "the good old days," criticizing current events from a standpoint imputed to people long since dead. Reference groups, then, arise through the internalization of norms; they constitute the structure of expectations imputed to some audience for whom one organizes his conduct.

THE CONSTRUCTION OF SOCIAL WORLDS

As Dewey emphasized, society exists in and through communication; common perspectives—common cultures—emerge through participation in common communication channels. It is through social participation that perspectives shared in a group are internalized. Despite the frequent recitation of this proposition, its full implications, especially for the analysis of mass societies, are not often appreciated. Variations in outlook arise through differential contact and association; the maintenance of social distance—through segregation, conflict, or simply the reading of different literature—leads to the formation of distinct cultures. Thus, people in different social classes develop different modes of life and outlook, not because of anything inherent in economic position, but because similarity of occupation and limitations set by income level dispose them to certain restricted communication channels. Those in different ethnic groups form their own distinctive cultures because their identifications incline them to interact intimately with each other and to maintain reserve before outsiders. Different intellectual traditions within social psychology—psychoanalysis, scale analysis, *Gestalt*, pragmatism—will remain separated as long as those in each tradition restrict their sympathetic attention to works of their own school and view others with contempt or hostility. Some social scientists are out of touch with the masses of the American people because they eschew the mass media, especially television, or expose themselves only condescendingly. Even the outlook that the *avant-garde* regards as "cosmopolitan" is culture-bound, for it also is a product of participation in restricted communication channels—books, magazines, meetings, exhibits, and taverns which are out of bounds for most people in the middle classes. Social participation may even be vicarious, as it is in the case of a medievalist who acquires his perspective solely through books.

Even casual observation reveals the amazing variety of standards by which Americans live. The inconsistencies and contradictions which characterize modern mass societies are products of the multitude of communication channels and the ease of participation in them. Studying relatively isolated societies, anthropologists can speak meaningfully of "culture areas" in geographical terms; in such societies common cultures have a territorial base, for only those who live together can interact. In modern industrial societies, however, because of the development of rapid transportation and the media of mass communication, people who are geographically dispersed can communicate effectively. Culture areas are coterminous with communication channels; since communication networks are no longer coterminous with territorial boundaries, culture areas overlap and have lost their territorial bases. Thus, next-door neighbors may be complete strangers; even in common parlance there is an intuitive recognition of the diversity of perspectives, and we speak meaningfully of people living in different social worlds— the academic world, the world of children, the world of fashion.

Modern mass societies, indeed, are made up of a bewildering variety of social worlds. Each is an organized outlook, built up by people in their interaction with one another; hence, each communication channel gives rise to a separate world. Probably the greatest sense of identification and solidarity is to be found in the various communal structures—the underworld, ethnic minorities, the social elite. Such communities are frequently spatially segregated, which isolates them further from the outer world, while the "grapevine" and foreign-language presses provide internal contacts. Another common type of social world consists of the associational structures—the world of medicine, of organized labor, of the theater, of café society. These are held together not only by various voluntary associations within each locality but also by periodicals like *Variety*, specialized journals, and feature sections in newspapers. Finally, there are the loosely connected universes of special interest—the world of sports, of the stamp collector, of the daytime serial—serviced by mass media programs and magazines like *Field and Stream*. Each of these worlds is a unity of order, a universe of regularized mutual response. Each is an area in which there is some structure which permits reasonable anticipation of the behavior of others, hence, an area in which one may act with a sense of security and confidence.[7] Each social world, then, is a culture area, the boundaries of which are set neither by territory nor by formal group membership but by the limits of effective communication.

Since there is a variety of communication channels, differing in stability and extent, social worlds differ in composition, size, and the territorial distribution of the participants. Some, like local cults, are small and concentrated; others, like the intellectual world, are vast and the participants dispersed. Worlds differ in the extent and clarity of their boundaries; each is confined by some kind of horizon, but this may be wide or narrow, clear or vague. The fact that social worlds are not coterminous with the universe of men is recognized; those in the underworld are well aware of the fact that outsiders do not share their values. Worlds differ in exclusiveness and in the extent to which they demand the loyalty of their participants. Most important of all, social worlds are not static entities; shared perspectives are continually being reconstituted. Worlds come into existence with the establishment of communication channels; when life conditions change, social relationships may also change, and these worlds may disappear.

Every social world has some kind of communication system—often nothing more than differential association—in which there develops a special universe of discourse, sometimes an argot. Special meanings and symbols further accentuate differences and increase social distance from outsiders. In each world there are special norms of conduct, a set of values, a special prestige ladder, characteristic career lines, and a common outlook toward life—a Weltanschauung. In the case of elites there may even arise a code of honor which holds only for those who belong, while others are dismissed as beings somewhat less than human from whom bad manners may be expected. A social world, then, is an order conceived which serves as the stage on which each participant seeks to carve out his career and to maintain and enhance his status.

One of the characteristics of life in modern mass societies is simultaneous participation in a variety of social worlds. Because of the ease with which the individual may expose himself to a number of com-

---

[7] Cf. K. Riezler, *Man: Mutable and Immutable* (Chicago: Henry Regnery Co., 1950), pp. 62–72; L. Landgrebe, "The World as a Phenomenological Problem," *Philosophy and Phenomenological Research*, I (1940), 38–58; and A. Schuetz, "The Stranger: An Essay in Social Psychology," *American Journal of Sociology*, XLIX (1944), 499–507.

munication channels, he may lead a segmentalized life, participating successively in a number of unrelated activities. Furthermore, the particular combination of social worlds differs from person to person; this is what led Simmel to declare that each stands at that point at which a unique combination of social circles intersects. The geometric analogy is a happy one, for it enables us to conceive the numerous possibilities of combinations and the different degrees of participation in each circle. To understand what a man does, we must get at his unique perspective—what he takes for granted and how he defines the situation—but in mass societies we must learn in addition the social world in which he is participating in a given act.

LOYALTY AND SELECTIVE RESPONSIVENESS

In a mass society where each person internalizes numerous perspectives there are bound to be some incongruities and conflicts. The overlapping of group affiliation and participation, however, need not lead to difficulties and is usually unnoticed. The reference groups of most persons are mutually sustaining. Thus, the soldier who volunteers for hazardous duty on the battlefield may provoke anxiety in his family but is not acting contrary to their values; both his family and his comrades admire courage and disdain cowardice. Behavior may be inconsistent, as in the case of the proverbial office tyrant who is meek before his wife, but it is not noticed if the transactions occur in dissociated contexts. Most people live more or less compartmentalized lives, shifting from one social world to another as they participate in a succession of transactions. In each world their roles are different, their relations to other participants are different, and they reveal a different facet of their personalities. Men have become so accustomed to this mode of life that they manage to conceive of themselves as reasonably consistent human beings in spite of this segmentalization and are generally not aware of the fact that their acts do not fit into a coherent pattern.

People become acutely aware of the existence of different outlooks only when they are successively caught in situations in which conflicting demands are made upon them, all of which cannot possibly be satisfied. While men generally avoid making difficult decisions, these dilemmas and contradictions of status may force a choice between two social worlds. These conflicts are essentially alternative ways of defining the same situation, arising from several possible perspectives. In the words of William James, "As a man I pity you, but as an official I must show you no mercy; as a politician I regard him as an ally, but as a moralist I loathe him." In playing roles in different social worlds, one imputes different expectations to others whose differences cannot always be compromised. The problem is that of selecting the perspective for defin-ing the situation. In Mead's terminology, which generalized other's role is to be taken? It is only in situations where alternative definitions are possible that problems of loyalty arise.

Generally such conflicts are ephemeral; in critical situations contra-dictions otherwise unnoticed are brought into the open, and painful choices are forced. In poorly integrated societies, however, some people find themselves continually beset with such conflicts. The Negro intel-lectual, children of mixed marriages or of immigrants, the foreman in a factory, the professional woman, the military chaplain—all live in the interstices of well-organized structures and are marginal men.[8] In most instances they manage to make their way through their compartment-alized lives, although personal maladjustments are apparently frequent. In extreme cases amnesia and dissociation of personality can occur.

Much of the interest in reference groups arises out of concern with situations in which a person is confronted with the necessity of choosing between two or more organized perspectives. The hypothesis has been advanced that the choice of reference groups—conformity to the norms of the group whose perspective is assumed—is a function of one's in-terpersonal relations; to what extent the culture of a group serves as the matrix for the organization of perceptual experience depends upon one's relationship and personal loyalty to others who share that outlook. Thus, when personal relations to others in the group deteriorate, as sometimes happens in a military unit after continued defeat, the norms become less binding, and the unit may disintegrate in panic. Similarly, with the transformation of personal relationships between parent and child in late adolescence, the desires and standards of the parents often become less obligatory.

It has been suggested further that choice of reference groups rests upon personal loyalty to significant others of that social world. "Sig-nificant others," for Sullivan, are those persons directly responsible for the internalization of norms. Socialization is a product of a gradual accumulation of experiences with certain people, particularly those with whom we stand in primary relations, and significant others are those who are actually involved in the cultivation of abilities, values, and outlook.[9] Crucial, apparently, is the character of one's emotional ties with them. Those who think the significant others have treated them with affection and consideration have a sense of personal obliga-tion that is binding under all circumstances, and they will be loyal even

---

[8] Cf. E. C. Hughes, "Dilemmas and Contradictions of Status," *American Journal of Sociology*, L (1945), 353–59, and E. V. Stonequist, *The Marginal Man* (New York: Charles Scribner's Sons, 1937).

[9] H. S. Sullivan, *Conceptions of Modern Psychiatry* (Washington, D.C.: W. H. White Psychiatric Foundation, 1947), pp. 18–22.

at great personal sacrifice. Since primary relations are not necessarily satisfactory, however, the reactions may be negative. A person who is well aware of the expectations of significant others may go out of his way to reject them. This may account for the bifurcation of orientation in minority groups, where some remain loyal to the parental culture while others seek desperately to become assimilated in the larger world. Some who withdraw from the uncertainties of real life may establish loyalties to perspectives acquired through vicarious relationships with characters encountered in books.[10]

Perspectives are continually subjected to the test of reality. All perception is hypothetical. Because of what is taken for granted from each standpoint, each situation is approached with a set of expectations; if transactions actually take place as anticipated, the perspective itself is reinforced. It is thus the confirming responses of other people that provide support for perspectives.[11] But in mass societies the responses of others vary, and in the study of reference groups the problem is that of ascertaining *whose* confirming responses will sustain a given point of view.

THE STUDY OF MASS SOCIETIES

Because of the differentiated character of modern mass societies, the concept of reference group, or some suitable substitute, will always have a central place in any realistic conceptual scheme for its analysis. As is pointed out above, it will be most useful if it is used to designate that group whose perspective is assumed by the actor as the frame of reference for the organization of his perceptual experience. Organized perspectives arise in and become shared through participation in common communication channels, and the diversity of mass societies arises from the multiplicity of channels and the ease with which one may participate in them.

Mass societies are not only diversified and pluralistic but also continually changing. The successive modification of life-conditions compels changes in social relationships, and any adequate analysis requires a study of these transformational processes themselves. Here the concept of reference group can be of crucial importance. For example, all forms of social mobility, from sudden conversions to gradual assimila-

10 Cf. R. R. Grinker and J. P. Spiegel, *Men under Stress* (Philadelphia: Blakiston Co., 1945), pp. 122–26; and E. A. Shils and M. Janowitz, "Cohesion and Disintegration in the Wehrmacht in World War II," *Public Opinion Quarterly*, XII (1948), 280–315.

11 Cf. G. H. Mead, *The Philosophy of the Act* (Chicago: University of Chicago Press, 1938), pp. 107–73; and L. Postman, "Toward a General Theory of Cognition," in J. H. Rohrer and M. Sherif (eds.), *Social Psychology at the Crossroads* (New York: Harper & Bros., 1951), pp. 242–72.

tion, may be regarded essentially as displacements of reference groups, for they involve a loss of responsiveness to the demands of one social world and the adoption of the perspective of another. It may be hypothesized that the disaffection occurs first on the level of personal relations, followed by a weakening sense of obligation, a rejection of old claims, and the establishment of new loyalties and incorporation of a new perspective. The conflicts that characterize all persons in marginal roles are of special interest in that they provide opportunities for cross-sectional analyses of the processes of social change.

In the analysis of the behavior of men in mass societies the crucial problem is that of ascertaining how a person defines the situation, which perspective he uses in arriving at such a definition, and who constitutes the audience whose responses provide the necessary confirmation and support for his position. This calls for focusing attention upon the expectations the actor imputes to others, the communication channels in which he participates, and his relations with those with whom he identifies himself. In the study of conflict, imagery provides a fertile source of data. At moments of indecision, when in doubt and confusion, who appears in imagery? In this manner the significant other can be identified.

An adequate analysis of modern mass societies requires the development of concepts and operations for the description of the manner in which each actor's orientation toward his world is successively reconstituted. Since perception is selective and perspectives differ, different items are noticed and a progressively diverse set of images arises, even among those exposed to the same media of mass communication. The concept of reference group summarizes differential associations and loyalties and thus facilitates the study of selective perception. It becomes, therefore, an indispensable tool for comprehending the diversity and dynamic character of the kind of society in which we live.

RETROSPECTIVE COMMENT

If Professor Shibutani were here to reflect on his article, "Reference Groups As Perspectives," he would be gratified with the substantive role his article has played in the development of reference group influence as an area of consumer behavior. In his article, Professor Shibutani advocated the adoption of an observationally derived perspective of reference groups and presented the following observationally derived definition: "A reference group is that group whose outlook is used by the actor as a frame of reference in the organization of his perceptual field."

One can only speculate on the changes Professor Shibutani would make in his article if he were updating it today. However, the orientation and content of his article together with subsequent developments in the literature of reference groups suggests conceptual and empirical research areas which he might have explored. It is likely that these areas would have included the reference group selection process, the influence of non-membership (aspiration) reference groups, and the relevance of role theory in explaining variation in reference group influence across behavioral and attitudinal situations.

The likelihood that Professor Shibutani would have investigated the reference group selection process is suggested by his focus on the norm internalization process in which the individual adopts the norms of the audience (groups) whose response is most relevant to his situationally defined goal(s). Professor Shibutani's recognition of the potential influence of non-membership reference groups suggests that he might have investigated aspiration reference groups (groups to which the individual aspires but does not yet belong). Recent developments in the literature indicate that individuals may internalize the norms of such groups as a means of attaining desired membership or formal identification status.

The relevance of role theory in developing the conceptual framework of reference group research is another area which might have attracted Professor Shibutani's attention. In this context, he might have viewed the specifications of a current, or aspired to role, as the primary source of norms to be internalized by the individual. Thus, the individual could be viewed as an actor playing to a self-selected reference group audience; and products and services could be viewed as the actor's props. Variation in group influence across behavioral acts, as well as attitudes, might then be explained as a function of variation in role relevance and role commitment. Seemingly inconsistent behavioral acts or attitudes could be viewed as being a function of the individual's occupancy of, or aspiration to, multiple reference groups with their concomitant role specifications.

In summary, it appears reasonable to suggest that Professor Shibutani might have considered the above areas in updating his article. Perhaps the only statement that can be made with certainty is that his update would have reflected his belief that the reference group concept facilitates understanding the manner in which an individual's orientation toward society is constituted and successively reconstituted, and thus is an important factor in our efforts to describe, understand and predict human behavior.—*Dr. Robert E. Witt*, Professor of Marketing and Chairman of the Department of Marketing, University of Texas at Austin

18. Effects of Group Influence on Consumer Brand Preferences

James E. Stafford

Most earlier marketing researchers described consumer brand preference behavior without attempting to uncover and analyze experimentally determinants of such brand preferences [2, 3]. With the advent of sophisticated mathematical models, however, renewed interest was shown in conducting experimental studies leading to an explanation of the process of brand preference behavior [4, 5, 8]. To date, the most important contributions of these studies have been their reliance on realism and their emphasis on brand loyalty as a probability process. For the most part, factors other than economic ones were not considered important, or at least they were de-emphasized. In recent years, however, marketing men generally have conceded that such social factors as acculturation, social class, ethnic groups and identification all play some role in consumer decision making. The question today is exactly how, in what way, and to what extent social factors influence consumer behavior.

A second thought which suggested this study revolves around the concept of group or interpersonal influence. From both a theoretical and empirical point of view, the literature of the behavioral sciences fully supports the idea that certain groups, and particularly certain individuals within the group, influence member behavior. While a great deal of marketing research has been conducted on various aspects of consumer behavior, there have been only a few analytical attempts [7, 9] to determine if such interpersonal interactions do, in fact, influence consumer behavior.

The lack of empirical research on determining whether small, informal, social groups influence the purchasing behavior of their members led to this design of an experiment which would, first, indicate whether this influence exists and, second, describe and explain the process of group influence on one particular type of consumer behavior—brand preferences. The main objective was to explore in as much detail

Reprinted by permission of the author and publisher from the Journal of Marketing Research, *published by the American Marketing Association, Vol. 3 (February 1966), pp. 68–75.*

as possible if and how a consumer's brand preferences might be conditioned by intergroup communications and the perception of brand preferences of fellow group members.

The overall design of the experiment consisted of sociometrically selecting ten groups of women who were close friends, neighbors, or relatives; who might go shopping together; and who were given a common experimental task to perform. The assumption was that the resulting groups were "real" in some sense other than that of being arbitrarily brought together for the study. This did not mean that the groups had to have traditions of long standing, but they had to have real interaction among the individuals making up the group.

By analyzing first the relationship between the groups and their subsequent observed brand preference behavior, it was hoped that the influence of groups on the brand preferences of their members could be shown statistically. Second, by analyzing the interaction processes of each group, it was also hoped to illustrate that the degree of influence exerted varies according to the internal cohesiveness[1] of the group, and according to the type and strength of informal leadership exhibited.

REVIEW OF GROUP THEORY

During the past two decades there has been a resurgence of interest in individual-group relationships. This resurgence continued to build momentum until, today, the study of small groups has become a central area of theorization and experimentation for social psychologists. The major character of this trend, as contrasted with the individualistic emphasis, is the realization that group situations generate differential effects of significant consequence. Group interaction is seen as a major determinant in attitude formation and attitude change, as well as for other phenomena (satisfaction of social needs) of importance to the individual.

As is typical in the behavioral sciences, there is no one accepted definition of "groups." The most common definition revolves around the term "reference groups" which can include groups to which a person actually belongs, to which he aspires to belong, or dissociative groups to which he aspires *not* to belong. Thus, for one member a group may be a membership group while for another it is a reference group. Most social psychologists consider reference groups as a person's major source of values, norms, and perspectives.

Reference groups influence behavior in two major ways. First, they

---

[1] Cohesiveness refers to the attraction a group has for its members. The greater the attractiveness of the group, the more cohesive the group.

influence *aspiration levels* and thus play a part in producing satisfaction or frustration. If the other members of a particular reference group (for cxample, neighbors) are wealthier, more famous, better gardeners, *etc.*, one may be dissatisfied with his own achievements and may strive to do as well as the others.

Second, reference groups influence *kinds* of behavior. They establish approved patterns of using one's wealth, of wearing one's prestige, of designing one's garden. They thus produce conformity as well as contentment (or discontentment). These two kinds of influence have, in general, a great deal in common. Both imply certain perceptions on the part of the individual, who attributes characteristics to the reference group which it may or may not actually have. Both involve psychological rewards and punishment.

Reference behavior itself is a cognitive process in which individuals evaluate their statuses, behavior, norms, and values by means of referents.[2] The four objects of evaluation—norms, values, statuses, and behavior—may be grouped into objective (statuses and behavior) and subjective (norms and values) categories. It is recognized that the contents of each category have important linkages with those of the other, but for purposes of analysis the distinction may be made.

Reference behavior is characterized by three general dimensions—knowledge, affectivity, and sanctions. These dimensions appear as interrelated variables which come into play in all forms of reference behavior.

For a phenomenon to be used, the individual must be aware (have knowledge) of its existence, and the degree and kind of knowledge serve as guides to his use of the referent. Through direct and indirect communication, members learn the norms and values of their informal groups and see how the normative structure is expressed in the status arrangements and corresponding behavior patterns.

The sanctions perceived by individuals constitute another dimension of reference behavior. The concept of referents indicates the existence of myriads of potential referents and, yet, the actual number of referents utilized by any one person is necessarily limited. When an individual perceives a potential referent, such as an informal social group, to be the source of positive sanctions (rewards) or negative sanctions (punishment or the withholding of anticipated rewards) which relate to himself, at that moment the informal group becomes an actual referent and is used in the evaluation of norms, values, status, and behavior.

[2] Referents are whatever individuals employ in evaluating their own statuses, behavior, norms, and values. In this paper the small, informal social group is the main referent being considered, although there are many other phenomena that one could use as referents.

The third dimension of reference behavior—affectivity—relates to the degree of identification a person has for a particular group. Recognition of the importance of a person's degree of identification to a reference group is very valuable to an understanding of how groups influence the behavior of their members.

Because of the segmentation of life in an industrialized, mass society, important decisions faced by an individual can involve the perspectives of many referents without any perceived conflicts between them. In general, the more restricted the application of results of a process of evaluation, the more limited will be the number of referents mobilized in the process. If, for example, an individual was planning a small purchase (a gallon of milk), he would probably utilize very few referents to make a decision. On the other hand, if he were planning to purchase a new car, then he would probably evaluate his decision alternatives by considering a much larger number of referents. While determination of any rank order of influence potential is very difficult to accomplish, some mention can be made of two other concepts which have evolved out of group theory, and which are quantitatively measurable—group cohesion and group leadership.

Informal structuring tends to occur in all groups after a period of time during which the members have interacted with one another. Homans contended that "the usual outcome of interaction is the formation of interpersonal bonds of affect and respect [6]." The recipient of affect and respect was said to have social rank within the group. Differential social ranks provided the basis for informal structuring.

Were all members of a group to like and respect each other highly, no substructures would be said to exist. This condition would define complete, 100 percent positive cohesion. All social ranks would be equal. If, on the other hand, every member ignored every other one, each member would be considered a separate substructure, a one-man clique. This would define the state of zero cohesion. Internal social influence would be equal to zero. Much evidence exists to support the

Table 18.1. ANALYSIS OF VARIANCE SUMMARY FOR THE INFLUENCE OF INFORMAL GROUPS ON BRAND PREFERENCES

Source of Variation	Sum of squares	Degrees of freedom	Variance estimates by pooling	F
Brands	22.90	3	7.60	.74
Groups	181.30	9	20.10	1.97[a]
Interaction	1,580.40	155	10.20	

[a] $p = .05$

Table 18.2. THE RELATIONSHIP BETWEEN COHESIVENESS AND THE BEST LIKED
BRAND OF EACH GROUP

Rank order of groups from highest to lowest in cohesiveness	Cohesiveness in mean lib scores	Percent best liked brand chosen by the group
1	3.00	66.6%
2	2.50	65.6
3	2.00	30.9
4	1.90	50.0
5	1.40	25.3
6.5	1.10	28.2
6.5	1.10	29.7
8	1.00	43.7
9	0.90	50.0
10	0.65	34.2

proposition that inter-group pressure to conform on matters of importance varies directly with cohesion. In a very cohesive group, a member
will experience a great deal of pressure to conform. In a less cohesive
group, pressure to conform is expected to vary directly with the amount
of deviation from the group norms, at least up to a point.

The concept of "group leaders" developed from the evolution of
role differentiation within the group. Except in very unusual circumstances, informal role differentiations are expected to occur in every
group. As a result of this role differentiation process, each person in the
group has a certain social rank or status. The more status an individual
has, the greater his prestige; the greater one's prestige, the higher he is
in the informal hierarchy and the more "social power" he possesses.
Social power has been defined as the total amount of opinion change
one person could induce another to make. The concept could, of course,
be broadened to include the overt as well as the convert changes a member can effect in another member of the group. When a group member has social power over other members, he also usually has high status
and is normally considered the group leader.

METHODOLOGY

OBJECTIVES AND HYPOTHESES

Considering the fertile field for research in consumer behavior offered
by reference group theory, it seemed very pertinent to relate reference
theory and consumer behavior in an empirical study. The first and fore-
most objective of the study, therefore, was to show statistically that

small, informal groups do influence certain aspects of consumer behavior. In hypothesis form, the first objective was:

1. Small, informal social groups exert influence toward conformity on member brand preferences.

The second and third objectives were closely related to the first. In fact, they could be considered secondary objectives. Assuming support for the first goal, this part of the study attempted to determine how and to what degree informal groups influence member behavior. From a theoretical standpoint, group cohesion and group leadership played important roles in forming group opinions and behavior patterns. Specifically, then, Hypotheses 2 and 3 were:

2. The degree of influence exerted on a member by the group is directly related to the "cohesiveness" of that group.

3. Within a group, the "leader" is the most influential member with respect to member behavior patterns in purchase situations (brand preferences in this study).

RESEARCH DESIGN

The research design attempted to analyze the relationship among several variables (group influences and brand preferences) under controlled but "real-life" conditions. The broad steps of the research were as follows:

1. Specification and delineation of the first major variable of interest—small, informal groups. A two-stage, systematic random sample of ten housewives from one Census tract in Austin, Texas, was used as a representative basis to obtain ten informal groups. Each member of the original sample was asked to take a sociometric test, which was used to determine the interpersonal relationships of interest and to disclose the feelings which individuals have toward each other in respect to a group situation they are considering at that moment. Since consumer behavior was the broad topic of study, each woman was asked to nominate four friends, relatives or neighbors with whom "she likes to or would be willing to go shopping." The use of an activity criterion, rather than a request for a general statement of friendship, was intended to reveal the specific basis on which a selection was made, as well as to uncover group interactions closely associated to some common activity like buying behavior. The end result of the sociometric test was ten groups of women who were friendly toward each other, who interacted, and who all were oriented toward one criterion—shopping behavior. The rest of the experiment dealt with how the influence

of interpersonal relationships on a person's brand preferences could be observed.

2. A particular product, bread, was selected as a vehicle for the brand preference study because of ease of handling, frequent use, and financial considerations. Thin sliced white bread from a local bakery was packaged in identical clear unmarked cellophane bags. Large labels (2″ × 2″) with the letters, "H," "L," "M," "P," were designated as "brands" to be placed on the bread. These four middle-alphabet consonants were chosen because, first, they were easy to remember and, second, they have about the same frequency of use in English. It was not assumed that these symbols (brands) were completely neutral because it is probable that no set of symbols could be neutral, equally pleasing, or have common meanings for all individuals.

3. The experiment itself was relatively simple. Called on at home twice a week (Tuesday and Friday) for eight weeks each of the forty-two women in the study was given her choice of the four previously unknown brands of bread. The four brands were placed on a tray so the participant could easily see and choose the one she wanted. In order to control for position bias, the position of the brands on the tray was varied each day in Latin square design. The women were not aware that all of the brands were from the same bakery, or that the study was concerned with analyzing inter-group influences. Rather, they were told the purpose of the study was to discover how women go about choosing a brand of bread from several about which they knew nothing.

4. At the end of the test period, each woman was given a short questionnaire covering brand preferences and personal opinions regarding the bread. The questionnaire also provided specific information for determining group cohesion, group leadership, and intergroup communication patterns.

5. Analysis of the data included determination of (a) group influences on brand choices and preferences; (b) influence of the degree of group cohesion on brand preferences; (c) influence of group leaders on brand choices of other group members, and (d) comparisons of actual brand choices with brand preferences.

RESULTS

By analyzing the similarities and differences of brand choice patterns within the entire sample and among the members of each group, it was expected to determine whether the group was in fact a source of influence on member brand preferences. On the assumption that the data were neither correlated nor binomial, two-way analysis of variance (F-test) was a valid tool to use to test the first hypothesis. If the study was properly designed to show that groups influence member brand preferences, then the statistical result should be a significant difference between the groups in the brands preferred. In other words, while within group brand preferences should be similar, the groups themselves should vary among one another with respect to brand preferences. The results are presented in Table 1.

Table 18.3. COMPARISONS OF BEST LIKED BRANDS OF LEADERS AND GROUPS TO GROUP COHESION

Rank order of groups from highest to lowest in cohesiveness	Cohesiveness in mean lib scores	Leader's best brand liked	Percent best liked brand chosen by leader	Entire group's best liked brand	Percent best liked brand chosen by group (leader excluded)
1	3.0	H	68%	H	56%
2	2.5	M	100	M	48
3	2.0	H	43	H	31
4	1.9	P	83	P	50
5	1.4	H	43	H	25
6.5	1.1	M	37	P	28
6.5	1.1	L	40	H	29
8	1.0	P	43	H	28
9	0.9	M	100	M	50
10	0.6	P	43	M	34

Statistically, the results of the analysis of variance test supported the first hypothesis. A significant difference was found between the groups with respect to preferred brands, while there was no significant difference between the brands themselves. Also, there was no significant interaction effect between brands and groups, thus disposing of one major source of statistical ambiguity. The first result, while explaining nothing of the determinants of group influence, did provide sufficient stimulus to carry on a more detailed analysis of the process of group influence.

While analysis of variance was a valuable and powerful tool in determining whether the groups did, in fact, influence member brand preferences, it provided no clues as to *how* this influence was initiated and whether this influence was exerted toward member conformity. Theoretically speaking, two factors—cohesiveness and informal leadership—have an important bearing on the effectiveness of internal group influences.

Essentially, group cohesiveness was measured by having each member of the group rate every other member of that group on a seven point bipolar scale which ranged from Best Friend (+3) to Hated (−3), with Don't Know (0) as the center point. The algebraic sum of points given by all group members was termed "Lib units [1]." The higher the mean Lib score for a group, the more cohesive (positive or negative) was the group.

Group leadership was defined operationally as the sum of three different sources of influence: attractiveness, expertness, and communications centrality. First, the attractiveness of each group member to every other group member was measured by taking the mean Lib score that person received on the group cohesion measurement. The individual who was most attractive or best liked by his group was considered to be a potential informal leader of the group. Second, expertness as a form of leadership was described rather arbitrarily as the woman in each group who had been a member of the first bread panel study conducted by Tucker [10]. Because of her previous experience on a similar study, it was believed that this individual might be considered an expert in this study, with her opinions being therefore more influential. Finally, the leader was defined as the individual in the central position of that group's communication network. Each woman was asked to tell how often (times per week) she called, was called by, or saw in person each of the other group members. By classifying this data, it was possible to describe rather accurately the communication patterns of each group. The women in the group with the highest frequency of communications (central position) was defined as the leader.

EFFECT OF COHESIVENESS ON BRAND PREFERENCES

The main function of this section of the study was to determine whether cohesiveness influenced the degree to which members would conform to each other's brand preferences. In other words, would members of more cohesive groups be more likely to prefer the same brand than members of less cohesive groups? A second consideration from a slightly different point of view from the above was: would members of more cohesive groups tend to be more or less brand loyal than members of less cohesive groups? Does increased cohesion lead to similarities in general behavior (brand loyalty) even though the loyalty may be expressed on different brands?

As shown in Table 2, there appeared at first to be no relationship between cohesiveness and similarity among member brand preferences. The two groups highest in cohesiveness also had the highest percent-

Table 18.4. THE INFLUENCE OF GROUP COHESIVENESS ON THE EXTENT OF STRENGTH OF BRAND LOYALTY

Rank order of groups from highest to lowest in cohesiveness	Percent of each group brand loyal	Mean length of group's brand loyalty runs
1	100%	8.0
2	100	10.5
3	50	4.0
4	80	7.0
5	60	2.6
6.5	100	5.2
6.5	40	2.6
8	100	9.7
9	100	6.0
10	60	3.6

age of mutually preferred brands. Groups 8 and 9, however, also exhibited high degree of internal similarity for the best liked brand. As a result, no concrete conclusions could be drawn from these data regarding the importance of cohesiveness in the effectiveness of group influence.

In an attempt to approach the determination of the influence of cohesiveness from a different direction, the collected data were reanalyzed and rearranged as shown in Table 3.

Since it was known that group cohesion and leadership were closely related, Table 3 was revised to include not only the group's best liked brand but also that of the leader's. Notice that in the five most cohesive groups, the preferred brand of the group and the leader were the same. In the five less cohesive groups there was only one occurrence of preference similarity (Group 9).

No relationship was discovered between the degree of cohesiveness and the extent and strength of brand loyalty[3] in the group. In Table 4, for example, two groups ranked low in cohesiveness (8th and 9th) both had as many members brand loyal as the two top ranked groups. Also shown in the table was the fact that the average length of a brand loyalty run varied indiscriminately regardless of cohesiveness.

In this study, cohesiveness appeared to have its most important function in providing an agreeable environment in which informal leaders could effectively operate.

[3] Brand loyalty has been operationally defined as "three consecutive choices of the same brand."

EFFECT OF GROUP LEADERSHIP ON BRAND PREFERENCES

Group leadership, as previously mentioned, was measured in three ways: by attraction, expertness, and position centrality in the communications network. Since each was an independent measurement, it was possible that any or all of them would delineate a different group leader. Table 5 was the result of a cross tabulation of the measurements.

Table 18.5. COMPARISONS OF THE RESULTS OF THE THREE GROUP LEADERSHIP MEASUREMENTS[a]

Group	Indi-vidual	A	E	C	Group	Indi-vidual	A	E	C
1	1	None	X	X	6	27	X	X	X
	2					33			
	3					40			
	4					28			
	5								
2	6		X	X		26	X	X	X
	7	X				34			
	8					25			
	9					28			
	44					17	—		
3	11	X	X	X	8	29	X	X	X
	12					35			
	13					30			
	14								
	15								
4	16	None	X		9	42	X	X	X
	10					41			
	36			X		21			
						31			
						32			
5	22	X	X	X	10	19			
	23					20	None	X	X
	24								
	43								
	18								

[a]Leadership measurements
A = attraction
E = expertness
C = communications centrality.

In six of the ten groups, the leader was the same individual regardless of the leadership measurement. In three of the other four groups it was impossible to obtain a meaningful measurement of individual attraction because (1) all of the members were related, or (2) all individuals in the group were liked by each other to about the same degree. The individual from each group ultimately selected as the leader for purposes of analysis was the member who had the highest average on the three measurements.

In order to substantiate the importance of informal leadership to effective group influence, one must refer back to Table 3. An important aspect of this table was that it indicated a definite relationship between how well the leader preferred his best liked brand and what brand was preferred (including the strength of this preference) by the other members of the group. In other words, regardless of the degree of cohesiveness, the more frequently the leader chose his best liked brand, the higher the likelihood that the rest of the group would prefer that brand more often than expected by chance. For example, in the group ranked ninth in cohesiveness, the leader selected one brand sixteen consecutive times; her fellow group members preferred the same brand 50 percent of the time when it was expected by chance only 25 percent of the time.

Table 6 indicates this relationship even more clearly. Working down the figures in the table, it is seen that the more frequently a leader chose one brand, the higher the probability that the rest of her group would like and take the same brand. Once the leader's preference for a certain brand dropped below 68 percent, the group's frequency and similarity of brand preference to that of the leader declined rapidly. In the four highest ranked groups, the leaders and members not only preferred the same best liked brand, but preferred them an exceptionally high percentage of the time compared to the rest of the groups. In only two of the six remaining groups did the leaders and other members prefer the same brand, and then only at percentage levels expected by chance.

To further substantiate the hypothesis that group leaders are a key element in understanding how groups influence the behavior of members, the data were analyzed in order to compare the leader's degree of brand loyalty[4] and the percentage of brand loyalty among the other members of the group. Table 7 summarizes the results of this analysis.

Once the leader's brand loyalty reached a certain degree of strength (5 consecutive times), then the probability was much greater that most of his group would also become brand loyal. Further increases, how-

---

[4] While brand loyalty has been operationally defined as three consecutive choices of the same brand, it is logically assumed in this discussion that a person who selected the same brand 16 times in a row has a much higher degree of brand loyalty than an individual who selects the same brand three consecutive times.

Table 18.6. COMPARISONS OF FREQUENCY OF CHOICE OF BEST LIKED BRANDS OF THE LEADER AND MEMBERS OF EACH GROUP

Group leader's best liked brand	Percent best liked brand chosen by leader (ranked from highest to lowest in percent of time chosen)	Entire group's best liked brand	Percent best liked brand chosen by group (leader excluded)
M	100%	M	50%
M	100	M	48
P	83	P	50
H	68	H	56
P	43	M	34
H	43	H	31
M	43	P	28
H	43	H	25
L	40	H	29
M	37	P	28

ever, in the leader's degree of brand loyalty had no measurable effect, since 100 percent brand loyalty was the highest that could be obtained.

CONCLUSION

The study led to the following tentative conclusions:

First, an analysis of variance test indicated that the informal groups had a definite influence on their members toward conformity behavior with respect to brands of bread preferred. At the same time, there was no significant preference shown for any one of the four brands used in the study. Interaction between the groups and brands was found not to be significant.

Second, it was hypothesized that the cohesiveness of a group would be an important determinant of the degree of brand loyalty exhibited by members. No statistical significance, however, was found between the level of cohesiveness and the degree of member brand loyalty. Only when cohesiveness and leadership were combined was any relationship with member brand loyalty uncovered. In more cohesive groups, the probability was much higher that the members would prefer the same brand as the group leader. Thus, cohesiveness appeared to have its most important function in providing an agreeable environment in which informal leaders could effectively operate.

Table 18.7. Comparison of the Degree of Brand Loyalty of the Group Leader with the Percentage of Brand Loyalty in the Group

Group leader's degree of brand loyalty (length of longest consecutive run of one brand)	Percent of group (excluding leader) becoming brand loyal (3 consecutive choices of one brand)	Number in group (n)
16	100%	2
15	100	5
12	75	5
9	100	3
6	100	3
5	100	5
3	50	5
3	25	5
2	45	5
2	55	4
		42

Finally, leaders were found to influence fellow group members in two ways. First, the higher the degree of brand loyalty exhibited by a group leader, the more likely were the other members to prefer the same brand. Second, the greater the degree of leader brand loyalty, the higher was the percentage of his group also becoming brand loyal. In other words, the extent and degree of brand loyalty within a group was closely related to the behavior of the informal leader.

Like most exploratory studies of this nature, this experiment had certain inherent limitations—the groups obtained may not have been the ones most relevant to the purchase of bread, the number of groups studied was small, and only one product was used. Similarly, the product itself (bread) was a limiting factor. Susceptibility to group influence probably varies across products with the more conspicuous or socially important products being more susceptible. Also, the influence of the leaders on member brand preferences might be much less in the "real world" where differences do exist among products. If these statements are true, then the product used in this study may have been one which maximized the difficulty of locating and measuring the interpersonal influences of group members. Since in this experiment, the influence of groups (and leaders) was substantiated on such a common and minor purchase as bread, then there is good reason for presuming similar influence on a broad spectrum of consumer behavior. One of its primary values of this type of interdisciplinary study lies is the fact that the results usually lead to interesting and provocative implications, as well as providing new avenues and directions for research. By altering the selection process of the informal groups, and by testing products other than bread, a more thorough understanding of social influence on consumer behavior should be possible.

RETROSPECTIVE COMMENT

In the past ten years since publication of this article, considerable progress has been made in the area of consumer behavior research, both from a theoretical and methodological perspective. After rereading the article, I was struck by the simplistic analytical approach that I used then as compared to the much more sophisticated techniques employed today. Despite this obvious shortcoming, plus several others that I will mention later, the overall research approach and theoretical framework are still quite sound. In this commentary, I will focus briefly on two areas. First, I will review the study conducted ten years ago, offer various criticisms, and suggest several changes that would be appropriate if one was planning to engage in this type of research today. Second, I will comment on the field of reference group theory and its application to consumer behavior.

The original study reported in *JMR* was derived from a dissertation supervised by W. T. Tucker at The University of Texas. Dr. Tucker was a believer in the need for a logical and sound theoretical basis to any type of behavior research. His insistence on this framework is in large measure the reason why this article might be considered a "classic". I, as well as many other behaviorally oriented researchers, owe a great debt to Dr. Tucker.

Early consumer research had a history of studying the impact or relationship of a particular independent variable chosen from the social science literature and a dependent variable chosen from consumer market behavior. An example would be the relationship between "colors" used in package design and brand choice behavior. While ultimately my study fell into this same category, its original thrust was to move beyond this approach. We have known for a long time that man is a social animal needing and enjoying interpersonal relations with other human beings. As a result, man's behavior could be influenced by these social interactions. Little attention, however, had been directed toward this concept by consumer researchers. It seemed to me at the time that an individual's behavior in the market place was just as likely to be influenced by his social interactions as any other type of behavior. In order to come up with a manageable dissertation, I finally narrowed the scope of the study to the following:

1. to determine in a field experiment if one type of social interaction—informal membership groups—could influence consumer brand preferences

2. to analyze and describe in detail the process of this influence.

As I have already mentioned, a rather large body of knowledge from the behavioral sciences already existed on this phenomenon. The main task here was to determine if and how it was applicable to consumer behavior. In turn, the field methodology employed was rather innovative at the time and particularly appropriate given the nature of the problem and objectives of the research. There are, however, several major areas within the research conducted that need to be reviewed and criticized. Many of these criticisms are adapted from a very excel-lent replication of this study which was conducted by Jeffrey Ford and Ellwood Ellis in 1972 while graduate students at the Ohio State University.[5]

The first major problem associated with this study is that the method utilized in establishing the ten basic social groups leaves some doubt as to whether they were, in fact, groups. The sociometric test (Moreno) employed here asked each of ten women to name four or five other women whom she liked to go shopping with. In other words, the Moreno test, as used here, measures only the feelings of the nominator toward the nominated and not the reverse. It was possible, therefore, to obtain "groups" which had little or no social interaction among most of the members except what occurred between the nominator and each of the other women. The term "groups" can mean many different things and if I were redoing this research I would pay much more attention to the selection of groups or the nomination of referent others.

A major variable in my study was determining who was the leader in each group and ascertaining what influence that individual had on the brand choices of the other group members. While I found a statistically significant relationship between the brand choice behavior of the leaders and members of the group, insufficient attention was directed toward determining whether group members were influenced by the leader's power and influence or whether the leader's behavior was a reflection of group norms. It is clear, therefore, that to determine the appropriate cause and effect relationship in this type of situation, additional data must be collected and analyzed.

In this particular study I am confident that the flow of communication, and influence, was from the leader toward the other members of the group. That this is true is both a strength and weakness of the

---

[5] Jeffrey D. Ford and Ellwood Ellis, "Another Look at the Effects of Group Influence on Consumer Brand Preferences," Unpublished Term Project, Ohio State University, 1972.

study. As I mentioned earlier, the groups were formed by having each of ten women nominate five other friends or relatives to participate in the study. As a result, these nominators were central to any communications network within the group. Since in most of the groups all members did not know and interact with all other members, the primary source of influence had to be the group leader rather than the reverse. Unfortunately, this group selection process could result in a false relationship between the brand choice behavior of group leaders and members and a danger of overgeneralizing the implications. There are many different ways of defining group and opinion leadership and a considerable body of literature has been developed since publication of this study which would lead one towards more appropriate operational definitions of leadership than was used in my study.

Another major problem area in my earlier study relates to the statistical analysis employed. In their replication in 1972, Ford and Ellis take vigorous exception to my use of the two-way analysis of variance. Basically, they argue that analysis of variance should not have been used to test for group influence but only for brand differences. Whether or not this conclusion is appropriate is subject to debate. The key point, however, is that given our advances in the quantitative analysis of data, there would be other more appropriate methods of analyzing the data. A variety of statistical techniques should be employed rather than emphasizing only one technique. For example, I did not attempt to use regression analysis on testing my hypothesis. Had I done so, at least one hypothesis (#2), which dealt with the relationship between group cohesiveness and brand loyalty, would have been found significant in two out of three test instances. These data, therefore, would have tended to offer further support for a later study conducted by Witt (1969) which dealt with this very problem.[6] In any case, I think the implication is clear; much more care must be given to choosing appropriate statistical techniques and utilizing them in a thorough manner.

Several other general problems should be noted. Only one product—bread—was used. While use of this product can be questioned in terms of its overall importance in the consumer's purchasing process, this problem is not a major one, although future research should extend into other product areas. Another problem area relates to the definition and subsequent treatment of brand loyalty. Some rather arbitrary definitions of brand loyalty were developed. While I think these definitions were reasonable and certainly operational, it would be foolish to assume that other definitions might not be better.

After ten years one is able to make a more objective view of earlier

6 Robert Witt, "Informal Social Group Influence on Consumer Brand Choice," *Journal of Marketing Research*, VI, No. 4 (November 1969), pp. 473–476.

research work, particularly a dissertation. As I have already indicated this research was, by no means, perfect or all conclusive. What it did do, was to stimulate a number of other excellent researchers to enter this field, engage in research, and publish manuscripts which have certainly thrust our knowledge about consumer behavior further ahead. If I were to redo this research, there are a number of things that I would do differently. However, I still feel pleased that in many respects this research was a pioneering effort in a fascinating area of consumer behavior.

The next area that I wish to discuss refers to the current status of reference group theory in consumer research. The consumer behavior literature did not give much emphasis to reference group influence until about 1956 when the Bourne article was published.[7] Between 1966 and 1970, however, at least thirty articles appeared utilizing the concept in one form or another.[8] Interestingly enough since 1970 the number of reference group based articles in the social science field as well as consumer behavior has dwindled dramatically. Why? Did this merely reflect a shift in research interest or did it indicate a more fundamental difficulty with the theoretical nature of the concept itself and with the design of appropriate research methodologies.

A review of the literature does surface numerous criticisms of the reference group concept. First, the underlying thrust of most of these arguments is that there is no clear cut definition, operational or otherwise, of the reference group concept. As a result, any attempt to synthesize the results of various studies becomes quite complex. The second major area of criticism is that the research efforts are characterized by certain methodological weaknesses and also suffer from the fact that they are not organized around one explicate model of man. The most fundamental and negative methodological feature of the reference group literature has been the superficiality of the research efforts to date. As a result many researchers jumped on the reference group bandwagon because the concept was new and unique to consumer behavior and any results would lead to publication. What is discouraging is the apparent lack of interest in a more intensified research approach to the influence of reference groups on consumer behavior. Reference behavior is very complex and much more involved than small group behavior or opinion leadership. Much more attention in the future must be directed at building and testing broader theoretical models of

[7] Francis S. Bourne, *Group Influence in Marketing and Public Relations.* Ann Arbor, Michigan: Foundation for Research on Human Behavior, 1956.

[8] See James E. Stafford and A. Benton Cocanougher, "Reference Group Theory", *Project on Synthesis of Knowledge of Consumer Behavior*, RANN Program, National Science Foundation, University of Illinois, to be published in 1976.

behavior based on empirical research much like those developed by Howard and Sheth, etc.

In my opinion reference group theory (1) has not received adequate attention from consumer researchers and theorists and (2) should be of more value in the formulation of models of consumer behavior. Unfortunately, no one in the consumer behavior field has tried to crystallize common denominators out of the vast body of literature available. A very fruitful area of exploration, therefore, would be to develop a model or models employing reference group theory as a linking system. For example, role theory focuses upon the social structure, self theory concentrates upon the individual, and the reference other orientation emphasizes a social-psychological linkage between the socio-cultural system and the individual. An integration of these concepts within a common framework would be an indispensable endeavor for a better understanding of consumer behavior.

Additional systematical research into several other areas would improve our understanding of reference group influence on consumer behavior. Our knowledge of this influence could be enlarged, for example, through (1) conducting more intensive and theoretically oriented studies exploring the relationships among socio-cultural systems, reference sets, normative influence and product purchase decision, (2) utilizing longitudinal research designs which focus on the varying influences of reference others across time and products, (3) the generation and testing of formal models of reference groups and their normative influence, (4) investigating the conditions under which consumers are influenced by reference others despite the absence of identification mechanism and (5) setting-up concentrated studies of the socialization process. In addition, more descriptive and cross-cultural studies would be useful. Reference relationships should not be studied in isolation. More information is needed detailing the functions, membership and non-membership statuses, and relative importance of the totality of reference others within different reference groups. This would provide needed insights into the processes whereby consumers become influenced by specific reference others at given points in time. In addition, consumer awareness must be approached in a more intensified manner. We need to know more about the extent to which the consumer is influenced by others of which he is not aware. Similarly, little attention has been directed at determining the conditions under which a consumer moves away from the influence of his reference others.

The reference group concept still offers a great deal of theoretical insight to the consumer behavior researcher. Despite the difficulties involved in conducting research in this area it is hoped that both model builders and empirical data collectors will re-evaluate the role of reference others in influencing consumer behavior.—*James E. Stafford,* Professor of Marketing and Advertising, University of Houston

REFERENCES

BONNEY, W. C. and C. E. George. *Measurement of Affective Adaptation Residuals,* Technical Report 5 (Office of Naval Research, Agricultural and Mechanical College of Texas), 1961.

BROWN, GEORGE. "Brand Loyalty—Fact or Fiction?" *Advertising Age,* 23 (June 9, 1952), 53–5.

CUNNINGHAM, ROSS. "Brand Loyalty—What, Where, How Much?" *Harvard Business Review,* 34 (January–February 1956), 116–28.

FRANK, RONALD E. "Brand Choice as a Probability Process," *Journal of Business,* 35 (January 1962), 43–56.

HARVEY, FRANK and Benjamin Lipstein. "The Dynamics of Brand Loyalty: A Markovian Process," *Operations Research,* 10 (January–February 1962), 19–40.

HOMANS, GEORGE. *Social Behavior: Its Elementary Forms,* New York: Harcourt, Brace and World, Inc., 1961, 118–9.

KATZ, ELIHU and P. F. Lazarsfeld, *Personal Influence,* Glencoe, Ill.: The Free Press of Glencoe, 1955.

KUEHN, A. A. "Consumer Brand Choice—A Learning Process?" in *Quantitative Techniques in Marketing Analysis,* R. E. Frank, A. A. Kuehn, and W. F. Massy, eds., Homewood, Ill.: Richard D. Irwin, Inc., 1962, 390–403.

SHAW, S. J. "Behavioral Science Offers Fresh Insights on New Product Acceptance," *Journal of Marketing,* 29 (January 1965), 9.

TUCKER, W. T. "The Development of Brand Loyalty," *Journal of Marketing Research,* 1 (August 1964), 32–5.

19. Dimensions of Marital Roles in Consumer Decision-Making

Harry L. Davis

INTRODUCTION

The literature on family role structure is characterized by diverse theories about the structure of marital roles in decision making. At one extreme are those researchers who assume unidimensionality, and whose studies describe families as "matriarchal," "patriarchal," and "companionship," e.g., Burgess and Locke, or who use "global influence questions," e.g., Heer and "overall power scores," e.g., Blood and Wolfe. Other sociologists recognize at least two power hierarchies within the family—e.g., the distinction between "instrumental" and "expressive" roles or Farber's dichotomy between "policy" and "routine household" decisions. Herbst suggests four bases for role differentiation: (1) household duties; (2) child control and care; (3) social activities; and (4) economic activities. At the other extreme is the even more highly differentiated role structure implicit in the marketing literature. For example, Sharp and Mott report that husbands exert more influence than wives in the purchase of automobiles, less influence than wives in deciding how much to spend on food, and equal influence in deciding about vacations and housing. Other studies, suggest a further factoring of decisions for single purchases into numerous components.

These alternative views of family role structure undoubtedly reflect the different orientations of sociological and marketing research. Measurement of family authority is usually a first step in many sociological studies, and it is used as the independent or dependent variable in subsequent analyses. This may explain why the dimensionality of roles itself has been the subject of such little *empirical* research. While the sociological literature is strong on theory and somewhat weak on data, the literature in marketing is just the reverse. Measurement of purchase influence for specific products is often the only objective of such research.

Both of these approaches leave important questions unanswered.

Reprinted by permission of the author and publisher from the Journal of Marketing Research, *published by the American Marketing Association, Vol. 7 (May 1970), pp. 168–177.*

Sociologists, for example, often establish typologies on an *a priori* basis and then "force" data into these classifications. Whether Herbst's economic activities do, in fact, represent a unidimensional area of family structure has not been subject to adequate empirical testing. The absence of any explicit theory in the marketing literature, on the other hand, seriously limits generalizations. The roles of husband, wife, or children are discussed only on a product-by-product basis. Researchers have not questioned whether decision making influence within the family could be described in terms of a fewer number of dimensions that would subsume several products or several steps in the decision process for a single product. The answer to this question has implications for market research in suggesting what kinds of questions need to be asked, to whom, and with what degree of specificity.

Contributing to these alternative conceptualizations is the use of widely differing sources of information about purchase influence. A sampling of research shows that data have been collected from wives only, husbands only, a matched group of husbands and wives, husbands and wives within the same family, and children.

The extent to which wives can accurately report purchase influence is subject to considerable confusion in the literature. Some researchers stress the similarity between husbands' and wives' responses. Wolgast found a high level of agreement in husbands' and wives' reports about relative influence in four economic decisions. She concludes that "husbands and wives reflect one another's judgments about perfectly." Blood and Wolfe justify the use of wives as sole respondent by the fact that "other studies show that husbands and wives usually agree sufficiently to make it possible to rely on one partner's responses." Heer also concludes that the agreement between husband and wife is "substantial though not unanimous." Others emphasize the inconvenience and cost associated with interviewing more than one respondent per family. Scanzoni, for example, reasons that the decision to obtain data from both spouses often necessitates a smaller sample size, which, in turn, will lower the generalizability of results.

At the same time, the literature also contains studies that point to the considerable disagreement between husband and wife in their reporting of purchase influence. Ferber obtained independent assessments of relative influence in eight consumer decisions from the adult members of 237 families. Finding little correspondence between husbands' and wives' answers (R^2 ranging from .02 to .29) he concluded that "the reliability of ratings of relative influence of different family members, or different sexes, on purchases obtained by direct questioning of one member of the family is highly limited." Several other studies have found that the percentage of couples whose responses agree averages only slightly more than 50%. And more recently, Morgan has observed that

Table 19.1. MARITAL ROLES IN SELECTED AUTOMOBILE AND FURNITURE PURCHASE
DECISIONS AS PERCEIVED BY HUSBANDS ($N = 97$)

	Patterns of influence (%)		
Who decided:	Husband has more influence than wife	Husband and wife have equal influence	Wife has more influence than husband
When to buy the automobile?	68	29	3
Where to buy the automobile?	62	35	3
How much to spend for the automobile?	62	37	1
What make of automobile to buy?	60	31	8
What model of automobile to buy?	41	50	9
What color of automobile to buy?	25	50	25
How much to spend for furniture?	22	47	31
When to buy furniture?	16	45	39
Where to buy the furniture?	7	53	40
What furniture to buy?	3	33	64
What style of furniture to buy?	2	26	72
What color and fabric to select?	2	16	82

couples are likely to agree more about each other's personality than they
do in reporting who decided about specific purchase decisions.

There is clearly a need to resolve the apparent confusion about the
sufficiency of wives' responses. An answer is important for research on
family decision making since role concensus itself may be related to the
balance of power between husband and wife. An answer is equally important to market researchers who must decide whether to interview
both spouses or only the wife.

This article is a response to these difficult problems surrounding the
description and measurement of family role structure. Specifically, this
article will consider these questions:

1. What are the dimensions of husband-wife roles in two consumer purchase decisions?

2. To what extent do husbands and wives agree in their perception
of roles?

METHOD

The data reported are drawn from a questionnaire administered to 100
families living in four Chicago suburbs. A small convenience sample
was obtained by contacting families through three churches (two Protestant and one Catholic) and a grade school P.T.A. Couples were so-

licited by means of a letter asking their cooperation in a research project on "family living" and "decision making." Both husband and wife were requested to come to the church or school at the same time in order to participate. Each spouse was directed to a separate room in order to fill out the questionnaire, making collaboration impossible.

Couples were asked a series of questions about the relative influence of husband and wife in two durable goods purchases—an automobile and living room furniture. Several interrelated decisions were included for each product. For the last automobile purchased, husband and wife were asked to report who decided: (1) when to purchase; (2) how much money to spend; (3) make; (4) model; (5) color; and (6) where to purchase. Similar decisions were investigated for the furniture purchase— who usually decides: (1) what furniture to purchase; (2) how much to spend; (3) where to purchase; (4) when to purchase; (5) style; and (6) color and fabric. The questions were rated on a 5-point scale (husband decided = 1; husband more influence than wife = 2; equal influence = 3; wife more influence than husband = 4; wife decided = 5). Since these five categories refer only to the roles of husband and wife, the response to any given question represents a respondent's perception of *relative* influence in the decision.

The selection of these two products and the techniques used to measure marital roles can be justified because both purchases represent important family decisions. Also, they usually involve substantial financial outlay, extended period of ownership, social importance, and joint use by several family members. In terms of other consumer research, both would undoubtedly be classified as "policy" or "major economic" decisions. Moreover, it is meaningful to speak of *marital* roles in reference to both decisions. Other studies have found that husbands and wives are the major participants in these purchases. This finding also supports the use of a simple rating scale limited to a measure of husband-wife influence.

The data presented in this paper differ in several ways from other studies. Whereas existing research has investigated marital roles across several economic decisions or for a single product purchase, these data can be analyzed both across and within product purchase decisions because of the use of the same question for each of the two products purchases and the same measure of influence for all 12 decisions. There are also responses to the same questions from both husband and wife, permitting comparison of husbands' responses as a group with wives', as well as between husband and wife within the same family. The extent of agreement can also be calculated for each of 12 decisions to determine whether the nature of the decision significantly affects the level of consensus.

Reliance on this small sample seems warranted in light of the exploratory nature of this study. No attempt is made to generalize the particular distribution of relative influence for any decision to all families. The interest is to consider the relationship between husbands' and wives' responses and between decisions within the same families. At the same time, the small sample size and the use of volunteer subjects urge caution in generalizing the findings.

FINDINGS

RELATIVE INFLUENCE IN PURCHASE DECISIONS

Tables 1 and 2 show the distribution of husbands' and wives' responses to questions about relative influence in 12 automobile and furniture purchase decisions.[1] The individual questions are listed in order of increasing wife influence based on the average score for each decision. Data from husbands are reported in Table 1; the wives' responses are shown in Table 2.

The tables reveal considerable variability in husband-wife roles in these decisions, and it would be misleading to generalize about husband

Table 19.2. MARITAL ROLES IN SELECTED AUTOMOBILE AND FURNITURE PURCHASE DECISIONS AS PERCEIVED BY WIVES ($N = 97$)

	Patterns of influence (%)		
Who decided:	*Husband has more influence than wife*	*Husband and wife have equal influence*	*Wife has more influence than husband*
When to buy the automobile?	68	30	2
Where to buy the automobile?	59	39	2
How much to spend for the automobile?	62	34	4
What make of automobile to buy?	50	50	—
What model of automobile to buy?	47	52	1
What color of automobile to buy?	25	63	12
How much to spend for furniture?	17	63	20
When to buy the furniture?	18	52	30
Where to buy the furniture?	6	61	33
What furniture to buy?	4	52	44
What style of furniture to buy?	2	45	53
What color and fabric to select?	2	24	74

[1] To simplify presentation, the original 5-point scale was collapsed by combining the categories "husband decided" with "husband more than wife," and "wife decided" with "wife more than husband." The distribution of responses between the two "extreme" response categories (1 and 2; 4 and 5) provides no additional insights for the purpose of the first analysis.

and wife roles in any absolute sense. For example, conclusions about which spouse makes "the furniture purchase decision" would necessarily depend on which particular decision was being made. Marked differences in the wife's influence can be seen by comparing decisions about how much to spend and when to buy with those concerning style, color and fabric. The same thing can be seen for the automobile purchase decisions. The percentage of husband-dominant families decreases from 60% in the decision about what make of automobile to buy to 25% in the decision about what color to select.

Also, one cannot generalize about roles in a particular decision without reference to the product being purchased. For example, compare the percentage of husband-dominant families in two decisions—where to buy the automobile and where to buy furniture. The former is characterized by a large proportion of husband-dominant families while in the latter, less than 10% of the families are husband-dominant. The same is true when comparing the decision about how much to spend for the automobile and furniture. The modal response is husband-dominant for automobiles but joint for furniture.

Finally, note the substantial variability in roles for individual decisions. Only three decisions have more than 65% of the families in any one of the three influence types. For the other decisions there is a considerable spread over two (and in some cases, three) categories. Reliance on the modal response in such cases to classify *decisions* as either husband-dominant, joint, or wife-dominant would actually conceal the considerable amount of variability in roles that exists between families.

PATTERNS OF RELATIVE INFLUENCE

The decision in the previous section has been limited to the distribution of relative influence for each decision. In this section consider the distribution of relative influence across all six automobile and furniture decisions simultaneously. The emphasis here is upon the *pattern* of husband-wife influence across several decisions. Under the assumption of unidimensionality, all families should fall into one of three different patterns—husband-dominant, wife-dominant or joint—across all decisions. Alternatively, a pattern might reflect a division of labor between husband and wife (e.g., some decisions shared while others the responsibility of one spouse) common to a large number of families.[2] The number of patterns and their frequency will tell more about the variability

---

[2] The analysis of these patterns across three or more decisions does not lend itself to the usual factor analytic or clustering techniques which begin with a matrix of intercorrelations between pairs of variables. Such techniques could conceal the presence of meaningful regularity in relative influence across decisions.

Table 19.3. Association (Gamma) Between Relative Influence In Selected Automobile and Furniture Purchase Decisions—Husbands' Responses (N = 97)

Decisions	Automobile decisions						Furniture decisions					
	1	2	3	4	5	6	7	8	9	10	11	12
Automobile decisions:												
1. When to buy?												
2. Where to buy?	.44											
3. How much to spend?	.69	.44										
4. What make to buy?	.36	.74	.49									
5. What model to buy?	.21	.63	.57	.74								
6. What color to buy?	.24	.52	.37	.54	.59							
Furniture decisions:												
7. How much to spend?	.15	−.34	−.05	−.38	−.34	−.14						
8. When to buy?	.30	−.12	.25	−.14	−.09	−.06	.53					
9. Where to buy?	−.06	−.17	−.10	−.20	−.06	.13	.62	.59				
10. What to buy?	.17	−.14	−.10	−.17	−.11	.01	.61	.47	.64			
11. What style to buy?	.01	−.17	−.23	−.23	−.27	−.01	.48	.20	.59	.80		
12. What color and fabric to select?	.01	.09	.05	−.09	−.04	.33	.33	.23	.54	.71	.81	

in marital roles across decisions and may suggest a way of classifying families into various influence or decision "types."

For the purpose of this analysis, the 5-point scale of relative influence was again collapsed into 3 points by combining "husband decided" with "husband more than wife" (scale positions 1 and 2) and "wife decided" with "wife more than husband" (scale positions 4 and 5). In addition, automobile and furniture decisions were considered separately, so that each pattern included only 6 decisions. Both of these actions should make any regularities in the data more apparent.

Even with these modifications, the data show considerable variability in the number of unique patterns. Husbands' and wives' responses to the 6 automobile decisions yielded 52 and 38 patterns respectively. Similar results were found for furniture decisions—50 patterns (husbands' responses) and 46 patterns (wives' responses). Since the total number of respondents was 97 for the automobile purchase and 98 for the furniture purchase, a different pattern of relative influence is found for about every two respondents.

A few patterns do account for considerably more than two respondents each. Three patterns account for 32% of all families in the case of the automobile purchase (husbands' responses). Two of these—all joint ($N = 6$) and all husband-dominant ($N = 13$)—indicate unidimensionality. The other pattern ($N = 12$) is husband-dominant with the exception of one joint decision ("What color of automobile to buy"). These same three patterns account for 45% of all families when the wives' responses are analyzed. The furniture purchase reveals somewhat more variability on this same criterion although four patterns continue to account for a large percentage of all families—31% (husband's responses) and 41% (wives' responses). The most frequent pattern as reported by both husbands and wives is wife dominance for all six decisions ($N = 14$ and $N = 12$ respectively). Six other unique patterns (with frequencies of five or more) occur only once.

This analysis provides little basis for developing family "types" based upon patterns of relative influence since one would have to overlook more than 50% of the sample. The variability described in the previous section when roles were examined by decision across families is also apparent when families are studied across decisions.

DIMENSIONS OF DECISION ROLES

The discussion to this point has emphasized the variability of marital roles in two consumer purchases. In this section consider the interrelationship of roles between these decisions and then group decisions together on the basis of their similarities. The objective is to identify and delineate "dimensions" of decision roles.

Table 19.4. ASSOCIATION (GAMMA) BETWEEN RELATIVE INFLUENCE IN SELECTED AUTOMOBILE AND FURNITURE PURCHASE DECISIONS—WIVES' RESPONSES (N = 97)

Decisions	Automobile decisions						Furniture decisions					
	1	2	3	4	5	6	7	8	9	10	11	12
Automobile decisions:												
1. When to buy?												
2. Where to buy?	.78											
3. How much to spend?	.79	.69										
4. What make to buy?	.73	.78	.51									
5. What model to buy?	.70	.71	.55	.92								
6. What color to buy?	.52	.65	.42	.72	.66							
Furniture decisions:												
7. How much to spend?	.13	−.01	.14	.10	.08	.13						
8. When to buy?	.02	−.11	.26	−.18	.01	−.10	.77					
9. Where to buy?	.12	−.12	−.04	−.03	.01	.05	.67	.56				
10. What to buy?	.01	−.14	−.07	−.07	.03	−.09	.75	.60	.77			
11. What style to buy?	.00	−.10	−.17	−.14	−.09	−.10	.46	.26	.65	.75		
12. What color and fabric to select?	.03	−.07	.01	.05	.08	.04	.55	.40	.67	.71	.85	

Table 3 (husbands' responses) and 4 (wives' responses) show the association between roles in 12 automobile and furniture purchase decisions. Gamma coefficients were computed from 5 x 5 contingency tables showing the distribution of relative influence for every pair of decisions.

Tables 3 and 4 reveal the same patterns for husbands and wives. The triangle in the upper left-hand corner of the two matrices shows the association between relative influence in six automobile purchase decisions. Relative influence in all of these decisions is positively associated. Moreover, the degree of association is generally high. Data from husbands yield gammas ranging from .21 to .74. The degree of association reported by wives is even stronger, ranging from .42 to .92. The same pattern characterizes the association between relative influence in furniture purchase decisions (see the triangle in the lower right-hand corner of each matrix). Although there is some variability in the size of these gammas, one would conclude that decision roles within these product purchases are strongly and positively related.

The relationship between relative influence in automobile and furniture decisions can be seen in the square or lower left-hand portion of the matrices in Tables 3 and 4. In contrast to the association among decision roles *within* each of the two product categories, there is little relationship *across* product categories. The majority of signs are negative, indicating an inverse relationship between influence in automobile purchase decisions and influence in the purchase of furniture. Moreover, the magnitude of gammas is low. The degree of association ranges from .00 to .26 for wives and from .01 to −.38 for husbands, showing that purchase influence for automobiles is not related to purchase influence for furniture.

In an effort to more adequately delineate dimensions of decision roles, both matrices were analyzed using a clustering technique developed by McQuitty. This technique groups decisions into clusters so that the associations between pairs of decisions within a given cluster are high, while the associations between decisions in different clusters are low. First the two decisions in the matrix having the highest association are combined, and then the association between this "new" two-decision cluster and each of the remaining decisions is determined.[3] The matrix is thus reduced by one row and one column. The same procedure is applied as many times as there are columns in the original matrix, each

---

[3] An example illustrating this procedure may be useful. In Table 4 decisions about make and model of automobile are the most highly associated (.92). The association between this cluster and the remaining ten decisions is in each case determined by the pair with the lowest association. For example, the association between make of automobile and when to buy is .73; the association between model of automobile and when to buy is .70. To satisfy the classification assumption as specified by McQuitty— i.e., the three automobile decisions about make, model and when to buy must have as many common characteristics as the pair with the fewest—.70 is selected.

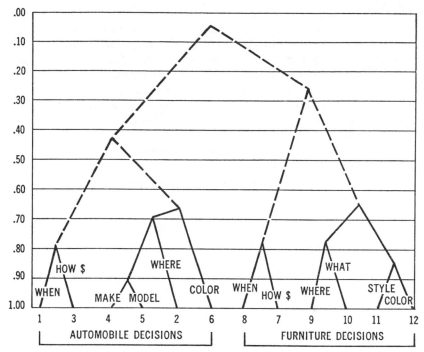

Figure 19.1. A CLASSIFICATION OF ROLES IN SELECTED AUTOMOBILE AND FURNITURE PURCHASE DECISIONS (WIVES' RESPONSES) (*N*=97)

time beginning with the two decisions (or two clusters) having the highest association. The association between the final two clusters is by definition the lowest gamma in the original matrix.

The results of this analysis can be seen in Figures 1 and 2, which give a graphic representation of how various decisions join together to form clusters. In addition, the height at which decisions or clusters merge represents the degree of association between them. Decisions were ordered along the x-axis to avoid intersecting lines as they were brought together.

Looking first at the wives' responses (Figure 1), four clusters of decisions are evident,[4] two of which represent product-related decisions in

[4] The stopping criteria for forming clusters of decisions is based upon the degree of association between decisions and/or clusters. The interrelationship of decisions through the formation of four clusters is high—greater than .60 for wives and .50 for husbands. Beyond this point, however, the association is markedly lower. In Figure 2, for example, the relationship between the two clusters of automobile decisions is only .21; the association between the two clusters of furniture decisions is also low—.20. It seems reasonable, therefore, to describe roles in these twelve purchase decisions in terms of four major dimensions.

the purchase of automobiles and furniture. One cluster includes four automobile decisions—what make and model of automobile to buy, where to buy it, and what color to select. Similar subdecisions also cluster together for the furniture purchase—what style and what color and fabric to select, what furniture to buy, and where to buy it. Decisions about the timing and expense of each purchase form the remaining two clusters. With one exception, the same dimensions of decision roles are present in the analysis of husbands' responses (Figure 2).[5]

Thus, two bases for role differentiation can be seen in these two product purchases—one basis being the product itself. Decision roles in the purchase of automobiles are not related to decision roles in the purchase of furniture. Within each of these product categories, roles are

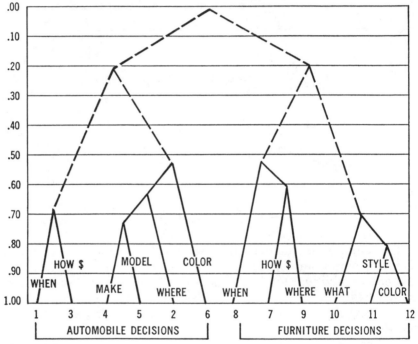

Figure 19.2. A CLASSIFICATION OF ROLES IN SELECTED AUTOMOBILE AND FURNITURE PURCHASE DECISIONS (HUSBANDS' RESPONSES) ($N=97$)

[5] The one exception is seen in the furniture decision clusters. Three decisions— what furniture to buy, what style and what color to select—form one cluster. The remaining three decisions (i.e., when to buy furniture, how much to spend and where to buy) group together into another. In contrast to the wives' perception of similarity between what furniture to buy and where to buy it, husbands perceive roles in deciding where to buy furniture as being more similar to the decision of how much to spend.

further differentiated by the nature of the decision. Roles in "product-selection" decisions (e.g., model, make, color) differ from roles in "allocation or "scheduling" decisions (e.g., how much to spend and when to buy).

ROLE CONSENSUS

The discussion to this point has considered the responses to questions about purchase influence separately for husbands and for wives. In this section turn to the question of whether or not husbands and wives considered as groups and as individual families agree in their perception of roles.

Table 5 is a summary of Tables 1 and 2 and shows the average relative influence in the 12 purchase decisions as reported by husbands and and wives. As before, the individual decisions are listed in order of increasing wife influence.

This table reveals a high level of agreement in husband-wife perception when viewed in these aggregate terms. Note first that the rank ordering of decisions in terms of increasing wife influence is identical for husbands and wives. Moreover, the differences between husbands' and wives' responses are not statistically significant on the basis of a multivariate test which considers all 12 decisions simultaneously ($F = .9041$; $df = 12, 187$; $p < .54$). It is not likely that the conclusions reached by advertisers would differ at all depending on whether they had examined the husbands' responses or the wives'.

Two noteworthy patterns can be detected in these data. First, the direction of differences between the mean response of husbands and wives is consistent across all 12 decisions. Either one or both spouses seem to be modest in the assessment of their own influence. That is, husbands attribute more influence to their wives than wives attribute to themselves, and/or vice-versa. Secondly, the largest disagreements between husbands and wives occur for decisions that involve what might be termed "aesthetic" considerations (e.g., what model and color of automobile to buy, what furniture, what style and what color of furniture to buy). One reason may be, for example, that a husband's assessment of his wife's importance in decisions requiring aesthetic skills tends to be biased upward as a result of cultural expectations about the "appropriate" role for women. Alternatively, a wife might bias downward her husband's participation in such decisions for the same reason.

The data contained in Table 5, of course, do not provide any evidence of the extent to which husbands and wives *within the same family* agree in their role perception. In an extreme case, husbands and wives could exhibit perfect agreement as groups but perfect disagreement on an

Table 19.5. AVERAGE RELATIVE INFLUENCE IN SELECTED AUTOMOBILE AND FURNI-
TURE PURCHASE DECISIONS AS PERCEIVED BY HUSBANDS AND WIVES

	Mean response from:		
Who decided:	Husbands (*N* = 97)	Wives (*N* = 97)	*Difference in means*
When to buy the automobile?	1.95	1.83	+.12
Where to buy the automobile?	1.97	1.95	+.02
How much to spend for the automobile?	2.05	1.98	+.07
What make of automobile to buy?	2.13	2.11	+.02
What model of automobile to buy?	2.41	2.17	+.24
What color of automobile to buy?	2.95	2.73	+.22
How much to spend for furniture?	3.17	3.04	+.13
When to buy the furniture?	3.27	3.18	+.09
Where to buy the furniture?	3.45	3.35	+.10
What furniture to buy?	3.80	3.55	+.25
What style of furniture to buy?	3.91	3.68	+.23
What color and fabric to select?	4.17	3.92	+.25

intrafamily comparison.[6] What can be said about the extent of role consensus within families? Is there the same high level of agreement that was characteristic of the aggregate comparisons?

Table 6 shows the extent of agreement between husbands and wives in the 6 automobile and 6 furniture decisions. The determination of whether or not a couple agrees was based upon a comparison of a 3-point (as opposed to the 5-point) scale. Disagreements, therefore, indicate a significant difference in perception. At the extreme, a difference of two scale points means that one spouse perceived a decision as husband-dominant while the other perceived it as wife-dominant. A disagreement between whether a decision was husband-dominant or joint (and wife-dominant or joint) is represented by a difference of one scale point.

The percentage of couples who agree about their roles in decision making averages 63% for the 6 automobile purchase decisions and 61% for the 6 furniture purchase decisions. The range of agreement is somewhat greater for the furniture decisions. Although these percentages are higher than the 33% expected by chance, these results raise considerable doubt about the validity of assuming that wives' responses are sufficient. In a large number of cases—ranging from 25% to 52% of the families—

---

[6] The distinction between these two definitions of agreement is sometimes confused in the literature. For example, Hill bases a decision to utilize the wife as respondent on Wolgast's study of economic decision making. She found, according to Hill, "the wife equally well informed, and more accurate in predicting plans than the husband" [9, p. 73]. This is hardly accurate, however, since Wolgast's findings were based upon a comparison of husbands as group with wives as a group—who, incidentally, were rarely from the same family.

one would obtain a *different* assessment of relative influence by asking the husband. To rely only on wives' responses would be both incomplete and possibly misleading. Hence, the similarity between husbands' and wives' responses when viewed in aggregate terms is clearly not present on a within-family comparison.

What can be said about the nature of the disagreements? Perhaps role consensus varies in some predictable ways by families, decisions, or relative influence. It is also possible that the disagreements are more or less random, reflecting an inherent ambiguity in questions about purchase influence.

The nature of the distribution of disagreements for each decision provides some evidence for this latter explanation. Notice that the great majority of disagreements are only one scale point. Moreover, the shape of the distributions tends to be symmetrical. Only in the case of three or four furniture purchase decisions is there any tendency for the disagreeing couples to over-represent those in which husbands attribute *more* influence to the wife than the wife attributes to herself. If there were a consistent bias in the way couples responded to these questions, it is likely that these distributions would have been more highly skewed.

Another possible explanation for disagreement is the presence of real conflict surrounding the decision. If a husband and wife disagreed about what make of car to buy and had reached a compromise, an assessment of "who decided" might be difficult since it would be subject to different interpretations. One might, therefore, anticipate a positive relationship between reported conflict and the extent of disagreement about who actually made the decision. The data do not conform to this expectation, however. While the six automobile decisions tend to be seen as relatively conflict-free, each furniture decision involves "some disagreement" in about 40% of the families on the average.[7] If different perceptions of roles really do arise from such conflicts, one should find lower consensus for furniture decisions than for automobile decisions. As seen in Table 6, this is not apparent. In fact, it is the similarity in the magnitude of role consensus across these decisions rather than any difference that is noteworthy.

A third possibility is that relative influence is itself related to the magnitude of role consensus. It might be, for example, that disagreeing couples share decisions more equally. Couples with highly specialized roles (i.e., husband-dominant or wife-dominant), on the other hand, might display high consensus given less ambiguity about "who decides."

---

[7] Using husbands' responses, the percentage of families who report disagreement in automobile decisions ranges from 3% to 13%. Disagreement is even less according to wives—from 2% to 8%. The percentage of families who report disagreement in furniture decisions ranges from 40% to 61% (husbands' responses) and from 25% to 51% (wives' responses).

In order to examine this possible relationship a comparison was made of average relative influence in each decision for three groups: (1) couples who agreed; (2) wives who disagreed with their husbands; and (3) husbands who disagreed with their wives. Differences in the mean values among these groups were not large. The only noteworthy pattern was the tendency for "disagreeing husbands" to attribute consistently more influence to wives than do their wives or the couples who agree. This finding suggests that the bias described earlier is due primarily to husbands rather than wives. It also suggests that relative influence has no relationship to the degree of consensus in the light of the husbands' consistent upward bias over both product categories.

Finally, is there any evidence that families tend to agree or disagree across several decisions? One simple test is merely to plot the number of disagreements (from 0 to 6) for each product. A bimodal distribution would be found if one group of families consistently agreed and another group consistently disagreed about their roles in these decisions. Regularity could also be represented by a relatively flat distribution in which couples formed a scale from high to low consensus. Rather than finding either of these two distributions, however, the data showed unimodal distributions for both automobile and furniture decisions with the mode in each case at two disagreements. Knowing that a couple disagreed about their roles in one decision does not increase the ability to predict whether they will agree or disagree about others.

The search for systematic differences in families, decisions, or relative influence as a basis for explaining the disagreement in spouses' perception of relative influence has produced largely negative results. It seems much more likely that disagreement reflects measurement error.

DISCUSSION

The multidimensional role structure evident in these two purchase decisions contrasts with the unidimensional or bidimensional authority structures posited in much of the existing sociological literature. Instrumental decisions, in Parsons' terminology, or economic decisions, as defined by Herbst of which the automobile and furniture decisions would seem to be a part, can be differentiated much further.[8] This finding also raises doubts about the common practice of summing over individual decisions in order to construct an "overall" power score for a family. There should be prior evidence that the decisions are, in fact, unidimensional. From a marketing point of view, the analysis suggests a *less* differ-

---

[8] This conclusion is consistent with several sociological studies that have found considerable role specialization within the family (Levinger [10]; Tharp [18]; and Wilkening and Bharadwaj [20]).

Table 19.6. EXTENT OF HUSBAND-WIFE AGREEMENT IN SELECTED AUTOMOBILE AND FURNITURE PURCHASE DECISIONS ($N = 97$)

Who decided:	Husband attributes less influence to wife than she attributes to herself		Husband and wife agree	Husband attributes more influence to wife than she attributes to herself	
	-2	-1		$+1$	$+2$
	%	%	%	%	%
When to buy the automobile?	2	14	66	16	2
How much to spend for the automobile?	1	22	63	12	2
What make of automobile to buy?	—	20	64	15	1
What model of automobile?	—	14	59	25	2
What color of automobile?	—	14	59	26	1
Where to buy the automobile?	—	18	68	13	1
What furniture to buy?	—	10	59	30	1
How much to spend for furniture?	1	18	57	21	3
Where to buy the furniture?	—	16	63	19	2
When to buy the furniture?	1	21	48	25	5
What style of furniture to buy?	—	10	62	28	—
What color and fabric to select?	—	9	75	16	—

entiated structure than that which is often implicit in the literature. It is possible to subsume several decisions under a more general category and hence begin to generalize about roles in consumer decisions. Of interest in future research is whether the same two clusters of product-related and allocation-related decisions are found for other product categories and whether these dimensions are sensitive to the demographic and social characteristics of families.

These results regarding role consensus have one direct implication for research. If the purpose of a study is merely to describe the relative influence of husbands and wives in various purchase decisions, then interview only one spouse. The conclusions reached by an advertiser in determining the appropriate audience for his message would not differ depending upon whether he had collected data from husbands or wives.

If, on the other hand, a study uses purchase influence as a basis for classifying families for the purpose of further investigation, then the extent of within-family agreement becomes critical. The responses of one spouse may consistently provide better predictions of other aspects of a family's consumption behavior. Moreover, independent reports from husband and wife provide a basis for estimating the validity of measures used in a study.

How can the level of role consensus be increased? The findings of this study suggest that the use of specific, as opposed to global, measures of purchase influence is not the answer. It would appear that disagreement reflects each spouse's differing interpretations about the meaning of influence rather than any systematic bias inherent in these questions, whether general or specific. Attempts to increase consensus about roles will require more attention to the dynamics of the decision process. Information about the nature and frequency of discussion prior to each decision, length of the planning period, importance of each decision, and details about search activities may permit construction of meaningful classifications. Even with improved methodological procedures, however, one should consider that each spouse may have different but *equally legitimate* perceptions of relative influence. If this is true, the now common search for one "objective reality" or for the spouse who is "right" is misguided.

REFERENCES

BLOOD, ROBERT O. and Donald M. Wolfe. *Husbands and Wives: The Dynamics of Married Living*, Glencoe, Illinois: The Free Press, 1960.

BURGESS, ERNEST W. and Harvey J. Locke. *The Family*, New York: American Book Company, 1960.

FARBER, BERNARD. "A Study of Dependence and Decision-Making in Marriage," unpublished Doctoral dissertation, University of Chicago, September, 1949.

FERBER, ROBERT. "On the Reliability of Purchase Influence Studies," *Journal of Marketing*, 19 (January 1955), 225–32.

HABERMAN, PAUL W. and Jack Elinson. "Family Income Reported in Surveys: Husbands Versus Wives," *Journal of Marketing Research*, 4 (May 1967), 191–4.

HEER, DAVID M. "Husband and Wife Perceptions of Family Power Structure," *Marriage and Family Living*, 36 (February 1962), 65–7.

———. "Dominance and the Working Wife," *Social Forces*, 36 (May 1958), 341–7.

HERBST, P. G. "The Measurement of Family Relationships," *Human Relations*, 5 (February 1952), 3–35.

HILL, REUBEN. "Patterns of Decision-Making and the Accumulation of Family Assets," in Nelson Foote, ed., *Household Decision-Making*, New York: New York University Press, 1961, 57–80.

LEVINGER, GEORGE. "Task and Social Behavior in Marriage," *Sociometry*, 27 (December 1964), 433–48.

Male vs. Female Influence on the Purchase of Selected Products as Revealed by an Exploratory Depth Interview Study with Husbands and Wives. New York: Fawcett Publications, 1958.

McCANN, GLEN C. "Consumer Decisions in the Rural Family in the South," paper presented at the annual meeting of the American Sociological Association, New York, August, 1960 (mimeographed).

McQUITTY, LOUIS L. "Hierarchical Syndrome Analysis," *Educational and Psychological Measurement*, 20 (Summer 1960), 293–304.

MORGAN, JAMES T. "Some Pilot Studies of Communication and Consensus in the Family," *Public Opinion Quarterly*, 32 (Spring 1968), 113–21.

PARSONS, TALCOTT and Robert F. Bales. *Family, Socialization, and Interaction Process*, Glencoe, Illinois: The Free Press, 1955.

SCANZONI, JOHN. "A Note on the Sufficiency of Wife Responses in Family Research," *Pacific Sociological Review*, 8 (Fall 1965), 109–15.

SHARP, HARRY and Paul Mott. "Consumer Decisions in the Metropolitan Family," *Journal of Marketing*, 21 (October 1956), 149–56.

THARP, ROLAND C. "Dimensions of Marriage Roles," *Marriage and Family Living*, 25 (November 1963), 389–404.

Time Magazine. "Family Decision-Making," Research Report 1428, 1967.

WILKENING, EUGENE A. and Lakschmi Bharadwaj. "Dimensions of Aspirations, Work Roles, and Decision-Making of Farm Husbands and Wives in Wisconsin," *Journal of Marriage and the Family*, 29 (November 1967), 703–11.

WOLGAST, ELIZABETH H. "Do Husbands or Wives Make the Purchasing Decisions?" *Journal of Marketing*, 23 (October 1958), 151–8.

20. The Significance of Social Stratification in Selling

Richard P. Coleman

Dating back to the late 1940's, advertisers and marketers have alternately flirted with and cooled on the notion that W. Lloyd Warner's social class concept[1] is an important analytic tool for their profession. The Warnerian idea that six social classes constitute the basic division of American Society has offered many attractions to marketing analysts when they have grown dissatisfied with simple income categories or census-type occupational categories and felt a need for more meaningful classifications, for categorizations of the citizenry which could prove more relevant to advertising and marketing problems. However, in the course of their attempts to apply the class concept, marketers have not always found it immediately and obviously relevant. Sometimes it has seemed to shed light on advertising and merchandising problems and at other times it hasn't—with the result that many analysts have gone away disenchanted, deciding that social classes are not much more useful than income categories and procedurally far more difficult to employ.

It is the thesis of this writer that the role of social class has too often been misunderstood or oversimplified, and that if the concept is applied in a more sophisticated and realistic fashion, it will shed light on a great many problems to which, at first glance, it has not seemed particularly relevant. What we propose to do here, then, is discuss and illustrate a few of these more subtle, more refined and (it must be acknowledged) more complicated ways of applying social class analyses to marketing and advertising problems. In other words, the purpose of this paper is to clarify *when* and *in what ways* social class concepts are significant in selling, and to suggest when they might not be as significant as other concepts, or at least need to be used in concert with other analytic categories.

[1] See W. Lloyd Warner, Marchia Meeker, Kenneth Eells, *Social Class in America* (Chicago: Science Research Associates, 1949).

Reprinted by permission of the author and publisher from Martin L. Bell (ed.), Marketing: A Maturing Discipline, *published by the American Marketing Association (1960), pp. 171–184.*

THE WARNERIAN SOCIAL CLASSES

The six social classes which are referred to in this paper are those which W. Lloyd Warner and his associates have observed in their analyses of such diverse communities as Newburyport, Massachusetts,[2] Natchez, Mississippi,[3] Morris, Illinois,[4] Kansas City, Missouri,[5] and Chicago. These social classes are groups of people who are more or less equal to one another in prestige and community status; they are people who readily and regularly interact among themselves in both formal and informal ways; they form a "class" also to the extent that they share the same goals and ways of looking at life. It is this latter fact about social classes which makes them significant to marketers and advertisers.

Briefly characterized, the six classes are as follows, starting from the highest one and going down.[6]

1. The Upper-Upper or "Social Register" Class is composed of locally prominent families, usually with at least second or third generation wealth. Almost inevitably, this is the smallest of the six classes—with probably no more than one-half of one per cent of the population able to claim membership in this class. The basic values of these people might be summarized in these phrases: living graciously, upholding the family reputation, reflecting the excellence of one's breeding, and displaying a sense of community responsibility.

2. The Lower-Upper or "Nouveau Riche" Class is made up of the more recently arrived and never-quite-accepted wealthy families. Included in this class are members of each city's "executive elite," as well as founders of large businesses and the newly well-to-do doctors and lawyers. At best only one and one-half per cent of Americans rank at this level—so that all told, no more than 2 per

[2] See W. Lloyd Warner and Paul Lunt, *The Social Life of a Modern Community* (New Haven: Yale University Press, 1941).

[3] See Allison Davis, Burleigh B. Gardner and Mary R. Gardner, *Deep South* (Chicago: University of Chicago Press, 1941).

[4] See W. Lloyd Warner and Associates, *Democracy in Jonesville* (New York: Harper & Brothers, 1949).

[5] The writer's observation on the Kansas City social class system will be included in a forthcoming volume on middle age in Kansas City, currently being prepared for publication by the Committee on Human Development of the University of Chicago.

[6] Some of the phrases and ideas in this characterization have been borrowed from Joseph A. Kahl's excellent synthesizing textbook, *The American Class Structure* (New York: Rinehart & Company, Inc., 1957).

cent of the population can be counted as belonging to one layer or the other of our Upper Class. The goals of people at this particular level are a blend of the Upper-Upper pursuit of gracious living and the Upper-Middle Class's drive for success.

3. In the Upper-Middle Class are moderately successful professional men and women, owners of medium-sized businesses and "organization men" at the managerial level; also included are those younger people in their twenties or very early thirties who are expected to arrive at this occupational status level—and possibly higher—by their middle or late thirties (that is, they are today's "junior executives" and "apprentice professionals" who grew up in such families and/or went to the "better" colleges). Ten per cent of Americans are part of this social class and the great majority of them are college educated.

The motivating concerns of people in this class are success at career (which is the husband's contribution to the family's status) and tastefully reflecting this success in social participation and home decor (which is the wife's primary responsibility). Cultivating charm and polish, plus a broad range of interests—either civic or cultural, or both—are also goals of the people in this class, just as in the Lower-Upper. For most marketing and advertising purposes, this class and the two above it can be linked together into a single category of "upper status people." The major differences between them—particularly between the Upper-Middle and the Lower-Upper —are in degree of "success" and the extent to which this has been translated into gracious living.

4. At the top of the "Average Man World" is the Lower-Middle Class. Approximately 30 per cent or 35 per cent of our citizenry can be considered members of this social class. For the most part they are drawn from the ranks of non-managerial office workers, small business owners, and those highly-paid blue-collar families who are concerned with being accepted and respected in white-collar dominated clubs, churches, and neighborhoods. The key word in understanding the motivations and goals of this class is Respectability, and a second important word is Striving. The men of this class are continually striving, within their limitations, to "do a good job" at their work, and both men and women are determined to be judged "respectable" in their personal behavior by their fellow citizens. Being "respectable" means that they live in well-maintained homes, neatly furnished, in neighborhoods which are more-or-less on the "right side of town." It also means that they will clothe themselves in coats, suits, and dresses from "nice stores" and save for a college education for their children.

5. At the lower half of the "Average Man World" is the Upper-Lower Class, sometimes referred to as "The Ordinary Working Class." Nearly 40 per cent of all Americans are in this class, making it the biggest. The proto-typical member of this class is a semi-skilled worker on one of the nation's assembly lines. Many of these "Ordinary Working Class" people make very good money, but do not bother with using it to become "respectable" in a middle-class way. Whether they just "get by" at work, or moonlight to make extra, Upper-Lowers are oriented more toward enjoying life and living well from day to day than saving for the future or caring what the middle class world thinks of them. They try to "keep in step with the times" (indeed, one might say the "times" are more important than the "Joneses" to this class), because they want to be at least Modern, if not Middle Class. That is, they try to take advantage of progress to live more comfortably and they work hard enough to keep themselves safely away from a slum level of existence.

6. The Lower-Lower Class of unskilled workers, unassimilated ethics, and the sporadically employed comprises about 15 per cent of the population, but this class has less than 7 or 8 per cent of the purchasing power, and will not concern us further here. Apathy, fatalism, and a point of view which justifies "getting your kicks whenever you can" characterize the approach toward life, and toward spending money, found among the people of this class.

Now, we do not mean to imply by these characterizations that the members of each class are always homogeneous in behavior. To suggest such would be to exaggerate greatly the meaning of social classes. To properly understand them, it must be recognized that there is a considerable variation in the way individual members of a class realize these class goals and express these values.

For example, within the Upper Middle and Lower Upper Class, there is one group—called Upper Bohemians[7] by Russell Lynes—for whom cultural pursuits are more important than belonging to a "good" country club. As a result, the tastes in furniture, housing accommodations, and recreations exhibited by the men and women of this "issues-and-culture set"—leaning toward the avant garde and eclectic, as they do—are apt to be very different from those practiced by the more conventional, bourgeois members of these status levels. Nevertheless, to both the Upper Bohemians and the Upper Conventionals, displaying "good taste" is quite important, with the differences between them not so much a question of good-versus-bad taste as one of whose form of good taste is preferred (though, to be sure, the Upper Bohemians are usually quite certain theirs is better).

[7] See Russell Lynes, *A Surfeit of Honey* (New York: Harper & Brothers, 1957).

Other sub-categories can be found in these higher classes and parallel kinds of sub-categories can be found in the Lower Middle and Upper Lower classes. Within the Upper Lower Class, for instance, there is a large number of people who are quite concerned with their respectability and spend much of their spare time in church trying to do something about it. Their respectability concerns are not quite like those of the Lower Middle Class, however, for they seem to care more about The Almighty's view of them than of their fellow man's. Thus, the Upper-Lower Class might, for certain analytic purposes, be sub-divided into Church-Going and Tavern-Hopping segments, although this would by no means exhaust all possibilities of sub-categorization here.

All of this is by way of indicating that the millions of individuals who compose each social class are not necessarily similar or identical in their consumption patterns, even though they are of equal status socially and share a set of goals and points of view which are class-wide. Thus far, the literature on social class in both marketing journals and sociological publications has emphasized the similarities of people within classes and rarely pointed out these variations. This has been necessary, of course, in order to properly introduce the concept and educate social scientists and marketers to its utility, but it has led on occasion to naive misuse of the concept and ultimate disillusion. In my view, it has come time for us to advance into a more sophisticated application of social class to marketing problems, which involves awareness of the differences as well as similarities within each class.

SOCIAL CLASS VERSUS INCOME

Let us proceed now to stating the basic significance of this class concept for people in the selling field. In the first place, it explains why income categories or divisions of Americans are quite often irrelevant in analyzing product markets, consumers' shopping habits and store preferences, and media consumption. For example, if you take three families, all earning around $8,000 a year, but each from a different social class, a radical difference in their ways of spending money will be observed.

An Upper-Middle Class family in this income bracket, which in this case might be a young lawyer and his wife or perhaps a college professor, is apt to be found spending a relatively large share of its resources on housing (in a "prestige" neighborhood), on rather expensive pieces of furniture, on clothing from quality stores, and on cultural amusements or club memberships. Meanwhile, the Lower-Middle Class family —headed, we will say, by an insurance salesman or a fairly successful grocery store owner, perhaps even a Diesel engineer—probably has a better house, but in not so fancy a neighborhood; it is apt to have as full a wardrobe though not so expensive, and probably more furniture though none by name designers. These people almost certainly have a much bigger savings account in the bank.

Finally, the Working Class family—with a cross-country truck driver or a highly-paid welder as its chief wage-earner—is apt to have less house and less neighborhood than the Lower-Middle or Upper-Middle family; but it will have a bigger, later model car, plus more expensive appliances in its kitchen and a bigger TV set in its living room. This family will spend less on clothing and furniture, but more on food if the number of children is greater, as is likely. One further difference: the man of the house probably spends much more on sports, attending baseball games (for example), going hunting and bowling, and perhaps owning a boat of some description.

The wives in these three families will be quite noticeably different in the kind of department stores they patronize, in the magazines they read, and in the advertising to which they pay attention. The clothing and furniture they select for themselves and their families will differ accordingly, and also because they are seeking quite different goals. This has become very clear in studies Social Research, Inc., has done for the *Chicago Tribune* on the clothing tastes of Chicagoland women, for the Kroehler Company on the place of furniture in American homes, and for MacFadden Publications on the purchasing patterns and motivations of their romance magazines' Working Class readers.[8] (These have been contrasted in turn with the motivations of Middle Class women who read service magazines.)

The Upper-Middle Class wife—even of the struggling young lawyer —usually buys all her public-appearance clothes at specialty shops or in the specialty departments of her community's best department stores; she feels constrained to choose her wardrobe according to rather carefully prescribed standards of appropriateness. In furnishing her home, she thoughtfully considers whether a given piece or a combination of pieces will serve as adequate testament to her aesthetic sensitivities, plus doing credit in turn to her husband's taste in wife-choosing. She pays careful attention to the dictates of the best shelter magazines, the "smart" interior decorators in town, the homes of other women in her class, and maybe that of the boss's wife.

The Lower-Middle Class woman is more single-mindedly concerned with furnishing her home so that it will be "pretty" in a way that suits her and hopefully might win praise from her friends and neighbors.

[8] This study has been published under the name *Workingman's Wife* (Oceana Press: New York City, 1959) by Lee Rainwater, Richard P. Coleman, and Gerald Handel.

She tries to get ideas from the medium-level shelter and service magazines and is perpetually depressed because her home isn't furnished as much like a dream house as she would like it to be. In this she is quite different from the Upper-Lower wife who is apt to care more about having a full arrary of expensive, gleaming white appliances in her kitchen than a doll's house of a living room. Where the Lower-Middle housewife usually has a definite style in mind which she's striving to follow, the Upper-Lower woman simply follows the lead of newspaper furniture advertising (and what she sees when window shopping) toward furniture which is "modern-looking," by which she means the "latest thing" that has hit the mass market.

A great many more examples of differences in consumption patterns by class levels could be given, but the principal ones have been well reported already—facetiously by Vance Packard and seriously by Pierre Martineau;[9] for further amplification on this point the latter source is recommended. The significance to merchandisers and advertisers of these findings about motivational differences between classes is fairly obvious, the major idea being that for many products, advertising appeals and merchandising techniques must be differentially geared to the points of view reflected in these three main social classes. Advertising of brands or goods aimed at a specific class must take into account the motivations of that class, and not try to sell everything as if it were the Upper Class or Upper-Middle status symbol.

Up to now, we've been talking about product areas—clothing, furniture, and residential neighborhoods—where the relationship between social class and quality of goods purchased is highest. In these things the so-called "Quality Market" and the Upper Middle (and higher) markets coincide. That is, the purchasers of highest quality clothing and highest quality furniture are more nearly from the Upper-Middle and Upper social classes than from the highest income categories, and so on it goes down the hierarchy. The correlation between price of goods purchased and social class is relatively quite high in these product areas while the correlation between price paid and annual income is lower than one might expect.

There is another group of products which are not linked in such a direct way with social class, but neither are they linked with income categories in any obvious relationship. The current car market provides an instructive example of this situation, for the nature of the market cannot be grasped by using one or the other concept exclusively. What is happening in today's car market can only be understood when income categories are placed into a social class framework.

[9] See Pierre Martineau, *Motivation in Advertising* (New York: McGraw-Hill Book Company, 1957) and "Social Classes and Spending Behavior," *The Journal of Marketing*, Vol. 23, No. 2, October 1958, pp. 121–130.

THE "OVERPRIVILEGED" AS "QUALITY MARKET"

Within each social class group there are families and individuals whose incomes are above average for their class. The Upper-Lower family with an income above $7,000 a year—sometimes a product of both husband and wife working, and sometimes not—is an example of this. So, too, is the Lower-Middle Class business owner or salesman who makes more than $10,000 a year, but has no interest in either the concerts or country clubs of Upper-Middledom and hence is still Lower Middle Class. The Upper Middle Class couple with more than $25,000 a year at its disposal but no desire to play the "society game" of subscription balls or private schools is also in this category. These are what might be called the "overprivileged" in the absolute sense, of course; they are "overprivileged," however, relative to what is required or needed by families in their class. After they have met the basic expectations and standards of their group in the housing, food, furnishing, and clothing areas, they have quite a bit of money left over which is their equivalent of "discretionary income."

In much the same way, each class has its "underprivileged" members; in the Upper-Middle Class these are the younger couples who haven't made the managerial ranks yet, the college professors, the genteel professionals, and a few downwardly mobile people from high-status backgrounds who are trying to hang on to what fragments of status they have left—for the most part these people are below the $12,000-a-year mark and they can barely meet some of the basic requirements of Upper-Middle life, much less experience any of its little luxuries; in the Lower-Middle Class these are the poorly paid bank tellers, the rows of bookkeepers in railroad offices, the school teachers with considerably more status aspiration than income; and the Upper-Lower Class it is almost any family earning less than $4,500 or $5,000 a year, at today's rates of pay in metropolitan areas.

In the middle of each class's income range are its "average" members, families who are neither underprivileged nor overprivileged by the standards of their class. You might think of this as the Upper-Middle Class family between $12,000 and $20,000 a year, the Lower-Middle family in the $7,000–$9,000 range, and the Upper-Lower family near $6,000 per annum. However, this word of caution is necessary: a lot of people in the middle income range of their class see themselves as underprivileged because they are aspiring to become one of the "overprivileged" in their class or to move on up the ladder to a higher class.

The relevance of all this to the car market is that when you look at this particular market today, you find it is the "average" members of each class, whether Upper-Middle, Lower-Middle, or Upper-Lower, who constitute the heart of the Low-Priced Three's audience; these are the people who are buying Fords and Chevrolets this year and last, and probably next. No longer is the Ford and Chevrolet market just a lower-middle income market, or (in class terms) a Lower-Middle or a Lower Class market. Rather, it is recruited from the middle income group *within each* social class. Indeed, the $15,000-a-year Upper-Middle "organization man" is apt to choose a Ford or Chevy from the Impala-Galaxie level or else a top-price station wagon once he ventures into this market, whereas the average-income Lower-Middle man will settle for a middle-series Bel Air or Fairlane 500, and the "average-income" Upper Lower guy either splurges for an Impala or "sensibly" contents himself with the spartan Biscayne.

While this has been happening to the Low-Priced Three makes the heart of the medium-price car market has relocated in the "overprivileged" segments of each class. Today, rich blue-collar workers are joining prosperous Lower-Middle Class salesmen and well-to-do Upper Middle Class business owners in buying Pontiacs, Buicks, Oldsmobiles, Chryslers, and even Cadillacs. In fact, what there is left of big-car lust in our society is found at peak strength among the "overprivileged" Upper-Lowers or else among men who have achieved higher status, but grew up as kids in the Upper-Lower class and have not forgotten their wide-eyed envy of the big car owner.

Finally, as you may have guessed by now, the compact car market's heart is to be found in the "underprivileged" segments of each class (here we are speaking of the market for a compact as a first car). The overwhelming majority of Rambler purchasers, Falcon buyers, and foreign economy car owners come from this socio-economic territory. Thus, it is not the really poor who are buying these cheapest, most economical cars—rather it is those who think of themselves as poor relative to their status aspirations and to their needs for a certain level of clothing, furniture, and housing which they could not afford if they bought a more expensive car.

The market for compacts as second cars is somewhat more complicated in its socio-economic geography, being located in the middle range of the Upper-Middle Class, and the "overprivileged" segment of the Lower-Middle. The "overprivileged" Upper Middle may have one as a third car, but he prefers either a T-Bird, a foreign sports car, a Pontiac convertible, or a beat-up station wagon as his second car, while the "overprivileged" Upper Lower is apt to go for a used standard if he wants a second car.

If marketers and advertisers had assumed that the market for compacts was going to be the lowest-income or lowest-status members of our society, they would have seriously miscalculated in their merchandising and advertising approach. Rambler, for one, did not make this mistake. American Motors advertised its cars as "bringing sense into the auto market" and thus enabled people who bought one to pride themselves on the high-minded rationality they had displayed. Rambler owners, as they drive down the street, are not ashamed that they couldn't afford better—instead, as the company has told them to be, they are proud that they did not yield, like their neighbors, to base emotional desires for a car bloated in size beyond necessity and loaded in gadgetry beyond reason. Compact car owners have their own form of snobbery—what might be called "sensibility snobbery"—with which to content themselves and justify their purchase.

This analysis of the car market is one example of what I mean by the sophisticated application of social class concepts to marketing and advertising problems. There are many products and many brands which, like cars, are more nearly symbols of higher status class within class than symbols of higher status per se. A color television set is such a product, or at least it was two years ago when Social Research, Inc., studied its market. At the time color television manufacturers were puzzled because sales were thinly spread throughout the income scale, without any noticeable increase in concentration until an extremely high level was reached. Furthermore, they were unable to see any particular relationship between social class and color set ownership, since about as many Upper-Lower Class people owned them as did Upper-Middles. However, when the two factors of income and class were put together, in the manner described above, it became clear that the color television market was concentrated among high-income or "overprivileged" members of each social class. Other products which bear this complicated relationship to class and income are the more costly brands and larger sizes of home appliances. Fairly expensive recreational equipment like outboard motor boats also tend to be in this category.

In summary, today's market for quality goods and quality brands is not necessarily drawn from what has historically been described as the "Quality Market" of Upper-Middle and Upper Class people, nor even necessarily from the highest income categories. Rather, in many instances, it is drawn from those people within each social level who have the most discretionary income available for enjoying life's little extras above and beyond the requirements of their class. Every merchandiser and advertiser ought to take a good hard look at what he is selling and ask himself if it bears this particular relationship to the class and income picture. If his product does, and if his brand is one of the more expensive, then he should merchandise it not as if it were just for social climbers or for the upper classes, but rather as part of the Better Life, U.S.A. If, on the other hand, his brand is one of the least expensive, then he is not just selling to the poor, but rather to those in all classes who feel it is only sensible on their part to settle for a brand such as his and save the difference for other things which are more important in their statement of social class aspiration and identity.

SOCIAL CLASS ISN'T ALWAYS IMPORTANT

Now, to make the picture complete, it must be pointed out that Social Research, Inc., has found some products in which the income factor is all-important and the social class variable is relevant only to the extent that it is correlated with income. Perhaps the most perfect example of this is the market for air conditioners in Southwestern cities. There, everybody—except the sickly and the extremely old-fashioned—agree that air conditioning one's home is imperative if summer is to be survived with any degree of comfort. Consequently the expensiveness of a family's air conditioning equipment—whether centrally installed, or window units to the number of four, three, two, or one—is directly correlated with family income. It is not merely a function of discretionary income—as in our example about purchase of medium-priced cars; it is instead almost completely a function of total annual income. If more Upper-Middles than Upper-Lowers are fully air-conditioned it is only because more of them can afford to be; it is not because Upper-Middles as a group are placing higher priority on the air-conditioned existence.

Undoubtedly air conditioners are not alone in being classless—so that one more thing the marketer who uses social class in a truly sophisticated way needs to understand is that there can be occasions when it is an irrelevant variable. Realizing this, he will not become disenchanted with social class when he finds a marketing problem where it does not shed light or where it does not seem pertinent. Of course, he will want to make sure that in advertising such a product there is indeed no need to take class into account. After all, some apparently classless products are properly sold to the market in a segmental approach, appealing first on one ground to one class, then on other grounds to another.

There are other products—and probably air conditioning is one of them and children's play clothes may be another—where this is not necessary. For such products some factor, such as physical comfort (in the one case) or simple durability (in the other), is so basic in the consumer's consideration that all other motivations pale into insignificance beside it. There are even products, like beer, where the democratic approach—that is, a tone of "let's-all-be-good-fellows-together" is exactly right and segmental appeals or snob stories are all wrong.

Another aspect to the sophisticated employment of social class refers back to the point made earlier that social class groups are not always homogeneous. It must be recognized that at times a product's market is formed by "highbrows" from the Upper-Upper Class on down to the Lower-Middle, or by "suburbanites" and suburban-minded people of all classes—in which case the social class variable may confuse a market analysis more than clarify it.

Particularly must merchandisers and market analysts beware of equating "Class" with "Brow"; for they are not synonymous. For example, the Upper-Middle Class and those above it are mainly middle-brow in taste (veering toward an all-American lower-middlebrow level of preferences in television shows and advertising messages) even though the majority of highbrows are found at this level. At times advertisers have made the mistake of assuming that the Upper-Middle Class should be appealed to in a highly sophisticated fashion—and though this is just fine if the product itself is likely to appeal primarily to the Manhattanized type of Upper-Middle, it is not correct if it is expected to sell to the kind of doctor in Dubuque who enjoys a visit to New York every now and then but would never want to live there.

In short, not only must the sophisticated marketer abandon social class in favor of income categories on occasion in his analysis and interpretation of a market, he must recognize that at times both income and class are superseded in importance by divisions of the public into brow levels, by divisions into "high mobiles" and "low mobiles," innovators and non-innovators, inner-directed and other-directed, urbanites, suburbanites, exurbanites, ruralites, and Floridians, or what have you. Usually, of course, fullest understanding of a market will require that social class be linked in with whichever sub-categorization proves pertinent from among those in the catalogue just recited, much as income and class were linked together for fullest comprehension of the car market.

As a final point, let it be noted that the way of life and the goals of people in each social class are in perpetual flux. Neither the "who" of each class nor "what motivates them" are constants to be assumed without continual re-evaluation. Right now, particularly, it is very clear that our society is changing. Every year the collar-color line is breaking down further. More blue-collar workers are becoming Middle Class as well as middle income and Modern, and a white-collar position is less and less a guarantee of Lower-Middle status. As a consequence of this, the Lower-Middle Class is perhaps somewhat more "materialistic" in outlook and slightly less "respectability" conscious than it was 25 years ago, or even 8. Meanwhile, for men and women to achieve Upper-Middle status without college backgrounds is becoming more and more difficult, so that this class is turning much more worldly-wise and well-read, much less conventionally bourgeois than it was in the zenith of Babbitt's day.

In short, the form of our society and its division into social classes is not fixed as of Yankee City in 1931, Jonesville in 1944, Kansas City in 1952, or St. Louis in 1960. We won't be able to say exactly the same things about either the classes themselves or their relationships to specific markets by next year at this time. This fact about the American class structure, than it is not static, that it is in the process of change, is in itself important to merchandisers, to advertisers, to anyone in selling. Among other things, it means that undoubtedly they have played a part in past changes and can play a leading role in directing future changes. But of more direct concern here, to the marketing analyst it means that if he allows his stratification concept to become dated, his use of it will cease as of that moment to be sophisticated.

RETROSPECTIVE COMMENT

In closing the above article—which originated as a speech to the A.M.A. in 1960—I warned the marketing analyst against allowing his or her "stratification concept to become dated." Now, I must open this Retrospective Commentary by suggesting that the Warnerian six-class view of American society forwarded in that paper has itself become a "dated" conception. As of the early-to-middle 1970s, American society appears more appropriately divided into three main classes—*Upper Americans*, *Middle Americans*, and *Lower Americans*—that are in turn subdivided into three or four lifestyle groupings. (This is the conclusion I have drawn from recent studies of stratification in Boston and Kansas City, more about which anon.) Once the market analyst has located these lifestyle groupings within the major three social classes and identified the membership, he can then proceed to examine consumer behavior much as was recommended before, determining when these class-and-lifestyle groupings are more relevant than income categories (or vice versa) to the understanding of consumer choices, and always looking for the possibility that a family's economic position as "overprivileged," "underprivileged," or "average" will prove the key.

The category of *Upper Americans*—as they emerged in my Boston/Kansas City research—embraces approximately the same types of people as were included in the Warnerian classes of Upper-Upper, Lower-Upper, and Upper-Middle, with these differences in arrangement and characterization: Upper Americans are today much more exclusively college-educated than in the 1930s and 1940s, and they divide themselves socially as much by lifestyle choices as by hierarchical rank. The rank is much as before: on top, a small *Social Register*, old-family group; next, the more recently prominent; and from there on down, status is a blend of income, educational credentials, and social ambition. Consumption behavior, however, is more closely correlated among these Upper Americans with type than rank, "type" referring here to identification either with The Gentility, The Academy, The Corporation, The Arts, Public Service, or The Entertainment World (to use shorthand phrases for six major groupings by lifestyle and/or career pattern). (*The Entertainment World* as used here reaches its social peak with a group dubbed *Celebrity Society* by the press, but includes quite broadly all persons of this Upper-American status whose lifestyle is characterized by sybaritic and exhibitionary pursuits, however vicarious versus real may be the experiencing of these pleasures). In each of these groupings of Upper Americans by type, there are people able to pursue the associated lifestyle with great affluence and elan, and then there are families barely able to manage it; what must be understood by the marketing analyst is that their goals are roughly the same, it is only their means that differ. Approximately 15 percent of the American public is both self-identified and socially accepted at this Upper level.

Middle Americans, comprising 65 or 70 percent of America's urban population, embrace the social levels formerly designated as Lower-Middle Class and Upper-Lower Class. As of Spring, 1975, average families of this status ranged in income by five thousand dollars up and down from a median of $14,300 a year, the Bureau of Labor Statistics' designated Moderate Standard of Living at that point in time. The financial elite of Middle Americans could then claim incomes of $20,000 or more, and in not a few cases way past $30,000—these we would designate "overprivileged" Middle Americans (to bring the income definition of the category up to date, if only for a few months). Meanwhile, "underprivileged" Middle Americans were those whose incomes fall below $9,200, the B.L.S.'s Austerity Level income for an urban family of four. Within this world of Middle Americans, two major lifestyle groupings can be observed: One is the descendant of the old, white-collar dominated Lower-Middle Class—its prime concern is *Respectability* in neighborhood, formal associations, and public appearance. The second continues to draw its consumption themes from the goals of *Modernity* and *Life Enjoyment* which emerged so strongly among unionized blue-collar workers of the Upper-Lower Class in the prosperous 1950s. Today these lifestyle divisions of Middle-Class and Working-Class Middle Americans are not necessarily tied to a white-collar/blue-collar occupational dichotomy, nor are they closely related to income. And it is not entirely clear that they are hierarchical either, since people of Middle American status now seem to look up and down at one another more according to standard-of-living than by what they do to earn that living or what they do with it for pleasure—at least, so they talk. In short, these lifestyle groupings of Middle Americans are not truly class strata or self-defined ranks; more nearly they are social science constructs.

The lowest of Lower Americans are those socially branded as *people on welfare*. More broadly, the very poor of all races and ethnic groups are societally identified as part of this stratum, plus the moderately poor of the minority-group bloc: Negroes, Mexican-Americans, Puerto Ricans, and American Indians. There are even fairly prosperous men and women whose consuming behavior reflects this self-identification: As "overprivileged" Lower Americans, their clothings styles, recreational expenditures, and locational choices draw primarily from their ethnic/racial identification and tend to be an affront to Middle-American concepts of "proper behavior." Lower Americans constitute no more than 15-to-20 percent of the population and in purchasing power they are even less important, representing no more than 7 or 8 percent of the national income.

The car market has long since ceased to serve as the classic example of how income position within social class determines consumer choices between makes and body size. By the late 1960s highly personal tastes expressed through body styles and make imagery—the choice of a truck-like vehicle versus a sports car versus a sedan or opting for a foreign make versus domestic—had come to dominate behavior in this market. Which appliance or motor-goods markets are now (1975) best understood by application of the income-in-class model I cannot specify, since I have been out of the market research industry since 1969. What I can assert with conviction, however, is that housing is a market where there always has been, and almost certainly will continue to be, an intimate relationship between class and income. Dating back to the first studies on social class in the 1920s, social scientists have been observing that neighborhood choice is basically governed by class identification and status aspirations, while choice of particular house or apartment is governed by pocketbook power. In my recent studies of status symbolism in Boston and Kansas City, this relationship remains strong: how people house themselves and where they choose to live in these metropolitan areas cannot fully be understood without taking both the variables of social status and economic standing into account.—*Richard P. Coleman, Social Research, Inc.*

21. Social Classes and Spending Behavior

Pierre Martineau

All societies place emphasis on some one structure which gives form to the total society and integrates all the other structures such as the family, the clique, voluntary association, caste, age, and sex groupings into a social unity.

Social stratification means any system of ranked statuses by which all the members of a society are placed in some kind of a superordinate and subordinate hierarchy. While money and occupation are important in the ranking process, there are many more factors, and these two alone do not establish social position. The concept of social class was designed to include this process of ranking people in superior and inferior social position by any and all factors.

CLASS SYSTEM

It has been argued that there cannot be a class system existent in America when most individuals do not have the slightest idea of its formal structure. Yet in actuality every individual senses that he is more at home with and more acceptable to certain groups than to others. In a study of department stores and shopping behavior, it was found that the Lower-Status woman is completely aware that, if she goes into High-Status department stores, the clerks will punish her in various subtle ways.

"The clerks treat you like a crumb," one woman expressed it. After trying vainly to be waited on, another woman bitterly complained that she was loftily told, "We thought you were a clerk."

The woman who is socially mobile gives considerable thought to the external symbols of status and she frequently tests her status by shopping in department stores which she thinks are commensurate with her changing position. She knows that, if she does not dress correctly, if she does not behave in a certain manner to the clerks, if she is awkward about the

Reprinted by permission of the publisher from the Journal of Marketing, *published by the American Marketing Association, Vol. 23 (October 1958), pp. 121–130.*

proper cues, then the other customers and the clerks will make it very clear that she does not belong.

In another study, very different attitudes in the purchase of furniture and appliances involving this matter of status were found. Middle-class people had no hesitancy in buying refrigerators and other appliances in discount houses and bargain stores because they felt that they could not "go wrong" with the nationally advertised names. But taste in furniture is much more elusive and subtle because the brand names are not known; and, therefore, one's taste is on trial. Rather than commit a glaring error in taste which would exhibit an ignorance of the correct status symbols, the same individual who buys appliances in a discount house generally retreats to a status store for buying furniture. She needs the support of the store's taste.

In a very real sense, everyone of us in his consumption patterns and style of life shows an awareness that there is some kind of a superiority-inferiority system operating, and that we must observe the symbolic patterns of our own class.

Lloyd Warner and Paul Lunt have described a six-class system: the Upper-Upper, or old families; Lower-Upper, or the newly arrived; Upper-Middle, mostly the professionals and successful businessmen; Lower-Middle, or the white collar salaried class; Upper-Lower, or the wage earner, skilled worker group; and Lower-Lower, or the unskilled labor group.[1] For practical purposes, in order to determine the individual's class position, Warner and his associates worked out a rating index, not based on amount of income but rather on type of income, type of occupation, house type, and place of residence.

Although the Warner thesis has been widely used in sociology, it has not generally been employed in marketing. As a matter of fact, some critics in the social sciences have held that, since Warner's thesis rested essentially on studies of smaller cities in the 10,000–25,000 class, this same system might not exist in the more complex metropolitan centers, or might not be unravelled by the same techniques. Furthermore, many marketers did not see the application of this dimension to the individual's economic behavior, since the studies of Warner and his associates had mostly been concerned with the differences in the broad patterns of living, the moral codes, etc.

SOCIAL CLASS IN CHICAGO

Under Warner's guidance, the *Chicago Tribune* has undertaken several extensive studies exploring social class in a metropolitan city, and its

[1] W. Lloyd Warner and Paul Lunt, *The Social Life of a Modern Community* (New

manifestations specifically in family buying patterns. The problem was to determine if such a social class system did exist in metropolitan Chicago, if the dimensions and the relationships were at all similar to the smaller cities which were studied before the far-reaching social changes of the past fifteen years. The studies were undertaken to see if there were any class significances in the individual family's spending-saving patterns, retail store loyalties, and his expressions of taste in typical areas such as automobiles, apparel, furniture, and house types.

It seems that many an economist overlooks the possibility of any psychological differences between individuals resulting from different class membership. It is assumed that a rich man is simply a poor man with more money and that, given the same income, the poor man would behave exactly like the rich man. The *Chicago Tribune* studies crystallize a wealth of evidence from other sources that this is just not so, and that the Lower-Status person is profoundly different in his mode of thinking and his way of handling the world from the Middle-Class individual. Where he buys and what he buys will differ not only by economics but in symbolic value.

It should be understood, of course, that there are no hard and fast lines between the classes. Implicit in the notion of social class in America is the possibility of movement from one class to another. The "office boy-to-president" saga is a cherished part of the American dream. Bobo Rockefeller illustrates the female counterpart: from coal miner's daughter to socialite. As a corollary of the explorations in class, the study also tried to be definitive about the phenomenon of social mobility—the movement from one class to another.

There are numerous studies of vertical mobility from the level of sociological analysis, mostly by comparing the individual's occupational status to that of his father. There are also studies at the level of psychological analysis. This study attempted to combine the two levels, to observe the individual's progress and also to understand something of the dynamics of the mobile person as compared to the stable individual. The attempt was to look both backward and forward: tracing such factors as occupation, place of residence, and religion back to parents and grandparents, and then where the family expected to be in the next five or ten years, what were the educational plans for each son, each daughter, a discussion of future goals.

Because this article is confined primarily to social class, this section may be concluded by saying that the studies show a very clear relationship between spend-saving aspirations and the factors of mobility-stability.

Haven: Yale University Press, 1950). Also, W. Lloyd Warner, Marchia Meeker, and Kenneth Eells, *Social Class in America* (Chicago: Science Research Associates, 1949).

FRAMEWORK OF STUDY

Following are Warner's hypotheses and assumptions for the study:

ASSUMPTIONS ABOUT SYMBOLS AND VALUES AND ABOUT
SAVING OF MONEY AND ACCUMULATION OF OBJECTS

Our society is acquisitive and pecuniary. On the one hand, the values and beliefs of Americans are pulled toward the pole of the accumulation of money by increasing the amount of money income and reducing its outgo. On the other hand, American values emphasize the accumulation of objects and products of technology for display and consumption. The self-regard and self-esteem of a person and his family, as well as the public esteem and respect of a valued social world around the accumulator, are increased or not by such symbols of accumulation and consumption.

The two sets of values, the accumulation of product symbols and the accumulation (saving) of money, may be, and usually are, in opposition.

General working hypotheses stemming from these assumptions were: (1) People are distributed along a range according to the two-value components, running from proportionately high savings, through mixed categories, to proportionately high accumulation of objects. (2) These value variations conform to social and personality factors present in all Americans.

ASSUMPTIONS ABOUT PRODUCT SYMBOLS, SAVERS, AND ACCUMULATIONS

American society is also characterized by social change, particularly technological change that moves in the direction of greater and greater production of more kinds and more numerous objects for consumption and accumulation.

Hypothesis: New varieties of objects will be most readily accepted by the accumulators, and most often opposed by the savers.

ASSUMPTIONS ABOUT SOCIAL VALUES OF ACCUMULATORS AND SAVERS

American society is characterized by basic cultural differences, one of them being social status. Social class levels are occupied by people, some of whom are upward mobile by intent and fact. Others are non-mobile, by intent and fact. The values which dictate judgments about actions, such as the kinds of objects which are consumed and accumulated, will vary by class level and the presence or absence of vertical mobility.

The personality components are distributed through the class levels and through the mobility types. By relating the social and personality components, it is possible to state a series of hypotheses about accumulators and savers as they are related to the object world around them, particularly to objects which are new and old to the culture, those which are imposing or not and those which are predominantly for display or for consumption.

At the direct, practical level, all of these theoretical questions can be summarized by one basic question: *What kinds of things are people likely to buy and not buy if they are in given class positions and if they are or are not socially mobile?* In other words, what is the effect on purchasing behavior of being in a particular social class, and being mobile or non-mobile?

If this is the crucial question, theoretically grounded, then a whole series of hypotheses can be laid out concerning values about money and values about buying various kinds of objects for consumption and for display. Some of these are:

1. There will be a relationship between values held by a particular subject and the extent to which particular products exemplify those values.

2. There is a differential hierarchy of things for which it is worth spending money.

3. Veblen's theory that conspicuous expenditure is largely applied to the Upper Class is erroneous. It runs all the way through our social system.

From these statements certain other hypotheses follow:

4. At different class levels, symbols of mobility will differ.

There is a differential hierarchy of things on which it is worth spending money. Class and mobility will be two of the dimensions that will differentiate—also personality and cultural background.

5. The place in the home where these symbols will be displayed will shift at different class levels.

The underlying assumption here is that there is a hierarchy of importance in the rooms of the house. This hierarchy varies with social class, mobility, age, ethnicity. The studies also revealed clear-cut patterns of taste for lamps, furnishings, house types, etc.

6. The non-mobile people tend to rationalize purchases in terms of cost or economy.

In other words, non-mobile people tend to be oriented more toward the pole of the accumulation of money. Purchases then, are rationalized in terms of the savings involved.

The basic thesis of all the hypotheses on mobility is this: Whereas the stable individual would emphasize saving and security, the behavior of the mobile individual is characterized by spending for various symbols of upward movement. All of the evidence turned up indicates that this difference in values does exist, and furthermore that notable differences in personality dynamics are involved. For instance, the analysis of how families would make investments shows that stable people overwhelmingly prefer insurance, the symbol of security. By contrast, the mobile people at all levels prefer stocks, which are risk-taking. In Warner's words, the mobile individual acts as if he were free, white, and twenty-one, completely able to handle the world, and perfectly willing to gamble on himself as a sure bet to succeed.

CLASS PLACEMENT

Returning to the factor of social class, in this study class placement was based on a multi-state probability area sample of metropolitan Chicago, involving 3,880 households. It was found that the matter of placement could not be done by the relatively simple scoring sufficient for the smaller cities. To secure house typings, it was necessary to provide the field investigators with photographs covering a wide range of dwelling types, all the way from exclusive apartments to rooms over stores. Because of the very complexity of metropolitan life, occupations provided the biggest problem. To solve this operational problem, it was necessary to construct an exhaustive list of occupational types involving degree of responsibility and training required by each. The data finally used to calculate the Index of Status Characteristics (ISC) were:

(weighted by 5)
Occupation (from 1 to 7 broad categories)
(weighted by 4)
Sources of Income (from 1 to 7 types)
(weighted by 3)
Housing Type (from 1 to 7 types)

The sum of the individual's weighted scores was used to predict his social class level as follows:[2]

[2] Dr. Bevode McCall helped to solve the ISC scoring problem for Metropolitan Chicago.

ISC Scores	*Predicted social class placement*
12-21	Upper Class
22-37	Upper-Middle Class
38-51	Lower-Middle Class
52-66	Upper-Lower Class
67-84	Lower-Lower Class

The study very clearly shows that there is a social-class system operative in a metropolitan area which can be delineated. Furthermore, class membership is an important determinant of the individual's economic behavior, even more so than in the smaller city. The one department store in the smaller city may satisfy almost everyone, whereas in the metropolitan city the stores become sharply differentiated.

This is the social-class structure of Metropolitan Chicago, typifying the transformation of the formerly agrarian Midwestern cities from Pittsburgh to Kansas City into a series of big milltowns:

Upper and Upper-Middle	8.1%
Lower-Middle	28.4%
Upper-Lower	44.0%
Lower-Lower	19.5%

While the Old Families and the Newly Arrived are still recognizable as types, they constitute less than 1 per cent of the population. A similar study in Kansas City turned up so few that they could not be counted at all. On the other hand, we see the emergence of a seventh class, the Upper-Lower "Stars" or Light-Blue Collar Workers. They are the spokesmen of the Upper-Lower Class groups—high income individuals, who have the income for more ostentatious living than the average factory worker but who lack the personal skills or desire for high status by social mobility.

There is certainly a rough correlation between income and social class. But social class is a much richer dimension of meaning. There are so many facets of behavior which are explicable only on a basis of social class dynamics. For instance, this analysis of the purchase of household appliances in Chicago over a four-year period shows a very different picture by income and by class:

Nine Appliance Types—Four-Year Period
By Income

Over $7,000	36.2%
4,000-6,999	46.0%
Under 4,000	17.8%

By Social Class

Upper and Upper-Middle	16.6%
Lower-Middle	29.2%
Upper-Lower	45.7%
Lower-Lower	8.5%

Income analysis shows that the lowest income group represents an understandably smaller market, but nevertheless a market. Social-class analysis highlights a fundamental difference in attitudes toward the home between the two lower classes. The Upper-Lower Class man sees his home as his castle, his anchor to the world, and he loads it down with hardware—solid heavy appliances—as his symbols of security. The Lower-Lower Class individual is far less interested in his castle, and is more likely to spend his income for flashy clothes or an automobile. He is less property-minded, and he has less feeling about buying and maintaining a home.

Several *Tribune* studies have explored the way of life and the buying behavior in many new suburbs and communities. All of them quickly become stratified along social-class and mobility dimensions, and, therefore, differ tremendously among themselves. *Fortune* has reported on Park Forest, Illinois, a middle-class suburb of 30,000 and only ten years old. It is characterized by high degrees of both upward and geographical mobility. The people are overwhelmingly those who had moved from other parts of the United States, who had few local roots, and who consequently wanted to integrate themselves in friendship groups. But this was not typical of the new Lower-Status suburbs where the women did relatively little fraternizing. It was not typical of the new Upper-Middle Class mobile suburbs where the people were preoccupied with status symbols, not in submerging themselves in the group.

One new community had crystallized as being for Higher-Status Negroes. This was a resettlement project with relatively high rents for Negroes. Eighty-five per cent of them had come from the South where social class was compressed. But, as soon as they came to Chicago, the class system opened up and they were anxious to establish a social distance between themselves and other Negroes. Almost all of them said they enjoyed the "peace and quiet" of their neighborhood, which was their way of insisting that they were not like the "noisy" lower-class Negroes. They deliberately avoided the stores patronized by other Negroes.

CHOICE OF STORE

All of these studies reveal the close relation between choice of store, patterns of spending, and class membership. In the probability sample delineating social class, such questions were asked in the total metropolitan area as:

"If you were shopping for a good dress, at which store would you be most likely to find what you wanted?"
"For an everyday dress?"

"For living room furniture?"

"At which store do you buy most of your groceries?"

To assume that all persons would wish to shop at the glamorous High-Status stores is utterly wrong. People are very realistic in the way they match their values and expectations with the status of the store. The woman shopper has a considerable range of ideas about department stores; but these generally become organized on a scale ranking from very High-Social Status to the Lowest-Status and prestige. The social status of the department store becomes the primary basis for its definition by the shopper. This is also true of men's and women's apparel stores, and furniture stores, on the basis of customer profits. The shopper is not going to take a chance feeling out of place by going to a store where she might not fit.

No matter what economics are involved, she asks herself who are the other customers in the store, what sort of treatment can she expect at the hands of the clerks, will the merchandise be the best of everything, or lower priced and hence lower quality? Stores are described as being for the rich, for the average ordinary people, or for those who have to stretch their pennies.

The most important function of retail advertising today, when prices and quality have become so standard, is to permit the shopper to make social-class identification. This she can do from the tone and physical character of the advertising. Of course, there is also the factor of psychological identification. Two people in the same social class may want different stores. One may prefer a conservative store, one may want the most advanced styling. But neither will go to stores where they do not "fit," in a social-class sense.

In contrast to the independent food retailer, who obviously adapts to the status of the neighborhood, the chain grocers generally invade many income areas with their stores. Nevertheless, customer profits show that each chain acquires a status definition. The two largest grocery chains in the Chicago area are A. & P. and Jewel; yet they draw very different customer bodies. A. & P. is strong with the mass market, whereas Jewel has its strength among the Middle Class.

While the national brand can and often does cut across classes, one can think of many product types and services which do have social class labels. The Upper-Middle Class person rarely travels by motor coach because none of his associates do so, even though there is certainly nothing wrong with this mode of transportation. On the other hand, even with low air-coach fares, one does not see many factory workers or day laborers on vacation around airports. Such sales successes as vodka and tonic water, and men's deodorants and foreign sports cars, were accomplished without benefit of much buying from this part of the market.

COMMUNICATION SKILLS

There is also a relation between class and communication abilities which has significance for marketing. The kind of super-sophisticated and clever advertising which appears in the *New Yorker* and *Esquire* is almost meaningless to Lower-Status people. They cannot comprehend the subtle humor; they are baffled by the bizarre art. They have a different symbol system, a very different approach to humor. In no sense does this imply that they lack intelligence or wit. Rather their communication skills have just been pressed into a different mold.

Here again, style of advertising helps the individual to make class identification. Most of the really big local television success stories in Chicago have been achieved by personalities who radiate to the mass that this is where they belong. These self-made businessmen who do the announcing for their own shows communicate wonderfully well with the mass audience. While many listeners switch off their lengthy and personal commercials, these same mannerisms tell the Lower-Status individual that here is someone just like himself, who understands him.

Social Research, Inc., has frequently discussed the class problem in marketing by dividing the population into Upper-Middle or quality market; the middle majority which combines both the Lower-Middle and Upper-Lower; and then the Lower-Lower. The distinction should be drawn between the Middle Classes and the Lower-Status groups. In several dozen of these store profiles, there is scarcely an instance where a store has appeal to the Lower-Middle and Upper-Lower classes with anything like the same strength.

It would be better to make the break between the Middle Class, representing one-third of the population and the Lower-Status or Working-Class or Wage-Earner group, representing two-thirds of metropolitan Chicago. This permits some psychological distinctions to be drawn between the Middle-Class individual and the individual who is not a part of the Middle-Class system of values. Even though this is the dominant American value system, even though Middle-Class Americans have been taught by their parents that it is the only value system, this Lower-Status individual does not necessarily subscribe to it.

WHO SAVES, WHO SPENDS?

Another important set of behavioral distinctions related to social class position was revealed in the "save-spend aspiration" study. The question was asked: "Suppose your income was doubled for the next ten years, what would you do with the increased income?" This is a fantasy question taken out of the realm of any pressing economic situation to reflect aspirations about money. The coding broke down the answers to this question into five general categories: (1) the mode of saving, (2) the purpose of saving, (3) spending which would consolidate past gains, meet present defensive needs, prepare for future self-advancement, (4) spending which is "self-indulgent-centered," (5) spending which is "house-centered."

Here are some of our findings:[3] The higher the individual's class position, the more likely is he to express some saving aspirations. Conversely, the lower his class position, the more likely is he to mention spending only. Moreover the higher the status, the more likely is the individual to specify *how* he will save his money, which is indicative of the more elaborate financial learning required of higher status.

Proceeding from the more general categories (such as saving versus spending only) to more specific categories (such as non-investment versus investment saving and the even more specific stock versus real estate investment, etc.) an increasingly sharper class differentiation is found. It is primarily *non-investment* saving which appeals to the Lower-Status person. Investment saving, on the other hand, appeals above all to the Upper-Status person.

Investors almost always specify how they will invest. And here in mode of investment are examples of the most sharply class-differentiated preferences. Intangible forms of investment like stock and insurance are very clearly distinguished as Upper-Status investments. Nearly four times as many Upper-Middles select insurance as would be expected by chance, whereas only one-fifth of the Lower-Lowers select it as would be expected by chance. By contrast, Lower-Status people have far greater preference for tangible investments, specifically ownership of real estate, a farm, or a business.

To sum up, Middle-Class people usually have a place in their aspirations for some form of saving. This saving is most often in the form of investment, where there is a risk, long-term involvement, and the possibility of higher return. Saving, investment saving, and intangible investment saving—successively each of these become for them increasingly symbols of their higher status.

The aspirations of the Lower-Status person are just as often for spending as they are for saving. This saving is usually a non-investment saving where there is almost no risk, funds can be quickly converted to spendable cash, and returns are small. When the Lower-Status person does invest his savings, he will be specific about the mode of investment, and is very likely to prefer something tangible and concrete—something he can point at and readily display.

Turning from mode of saving to purpose of saving, very significant

[3] The saving-spending aspiration analysis was carried out by Roger Coup, graduate student at the University of Chicago.

class relationships are likewise evident. Consider the verbalization of saving purpose. Lower-Status people typically explain why one should save—why the very act of saving is important. On the other hand, Middle-Class people do not, as if saving is an end-in-itself, the merits of which are obvious and need not be justified.

Spending is the other side of the coin. Analysis of what people say they will spend for shows similar class-related desires. All classes mention concrete, material artifacts such as a new car, some new appliance. But the Lower-Status people stop here. Their accumulations are artifact-centered, whereas Middle-Class spending-mentions are experience-centered. This is spending where one is left typically with only a memory. It would include hobbies, recreation, self-education and travel. The wish to travel, and particularly foreign travel, is almost totally a Middle-Class aspiration.

Even in their fantasies, people are governed by class membership. In his daydreaming and wishful thinking, the Lower-Status individual will aspire in different patterns from the Middle-Class individual.

PSYCHOLOGICAL DIFFERENCES

This spending-saving analysis has very obvious psychological implications to differentiate between the classes. Saving itself generally suggests foresightedness, the ability to perceive long-term needs and goals. Non-investment saving has the characteristics of little risk-taking and of ready conversion, at no loss, into immediate expenditures—the money can be drawn out of the account whenever the bank is open. Investment spending, on the other hand, has the characteristics of risk-taking (a gamble for greater returns) and of delayed conversion, with possible loss, to expenditures on immediate needs.

Here are some psychological contrasts between two different social groups:

Middle-Class
1. Pointed to the future
2. His viewpoint embraces a long expanse of time
3. More urban identification
4. Stresses rationality
5. Has a well-structured sense of the universe
6. Horizons vastly extended or not limited
7. Greater sense of choice-making
8. Self-confident, willing to take risks
9. Immaterial and abstract in his thinking
10. Sees himself tied to national happenings

Lower-Status
1. Pointed to the present and past
2. Lives and thinks in a short expanse of time

3. More rural in identification
4. Non-rational essentially
5. Vague and unclear structuring of the world
6. Horizons sharply defined and limited
7. Limited sense of choice-making
8. Very much concerned with security and insecurity
9. Concrete and perceptive in his thinking
10. World revolves around his family and body

CONCLUSION

The essential purpose of this article was to develop three basic premises which are highly significant for marketing:

1. There is a social-class system operative in metropolitan markets, which can be isolated and described.

2. It is important to realize that there are far-reaching psychological difference between the various classes.

They do not handle the world in the same fashion. They tend not to think in the same way. As one tries to communicate with the Lower-Status group, it is imperative to sense that their goals and mental processes differ from the Middle-Class group.

3. Consumption patterns operate as prestige symbols to define class membership, which is a more significant determinant of economic behavior than mere income.

Each major department store, furniture store, and chain-grocery store has a different "pulling power" on different status groups. The usual customers of a store gradually direct the store's merchandising policies into a pattern which works. The interaction between store policy and consumer acceptance results in the elimination of certain customer groups and the attraction of others, with a resulting equilibration around a reasonably stable core of specific customer groups who think of the store as appropriate for them.

Income has always been the marketer's handiest index to family consumption standards. But it is a far from accurate index. For instance, the bulk of the population in a metropolitan market today will fall in the middle-income ranges. This will comprise not only the traditional white collar worker, but the unionized craftsman and the semi-skilled worker with their tremendous income gains of the past decade. Income-wise, they may be in the same category. But their buying behavior, their tastes, their spending-saving aspirations can be poles apart. Social-class position and mobility-stability dimensions will reflect in much greater depth each individual's style of life.

RETROSPECTIVE COMMENT

In order to establish just how classic is Martineau's contribution, it is necessary to recall (or reveal, depending on your age) the state of the art in consumer research at the time his article appeared. The 1950's was a decade of push and shove between qualitative researchers and those who thought them clever, but irrelevant hucksters. Cartoons and bad jokes about motivation research abounded.

History tends to stereotype, the dichotomize, and this episode was no exception. It wasn't so much that quantitative researchers had all the chips—essentially, their case was built on socioeconomic measures, large samples, and first generation computers; the multivariate revolution had yet to occur. But they had *tradition* which, in commercial research circles, is a heavy, heavy pedigree. To side with the qualitative people, then, was quite literally to place your reputation in jeopardy. Would *you* want to be labeled a "hidden persuader?" If you worked for a newspaper?

However trivial hindsight seems to render this controversy, Martineau found himself in the midst of it. But he was so intensely practical it hardly bothered him. There was no question about his position—he was clearly in the qualitative camp—but he was never pedantic in his rationale. He was attempting to understand human behavior, and he saw little point to a holy war with methodology as its locus. Had he opted for confrontation, he could have drawn upon some formidable allies— Lloyd Warner (whose concept of social class attracted him) and Burleigh Gardner and Sidney Levy of Social Research, Inc. (the research firm engaged to perform the many studies). These people served largely to feed Martineau with the empirical grist he needed as he stumped (his *Motivation in Adverstising* plus numerous speeches and articles) for "soft data" as a (but never the *only*) key to understanding consumers. If ever there was a gatekeeper it was Martineau.

Is the 1958 article dated? Only in the sense that certain parts of a classic automobile need periodic maintenance. Is it a seminal paper? Martineau would probably laugh uproariously, regarding such an appellation as posthumous obsequiousness—in spite of the fact that advertising, consumer behavior, and marketing books continue to cite his work. No, he likely would dig in, punctuating what he said and did *not* say in 1958, and interpret the current world something like this:

> *Are there still social classes in America?* Yes; in spite of several proclaimed policies to vitiate them. Don't be fooled because incomes seem to have become more uniformly distributed over the past generation. The highest income bracket is open-ended and not really that high. A lot is hidden in a $10,000-and-over annual income

category. Moreover, some communities have more than one social-class structure. Unless and until *all* segments of a community can receive "unearned" rewards (inherited wealth or position that is recognized as legitimate by the majority), each segment is likely to establish its own status hierarchy. Witness the efforts of Jews and blacks today, and those of the Irish historically.

Why doesn't social class always work? To begin, explicate your assumption. By "always work" you must mean to serve as a viable method for segmenting markets. In that context there are three reasons. First, since social class is an indication of life style, there is no particular reason to expect that all products used to sustain respective life styles must be mutually exlusive. The 1958 article doesn't contend that social classes are disparate; indeed, it mentions the obverse and emphasizes the importance of mobility. Second, social class means more than just the level of a family's income. Indeed, if people insist on inventing their own versions of "social class" they shouldn't expect to be able to replicate the 1958 results except by fortuitous circumstance. Third, when social class seems not to "work"—in addition to the reasons just cited—it could well be that it *is* working, except you can't see how. Remember, a given product can be acquired by two very different people, in very different ways, for very different reasons. If you look only at the two different people, each with the identical product, you're apt to be mislead seriously and inadvertently deny everything you know about consumer psychology.

Is social class as simple and straightforward a phenomenon as you seem to suggest? It is neither simple nor straightforward; no one wears identifying shibboleths. The differences between classes are subtle and the relationships within classes are almost cryptic to the outsider. Dick Cavett, while a scholarship student at Yale, demurred that he'd "highed," when asked—quite matter-of-factly— where he had prepped. What else need be said?

To Martineau, the suggestion that his contribution was prescient would likely have been dismissed as an exercise in hyperbole. From his perspective, income-class was an overworked predictor and he sought something better. But he knew that "better" had to mean intuitively as well as statistically superior. His persistence in working with blue-chip researchers and his unwillingness to relent until the task was accomplished is not appreciated by the generation of students who take "social class" for granted. But the Tribune Tower periodically shakes in respect.—*Dr. Jerome B. Kernan*, Professor of Behavioral Analysis, University of Cincinnati

22. Social Class and Life Cycle as Predictors of Shopping Behavior

Stuart U. Rich and Subhash C. Jain

This article is concerned with application of concepts of social class and life cycle to consumer shopping behavior for the purposes of segmenting the market. That these concepts help in understanding the consumer is generally accepted. As Martineau said,

> The friends we choose, the neighborhoods we live in, the way we spend and save our money, the educational plans we have for our children are determined in large degree along social class lines. A rich man is not just a poor man with more money. He probably has different ideals, different personality forces, different church membership, and many different notions of right and wrong, all largely stemming from social class differentials. With its disciplinary pressures of approval and disapproval, belonging versus ostracism, social class is a major factor shaping the individual's style of life.

Thus for a marketing program to be effective, it must be designed to reach the social class that fits one's product or service. Similarly, life cycle has been used as an independent variable in analyzing housing needs and uses, income, finances, and the purchase of a standard package of items to be consumed at each stage in life.

However, recent changes in social and economic circumstances of consumers—such as increase in discretionary income, leisure time, opportunities for higher education, increasing social benefits, movements to suburbia—have raised some doubts about the effectiveness of social class and life cycle to explain consumer behavior. Several articles in academic and professional journals indicate how people supposedly of different classes tend to resemble each other in the market place. This was also reflected in the *Wall Street Journal*.

> It is no news that blue-collar pay is rising. It's not even particularly news that blue-collar workers have been raising their pay somewhat faster than white-collar workers. The extent to which these blue-collar increases have

Reprinted by permission of the authors and publisher from the Journal of Marketing Research, *published by the American Marketing Association, Vol. 5 (February 1968), pp. 41–49.*

been creating what is in effect a new class blending traditional blue-collar and white-collar spending habits, social customs and ways of thinking, is perhaps not so well realized. But recently this has become the most striking of all blue-collar trends.

A similar trend has been noted about life cycle. As a J. C. Penney's executive said,

> The youth market is influenced by the population explosion, education which teaches reason rather than memorization, sweeping changes in social attitudes. Young people have a "no depression complex," a refreshing honesty and self-effacing humor. They also have a higher level of "taste achievement" which they have acquired themselves. The youth market is witty, worldly, and has money to spend. This market has influence on all the other markets (parents, young adults, older people who respond to youth).[1]

In summary, the traditional distinctions between the various social classes and stages in the family life cycle seem to be quickly diminishing. The main objective of this article is to report the findings of a study done to test the usefulness of social class and life cycle in understanding consumer behavior during changing socioeconomic conditions.[2] In presenting our findings, other studies, and certain statements, and assertions will be referred to which our empirical findings support or refute.

METHOD

The data used in this study were originally collected by one of the authors for a comprehensive work in 1963 on shopping behavior of department store customers. The data consisted of about 4,000 personal and telephone interviews in Cleveland and New York. For this article part of the data was reanalyzed, namely the results of 1,056 personal interviews with a probability sample representing all women 20 years of age and older residing in the Cleveland standard metropolitan statistical area. In collecting the original data, a random procedure divided this Cleveland area into 19 zones and selected a sample of places —one place in each zone. This random procedure was repeated and a second, independent sample was drawn, providing a replicated probability sample.[3]

The two major variables used here were social class and family life cycle. Social class was stratified by a multiple-item index, Warner's In-

---

[1] For additional information see: "Experts Set Youth Market Guidelines."
[2] This study was done for a doctoral dissertation.
[3] For a step-by-step description of the research procedure used, including sample design, see "Technical Appendix on Research Methodology" (22).

dex of Status Characteristics widely used in social research.[4] In this index Warner had four variables, source of income, occupation, dwelling area, and house type. This index was modified and source of income and house type were replaced with the amount of income and education of family head. Warner originally used source of income only because of the difficulty in obtaining income amount. It has been found that house type, which is mainly a reflection of house value is mainly dependent on occupation. If house type and occupation were used, occupation would have been weighed very heavily. Therefore, education—also an important determinant of social class—was substituted for house type.

To measure life cycle, the following breakdown was used: under 40 without children, under 40 with children, 40 and over without children, 40 and over with children. This gave a measure of the effects of age, married status, and children in the household—all important determinants of shopping behavior. Using 40 as the dividing point for age indicated whether there were preschool children in the household, another important factor influencing shopping habits.

Highlights of the differences in shopping behavior of women in various social classes and stages in the life cycle are described here. Chi-square tests were used to ascertain which of these differences were significant at the .05 level and to determine, for instance, whether social class affected women's interest in fashion and choice of shopping companions.

FACTORS AFFECTING SHOPPING

INTEREST IN FASHION

If traditional distinctions between the women in various social classes and stages of the life cycle are disappearing an indication would be expected in women's interest in fashion. Respondents' interest in fashion was measured from these five statements, each printed on a separate card and handed to the respondent. She was asked to state her preferences, which were noted by the interviewer.

1. I read the fashion news regularly and try to keep my wardrobe up to date with fashion trends.
2. I keep up to date on all fashion changes although I don't always attempt to dress according to these changes.
3. I check to see what is currently fashionable only when I need to buy some new clothes.

4 For a full discussion of different methods of social stratification and how and why we used Warner's Index, see Jain, Subhash, "A Critical Analysis of Life Cycle and Social Class Concepts in Understanding Consumer Shopping Behavior."

4. I don't pay much attention to fashion trends unless a major change takes place.

5. I am not at all interested in fashion trends.

In Table 1, the fashion interests of the women belonging to various social classes are compared. Fashion plays an important part in the lives of all women regardless of class. Except for the lower-lower class, in which a slightly higher percentage of women than in other classes showed no interest in fashion at all, very small percentages of women among all other classes found fashion uninteresting.

King made essentially the same point, emphasizing the broad appeal of fashion. This finding supports Weiss's remark "Fashion today is the prerogative of a substantial majority of our population—men, women and children." However, these findings do not entirely agree with the traditional research of Barber and Lobel who found that social class differences determined the definition of women's fashion. Although this was true for knowing fashion changes, it did not apply to keeping the wardrobe up to date, which concerned all women.

The present survey also showed that women in different stages of the life cycle did not vary significantly in their fashion interests. For instance, 48 percent of women 40 or over with children either read the fashion news regularly or kept up to date on all fashion trends compared with 50 percent of women under 40 with children. Katz and Lazarsfeld, however, found that interest in fashion declined with the life cycle.

Table 2 summarizes the methods that women in various social classes used for following fashion trends. Except for watching television and listening to the radio, where the differences between social classes were not significant, the helpfulness of the various methods shown in keeping women up to date on fashion changes increased with social class level. The rate of increase varied, however, with different methods. For example, in the category "discussing fashion with others," there was relatively little difference between the lower and middle classes. In "looking at newspaper ads," there was a sharp rise in helpfulness from the lower-lower class to the upper-upper class, but the difference is not particularly significant until the upper-upper class. In summary, the traditional view of greater fashion interest for higher social classes generally holds true for particular methods used to keep informed of fashion although the increase in interest is seldom in any direct proportion to the increase in social level.

Unlike social class, life cycle did not affect fashion interest. There were no significant differences in the methods used by women in various stages of the family life cycle for being informed of fashion changes.

Table 22.1. INTEREST IN WOMEN'S FASHIONS BY CLEVELAND WOMEN SHOPPERS, BY
SOCIAL CLASS

Statement on degree of interest	Social class					
	L-L	U-L	L-M	U-M	L-U	U-U
Read news regularly and keep wardrobe up to date	14%	8%	9%	10%	19%	9%
Keep abreast of changes but not always follow	19	29	42	50	47	64
Check what is fashionable only if buy new clothes	15	22	15	17	17	9
Only pay attention to major fashion changes	22	23	19	14	14	18
Not at all interested in fashion trends	24	16	12	9	3	—b
Don't know	6	2	3	—	—	—
Total	100%	100%	100%	100%	100%	100%
Number of cases	132	346	265	206	36	11

[a]In this and subsequent tables, L = lower, M = middle and U = upper.
[b]In this and subsequent tables, a dash represents less than .5 percent.

SOURCES OF SHOPPER INFORMATION

Newspaper ads are an important source of shoppers' information.
The degree of helpfulness which women attributed to newspaper advertising was analyzed. Women in various social classes seemed to find
newspaper ads helpful to about the same degree, except a slightly
greater percentage of women in the lower-lower class found them somewhat more helpful.

Another measure used to study the importance of newspaper ads
was to analyze the regularity with which women in different social
classes looked at newspaper ads. Here again, women of different status
groups showed no significant differences in the regularity of their looking at newspaper ads. These results agreed with findings of a recent
study reported in *Editor and Publisher*:

The daily newspaper's coverage of the market place on the average day is
nearly universal. Almost every household, 87%, gets a newspaper. . . . The
mass exposure opportunity represented by this high percentage of page
opening is remarkably consistent for men and women of all ages, incomes,
educational attainments and geographical locations.

Carman has reported a similar finding about the importance of newspaper ads as a source of information for members of different social classes.

Among women in the various stages of the family life cycle, those with children considered the newspaper ads more helpful. For instance, 88 percent of the women 40 and over with children found ads helpful compared with 73 percent of those without children. Among the women under 40 with and without children, the percentages were 81 and 70, respectively. Further analysis showed that women with children looked at newspaper ads more often than those without children. Age itself had little effect on either the regularity of looking at ads in newspapers or the helpfulness attributed to these ads.

This finding about life cycle differs from what Miller pointed out in 1954,

> The younger housewives are easier to educate to an awareness of product and brand; it is easier to get across to the younger housewives the reasons why they should try it or buy it; and the younger housewives are less fixed in their buying habits and brand loyalty, and will be more inclined to change their buying patterns in response to advertising.

Again we note that some of the traditional distinctions among the social classes and stages in the family life cycle may be disappearing.

INTERPERSONAL INFLUENCES IN SHOPPING

Interpersonal influences play an important part in shopping decisions. For practical application to marketing, it is necessary to know who these influencers are for each segment of the market. The traditional view has been that upper classes interacted more with members of the immediate family and put great emphasis on lineage. The middle class, though, was generally considered self-directing, had initiative, and was dependent on themselves and their friends more than on relatives. Like the upper classes, the lower classes depended on relatives and family members more often. Our findings differed in some respects from this view.

Tables 3 and 4 present data on the impact of interpersonal influences on shopping decisions under two categories, helpfulness attributed to discussing shopping with others and persons with whom respondents usually shopped. In both categories, women in various social classes showed no significant difference in the influence of friends on shopping. The husband was slightly more important as a shopping influence for the middle and upper classes than for the lower classes, and by the middle and upper classes. However, mother and other family members

Table 22.2. METHODS HELPFUL TO CLEVELAND WOMEN ON FASHION TRENDS, BY
SOCIAL CLASS

Method	Social class					
	L-L	*U-L*	*L-M*	*U-M*	*L-U*	*U-U*
Going to fashion shows	5%	3%	7%	9%	22%	18%
Reading fashion magazines	14	13	11	23	36	27
Reading other magazines	17	18	26	31	28	46
Reading fashion articles in papers	22	34	46	45	56	64
Looking at newspaper ads	39	57	60	68	67	91
Going shopping	36	50	53	63	75	73
Discussing fashion with others	21	22	29	34	36	46
Observing what others wear	22	36	81	51	58	55
Watching television	32	28	25	26	25	46
Listening to the radio	2	5	5	2	8	—
Don't know	3	1	1	—	—	—
No interest in fashion	30	18	14	10	3	—
Total[a]	243%	285%	358%	362%	414%	466%
Number of cases	132	346	265	206	36	11

[a]Total exceeds 100 percent because of multiple responses.

were not mentioned to any large extent by the lower classes as traditional research would indicate.

Note also in Table 3 that the proportion of women who attributed no help to discussing shopping with others was not significantly different for the three classes. This does not agree with what Rainwater, Coleman, and Handel said, "the working class largely depended on word-of-mouth recommendation before making major purchases."

SHOPPING ENJOYMENT

Most women enjoyed shopping regardless of their social class. However, women in different social classes had varying reasons for enjoying shopping. Some reasons—such as the recreational and social aspects of shopping, seeing new things and getting new ideas, and bargain hunting and comparing merchandise—were mentioned by all social classes without any significant difference. Another reason, namely acquiring new clothes or household things, was more enjoyable for the two lower classes. However, a pleasant store atmosphere, display and excitement were specified as reasons for enjoying shopping by a greater proportion of women in the upper-middle, lower-upper, and upper-upper classes. Stone and Form found that enjoyment in shopping was not a function of social status. This was in accord with our general finding on shopping enjoyment although, as just noted, the reasons for enjoyment sometimes varied among social classes.

Life cycle did not have any effect on the enjoyment of shopping for clothing and household items. For instance, 38 percent of the women over 40 with children enjoyed shopping for such reasons as pleasant store atmosphere, displays, and excitement compared with 36 percent in this age group without children. For women under 40 without children, the percentages were 37 and 41, respectively.

Stone and Form claimed that younger women with children enjoyed shopping more than other women. In this study, neither age nor the presence of children in the family seemed to make any difference for women in their enjoyment of shopping.

SHOPPING FREQUENCY

The frequency with which women shopped during the year was significantly associated with social class. For example, 38 percent of the women in the upper class and 34 percent in the middle class shopped 52 or more times a year compared with 24 percent in the lower class. These findings do not match those of Stone and Form. According to

Table 22.3. DISCUSSION OF SHOPPING WITH OTHERS, CLEVELAND WOMEN, BY SOCIAL CLASS

	Social class[a]		
Consider it helpful with	*Lower*	*Middle*	*Upper*
Friends	34%	37%	50%
Husband	13	18	24
Mother	5	5	6
Other family members	20	14	18
No one	36	39	32
Total[b]	108%	113%	130%
Number of cases	478	471	47

[a]Significant differences were noted even when we divided the respondents into six social classes. However, to save space here in some instances only three classes are shown.

[b]Total exceeds 100 percent because of multiple responses.

them, women in either the upper or the middle class shopped less often than women in the lower or working class.

Younger women shopped more often than older women, but presence of children did not make any significant difference within the two age groups (Table 5). Stone and Form found the frequency of shopping trips mainly dependent on children in the family.

IMPORTANCE OF SHOPPING QUICKLY

The higher the social status of a woman, the more she considered it important to shop quickly. Thus 39 percent of upper class women regarded it important to always shop quickly though only 30 percent in the lower class and 34 percent in the middle class did. Only 10 percent of upper class women felt it was not important to shop quickly compared with 19 percent and 29 percent in the middle and lower classes, respectively. According to Stone and Form, however, the upper and lower classes spent more time shopping than did the middle class. Huff found that women of high social status spent the most time on an average shopping trip.

For life cycle, Sone and Form found that women in their forties felt most hurried, and women in their twenties were divided evenly between those who felt they had adequate time and those who did not. In their study age was found to be the determining factor of the importance of shopping quickly. In this study, women under and over 40 with children put more stress on quick shopping than those without children. These findings thus show different behavior patterns about the importance of shopping quickly.

BROWSING

Tendency to browse without buying anything was more prominent among the upper-lower (41 percent), lower-middle (44 percent), and upper-middle (42 percent) classes. Yet women in the lower-lower, lower-upper, and upper-upper classes mentioned it less often (Table 6). Stone and Form discovered that lower class women did more browsing than middle and upper class women, a finding obviously different from this study's.

Further, women under 40 with or without children, browsed more (24 percent and 22 percent, respectively) than women 40 and over (12 percent for those with and without children); but Stone and Form did not find the life cycle to have any relationship here. Again, traditional distinctions among the various social classes and stages in the family life cycle may be changing.

DOWNTOWN SHOPPING

Several authors have reported how the continued expansion of the shopping centers has challenged the traditional role of the downtown area. In this study, the lower the social status, the greater the proportion of downtown shopping (Table 7). Sixty-eight percent of lower-lower class women were designated as high downtown shoppers, only 22 percent of the lower-upper class and 18 percent of the upper-upper class were considered to be so. This finding is different from that reported in *Workingman's Wife*, "A comparison between the shopping of middle class women and working class women shows the provinciality of the latter. Fewer working class than middle class women classify themselves as 'regular shoppers' in the central business districts." Thus there is a change in downtown clientele. Once the upper class shopped downtown more often; now it may be the lower classes who patronize downtown more.

This also suggests that suburban shopping centers are becoming increasingly more important for the upper classes. This has been noted in *Women's Wear Daily*, "It is a mistake to promote just $25 dresses in a suburban store. . . . We have found, from experience, that higher price clothes do sell in depth in the suburbs."

Cross tabulations by life cycle showed a tendency for young people to patronize shopping centers more than older people, as suggested by other findings.

No significant differences on downtown shopping existed among the women in the various social classes living in the city. However, among the suburbanites, social class was inversely related to downtown shopping. For instance, among the city dwellers about 60 percent of the women in the two lower and two middle classes were ranked as high downtown shoppers. Yet, among the out-of-city residents 43 percent of lower-lower class women and 37 percent of upper-lower class were considered high in-town shoppers; only 32 percent in the lower-middle and 27 percent in the upper-middle class were high downtown shoppers. The percentages for the two upper classes further decreased to 22 percent and 18 percent, respectively.

In contrast, about 70 percent of the women in the two upper classes (living in the suburbs) were low downtown shoppers though the same percentage was 29 percent for the lower-lower class and 40 percent for the upper-lower class. However, when the high and low categories were considered together and compared with the "none" group, downtown shopping by suburbanites increased in each higher social class.

In general, a greater proportion of higher class women shop downtown, but women in the lower classes appear to shop more intensively in the central business district.

Table 22.4. PERSONS WITH WHOM CLEVELAND WOMEN USUALLY SHOP, BY SOCIAL CLASS

Usually shop with	Social class					
	L-L	*U-L*	*L-M*	*U-M*	*L-U*	*U-U*
Friends	32%	31%	26%	34%	39%	46%
Husband	20	25	32	35	33	9
Mother	5	7	9	9	3	—
Children	10	15	22	23	28	—
Other family members	21	23	16	10	8	18
No one in particular	26	20	17	10	17	36
Never shops with others	—	2	1	2	—	—
Total[a]	114%	123%	123%	135%	128%	109%
Number of cases	132	346	265	206	36	11

[a]Total exceeds 100 percent because of multiple responses.

TYPE OF STORE PREFERRED

As seen in Table 8, higher class women more often named the regular department store as their favorite. The department store maintained a broad image as a favorite store since 51 percent of the lower-lower class women and 60 percent of the upper-lower class designated it their favorite store. A greater percentage of lower-lower (14 percent) and upper-lower (11 percent) women favored the discount store than did women in either the middle or upper classes.

Several writers have emphasized that women in various social classes differ in the department stores they patronize and have different expectations about each store. Therefore, the authors looked at the particular stores which women named as their favorites among the different regular department stores. Three department stores in Cleveland were mentioned far more often than others, and these were called a high fashion, a price appeal, or a broad appeal store.

As shown in Table 9, the high fashion store became more important for each higher class. But, the price appeal store was inversely related to social class. The broad appeal store was mentioned by the two middle classes more often. These findings generally agreed with what Martineau discovered:

> the blue collar individual, as his family income goes up, proceeds from cars to appliances to home ownership to apparel. He and his family are candidates for almost any store, and the most successful stores which would traditionally appeal to them have held them by steadily trading up, both in merchandise, store facilities and their image.... The point again is that this person has changed. He is not the same guy. He has long since satisfied his needs and wants and now he is interested in satisfying his wishes.

The high preference of the lower class shoppers for the regular department stores is therefore not surprising.

The kind of department store women in the various social classes mentioned most often was also analyzed for the following kinds of merchandise: women's better dresses; house dresses and underwear; children's clothing; men's socks and shirts; furniture; large appliances; towels, sheets, blankets and spreads; and small electrical appliances and kitchen utensils. Here again the two upper classes specified the high fashion store as their favorite for the first five of these eight kinds of merchandise. Women in the two lower classes shopped at the price appeal store most of the time for all items.

Analysis of the favorite store of women in various stages of the life cycle showed that the regular department store ranked high among all women except that younger women with children showed somewhat

Table 22.5. FREQUENCY OF SHOPPING TRIPS OF CLEVELAND WOMEN, BY LIFE CYCLE

	Stage in life cycle			
	Under 40		*40 and over*	
Times per year	*No child*	*Child*	*No child*	*Child*
52 or more	30%	30%	25%	31%
24 to 51	33	25	17	20
12 to 23	23	28	18	21
6 to 11	2	4	6	7
1 to 5	12	12	27	21
Less than once	—	—	2	—
Never	—	—	1	—
Don't know	—	1	4	—
Total	100%	100%	100%	100%
Number of cases	66	474	240	276

Table 22.6. BROWSING OF CLEVELAND WOMEN, BY SOCIAL CLASS

	Social class					
Regularity of occurrence	*L-L*	*U-L*	*L-M*	*U-M*	*L-U*	*U-U*
Regularly or fairly often	29%	41%	44%	42%	22%	18%
Once in awhile	30	37	35	36	31	27
Never	40	21	20	22	44	55
Don't know	1	1	1	—	3	—
Total	100%	100%	100%	100%	100%	100%
Number of cases	132	346	265	206	36	11

less preference for it. Table 10 shows that 57 percent of the younger women with children and 65 percent of the younger women without children mentioned the regular department store as their favorite. Discount stores were preferred by the younger women a little more than by the older ones. No significant differences were revealed between the types of stores favored by women in various stages of the family life cycle for the eight kinds of merchandise individually.

CONCLUSION

Socioeconomic changes in income, education, leisure time, and movement to suburbia cut across traditional class lines and various stages in the life cycle. Some authors like Rainwater, Coleman, and Handel have found social class a significant factor in determining consumer behavior. However recent writings seem to indicate that social class distinctions have been obscured by rising incomes and educational levels.

Our empirical findings tend to support the second viewpoint. The random sampling procedure used assured every Cleveland woman 20 years of age or older an equal chance of being selected, and interviewer bias was closely controlled. Hence we are able to generalize about shopping behavior in Cleveland. Admittedly, all findings cannot be applied to women in other cities. However in the original study, which included Cleveland and New York-northeastern New Jersey metropolitan areas, many patterns of shopping behavior for women in particular income or life cycle categories were almost identical in the two areas despite the contrasting patterns of size, geographical location, demography, and kinds of stores found in these two cities.

Table 22.7. SHOPPING DONE DOWNTOWN BY CLEVELAND WOMEN, BY SOCIAL CLASS

Proportion of downtown shopping[a]	Social class					
	L-L	*U-L*	*L-M*	*U-M*	*L-U*	*U-U*
High	68%	50%	42%	33%	22%	18%
Low	19	33	37	50	59	64
None	11	15	19	15	16	18
Don't know	2	2	2	2	3	—
Total	100%	100%	100%	100%	100%	100%
Number of cases	132	346	265	206	36	11

[a]High downtown shoppers shop downtown half or more of the time; Low downtown Shoppers, one-quarter or less of the time; None means women who do not shop downtown.

Spot checks made of Cleveland and New York women in the present study again produced similar results. For instance, among women under 40 with children in Cleveland, 30 percent shopped 52 or more times

Table 22.8. KIND OF FAVORITE STORE OF CLEVELAND WOMEN, BY SOCIAL CLASS

	Social class					
Kind of store	*L-L*	*U-L*	*L-M*	*U-M*	*L-U*	*U-U*
Regular department	51%	60%	77%	83%	88%	91%
Discount department	14	11	6	2	—	9
Variety and junior department	2	6	6	5	—	—
Mail order	9	14	5	2	3	—
Medium to low specialty	2	2	1	—	6	—
Neighborhood	11	2	1	1	3	—
Others	11	5	4	7	—	—
Total	100%	100%	100%	100%	100%	100%
Number of cases	132	346	265	206	36	11

Table 22.9. KIND OF DEPARTMENT STORE FAVORED BY CLEVELAND WOMEN

	Social class					
Kind of department store	*L-L*	*U-L*	*L-M*	*U-M*	*L-U*	*U-U*
High fashion store	4%	7%	22%	34%	70%	67%
Price appeal store	74	63	36	24	19	18
Broad appeal store	22	30	42	42	11	15
Total	100%	100%	100%	100%	100%	100%
Number of cases	67	208	204	71	32	10

Table 22.10. KIND OF FAVORITE STORE OF CLEVELAND WOMEN, BY LIFE CYCLE

	Stage in life cycle			
	Under 40		40 and over	
Kind of favorite store	*No child*	*Child*	*No child*	*Child*
Department	65%	57%	83%	79%
Discount	9	13	2	2
Mail order	5	11	2	7
All others	21	19	13	12
Total	100%	100%	100%	100%
Number of cases	66	474	240	276

per year compared with 34 percent for this group in New York. For women 40 and over with children, the percentages were 31 and 30 for the two cities. On the importance of being able to shop quickly, 30 percent of the lower social class women in Cleveland felt this was always important, as did 34 percent of the middle class women and 39 percent of the upper class women. In New York these percentages were 29, 36, and 39, respectively. In other words, there seems to be evidence that many of the shopping behavior patterns of Cleveland women exist in other cities.

The findings thus question the usefulness of life cycle and social class concepts in understanding consumer behavior in view of recent changes in income, education, leisure time, movement to suburbia, and other factors. Students of marketing and store executives may need to reconsider how far these sociological concepts should be used for segmentation purposes and what their probable impact will be on marketing policies and programs.

RETROSPECTIVE COMMENT

In our article, "Social Class and Life Cycle as Predictors of Shopping Behavior," based on research data collected in 1963, Jain and I described how major social, economic, and demographic factors affected consumer shopping behavior. These factors had a leveling effect on consumer behavior such that markets could no longer be clearly segregated according to social class and stage in family life cycle.

What are the new factors today which affect consumer shopping behavior? Are these factors causing a continuation of the leveling effect noted above? Within the limited scope of this commentary I can only note what some of the major factors are, and give a few examples of how they seem to be affecting shopping behavior. More definitive answers to the above questions would require a study approximating the magnitude of our earlier one, which no researcher has as yet undertaken.

The major social, economic, and demographic forces today which have an impact on consumer behavior in the market place are: (1) Responsiveness of the government to demands by low income and minority groups for social benefits and programs which will put them in the mainstream of middle class economic life; (2) Stagflation, that is, slow growth for the economy as a whole, with some industries registering little or no growth, but with continued high inflation for all segments of the economy; (3) Energy shortage and high costs of energy; (4) Environmentalism, with attendant "life simplification" and "return to nature" trends; (5) Women's liberation, with accompanying pattern of husband and wife partnership and a blurring of the distinction between "working" and "non-working" women; (6) Consumerism, with attendant demand for products and services that live up to manufacturers' and retailers' claims; (7) A blurring of the distinction between various stages of the family life cycle—for example, there are as many women in the country with neither husbands nor children as there are married women with children under eighteen living at home; (8) Decline in birth and fertility rates, with change in popular attitude toward family size; and (9) Household formations by the baby boom children of the latter half of the 1940's and first half of the 1950's.

As a result of the above factors, today's consumers are economizing, bargain-hunting, and repairing the once-discardable. They are showing a growing preference for products that offer economy, simplicity, and functionalism. They are shopping more at discount stores, cutting back on the purchase of discretionary goods and services, and economizing on the use of electricity. They are taking pride in becoming better, less gullible shoppers. These patterns of behavior are becoming increasingly evident among consumers in all social classes and in all stages of the family life cycle. In other words, the leveling effect noted in the early 1960's, is still evident in the mid-1970's, now caused by a new set of economic, social, and demographic factors. The main difference, however, is that in the 1960's the life style of the upper middle class was a model for people in lower classes to level up to, whereas today there is at least a partial reversal of this pattern. Many middle and upper middle-class families are shifting to a lower or working-class pattern of consumption in their search for a simpler life, or just to cope with problems of scarcity, inflation, and threat of unemployment.

As for consumers in different stages of the family life cycle, some of the anti-materialism values of the youth culture have been adopted by older persons. At the same time, however, current economic pressures have caused many young people—particularly those now forming households—to return to the values represented by the Protestant work ethic, such as the belief that hard work pays off, and that part of earnings should regularly be put into savings even if it means sacrifice. *Stuart U. Rich,* Professor of Marketing, School of Business Administration, University of Oregon

REFERENCES

BARBER, BERNARD and Lyle S. Lobel. "Fashion in Women's Clothes and the American Social System," *Social Forces*, 31 (December 1952), 124–31.

CARMAN, JAMES M. *The Application of Social Class in Market Segmentation,* Berkeley, Calif.: University of California, 1965.

CLARK, LINCOLN, ed. *The Life Cycle and Consumer Behavior*, Vol. 2, New York: New York University Press, 1955.

COLEMAN, RICHARD P. "The Significance of Social Stratification in Selling," in Martin L. Bell, ed., *Marketing: A Maturing Discipline*, Chicago: American Marketing Association, December 1960, 177.

DAVIDSON, THOMAS LEA. *Some Effects of the Growth of Planned and Controlled Shopping Centers on Small Retailers*, Washington, D.C.: Small Business Administration, 1960.

Editors of *Fortune, Market for the Sixties*. New York: Harper and Row, 1960.

"Experts Set Youth Market Guidelines," *Women's Wear Daily*, 113 (October 18, 1966), 19.

HOLLINGSHEAD, AUGUST B. "Class Differences in Family Stability," in Reinhard Bendix and Seymour Martin Lipset, eds., *Class, Status and Power*, New York: The Free Press, 1965.

HUFF, DAVID L. "Geographical Aspects of Consumer Behavior," *University of Washington Business Review*, 18 (June 1959), 27–35.

JAIN, SUBHASH. "A Critical Analysis of Life Cycle and Social Class Concepts in Understanding Consumer Shopping Behavior," Unpublished doctoral dissertation, University of Oregon, 1966.

JOHANSSEN, C. T. *The Shopping Center Versus Downtown*, Columbus, Ohio: The Ohio State University, 1955.

KATZ, ELIHU and Paul F. Lazarsfeld. *Personal Influence*, Glencoe, Ill.: The Free Press, 1955, 263–8.

KING, CHARLES W. "Fashion Adoption: A Rebuttal to the Trickle Down Theory," *Proceedings*, Summer Conference, American Marketing Association, June 1964, 108–25.

KLEIN, FREDERICK C. "Rising Pay Lifts More Blue Collar Men into a New Affluent Class," *The Wall Street Journal*, 165 (April 5, 1965).

MARTINEAU, PIERRE. "Customer Shopping Center Habits Change Retailing," *Editor & Publisher*, 96 (October 26, 1963), 16, 56.

Motivation in Advertising. New York: McGraw-Hill Book Company, 1957, 166–7.

MILLER, DONALD L. "The Life Cycle and the Importance of Advertising," in Lincoln Clark, ed., *The Life Cycle and Consumer Behavior*, Vol. 2, New York: New York University Press, 1955.

PACKARD, VANCE. *The Status Seekers*, New York: Pocket Books, Inc., 1961, 113.

PETERSON, PETER G. "Conventional Wisdom and the Sixties," *Journal of Marketing*, 26 (April 1962), 63–5.

PROKOP, TRUDY. "Jack Weiss: No Gambler, But a Man of Decision," *Women's Wear Daily*, 113 (November 28, 1966), 40.

RAINWATER, LEE, Richard Coleman, and Gerald Handel. *Workingman's Wife*, New York: MacFadden-Bartell Corp., 1962.

RICH, STUART U. *Shopping Behavior of Department Store Customers*, Boston, Mass.: Division of Research, Graduate School of Business Administration, Harvard University, 1963.

STERNLIEB, GEORGE. *The Future of the Downtown Department Store*, Cambridge, Mass.: Harvard University, 1962.

STONE, GREGORY P. and William H. Form. *The Local Community Clothing Market: A Study of the Social and Social Psychological Contexts of Shopping*, East Lansing, Mich.: Michigan State University, 1957, 20.

"Survey Proves High Exposure for Ads on Newspaper Pages." *Editor & Publisher*, 97 (October 3, 1964), 17–8.

TAYLOR, THAYER C. "Selling Where the Money Is," *Sales Management*, 91 (October 18, 1963), 37–41, 122, 124, 126.
———. "The I AM ME Consumer," *Business Week* (December 23, 1961), 38–39.
WARNER, W. LLOYD, M. Meeker and K. Eells. *Social Class in America*, Chicago: Social Research, Inc., 1949.
WEISS, EDWARD B. "The Revolution in Fashion Distribution," *Advertising Age*, 34 (June 24, 1963), 104–5.

23. The Silent Language in Overseas Business

Edward T. Hall

With few exceptions, Americans are relative newcomers on the international business scene. Today, as in Mark Twain's time, we are all too often "innocents abroad," in an era when naiveté and blundering in foreign business dealings may have serious political repercussions.

When the American executive travels abroad to do business, he is frequently shocked to discover to what extent the many variables of foreign behavior and custom complicate his efforts. Although the American has recognized, certainly, that even the man next door has many minor traits which make him somewhat peculiar, for some reason he has failed to appreciate how different foreign businessmen and their practices will seem to him.

He should understand that the various peoples around the world have worked out and integrated into their subconscious literally thousands of behavior patterns that they take for granted in each other.[1] Then, when the stranger enters, and behaves differently from the local norm, he often quite unintentionally insults, annoys, or amuses the native with whom he is attempting to do business. For example: In the United States, a corporation executive knows what is meant when a client lets a month go by before replying to a business proposal. On the other hand, he senses an eagerness to do business if he is immediately ushered into the client's office. In both instances, he is reacting to subtle cues in the timing of interaction, cues which he depends on to chart his course of action.

Abroad, however, all this changes. The American executive learns that the Latin Americans are casual about time and that if he waits an hour in the outer office before seeing the Deputy Minister of Finance,

[1] For details, see my book, *The Silent Language* (New York: Doubleday & Company, Inc., 1959).

---

it does not necessarily mean he is not getting anywhere. There people are so important that nobody can bear to tear himself away; because of the resultant interruptions and conversational detours, everybody is constantly getting behind. What the American does not know is the point at which the waiting becomes significant. In another instance, after traveling 7,000 miles an American walks into the office of a highly recommended Arab businessman on whom he will have to depend completely. What he sees does not breed confidence. The office is reached by walking through a suspicious-looking coffeehouse in an old, dilapidated building situated in a crowded non-European section of town. The elevator, rising from dark, smelly corridors, is rickety and equally foul. When he gets to the office itself, he is shocked to find it small, crowded, and confused. Papers are stacked all over the desk and table tops—even scattered on the floor in irregular piles.

The Arab merchant he has come to see had met him at the airport the night before and sent his driver to the hotel this morning to pick him up. But now, after the American's rush, the Arab is tied up with something else. Even when they finally start talking business, there are constant interruptions. If the American is at all sensitive to his environment, everything around him signals, "What am I getting into?"

Before leaving home he was told that things would be different, but how different? The hotel is modern enough. The shops in the new part of town have many more American and European trade goods than he had anticipated. His first impression was that doing business in the Middle East would not present any new problems. Now he is beginning to have doubts. One minute everything looks familiar and he is on firm ground; the next, familiar landmarks are gone. His greatest problem is that so much assails his senses all at once that he does not know where to start looking for something that will tell him where he stands. He needs a frame of reference—a way of sorting out what is significant and relevant.

That is why it is so important for American businessmen to have a real understanding of the various social, cultural, and economic differences they will face when they attempt to do business in foreign countries. To help give some frame of reference, this article will map out a few areas of human activity that have largely been unstudied.

The topics I will discuss are certainly not presented as the last word on the subject, but they have proved to be highly reliable points at which to begin to gain an understanding of foreign cultures. While additional research will undoubtedly turn up other items just as relevant, at present I think the businessman can do well to begin by appreciating cultural differences in matters concerning the language of time, of space, of material possessions, of friendship patterns, and of agreements.

LANGUAGE OF TIME

Everywhere in the world people use time to communicate with each other. There are different languages of time just as there are different spoken languages. The unspoken languages are informal; yet the rules governing their interpretation are surprisingly *ironbound*.

In the United States, a delay in answering a communication can result from a large volume of business causing the request to be postponed until the backlog is cleared away, from poor organization, or possibly from technical complexity requiring deep analysis. But if the person awaiting the answer or decision rules out these reasons, then the delay means to him that the matter has low priority on the part of the other person—lack of interest. On the other hand, a similar delay in a foreign country may mean something altogether different. Thus: In Ethiopia, the time required for a decision is directly proportional to its importance. This is so much the case that low-level bureaucrats there have a way of trying to elevate the prestige of their work by taking a long time to make up their minds. (Americans in that part of the world are innocently prone to downgrade their work in the local people's eyes by trying to speed things up.) In the Arab East, time does not generally include schedules as Americans know and use them. The time required to get something accomplished depends on the relationship. More important people get fast service from less important people, and conversely. Close relatives take absolute priority; nonrelatives are kept waiting.

In the United States, giving a person a deadline is a way of indicating the degree of urgency or relative importance of the work. But in the Middle East, the American runs into a cultural trap the minute he opens his mouth. "Mr. Aziz will have to make up his mind in a hurry because my board meets next week and I have to have an answer by then," is taken as indicating the American is overly demanding and is exerting undue pressue. "I am going to Damascus tomorrow morning and will have to have my car tonight," is a sure way to get the mechanic to stop work, because to give another person a deadline in this part of the world is to be rude, pushy, and demanding.

An Arab's evasiveness as to when something is going to happen does not mean he does not want to do business; it only means he is avoiding unpleasantness and is side-stepping possible commitments which he takes more seriously than we do. For example: The Arabs themselves at times find it impossible to communicate even to each other that some processes cannot be hurried, and are controlled by built-in schedules. This is obvious enough to the Westerner but not to the Arab. A highly placed public official in Baghdad precipitated a bitter family dispute because his nephew, a biochemist, could not speed up the complete analysis of the uncle's blood. He accused the nephew of putting other less important people before him and of not caring. Nothing could sway the uncle, who could not grasp the fact that there is such a thing as an *inherent* schedule.

With us the more important an event is, the further ahead we schedule it, which is why we find it insulting to be asked to a party at the last minute. In planning future events with Arabs, it pays to hold the lead time to a week or less because other factors may intervene or take precedence.

Again, time spent waiting in an American's outer office is a sure indicator of what one person thinks of another or how important he feels the other's business to be. This is so much the case that most Americans cannot help getting angry after waiting 30 minutes; one may even feel such a delay is an insult, and will walk out. In Latin America, on the other hand, one learns that it does not mean anything to wait in an outer office. An American businessman with years of experience in Mexico once told me, "You know, I have spent two hours cooling my heels in an executive's outer office. It took me a long time to learn to keep my blood pressure down. Even now, I find it hard to convince myself they are still interested when they keep me waiting."

The Japanese handle time in ways which are almost inexplicable to the Western European and particularly the American. A delay of years with them does not mean that they have lost interest. It only means that they are building up to something. They have learned that Americans are vulnerable to long waits. One of them expressed it, "You Americans have one terrible weakness. If we make you wait long enough, you will agree to anything."

Indians of South Asia have an elastic view of time as compared to our own. Delays do not, therefore, have the same meaning to them. Nor does indefiniteness in pinpointing appointments mean that they are evasive. Two Americans meeting will say, "We should get together sometime," thereby setting a low priority on the meeting. The Indian who says, "Come over and see me, see me anytime", means just that.

Americans make a place at the table which may or may not mean a place made in the heart. But when the Indian makes a place in his time, it is yours to fill in every sense of the word if you realize that by so doing you have crossed a boundary and are now friends with him. The point of all this is that time communicates just as surely as do words and that the vocabulary of time is different around the world. The principle to be remembered is that time has different meanings in each country.

LANGUAGE OF SPACE

Like time, the language of space is different wherever one goes. The American businessman, familiar with the pattern of American corporate life, has no difficulty in appraising the relative importance of someone else, simply by noting the size of his office in relation to other offices around him: our pattern calls for the president or the chairman of the board to have the biggest office. The executive vice president will have the next largest, and so on down the line until you end up in the "bull pen." More important offices are usually located at the corners of buildings and on the upper floors. Executive suites will be on the top floor. The relative rank of vice presidents will be reflected in where they are placed along "Executive Row."

The French, on the other hand, are much more likely to lay out space as a network of connecting points of influence, activity, or interest. The French supervisor will ordinarily be found in the middle of his subordinates where he can control them.

Americans who are crowded will often feel that their status in the organization is suffering. As one would expect in the Arab world, the location of an office and its size constitute a poor index of the importance of the man who occupies it. What we experience as crowded, the Arab will often regard as spacious. The same is true in Spanish cultures. A Latin American official illustrated the Spanish view of this point while showing me around a plant. Opening the door to an 18-by-20-foot office in which seventeen clerks and their desks were placed, he said, "See, we have nice spacious offices. Lots of space for everyone."

The American will look at a Japanese room and remark how bare it is. Similarly, the Japanese look at our rooms and comment, "How bare!" Furniture in the American home tends to be placed along the walls (around the edge). Japanese have their charcoal pit where the family gathers in the *middle* of the room. The top floor of Japanese department stores is not reserved for the chief executive—it is the bargain roof!

In the Middle East and Latin America, the businessman is likely to feel left out in time and overcrowded in space. People get too close to him, lay their hands on him, and generally crowd his physical being. In Scandinavia and Germany, he feels more at home, but at the same time the people are a little cold and distant. It is space itself that conveys this feeling.

In the United States, because of our tendency to zone activities, nearness carries rights of familiarity so that the neighbor can borrow material possessions and invade time. This is not true in England. Propinquity entitles you to nothing. American Air Force personnel stationed there complain because they have to make an appointment for their children to play with the neighbor's child next door.

Conversation distance between two people is learned early in life by copying elders. Its controlling patterns operate almost totally unconsciously. In the United States, in contrast to many foreign countries, men avoid excessive touching. Regular business is conducted at distances such as 5 feet to 8 feet; highly personal business, 18 inches to 3 feet—not 2 or 3 inches.

In the United States, it is perfectly possible for an experienced executive to schedule the steps of negotiation in time and space so that most people feel comfortable about what is happening. Business transactions progress in stages from across the desk to beside the desk, to the coffee table, then on to the conference table, the luncheon table, or the golf course, or even into the home—all according to a complex set of hidden rules which we obey instinctively.

Even in the United States, however, an executive may slip when he moves into new and unfamiliar realms, when dealing with a new group, doing business with a new company, or moving to a new place in the industrial hierarchy. In a new country the danger is magnified. For example, in India it is considered improper to discuss business in the home on social occasions. One never invites a business acquaintance to the home for the purpose of furthering business aims. That would be a violation of sacred hospitality rules.

LANGUAGE OF THINGS

Americans are often contrasted with the rest of the world in terms of material possessions. We are accused of being materialistic, gadget-crazy. And, as a matter of fact, we have developed material things for some very interesting reasons. Lacking a fixed class system and having an extremely mobile population, Americans have become highly sensitive to how others make use of material possessions. We use everything from clothes to houses as a highly evolved and complex means of ascertaining each other's status. Ours is a rapidly shifting system in which both styles and people move up or down. For example: The Cadillac ad men feel that not only is it natural but quite insightful of them to show a picture of a Cadillac and a well-turned out gentleman in his early fifties opening the door. The caption underneath reads, "You already know a great deal about the man." Following this same pattern, the head of a big union spends an excess of $100,000 furnishing his office so that the president of United States Steel cannot look down on him. Good materials, large space, and the proper surroundings signify that the people who occupy the premises are solid citizens, that they are dependable and successful.

The French, the English, and the Germans have entirely different ways of using their material possessions. What stands for the height of dependability and respectability with the English would be old-fashioned and backward to us. The Japanese take pride in often inexpensive but tasteful arrangements that are used to produce the proper emotional setting.

Middle East businessmen look for something else—family, connections, friendship. They do not use the furnishings of their office as part of their status system; nor do they expect to impress a client by these means or to fool a banker into lending more money than he should. They like good things, too, but feel that they, as persons, should be known and not judged solely by what the public sees.

One of the most common criticisms of American relations abroad, both commercial and governmental, is that we usually think in terms of material things. "Money talks," says the American, who goes on talking the language of money abroad, in the belief that money talks the *same* language all over the world. A common practice in the United States is to try to buy loyalty with high salaries. In foreign countries, this maneuver almost never works, for money and material possessions stand for something different there than they do in America.

LANGUAGE OF FRIENDSHIP

The American finds his friends next door and among those with whom he works. It has been noted that we take people up quickly and drop them just as quickly. Occasionally a friendship formed during school-days will persist, but this is rare. For us there are few well-defined rules governing the obligations of friendship. It is difficult to say at which point our friendship gives way to business opportunism or pressure from above. In this we differ from many other people in the world. As a general rule in foreign countries friendships are not formed as quickly as in the United States but go much deeper, last longer, and involve real obligations. For example:

> It is important to stress that in the Middle East and Latin America your "friends" will not let you down. The fact that they personally are feeling the pinch is never an excuse for failing their friends. They are supposed to look out for your interests.

Friends and family around the world represent a sort of social insurance that would be difficult to find in the United States. We do not use our friends to help us out in disaster as much as we do as a means of getting ahead—or, at least, of getting the job done. The United States systems work by means of a series of closely tabulated favors and obligations carefully doled out where they will do the most good. And the least that we expect in exchange for a favor is gratitude.

The opposite is the case in India, where the friend's role is to "sense" a person's need and do something about it. The idea of reciprocity as we know it is unheard of. An American in India will have difficulty if he attempts to follow American friendship patterns. He gains nothing by extending himself in behalf of others, least of all gratitude, because the Indian assumes that what he does for others he does for the good of his own psyche. He will find it impossible to make friends quickly and is unlikely to allow sufficient time for friendships to ripen. He will also note that as he gets to know people better, they may become more critical of him, a fact that he finds hard to take. What he does not know is that one sign of friendship in India is speaking one's mind.

LANGUAGE OF AGREEMENTS

While it is important for American businessmen abroad to understand the symbolic meanings of friendship rules, time, space, and material possessions, it is just as important for executives to know the rules for negotiating agreements in various countries. Even if they cannot be expected to know the details of each nation's commercial legal practices, just the awareness of and the expectation of the existence of differences will climinate much complication.

Actually, no society can exist on a high commercial level without a highly developed working base on which agreements can rest. This base may be one or a combination of three types:

1. Rules that are spelled out technically as law or regulation.
2. Moral practices mutually agreed on and taught to the young as a set of principles.
3. Informal customs to which everyone conforms without being able to state the exact rules.

Some societies favor one, some another. Ours, particularly in the business world, lays heavy emphasis on the first variety. Few Americans will conduct any business nowadays without some written agreement or contract.

Varying from culture to culture will be the circumstances under which such rules apply. Americans consider that negotiations have more or less ceased when the contract is signed. With the Greeks, on the other hand, the contract is seen as a sort of way station on the route to negotiation that will cease only when the work is completed. The contract is nothing more than a charter for serious negotiations. In the Arab world, once a man's word is given in a particular kind of way, it is just as binding, if not more so, than most of our written contracts. The written contract, therefore, violates the Moslem's sensitivities and reflects on his honor. Unfortunately, the situation is now so hopelessly confused that neither system can be counted on to prevail consistently.

Informal patterns and unstated agreements often lead to untold difficulty in the cross-cultural situation. Take the case of the before-and-after patterns where there is a wide discrepancy between the American's expectations and those of the Arab: In the United States, when you engage a specialist such as a lawyer or a doctor, require any standard service, or even take a taxi, you make several assumptions: (a) the charge will be fair; (b) it will be in proportion to the services rendered; and (c) it will bear a close relationship to the "going rate."

You wait until after the services are performed before asking what the tab will be. If the charge is too high in the light of the above assumptions, you feel you have been cheated. You can complain, or can say nothing, pay up, and take your business elsewhere the next time.

As one would expect in the Middle East, basic differences emerge which lead to difficulty if not understood. For instance, when taking a cab in Beirut it is well to know the going rate as a point around which to bargain and for settling the charge, which must be fixed before engaging the cab.

If you have not fixed the rate *in advance*, there is a complete change and an entirely different set of rules will apply. According to these rules, the going rate plays no part whatsoever. The whole relationship is altered. The sky is the limit, and the customer has no kick coming. I have seen taxi drivers shouting at the top of their lungs, waving their arms, following a redfaced American with his head pulled down between his shoulders, demanding for a two-pound ride ten Lebanese pounds which the American eventually had to pay.

It is difficult for the American to accommodate his frame of reference to the fact that what constitutes one thing to him, namely, a taxi ride, is to the Arab two very different operations involving two different sets of relationships and two sets of rules. The crucial factor is whether the bargaining is done at the beginning or the end of the ride! As a matter of fact, you cannot bargain at the end. What the driver asks for he is entitled to!

One of the greatest difficulties Americans have abroad stems from the fact that we often think we have a commitment when we do not. The second complication on this same topic is the other side of the coin, i.e., when others think we have agreed to things that we have not. Our own failure to recognize binding obligations, plus our custom of setting organizational goals ahead of everything else, has put us in hot water far too often.

People sometimes do not keep agreements with us because we do not keep agreements with them. As a general rule, the American treats the agreement as something he may eventually have to break. For example:

> Once while I was visiting an American post in Latin America, the Ambassador sent the Spanish version of a trade treaty down to his language officer with instructions to write in some "weasel words." To his dismay, he was told, "There are no weasel words in Spanish."

A personnel officer of a large corporation in Iran made an agreement with local employees that American employees would not receive preferential treatment. When the first American employee arrived, it was learned quickly that in the United States he had been covered by a variety of health plans that were not available to Iranians. And this led to immediate protests from the Iranians which were never satisfied. The personnel officer never really grasped the fact that he had violated an ironbound contract.

Certainly, this is the most important generalization to be drawn by American businessmen from this discussion of agreements: there are many times when we are vulnerable *even when judged by our own standards.* Many instances of actual sharp practices by American companies are well known abroad and are giving American business a bad name. The cure for such questionable behavior is simple. The companies concerned usually have it within their power to discharge offenders and to foster within their organization an atmosphere in which only honesty and fairness can thrive.

But the cure for ignorance of the social and legal rules which underlie business agreements is not so easy. This is because:

1. The subject is complex.
2. Little research has been conducted to determine the culturally different concepts of what is an agreement.
3. The people of each country think that their own code is the only one, and that everything else is dishonest.
4. Each code is different from our own; and the farther away one is traveling from Western Europe, the greater the difference is.

But the little that has already been learned about this subject indicates that as a problem it is not insoluble and will yield to research. Since it is probably one of the more relevant and immediately applicable areas of interest to modern business, it would certainly be advisable for companies with large foreign operations to sponsor some serious research in this vital field.

A CASE IN POINT

Thus far, I have been concerned with developing the five check points around which a real understanding of foreign cultures can begin. But the problems that arise from a faulty understanding of the silent language of foreign custom are human problems and perhaps can best be dramatized by an actual case.

A Latin American republic had decided to modernize one of its communication networks to the tune of several million dollars. Because of its reputation for quality and price, the inside track was quickly taken by American company "Y."

The company, having been sounded out informally, considered the size of the order and decided to bypass its regular Latin American representative and send instead its sales manager. The following describes what took place.

The sales manager arrived and checked in at the leading hotel. He immediately had some difficulty pinning down just who it was he had to see about his business. After several days without results, he called at the American Embassy where he found that the commercial attaché had the up-to-the-minute information he needed. The commercial attaché listened to his story. Realizing that the sales manager had already made a number of mistakes, but figuring that the Latins were used to American blundering, the attaché reasoned that all was not lost. He informed the sales manager that the Minister of Communications was the key man and that whoever got the nod from him would get the contract. He also briefed the sales manager on methods of conducting business in Latin America and offered some pointers about dealing with the minister.

The attaché's advice ran somewhat as follows:

1. "You don't do business here the way you do in the States; it is necessary to spend much more time. You have to get to know your man and vice versa.

2. "You must meet with him *several times* before you talk business. I will tell you at what point you can bring up the subject. Take your cues from me. [Our American sales manager at this point made a few observations to himself about "cookie pushers" and wondered how many payrolls had been met by the commercial attaché.]

3. "Take the price list and put in your pocket. Don't get it out until I tell you to. Down here price is only one of the many things taken into account before closing a deal. In the United States, your past experience will prompt you to act according to a certain set of principles, but many of these principles will *not* work here. Every time you feel the urge to act or to say something look at me. Suppress the urge and take your cues from me. This is very important.

4. "Down here people like to do business with men who *are* somebody. In order to be somebody, it is well to have written a book, to have lectured at a university, or to have developed your intellect in some way. The man you are going to see is a poet. He has published several volumes of poetry. Like many Latin Americans, he prizes poetry highly. You will find that he will spend a good deal of business time quoting his poetry to you, and he will take great pleasure in this.

5. "You will also note that the people here are very proud of their Spanish blood, but they are also exceedingly proud of their

liberation from Spain and their independence. The fact that they are a democracy, that they are free, and also that they are no longer a colony is very, very important to them. They are warm and friendly and enthusiastic if they like you. If they don't they are cold and withdrawn.

6. "And another thing, time down here means something different. It works in a different way. You know how it is back in the States when a certain type blurts out whatever is on his mind without waiting to see if the situation is right. He is considered an impatient bore and somewhat egocentric. Well, down here, you have to wait much, much longer, and I really mean *much, much* longer, before you can begin to talk about the reason for your visit.

7. There is another point I want to caution you about. At home, the man who sells takes the initiative. Here, *they* tell you when they are ready to do business. But, most of all, don't discuss price until you are asked and don't rush things."

THE PITCH

The next day the commercial attaché introduced the sales manager to the Minister of Communications. First, there was a long wait in the outer office while people kept coming in and out. The sales manager looked at his watch, fidgeted, and finally asked whether the minister was really expecting him. The reply he received was scarcely reassuring, "Oh yes, he is expecting you but several things have come up that require his attention. Besides, one gets used to waiting down here." The sales manager irritably replied, "But doesn't he know I flew all the way down here from the United States to see him, and I have spent over a week already of my valuable time trying to find him?" "Yes, I know," was the answer, "but things just move much more slowly here."

At the end of about 30 minutes, the minister emerged from the office, greeted the commercial attaché with a *doble abrazo*, throwing his arms around him and patting him on the back as though they were long-lost brothers. Now, turning and smiling, the minister extended his hand to the sales manager, who, by this time, was feeling rather miffed because he had been kept in the outer office so long.

After what seemed to be an all too short chat, the minister rose, suggesting a well-known café where they might meet for dinner the next evening. The sales manager expected, of course, that, considering the nature of their business and the size of the order, he might be taken to the minister's home, not realizing that the Latin home is reserved for family and very close friends.

Until now, nothing at all had been said about the reason for the sales manager's visit, a fact which bothered him somewhat. The whole set-up seemed wrong; neither did he like the idea of wasting another day in town. He told the home office before he left that he would be gone for a week or ten days at most, and made a mental note that he would clean this order up in three days and enjoy a few days in Acapulco or Mexico City. Now the week had already gone and he would be lucky if he made it home in ten days.

Voicing his misgivings to the commercial attaché, he wanted to know if the minister really meant business, and, if he did, why could they not get together and talk about it? The commercial attaché by now was beginning to show the strain of constantly having to reassure the sales manager. Nevertheless, he tried again:

> What you don't realize is that part of the time we are waiting, the minister was rearranging a very tight schedule so that he could spend tomorrow night with you. You see, down here they don't delegate responsibility the way we do in the States. They exercise much tighter control than we do. As a consequence, this man spends up to 15 hours a day at his desk. It may not look like it to you, but I assure you he really means business. He wants to give your company the order; if you play your cards right, you will get it.

The next evening provided more of the same. Much conversation about food and music, about many people the sales manager had never heard of. They went to a night club, where the sales manager brightened up and began to think that perhaps he and the minister might have something in common after all. It bothered him, however, that the principal reason for his visit was not even alluded to tangentially. But every time he started to talk about electronics, the commercial attaché would nudge him and proceed to change the subject.

The next meeting was for morning coffee at a café. By now the sales manager was having difficulty hiding his impatience. To make matters worse, the minister had a mannerism which he did not like. When they talked, he was likely to put his hand on him; he would take hold of his arm and get so close that he almost "spat" in his face. As a consequence, the sales manager was kept busy trying to dodge and back up.

Following coffee, there was a walk in a nearby park. The minister expounded on the shrubs, the birds, and the beauties of nature, and at one spot he stopped to point at a statue and said: "There is a statue of the world's greatest hero, the liberator of mankind!" At this point, the worst happened, for the sales manager asked who the statue was of and, being given the name of a famous Latin American patriot, said "I never heard of him," and walked on.

THE FAILURE

It is quite clear from this that the sales manager did not get the order, which went to a Swedish concern. The American, moreover, was never able to see the minister again. Why did the minister feel the way he did? His reasoning went somewhat as follows:

> I like the American's equipment and it makes sense to deal with North Americans who are near us and whose price is right. But I could never be friends with this man. He is not my kind of human being and we have nothing in common. He is not *simpatico*. If I can't be friends and he is not *simpatico*, I can't depend on him to treat me right. I tried everything, every conceivable situation, and only once did we seem to understand each other. If we could be friends, he would feel obligated to me and his obligation would give me some control. Without control, how do I know he will deliver what he says he will at the price he quotes?

Of course, what the minister did not know was that the price was quite firm, and that quality control was a matter of company policy. He did not realize that the sales manager was a member of an organization, and that the man is always subordinate to the organization in the United States. Next year maybe the sales manager would not even be representing the company, but would be replaced. Further, if he wanted someone to depend on, his best bet would be to hire a good American lawyer to represent him and write a binding contract.

In this instance, both sides suffered. The American felt he was being slighted and put off, and did not see how there could possibly be any connection between poetry and doing business or why it should all take so long. He interpreted the delay as a form of polite brushoff. Even if things had gone differently and there had been a contract, it is doubtful that the minister would have trusted the contract as much as he would a man whom he considered his friend. Throughout Latin America, the law is made livable and contracts workable by having friends and relatives operating from the inside. Lacking a friend, someone who would look out for his interests, the minister did not want to take a chance. He stated this simply and directly.

CONCLUSION

The case just described has of necessity been oversimplified. The danger is that the reader will say, "Oh, I see. All you really have to do is be friends." At which point the expert will step in and reply: "Yes, of course, but what you don't realize is that in Latin America being a friend involves much more than it does in the United States and is an entirely different proposition. A friendship implies obligations. You go about it differently. It involves much more than being nice, visiting, and playing golf. You would not want to enter into friendship lightly."

The point is simply this. It takes years and years to develop a sound foundation for doing business in a given country. Much that is done seems silly or strange to the home office. Indeed, the most common error made by home offices, once they have found representatives who can get results, is failure to take their advice and allow sufficient time for representatives to develop the proper contacts.

The second most common error, if that is what it can be called, is ignorance of the secret and hidden language of foreign cultures. In this article I have tried to show how five key topics—time, space, material possessions, friendship patterns, and business agreements—offer a starting point from which companies can begin to acquire the understanding necessary to do business in foreign countries.

Our present knowledge is meager, and much more research is needed before the businessman of the future can go abroad fully equipped for his work. Not only will he need to be well versed in the economics, law, and politics of the area, but he will have to understand, if not speak, the silent languages of other cultures.

RETROSPECTIVE COMMENT

Culture evolution is quite slow and decades and centuries are but minutes and hours in a cultural-historical context. The unchanging nature of culture is one of the distinguishing characteristics of traditional societies—a definition that aptly applies to more than half the world's population, and includes most of Asia, Latin America, parts of Western Europe, and Africa (where large segments of the continent would be considered tribal or pre-traditional in anthropological terms). Culture is the means by which a set of people define and describe their way of life, as distinguished from some other group. It consists of all those things, tangible and intangible, that give expression to a person's human experience, his place in society, criteria for interpersonal relationships, and the basis for socialization and institutional development in a society. It includes values and beliefs, language and other forms of symbolic communication, traditions and historical experience, accepted forms and norms of reward and punishment for socially accepted or deviant behavior.

External events and interraction with other cultures do have an influence on a given culture and its values. However, while the changes in outer manifestation of behavior are more pronounced, underlying values change very slowly and in a manner that is difficult, if not impossible, to predict. Thus, in the context of one's life span of experience it is safer to assume and treat different cultures as constants in dealing with people from different societies.

The point being made here is that cultural differences between various societies have not diminished since Edward Hall's excellent and thought provoking article "Silent Language of Overseas Business" appeared in *Harvard Business Review* issue of May–June, 1960. On the other hand the interaction between the industrialized societies of the West and the traditional, but resource rich and developing, societies in other parts of the world, has vastly increased and become more complex with some shift in the balance of power. U.S. and European businessmen and government policy makers are having to learn about the differences between a Saudi Arabian and an Iranian, and remember and distinguish between such previously unheard of countries as Zaire, Zambia, Senegal, and Tanzania.

Unfortunately, to the uninitiated and uninformed, the similarities in external forms or symbols of behavior signify a basic similarity in underlying cultural values. This often leads to behavior patterns which are offensive to the people with different cultural traits, and are most assuredly counterproductive for the initiator. A rigid attitude about the rightness of one's viewpoint is the hallmark of either an ignorant or an arrogant person. If the experience of the last decade is any guide, it would appear that American businessmen have neither devoted greater attention nor learnt much about the significance of cultural differences that exist between various societies of the world. Confident in his advanced technological skills, which he equates with "advanced and progressive management and society," the American executive tends to exhibit extreme impatience in understanding a different culture, which he is more likely to dismiss as exotic, inscrutable, or primitive, and therefore, incomprehensible. After such a short shrift, he then proceeds to acquire a nodding acquaintance with the rhetoric and rituals of another culture believing that they would provide him with adequate tools to deal with these people.

I believe Hall's article and the book *The Silent Language* (New York: Doubleday, 1959) on which it was based have been misinterpreted and their deeper meaning largely ignored by American businessmen. Instead of learning about the fundamental traits and characteristics of a culture and how they effect behavior, they have emphasized the learning of external mores and rituals in the mistaken belief that a Pavlovian dog would be indistinguishable from a human being. High priced seminars and courses abound where executives are taught about the customs and forms of behavior in other countries.

Clearly, there is a wealth of good material available in such academic disciplines as cultural anthropology and sociology. However, a typical businessman is generally unfamiliar with it. His experiential framework in terms of career and organizational constraints makes it difficult for him to devote either the time or the resources to any meaningful learning.

Recently there have been some attempts at explaining differences in behavior patterns as related to substantive variations in cultural norms. For example, Peter Drucker in his article, "What Can We Learn from Japanese Management," *Harvard Business Review* (March–April, 1971), analyzes Japanese management practices and how they make sense in terms of Japanese cultural values and traditions. He rightly points out that what appears to a Western executive to be the antithesis of good management practice, nevertheless is extremely successful in Japan because it is in harmony with the cultural norms and social behavior patterns of the Japanese people. In my own book *Japanese Business and Social Conflict: A Comparative Analysis of Response Patterns With American Business* (Cambridge, Mass.: Ballinger Publishing Company, 1975), I have attempted to analyze the nature of responses by Japanese business to such social problems e.g., pollution, consumerism, and business-government relations in terms of underlying cultural traits.

There are no short cuts to learning of cultures and there are no substitutes to such learning. I am sure Dr. Hall would agree with me. It calls for a heavy investment of time and resources which U.S. multinational corporations must commit if they wish to build lasting and successful relations with other countries. The types of changes and resources needed for such an effort are quite important and will no doubt receive increasing attention in the professional journals once the need for such cultural learning has been recognized and become impelling.—*Dr. S. Prakash Sethi*, Visiting Professor of Management Policy, School of Management, Boston University, Boston, and Professor of Business Administration, University of California, Berkeley

24. The Marketing Dilemma of Negroes

*Raymond A. Bauer, Scott M. Cunningham,
and Lawrence H. Wortzel*

The distinctive nature of the Negro revolution is that it is not a revolution to overthrow the established order so much as it is a revolution to achieve full membership in that order.

Because material goods have such an important symbolic role in American society, the acquisition of material goods should be symbolic to the Negro of his achievement of full status. This is not to say that all product categories have such a symbolic function for Negroes. In general, though, the symbolic status attributed to products by Negroes parallels that attributed to these products by whites.

Some exceptions, however, give the Negro market some distinctive characteristics. For example, it would appear that toilet soap, particularly as associated with deodorizing properties, has special importance for Negro women as compared with white women. Perhaps this is only a reflection of the middle-class dictum about cleanliness being next to godliness, perhaps also a reaction to the belief that Negroes smell different than whites.

The background of both the Negro revolution and the Negro's behavior in the marketplace is, of course, his relatively low socioeconomic status. Despite an absolute income increase in Negro income since World War II, it is a moot point as to whether the Negro's relative position has improved. While two-thirds of Negroes reported a family income below $4,500 in the 1960 census, only one-third of the white families did so. Negro educational occupational, and housing deprivations are also severe. These are some of the factors which account for the Negroes' increasing concentration in Northern urban "ghettos."

The socio-economic factors are so important that it may be asked whether there is a Negro market in any meaningful sense. Are there any special characteristics which distinguish the Negro from any other

Reprinted by permission of the authors and publisher from the Journal of Marketing, *published by the American Marketing Association, Vol. 29 (July 1965), pp. 1–6.*

lower-income, lower-educated, and geographically concentrated group?

The answer is yes. And while income and education are the most important factors, they are not the only ones.

SOURCES OF DATA

The hypotheses developed here are derived from reanalyses of over a dozen surveys, both local and national, which have been studied during a period beginning in 1962.

To preserve continuity for the reader, the illustrative data will be drawn from only two studies: a survey of women's shopping habits in New York and Cleveland,[1] and a survey of male buyers of Scotch in Northern urban areas.[2] Many of the same patterns noted have been found in cross-sectional samples of the U.S. Negro and white population, as well as in some local surveys.

BASIC DILEMMA OF NEGROES

Negroes as a group have accepted the values of the majority white middle-class culture, but are at a disadvantage in acquiring the goods which represent some of these values.

In other words, *the basic dilemma of Negroes is whether to strive against odds to attain these middle-class values (and the goods which come with them), or to give in and live without most of them.*

It is easy to listen to the rising, increasingly militant, voices of American Negroes combined with the voices of American nationalism, and to conclude that the American Negro has not accepted white middle-class values, or that he may even be alienated from the white culture. However, even the publications of the Black Muslims reveal strong emphasis on the values of temperance and achievement, along with some racist content.

Certainly it is the consensus of both Negro and white students of the American Negro that Negroes have accepted white middle-class values.[3]

For convenience, we have been discussing Negroes and whites as though they were two distinct groups, each of which is in turn homo-

---

[1] Stuart U. Rich, with the assistance of Bernard Portis, Jr., *Shopping Behavior of Department Store Customers.* (Boston: Division of Research, Harvard University Graduate School of Business Administration, 1963.) The data presented are a result of reanalysis of the original data, and not to be found in Rich and Portis.

[2] Made available through the cooperation of Browne-Vintners, Inc., distributors of White Horse Scotch.

[3] For example, Thomas F. Pettigrew, *A Profile of the Negro American* (Princeton: D. Van Nostrand Company, Inc., 1964), Chapters 1 and 2.

Table 24.1. Negro Versus White Spending Behavior[a] Controlled by Income

	Negro spending versus white spending
Food	Less
Housing	Less
Clothing	More
Recreation and leisure	Mixed
Home furnishing	More
Medical	Less
Auto transportation	Less
Non-Auto	More
Savings	More
Insurance	Less

[a]Source: Marcus Alexis: "Some Negro-White Differences in Consumption," *American Journal of Economics and Sociology*, Vol. 21 (January, 1962), pp. 11–28.

geneous. This is, of course, not so; but we are trying to emphasize some major trends and certainly various Negroes respond differently to the "basic dilemma" mentioned above.

DIFFERENCES IN CONSUMPTION PATTERNS

Any discussion of the Negro market needs to be based on general differences in Negro-white consumption patterns. A combination of societal restraints and cultural traditions leads Negroes to underspend, as compared with whites of equal income, in four major areas: housing, automobile transportation, food, and medical care (excluding certain categories of proprietary medicines). See Table 1.

This pattern of spending less on housing, automobile transportation, food, and medical care makes available to Negroes *proportionately* more money for the purchase of goods than is available to whites of comparable income. Thus, Negroes at a given level of income repeatedly have been found to spend more on clothing, furniture, and alcoholic beverages than do whites of the same income.

SYMBOLIC IMPORTANCE OF GOODS

The once prevalent stereotype that Negroes were uninterested in, or incompetent to judge, the quality of goods has long been displaced—with the contrary image now of Negroes being extremely interested in quality, and being even more concerned with the symbolic value of goods than are whites. Although this idea may sometimes be overdrawn,

Table 24.2. PROPORTION OF NEGRO AND WHITE WOMEN SHOWING "HIGH-FASHION INTEREST"[a]

Family income	Negro women %	Negro women No.	White women %	White women No.
Under $3,000	34%	(113)	21%	(216)
$3,000– 4,999	38	(115)	36	(416)
$5,000– 7,500	56	(99)	47	(938)

[a] Of the Negro women who had $3,000 family income, 34% were "high fashion" in orientation.

it seems close to the truth. Table 2 shows the proportion of white and Negro women in New York and Cleveland who scored high on a scale of fashion-consciousness.[4] Negro women were at least as fashion-conscious or more so than white women.

For another product category, liquor, a Negro family is likely to spend about 1.25 times as much money on alcoholic beverages as a white family with the same per capita income.[5] But the figures on buying Scotch are even more interesting.

Negroes drink at least 25% of the Scotch consumed in the United States, although they represent only 11% of the population. *Chicago Tribune* panel data (1961) indicate that 16.8% of Negro families report buying Scotch, compared with 9.3% of white families. The distributors of White Horse have found that the average Negro Scotch drinker reports drinking almost twice as many drinks of Scotch per week as the average white Scotch drinker.

These data suggest that Negro *per capita* consumption of Scotch is *three times* as much as that consumed by whites. Other estimates have been of the same order.

Is Scotch related to status among Negroes? On a series of questions generally assumed to be related to the idea of Scotch as a high-status drink, Negroes indicate that drinking of Scotch is associated with high status. But perhaps a more crucial question is whether these attitudes vary according to whether a Negro sees himself moving upward or downward in society. We find that self-perceived mobility—that is, perceiving one's self as higher, the same, or lower in social class than one's father—is closely related to attitudes toward Scotch and toward reporting that one is a regular Scotch drinker.

Within the Negro group, such attitudes are much more highly correlated with self-perceived mobility than with present income. Those Ne-

[4] Same reference as footnote 1.
[5] George Fisk, *Leisure Spending Behavior* (Philadelphia: University of Pennsylvania Press, 1963), p. 145.

groes who see themselves as moving upward from their fathers' position in society are most likely to give answers which indicate they regard Scotch as a "status" drink, and are most likely to report being regular Scotch drinkers.

SEGMENTATION WITHIN THE NEGRO MARKET

To repeat what was stated above, the "basic dilemma" of the Negro is whether to strive against odds for middle-class values as reflected in material goods, or to give in and live more for the moment. It is the response of Negroes to this dilemma that creates two categories of persons whom we have labeled "strivers" and "nonstrivers." In turn, their responses to goods of high symbolic value, leads to an interesting segmentation of the Negro market.

Let us assume, therefore, that Negro women who are high on the scale of fashion-consciousness and Negro men who report they are regular Scotch drinkers are "strivers," and that the others are "nonstrivers," and then see where this leads us.

Table 3 shows relationships between fashion interest and social activities outside the respondent's family. The pattern suggested by these data is: Among white women, social activities outside the family are almost entirely a function of family income, whereas for Negro women, once they have been identified by degree of interest in fashion, income no longer plays a role in the Negro group.

In every income category, those Negro women high on fashion-consciousness are twice as likely to take part in social activities outside the family as are low-fashion-conscious Negro women.

These data indicate that by comparing Negro women on the basis of interest in fashion, we have identified women with two basically different orientations toward the world outside the family. One group is actively engaged with the outside world; the other is more withdrawn

Table 24.3. SOCIAL ACTIVITIES OUTSIDE THE FAMILY

	Negroes				Whites			
Income	High fashion	No.	Low fashion	No.	High fashion	No.	Low fashion	No.
Under $3,000	54%[a]	(38)	25%	(46)	30%	(45)	29%	(120)
$3,000–$5,000	46	(44)	21	(27)	44	(150)	38	(161)
$5,000–$7,000	53	(56)	28	(24)	54	(440)	48	(281)

[a]Of 38 high-fashion Negroes who had income under $3,000, 54% were involved in community activities.

from the world. This proposition would not be so interesting if it were not for the fact that this is *not* true for the white women in this sample.

The same sort of relationship holds for a whole series of questions on shopping habits: High-fashion-conscious Negro women are more than twice as likely as low-fashion-conscious Negro women to report that they shop with others. Also, they are likely to combine shopping with social and recreational activities (see Table 4).

In short, the high-fashion-conscious Negro women (in the Rich-and-Portis shopping study) express their greater involvement with the world outside of the family in their shopping activities. Such differences among white women are in the same direction; but the differences, in general, are less than half the magnitude, either absolutely or relatively, as those among Negro women.

Thus, the Negro strivers are more actively engaged in the world about them than the nonstrivers; and shopping and attitudes toward symbolically important goods (interest in fashion) reflect this "striving" attitude.

ANXIETY ABOUT SHOPPING

Shopping can be an especially serious business for a social group that is moving up in society and very concerned with whether their funds are sufficient for buying the goods to which they aspire. We have found the Negro women are less likely to mention the secondary aspects of shopping—convenience, politeness of salesgirls, crowds, and so on—than white women. Rather, Negro women concentrate more on the economic transaction of exchanging dollars for goods. Compared with white women, what Negroes *like* best about shopping is getting new things and finding

Table 24.4. COMBINING SHOPPING WITH OTHER ACTIVITIES CONTROLLED BY INCOME

| | Negroes | | Whites | |
| | Fashion-consciousness | | Fashion-consciousness | |
Activity while shopping[a]	High	Low	High	Low
Lunches	11%[b]	3%	7%	3%
Theatre	15	4	4	4
Seeing friends	7	—	6	3
Errands	3	5	2	3
Other	5	3	7	4
Don't combine shopping with other activities	60	84	73	83
Number =	(136)	(98)	(626)	(581)

[a]Multiple responses permitted.

[b]Of the 136 high-fashion-conscious Negro women, 11% reported eating lunch when they went shopping.

Table 24.5. PROPORTION HAVING DIFFICULTY MAKING SHOPPING DECISIONS
CONTROLLED BY INCOME

	Negroes Fashion-consciousness		Whites Fashion-consciousness	
	High	*Low*	*High*	*Low*
	39%[a]	29%	25%	23%
N =	(158)	(110)	(1,472)	(979)

[a] Of the 158 high-fashion-conscious Negroes, 39% reported having difficulty making shopping decision.

bargains; but they also are more likely to say that what they *dislike* about shopping is spending money!

Our discussion of shopping as an especially serious business for Negroes leads us to the expectation that there is a greater degree of anxiety among Negroes with respect to making shopping decisions generally. Table 5 shows that Negro women in general report greater difficulty than white women, in making buying decisions. This becomes most acute among those Negroes who are "most involved" in the product category. The Negro women "strivers" are more committed to goods of high symbolic value (we identified them by their interest in fashion), more involved with the world outside the family, and show more concern over making shopping decisions.

A parallel may be found in the market for Scotch. Negroes are more likely than whites to report having an established brand preference, and at least as likely to specify a particular brand of Scotch when ordering a drink (see Table 6). Furthermore, the regular Scotch drinkers,

Table 24.6. BRAND PREFERENCE FOR SCOTCH CONTROLLED BY INCOME

	Negro drinkers		White drinkers	
	Regular	*Occasional*	*Regular*	*Occasional*
Brand preferences "firmly established"	71%[a]	51%	67%	46%
(No. =)	(94)	(107)	(243)	(375)
Specify brand of Scotch when ordering in bars, clubs, restaurants	79%[b]	64%	77%	55%
(No. =)	(93)	(101)	(241)	(389)

[a] Of the 94 Negro regular Scotch drinkers, 71% claim that their brand preferences are firmly established.

[b] Of the 93 Negro regular Scotch drinkers, 79% claim to specify a particular brand of Scotch when ordering in bars.

both Negro and white, are more brand-conscious than occasional Scotch drinkers.

In response to the statement: "To obtain a good Scotch you have to order an old reliable brand," the regular drinkers among the whites are somewhat more likely to reject this statement.

This pattern conforms to a trend that has been discussed in marketing circles, namely, that persons more experienced with a product type probably will display their "expertise" by departing from accepted brands. But among Negroes, the reverse is true in the present instance. It is the regular drinkers, those most engaged in the product category, who report being reliant on the brand-name for assurance of getting a good Scotch (see Table 7).

The inference we draw is that the regular Negro drinker of Scotch, in contrast with his white "opposite number," is more anxious about the possibility of making a mistake. His greater familiarity with the product (compared with the occasional drinker) does not decrease his reliance on brand names to avoid a mistake. This is analogous to the finding above, that fashion-conscious Negro women are more likely to report having difficulties in making buying decisions.

DISCUSSIONS

We have indicated that Negroes show a simultaneous high degree of involvement in material goods of high symbolic value, and a degree of anxiety associated with exchanging scarce resources for goods about which one does not want to make a mistake. Among Negroes, this leads to a good deal of talking about shopping. Negro women are more likely to say they find it useful to talk with someone when they have trouble making shopping decisions than are white women (52% v. 36%).

Furthermore, to the extent that they are involved with the world outside their family, they are more likely to turn to it for guidance. As can be seen from Table 8, high-fashion-conscious Negro women are more

Table 24.7. RELIANCE ON BRAND NAME CONTROLLED BY INCOME

	Negro drinkers		White drinkers	
	Regular	Occasional	Regular	Occasional
State that to obtain a good Scotch you have to order an old reliable brand (No. =)	61%[a] (98)	53% (114)	49% (247)	60% (416)

[a]Of the 98 Negro regular drinkers of Scotch, 61% agreed with the statement.

Table 24.8. (1) PROPORTION FINDING IT HELPFUL TO DISCUSS SHOPPING WITH VARIOUS TYPES OF PERSONS

Person	Negroes		Whites	
	Fashion-consciousness		Fashion-consciousness	
	High	Low	High	Low
Friend	55%[a]	32%	30%	20%
Husband	5	8	9	11
Other or no one	45	60	51	69
(No. =)	(158)	(110)	(1472)	(979)

[a]Of the 158 Negroes who were high-fashion-conscious, 55% found it helpful to discuss shopping with their friends.

(2) CHOICE OF SHOPPING COMPANIONS

Companion	Negroes		Whites	
	Fashion-consciousness		Fashion-consciousness	
	High	Low	High	Low
Friend	48%[a]	34%	37%	27%
Husband	9	32	23	24
Other or no one	43	34	40	49
(No. =)	(98)	(56)	(517)	(400)

[a]Of the 98 high-fashion Negroes who took someone with them when shopping, 48% selected a friend as a companion.

likely to talk with and go shopping with friends than with husbands. This trend is not nearly so strong among the white group.

As to the market for Scotch, Negroes are more likely to report that they initiated and took part in discussions about brands of Scotch. Furthermore, regular drinkers (both Negro and white) are generally more likely to take part in such discussions than occasional drinkers.

Since regular Scotch drinkers have more friends who are also regular Scotch drinkers, they have more opportunities to talk about Scotch than do occasional Scotch drinkers (and in fact they do talk more). After performing a statistical manipulation to equalize the number of regular Scotch drinkers each group has among its friends, we can look at their discussion habits as they would be if everyone had about the same opportunity to talk. This is the basis for the data presented in Table 9.

The data in this table indicate that the regular Negro drinkers of Scotch are *not* appreciably more likely to report having heard of a brand recommended than the occasional drinkers of Scotch among the Negroes. However, they are at least four times as likely as occasional drinkers to report having heard a brand criticized.

Table 24.9. WORD-OF-MOUTH ACTIVITY RELATIVE TO SCOTCH CONTROLLED BY FRIENDSHIP PATTERNS

	Negro drinkers		*White drinkers*	
	Regular	*Occasional*	*Regular*	*Occasional*
Heard brand recommended	42%	39%	51%	39%
Heard brand criticized	25	6	21	11
(No. =)	(98)	(114)	(247)	(416)

This suggests that the regular Negro drinkers of Scotch are principally concerned with information that will help them to avoid mistakes. This fits with the picture sketched above of the regular Negro drinkers of Scotch being especially anxious about not making mistakes.

IMPLICATIONS

The data about drinking of Scotch fit the contemporary stereotype of high brand loyalty among Negroes. However, an all embracing notion of Negroes being brand loyal is, judging from our other studies, often too simple.

There are whole product categories, for example, facial tissues, which appear *not* to have high symbolic value with respect to middle-class cultural values (at least in the eyes of Negroes). In this product category none of the phenomena discussed with respect to Scotch and fashion have been found.

Furthermore, the Negro market is by no means homogeneous as to involvement with products of high symbolic importance. In fact, it is split between the strivers and nonstrivers.

Again, in some product categories, such as women's fashion, the same dynamics that might elsewhere lead the strivers among the Negroes to rely on brand names for reassurance drives them rather to other sources of information such as talking with friends.

Finally, in areas where brand names are important, Negroes tend to be brand-conscious, rather than brand-loyal. In the Scotch market we found evidence of Negroes being under cross-pressures—on the one hand, they had their own favorite brands; but on the other hand, they also reported being involved in many more discussions in which competing brands were recommended.

Compared with whites, Negroes show more concern, more anxiety, and more ambivalance over spending money for material goods. In this connection, it will be remembered that what the women liked most about shopping was getting things, and what they liked least was spending money.

While some Negroes will become increasingly secure in their status, it is probable that a growing proportion will become strivers as their expectations rise to the point where they work for a full place in American life. The proportion of nonstrivers will probably decrease as aspirations rise in general. But until Negroes' opportunities are brought in line with their aspirations, the basic dilemma we have discussed will remain.

RETROSPECTIVE COMMENT

"Marketing Dilemma of Negroes" resulted from the desire of Cunningham, Wortzel, and me to cut a little deeper into a faddish area of marketing concern where the research was generally extraordinarily sloppy and shallow.

Probably our main contribution was the introduction of the dicotomy of "strivers" and "non-strivers." Conceptually this concept held out and it makes a good deal of sense as a reflection of the distinctive socioeconomic plight of blacks and other minorities.

I would hasten to indicate that there is a crucial difference between our position and that of other writers such as Banfield. Banfield interprets the behavior in the plight of the poor as a result of the short time horizon. Psychologists have long been aware of the fact that objective conditions affect expectations and that poor expectations in a situation such as we are talking about produce short time horizons.

While the concept has held up conceptually, there are flaws in the measurement instrument we used in this particular article. The reader who has serious concerns for this phenomenon should consult Chapter Two of *Studies in the Negro Market* by Bauer and Cunningham, published by the Marketing Science Institute in 1970.—*Raymond A. Bauer*

PART III. QUESTIONS FOR DISCUSSION

1. Under what conditions will reference group influence be great?

2. What are the key bases for role differentiations between husband and wife in purchase decision processes?

3. Why is family life cycle a better means of segmentation than such traditional demographic variables as age and marital status?

4. Explain the "overprivileged market" in social class strata? How

might the overprivilege market's spending patterns differ from other members of the same stratum?

5. Contrast the conclusions of the Martineau article with that of Rich and Jain.

6. Define culture. How is culture different from subculture?

7. What steps are Black Americans taking to overcome the basic dilemma described in the Bauer, Cunningham, and Wortzel article?

Part IV.
Personal Influence Patterns

Interpersonal communications makes possible both the dissemination of new information and personal influence by one or more communicators which results in changed attitudes and/or behavior. The operation of personal influence is often casual rather than deliberate and it is a difficult component of the consumer decision-process to control. Nevertheless, the personal influence component may be the crucial input in individual decision-making.

The opening selection by Elihu Katz discusses the well-known *two-step flow of communications* hypothesis. The concept argues that communications flows indirectly to most individuals, starting with mass media and then flowing to opinion leaders in each social system and from them to others in the social system.

The second selection treats the variables involved in the adoption of new products by the individual, while the final selection by Saxon Graham analyzes the diffusion of innovations throughout a social system.

25. The Two-Step Flow of Communications: An Up-to-Date Report on an Hypothesis

Elihu Katz

Analysis of the process of decision-making during the course of an election campaign led the authors of *The People's Choice* to suggest that the flow of mass communications may be less direct than was commonly supposed. It may be, they proposed, that influences stemming from the mass media first reach "opinion leaders" who, in turn, pass on what they read and hear to those of their every-day associates for whom they are influential. This hypothesis was called "the two-step flow of communication."[1]

The hypothesis aroused considerable interest. The authors themselves were intrigued by its implications for democratic society. It was a healthy sign, they felt, that people were still most successfully persuaded by give-and-take with other people and that the influence of the mass media was less automatic and less potent than had been assumed. For social theory, and for the design of communications research, the hypothesis suggested that the image of modern urban society needed revision. The image of the audience as a mass of disconnected individuals hooked up to the media but not to each other could not be reconciled with the idea of a two-step flow of communication implying, as it did, networks of interconnected individuals through which mass communications are channeled.

Of all the ideas in *The People's Choice*, however, the two-step flow hypothesis is probably the one that was least well documented by empirical data. And the reason for this is clear: the design of the study did not anticipate the importance which interpersonal relations would as-

[1] Paul F. Lazarsfeld, Bernard Berelson and Hazel Gaudet, *The People's Choice*, New York: Columbia University Press, 1948 (2nd edition), p. 151.

Reprinted by special permission from Public Opinion Quarterly, *Vol. 21 (Spring 1957).*

This may be identified as Publication No. A-225 of the Bureau of Applied Social Research, Columbia University. It is an abridged version of a chapter in the author's "Interpersonal Relations and Mass Communications: Studies in the Flow of Influence," unpublished Ph.D. thesis, Columbia University, 1956. The advice and encouragement of Dr. Paul F. Lazarsfeld in the writing of this thesis are gratefully acknowledged.

sume in the analysis of the data. Given the image of the atomized audience which characterized so much of mass media research, the surprising thing is that interpersonal influence attracted the attention of the researchers at all.[2]

In the almost seventeen years since the voting study was undertaken, several studies at the Bureau of Applied Social Research of Columbia University have attempted to examine the hypothesis and to build upon it. Four such studies will be singled out for review. These are Merton's study of interpersonal influence and communications behavior in Rovere;[3] the Decatur study of decision-making in marketing, fashions, movie-going and public affairs, reported by Katz and Lazarsfeld;[4] the Elmira study of the 1948 election campaign reported by Berelson, Lazarsfeld and McPhee;[5] and, finally, very recent study by Coleman, Katz and Menzel on the diffusion of a new drug among doctors.[6]

These studies will serve as a framework within which an attempt will be made to report on the present state of the two-step flow hypothesis, to examine the extent to which it has found confirmation and the ways in which it has been extended, contracted and reformulated. More than that, the studies will be drawn upon to highlight the successive strategies which have been developed in attempting to take systematic account of interpersonal relations in the design of communications research, aiming ultimately at a sort of "survey sociometry." Finally, these studies, plus others which will be referred to in passing, will provide an unusual opportunity to reflect upon problems in the continuity of social research.[7]

[2] For the discussion of the image of the atomized audience and the contravening empirical evidence, see Elihu Katz and Paul F. Lazarsfeld, *Personal Influence: The Part Played by People in the Flow of Mass Communications*, Glencoe, Illinois: The Free Press, 1955, pp. 15–42; Eliot Friedson, "Communications Research and the Concept of the Mass," *American Sociological Review*, Vol. 18 (1953), pp. 313–317; and Morris Janowitz, *The Urban Press in a Community Setting*, Glencoe, Illinois: The Free Press, 1952.

[3] Robert K. Merton, "Patterns of Influence: A Study of Interpersonal Influence and Communications Behavior in a Local Community," in Paul F. Lazarsfeld and Frank N. Stanton, eds., *Communications Research, 1948–9*, New York: Harper and Brothers, 1949, pp. 180–219.

[4] Elihu Katz and Paul F. Lazarsfeld, *op. cit.*, Part Two.

[5] Bernard R. Berelson, Paul F. Lazarsfeld and William N. McPhee, *Voting: A Study of Opinion Formation in a Presidential Campaign*, Chicago: University of Chicago Press, 1954.

[6] A report on the pilot phase of this study is to be found in Herbert Menzel and Elihu Katz, "Social Relations and Innovation in the Medical Profession," *Public Opinion Quarterly*, Vol. 19 (1955), pp. 337–52; a volume and various articles on the full study are now in preparation.

[7] Other authors who have drawn upon the concepts of opinion leadership and the two-step flow of communication, and developed them further, are Matilda and John Riley, "A Sociological Approach to Communications Research," *Public Opinion Quarterly*, Vol. 15 (1951), pp. 445–460; S. N. Eisenstadt, "Communications Processes Among Immigrants in Israel," *Public Opinion Quarterly*, Vol. 16 (1952), pp. 42–58

FINDINGS OF *The People's Choice*

The starting point for this review must be an examination of the evidence in the 1940 voting study which led to the original formulation of the hypothesis. Essentially, three distinct sets of findings seem to have been involved. The first had to do with *the impact of personal influence.* It is reported that people who made up their minds late in the campaign, and those who changed their minds during the course of the campaign, were more likely than other people to mention personal influence as having figured in their decisions. The political pressure brought to bear by everyday groups such as family and friends is illustrated by reference to the political homogeneity which characterizes such groups. What's more, on an average day, a greater number of people reported participating in discussion of the election than hearing a campaign speech or reading a newspaper editorial. From all of this, the authors conclude that personal contacts appear to have been both more frequent and more effective than the mass media in influencing voting decisions.[8]

The second ingredient that went into the formulation of the hypothesis concerned *the flow of personal influence.* Given the apparent importance of interpersonal influence, the obvious next step was to ask whether some people were more important than others in the transmission of influence. The study sought to single out the "opinion leaders" by two questions: "Have you recently tried to convince anyone of your political ideas?", and "Has anyone recently asked you for your advice on a political question?" Comparing the opinion leaders with others, they found the opinion leaders more interested in the election. And from the almost even distribution of opinion leaders throughout every class and occupation, as well as the frequent mention by decision-makers of the influence of friends, co-workers and relatives, it was concluded opinion leaders are to be found on every level of society and presumably, therefore, are very much like the people whom they influence.[9]

---

and "Communication Systems and Social Structure: An Exploratory Study," *Public Opinion Quarterly,* Vol. 19 (1955), pp. 153–167; David Riesman, *The Lonely Crowd,* New Haven: Yale University Press, 1950; Leo A. Handel, *Hollywood Looks at its Audience,* Urbana: University of Illinois Press, 1950. The program of research in international communications at the Bureau of Applied Social Research has given considerable attention to opinion leadership; see Charles Y. Glock, "The Comparative Study of Communications and Opinion Formation," *Public Opinion Quarterly,* Vol. 16 (1952–53), pp. 512–523; J. M. Stycos, "Patterns of Communication in a Rural Greek Village," *Public Opinion Quarterly,* Vol. 16 (1952), pp. 59–70; and the forthcoming book by Daniel Lerner, Paul Berkman and Lucille Pevsner, *Modernizing the Middle East.* Forthcoming studies by Peter H. Rossi and by Robert D. Leigh and Martin A. Trow are also concerned with the interplay of personal and mass media influences in local communities.

8 Lazarsfeld, Berelson and Gaudet, *op. cit.,* pp. 135–152.

9 *Ibid.,* pp. 50–51.

A further comparison of leaders and others with respect to mass media habits provides the third ingredient: *the opinion leaders and the mass media*. Compared with the rest of the population, opinion leaders were found to be considerably more exposed to the radio, to the newspapers and to magazines, that is, to the formal media of communication.[10]

Now the argument is clear: If word-of-mouth is so important, and if word-of-mouth specialists are widely dispersed, and if these specialists are more exposed to the media than the people whom they influence, then perhaps "ideas often flow from radio and print to opinion leaders and from these to the less active sections of the population."[11]

DESIGN OF THE VOTING STUDY

For studying the flow of influence as it impinges on the making of decisions, the study design of *The People's Choice* had several advantages. Most important was the panel method which made it possible to locate changes almost as soon as they occurred and then to correlate change with the influences reaching the decision-maker. Secondly, the unit of effect, the decision, was a tangible indicator of change which could readily be recorded. But for studying that part of the flow of influence which had to do with contacts among people, the study design fell short, since it called for a random sample of individuals abstracted from their social environments. It is this traditional element in the design of survey research which explains the leap that had to be made from the available data to the hypothesis of the two-step flow of communication.

Because every man in a random sample can speak only for himself, opinion leaders in the 1940 voting study had to be located by self-designation, that is, on the basis of their own answers to the two advice-giving questions cited above.[12] In effect, respondents were simply asked to report whether or not they were opinion leaders. Much more important than the obvious problem of validity posed by this technique is the fact that it does not permit a comparison of leaders with their respective followers, but only of leaders and non-leaders in general. The data, in other words, consist only of two statistical groupings: people who said they were advice-givers and those who did not. Therefore, the fact that leaders were more interested in the election than non-leaders cannot be

10 *Ibid.*, p. 51.

11 *Ibid.*, p. 151.

12 Strictly speaking, of course, if a respondent reports whether or not he is a leader he is not speaking for himself but for his followers, real or imagined. Furthermore, it ought to be pointed out for the record that it is sometimes possible for a respondent to speak for others besides himself. The voting studies, for example, ask respondents to report the vote-intentions of other family members, of friends, of co-workers, though this procedure is of undetermined validity.

taken to mean that influence flows from more interested persons to less interested ones. To state the problem drastically, it may even be that the leaders influence only each other, while the uninterested non-leaders stand outside the influence market altogether. Nevertheless, the temptation to assume that the non-leaders are the followers of the leaders is very great, and while *The People's Choice* is quite careful about this, it cannot help but succumb.[13] Thus, from the fact that the opinion leaders were more exposed to the mass media than the non-leaders came the suggestion of the two-step flow of communication; yet, manifestly, it can be true only if the non-leaders are, in fact, followers of the leaders.

The authors themselves point out that a far better method would have been based on "asking people to whom they turn for advice on the issue at hand and then investigating the interaction between advisers and advisees. But that procedure would be extremely difficult, if not impossible, since few of the related 'leaders' and 'followers' would happen to be included in the sample."[14] As will be shown immediately, this is perhaps the most important problem which succeeding studies have attempted to solve.

DESIGN OF THREE SUBSEQUENT STUDIES

To this point, two aspects of the original statement of the two-step flow hypothesis have been reviewed. First of all, the hypothesis has been shown to have three distinct components, concerning respectively the impact of personal influence; the flow of personal influence; and the relationship of opinion leaders to the mass media. The evidence underlying each has been examined. Secondly, the design of the study has been recalled in order to point up the difficulty that arises from attempting to cope with the fundamentally new problem of incorporating *both* partners to an influence transaction into a cross-sectional study.

From this point forward, the major focus will turn to those studies that have succeeded *The People's Choice*. We will first report the different ways in which three of the four studies selected for review approached the problem of designing research on interpersonal influence.[15]

13 There is an alternative procedure which is something of an improvement. Respondents can be asked not only whether they have given advice but whether they have taken advice. This was done in the Decatur and Elmira studies which are cited below. Thus the non-leaders can be classified in terms of whether or not they are in the influence market at all, that is, whether or not they are "followers."

14 Lazarsfeld, Berelson and Gaudet, *op. cit.*, pp. 49–50.

15 The Elmira study will be omitted at this point because its design is essentially the same as that of the 1940 voting study except for the important fact that it obtained from each respondent considerably more information about the vote-intentions of others in his environment, the kinds of people he talks with, etc., than was done in *The People's Choice*.

Thereafter, the substantive findings of the several studies will be reviewed and evaluated so as to constitute an up-to-date report on the accumulating evidence for and against the hypothesis of the two-step flow of communication.

THE ROVERE STUDY

Undertaken just as the 1940 voting study was being completed, the earliest of the three studies was conducted in a small town in New Jersey. It began by asking a sample of 86 respondents to name the people to whom they turned for information and advice regarding a variety of matters. Hundreds of names were mentioned in response, and those who were designated four times or more were considered opinion leaders. The influentials were then sought out and interviewed.[16]

Here, then, is the initial attempt, on a pilot scale, to solve the problem of research design posed by *The People's Choice*. To locate influentials, this study suggests, begin by asking somebody, "Who influences you?" and proceed from the persons influenced to those who are designated as influential.

Two important differences between this study and the 1940 voting study must be pointed out. First, there is a difference in the conception of opinion leadership. Whereas the voting study regards any advice-giver as an opinion leader if he influences even one other person (such as a husband telling his wife for whom to vote), the leaders singled out by the criterion employed in Rovere were almost certainly wielders of wider influence.

Secondly, the voting study, at least by implication, was interested in such questions as the extent of the role of interpersonal influence in decision-making and its relative effectiveness compared to the mass media. The Rovere study took for granted the importance of this kind of influence, and proceeded to try to find the people who play key roles in its transmission.

A final point to make in connection with the design of this study is that it makes use of the initial interviews almost exclusively to *locate* opinion leaders and hardly at all to explore the *relationships* between leaders and followers. Once the leaders were designated, almost exclusive attention was given to classifying them into different types, studying the communications behavior of the different types and the interaction among the leaders themselves, but very little attention was given to the interaction between the leaders and the original informants who designated them.

16 Merton, *op. cit.*, pp. 184–185.

THE DECATUR STUDY

The Decatur study carried out in 1945–46, tried to go a step further.[17] Like the voting study, but unlike Rovere, it tried to account for decisions—specific instances in which the effect of various influences could be discerned and assessed. Like Rovere, but unlike the voting study, it provided for interviews with the persons whom individuals in the initial sample had credited as influential in the making of recent decisions (in the realms of marketing, movie-going, and public affairs). The focus of the study this time was not on the opinion leaders alone, but (1) on the relative importance of personal influence and (2) on the person who named the leader as well as the leader—the advisor-advisee dyad.

Ideally, then, this study could ask whether opinion leaders tended to be from the same social class as their followers or whether the tendency was for influence to flow from the upper classes downwards. Were members of the dyads likely to be of the same age, the same sex, etc.? Was the leader more interested in the particular sphere of influence than his advisee? Was he more likely to be exposed to the mass media?

Just as the dyad could be constructed by proceeding from an advisee to his adviser, it was also possible to begin the other way around by talking first to a person who claimed to have acted as an adviser, and then locating the person he said he had influenced. The Decatur study tried this too. Using the same kind of self-designating questions employed in the voting study, persons who designated themselves as influential were asked to indicate the names of those whom they had influenced. By "snowballing" to the people thus designated, there arose the opportunity not only to study the interaction between adviser and advisee but also to explore the extent to which people who designated themselves as influential were confirmed in their self-evaluations by those whom they allegedly had influenced. Proceeding in this way, the researchers hoped to be able to say something about the validity of the self-designating technique.[18]

The authors of *The People's Choice* had said that "asking people to whom they turn and then investigating the interaction between advisers and advisees . . . would be extremely difficult if not impossible." And, in fact, it proved to be extremely difficult. Many problems were encountered in the field work, the result of which was that not all the

---

[17] Katz and Lazarsfeld, *op. cit.*, Part Two.

[18] About two-thirds of the alleged influences confirmed the fact that a conversation had taken place between themselves and the self-designated influential on the subject-matter in question. Of these, about 80 per cent further confirmed that they had received advice. The extent of confirmation is considerably less in the realm of public affairs than it is in marketing or fashion, *ibid.*, pp. 149–161 and 353–362.

"snowball" interviews could be completed.[19] In many parts of the analysis of the data, therefore, it was necessary to revert to comparisons of leaders and non-leaders, imputing greater influence to groups with higher concentrations of self-designated leadership. Yet, in principle, it was demonstrated that a study design taking account of interpersonal relations was both possible and profitable to execute.

But about the time it became evident that this goal was within reach, the goal itself began to change. It began to seem desirable to take account of chains of influence longer than those involved in the dyad; and hence to view the adviser-advisee dyad as one component of a more elaborately structured social group.

These changes came about gradually and for a variety of reasons. First of all, findings from the Decatur study and from the later Elmira study revealed that the opinion leaders themselves often reported that their own decisions were influenced by still other people.[20] It began to seem desirable, therefore, to think in terms of the opinion leaders of opinion leaders.[21] Secondly, it became clear that opinion leadership could not be viewed as a "trait" which some people possess and others do not, although the voting study sometimes implied this view. Instead, it seemed quite apparent that the opinion leader is influential at certain times and with respect to certain substantive areas by virtue of the fact that he is "empowered" to be so by other members of his group. Why certain people are chosen must be accounted for not only in demographic terms (social status, sex, age, etc.) but also in terms of the structure and values of the groups of which both adviser and advisee are members. Thus, the unexpected rise of young men to opinion leadership in traditional groups, when these groups faced the new situations of urbanization and industrialization, can be understood only against the background of old and new patterns of social relations within the group and of old and new patterns of orientation to the world outside the group.[22] Reviewing the literature of small group research hastened the formulation of this conception.[23]

One other factor shaped the direction of the new program as well. Reflecting upon the Decatur study, it became clear that while one could

[19] Partly this was due to inability to locate the designated people, but partly, too, to the fact that original respondents did not always know the person who had influenced them as is obvious, for example, in the case of a woman copying another woman's hat style, etc. See *ibid.*, pp. 362–363.

[20] *Ibid.*, p. 318; Berelson, Lazarsfeld and McPhee, *op. cit.*, p. 110.

[21] This was actually tried at one point in the Decatur study. See Katz and Lazarsfeld, *op cit.*, pp. 283–287.

[22] See, for example, the articles by Eisenstadt, *op. cit.*, and Glock, *op. cit.*; the Rovere study, too, takes careful account of the structure of social relations and values in which influentials are embedded, and discusses the various avenues to influentiality open to different kinds of people.

[23] Reported in Part I of Katz and Lazarsfeld, *op. cit.*

talk about the role of various influences in the making of fashion *decisions by individuals*, the study design was not adequate for the study of fashion in the aggregate—*fashion as a process of diffusion*—as long as it did not take account of either the content of the decision or the time factor involved. The decisions of the "fashion changers" studied in Decatur might have cancelled each other out: while Mrs. X reported a change from Fashion A to Fashion B, Mrs. Y might have been reporting a change from B to A. What is true for fashion is true for any other diffusion phenomenon: to study it, one must trace the flow of some specific item over time. Combining this interest in diffusion with that of studying the role of more elaborate social networks of communication gave birth to a new study which focused on (1) a specific item, (2) diffusion over time, (3) through the social structure of an entire community.

THE DRUG STUDY

This study was conducted to determine the way in which doctors make decisions to adopt new drugs. This time, when it came to designing a study which would take account of the possible role of interpersonal influence among physicians, it became clear that there were so few physicians (less than one and one-half per 1000 population) that it was feasible to interview all members of the medical profession in several cities. If all doctors (or all doctors in specialties concerned with the issue at hand) could be interviewed, then there would be no doubt that all adviser-advisee pairs would fall within the sample. All such pairs could then be located within the context of larger social groupings of doctors, which could be measured by sociometric methods.

Doctors in the relevant specialties in four midwestern cities were interviewed. In addition to questions on background, attitudes, drug-use, exposure to various sources of information and influence, and the like, each doctor was also asked to name the three colleagues he saw most often socially, the three colleagues with whom he talked most frequently about cases, and the three colleagues to whom he looked for information and advice.[24]

In addition to the opportunity of mapping the networks of interpersonal relations, the drug study also provided for the two other factors necessary for a true diffusion study: attention to a specific item in the course of gaining acceptance, and a record of this diffusion over time. This was accomplished by means of an audit of prescriptions on file in the local pharmacies of the cities studied, which made it possible to date each doctor's earliest use of a particular new drug—a drug which had gained widespread acceptance a few months before the study had

[24] See footnote 6.

begun. Each doctor could thus be classified in terms of the promptness of his decision to respond to the innovation, and in terms of other information provided by the prescription audit.

Altogether, compared with the earlier studies, the drug study imposes a more objective framework—both psychological and sociological—on the decision. First of all, the decision-maker himself is not the only source of information concerning his decision. Objective data from the prescription record are used as well. Secondly, the role of different influences is assessed not only on the basis of the decision-maker's own reconstruction of the event, but also on the basis of objective correlations from which inferences concerning the flow of influence can be drawn. For example, doctors who adopted the new drug early were more likely to be participants in out-of-town medical specialty meetings than those who adopted it later.

Similarly, it is possible to infer the role of social relations in doctor's decision-making not only from the doctor's own testimony concerning the role of social influences but also from the doctor's "location" in the interpersonal networks mapped by the sociometric questions. Thus, on the basis of sociometric data, it is possible to classify doctors according to their integration into the medical community, or the degree of their influence, as measured by *the number of times* they are named by their colleagues as friends, discussion-partners, and consultants. They can also be classified according to their membership in one or another network or clique, as indicated by *who* names them. Using the first measure makes it possible to investigate whether or not the more influential doctors adopt a drug earlier than those who are less influential. From the second kind of analysis one can learn, for example, whether or not those doctors who belong to the same sub-groups have similar drug-use patterns. In this way, it becomes possible to weave back and forth between the doctor's own testimony about his decisions and the influences involved, on the one hand, and the more objective record of his decisions and of the influences to which he has been exposed, on the other hand.

Note that the networks of social relations in this study are mapped "prior" to the introduction of the new drug being studied, in the sense that friendship, consultation, and so on, are recorded independently of any particular decision the doctor has made. The study is concerned with the potential relevance of various parts of these sociometric structures to the transmission of influence. For example, it is possible to point to the parts of the structure which are "activated" upon the introduction of a new drug, and to describe the sequence of diffusion of the drug as it gains acceptance by individuals and groups in the community. While the Decatur study could hope to examine only the particular face-to-face relationship which had been influential in a given decision, the drug study can locate this relationship against the background of the entire web of *potentially* relevant relationships within which the doctor is embedded.

THE FINDINGS OF STUDIES SUBSEQUENT TO *THE PEOPLE'S CHOICE*

Having examined the *designs* of these studies, the next step is to explore their *findings* insofar as these are relevant to the hypothesis about the two-step flow of communication. It will be useful to return to the three categories already singled out in discussing *The People's Choice*: (1) the impact of personal influence; (2) the flow of personal influence; and (3) opinion leaders and the mass media. Evidence from the three studies just reported, as well as from the 1948 Elmira study[25] and from others, will be brought together here; but in every case the characteristics of each study's design must be borne in mind in evaluating the evidence presented.

THE IMPACT OF PERSONAL INFLUENCE

Personal and the Mass Media Influence. The 1940 study indicated that personal influence affected voting decisions more than the mass media did, particularly in the case of those who changed their minds during the course of the campaign. The Decatur study went on to explore the relative impact of personal influences and the mass media in three other realms: marketing, fashions and movie-going. Basing its conclusions on the testimony of the decision-makers themselves, and using an instrument for evaluating the relative effectiveness of the various media which entered into the decisions, the Decatur study again found that personal influence figured both more frequently and more effectively than any of the mass media.[26]

In the analysis to date, the drug study has not approached the problem of the relative effectiveness of the various media from the point of view of the doctor's own reconstruction of what went into the making of his decision. Comparing mere frequency of mention of different media, it is clear that colleagues are by no means the most frequently mentioned source. Nevertheless, exploration of the factors related to whether the doctor's decision to adopt the drug came early or late indicates that the factor most strongly associated with the time of adoption of the new drug is the extent of the doctor's integration in the medical community. That is, the more frequently a doctor is named by his colleagues as a

25 Berelson, Lazarsfeld, and McPhee, *op. cit.*
26 Katz and Lazarsfeld, *op. cit.*, pp. 169–186.

friend or a discussion partner, the more likely he is to be an innovator with respect to the new drug. Extent of integration proves to be a more important factor than any background factor (such as age, medical school, or income of patients), or any other source of influence (such as readership of medical journals) that was examined.

Investigation of why integration is related to innovation suggests two central factors: (1) interpersonal communication—doctors who are integrated are more in touch and more up-to-date; and (2) social support—doctors who are integrated feel more secure when facing the risks of innovation in medicine.[27] Thus the drug study, too, provides evidence of the strong impact of personal relations—even in the making of scientific decisions.

Homogeneity of Opinion in Primary Groups. The effectiveness of interpersonal influence, as it is revealed in the studies under review, is reflected in the homogeneity of opinions and actions in primary groups. The medium of primary group communication is, by definition, person-to-person. Both of the voting studies indicate the high degree of homogeneity of political opinion among members of the same families, and among co-workers and friends. The effectiveness of such primary groups in pulling potential deviates back into line is demonstrated by the fact that those who changed their vote intentions were largely people who, early in the campaign, had reported that they intended to vote differently from their family or friends.[28]

The drug study, too, was able to examine the extent of homogeneity in the behavior of sociometrically related doctors, and was able to demonstrate that there were situations where similar behavior could be deserved. For example, it was found that, when called upon to treat the more puzzling diseases, doctors were likely to prescribe the same drug as their sociometric colleagues. The study also showed that, very early in the history of a new drug, innovating doctors who were sociometrically connected tended to adopt the new drug at virtually the same time. This phenomenon of homogeneity of opinion or behavior among interacting individuals confronting an unclear or uncertain situation which calls for action has often been studied by sociologists and social psychologists.[29]

[27] On the relationship between social integration and self-confidence in a work situation, see Peter M. Blau, *The Dynamics of Bureaucracy*, Chicago: University of Chicago Press, 1955, pp. 126–129.

[28] Lazarsfeld, Berelson and Gaudet, *op. cit.*, pp. 137–145; Berelson, Lazarsfeld and McPhee, *op. cit.*, pp. 94–101, 120–122.

[29] That men, faced with an unstructured situation, look to each other to establish a "social reality" in terms of which they act, is a central theme in the work of Durkheim, Kurt Lewin and his disciples, H. S. Sullivan ("consensual validation"), and in the studies of Sherif, Asch and others.

The Various Roles of the Media. The 1940 voting study explored some of the reasons why personal influence might be expected to be more influential in changing opinions than the mass media: It is often non-purposive; it is flexible; it is trustworthy. It was suggested that the mass media more often play a reinforcing role in the strengthening of pre-dispositions and of decisions already taken. Nevertheless, it was assumed that the various media and personal influence are essentially competi-tive, in the sense that a given decision is influenced by one *or* the other. The Decatur study tended toward this assumption too, but at one point the study does attempt to show that different media play different parts in the decision-making process and take patterned positions in a se-quence of several influences. The drug study elaborates on the roles of the media even further, distinguishing between media that "inform" and media that "legitimate" decisions. Thus in doctors' decisions, pro-fessional media (including colleagues) seem to play a legitimating role, while commercial media play an informing role.

THE FLOW OF PERSONAL INFLUENCE

The 1940 voting study found that opinion leaders were not concen-trated in the upper brackets of the population but were located in almost equal proportions in every social group and stratum. This find-ing led to efforts in subsequent studies to establish the extent to which this was true in areas other than election campaigns and also to ascertain what it is that *does* distinguish opinion leaders from those whom they influence.

The first thing that is clear from the series of studies under review is that the subject matter concerning which influence is transmitted has a lot to do with determining who will lead and who follow. Thus, the Rovere study suggests that within the broad sphere of public affairs one set of influentials is occupied with "local" affairs and another with "cosmopolitan" affairs.[30] The Decatur study suggests that in marketing, for example, there is a concentration of opinion leadership among older women with larger families, while in fashions and movie-going it is the young, unmarried girl who has a disproportionate chance of being turned to for advice. There is very little overlap of leadership: a leader in one sphere is not likely to be influential in another unrelated sphere as well.[31]

Yet, even when leadership in one or another sphere is heavily concen-trated among the members of a particular group—as was the case with marketing leadership in Decatur—the evidence suggests that people still

[30] Merton, *op. cit.*, pp. 187–188.
[31] For a summary of the Decatur findings on the flow of interpersonal influence, see Katz and Lazarsfeld, *op. cit.*, pp. 327–334.

talk, most of all, to others like themselves. Thus, while the marketing leaders among the older "large-family wives" also influenced other kinds of women, most of their influence was directed to women of their own age with equally large families. In marketing, fashions, and movie-going, furthermore, there was no appreciable concentration of influentials in any of the three socio-economic levels. Only in public affairs was there a concentration of leadership in the highest status, and there was some slight evidence that influence flows from this group to individuals of lower status. The Elmira study also found opinion-leaders in similar proportions on every socio-economic and occupational level and found that conversations concerning the campaign went on, typically, between people of similar age, occupation, and *political* opinion.

What makes for the concentration of certain kinds of opinion leadership within certain groups? And when influential and influencee are outwardly alike—as they so often seem to be—what, if anything, distinguishes one from the other? Broadly, it appears that influence is related (1) to the *personification of certain values* (who one is); (2) to *competence* (what one knows); and (3) to *strategic social location* (whom one knows). Social location, in turn, divides into whom one knows within a group; and "outside."

Influence is often successfully transmitted because the influencee wants to be as much like the influential as possible.[32] That the young, unmarried girls are fashion leaders can be understood easily in a culture where youth and youthfulness are supreme values. This is an example where "who one is" counts very heavily.

But "what one knows" is no less important.[33] The fact is that older women, by virtue of their greater experience, are looked to as marketing advisers and that specialists in internal medicine—the most "scientific" of the practicing physicians—are the most frequently mentioned opinion leaders among the doctors. The influence of young people in the realm of movie-going can also be understood best in terms of their familiarity with the motion picture world. The Elmira study found slightly greater concentrations of opinion leadership among the more educated people on each socioeconomic level, again implying the importance of competence. Finally, the influence of the "cosmopolitans" in Rovere rested on the presumption that they had large amounts of information.

[32] That leaders are, in a certain sense, the most conformist members of their groups—upholding whatever norms and values are central to the group—is a proposition which further illustrates this point. For an empirical illustration from a highly relevent study, see C. Paul Marsh and A. Lee Coleman, "Farmers' Practice Adoption Rates in Relation to Adoption Rates of Leaders," *Rural Sociology*, Vol. 19 (1954), pp. 180–183.

[33] The distinction between "what" and "whom" one knows is used by Merton, *op. cit.*, p. 197.

It is, however, not enough to be a person whom others want to emulate, or to be competent. One must also be accessible. Thus, the Decatur study finds gregariousness—"whom one knows"—related to every kind of leadership. The Rovere study reports that the leadership of the "local" influentials is based on their central location in the web of interpersonal contacts. Similarly, studies of rumor transmission have singled out those who are "socially active" as agents of rumor.[34]

Of course, the importance of whom one knows is not simply a matter of the number of people with whom an opinion leader is in contact. It is also a question of whether the people with whom he is in touch happen to be interested in the area in which his leadership is likely to be sought. For this reason, it is quite clear that the greater interest of opinion leaders in the subjects over which they exert influence is not a sufficient explanation of their influence. While the voting studies as well as the Decatur study show leaders to be more interested, the Decatur study goes on to show that interest alone is not the determining factor.[35] In fashion, for example, a young unmarried girl is considerably more likely to be influential than a matron with an equally great interest in clothes. The reason, it is suggested, is that a girl who is interested in fashion is much more likely than a matron with an equally high interest to know other people who share her preoccupation, and thus is more likely than the matron to have followers who are interested enough to ask for her advice. In other words, it takes two to be a leader—a leader and a follower.

Finally, there is the second aspect of "whom one knows." An individual may be influential not only because people within his group look to him for advice but also because of whom he knows outside his group.[36] Both the Elmira and Decatur studies found that men are more likely than women to be opinion leaders in the realm of public affairs and this, it is suggested, is because they have more of a chance to get outside the home to meet people and talk politics. Similarly, the Elmira study indicated that opinion leaders belonged to more organizations, more often knew workers for the political parties, and so on, than did others. The drug study found that influential doctors could be characterized in terms of such things as their more frequent attendance at out-of-town meetings and the diversity of places with which they maintained contact, particularly far-away places. It is interesting that a study of the

[34] Gordon W. Allport and Leo J. Postman, *The Psychology of Rumor*, New York: Henry Holt, 1943, p. 183.

[35] Katz and Lazarsfeld, *op. cit.*, pp. 249–252.

[36] It is interesting that a number of studies have found that the most integrated persons within a group are also likely to have more contacts outside the group than others. One might have expected the more marginal members to have more contacts outside. For example, see Blau, *op. cit.*, 128.

farmer-innovators responsible for the diffusion of hybrid seed-corn in Iowa concluded that these leaders also could be characterized in terms of the relative frequency of their trips out of town.[37]

THE OPINION LEADERS AND THE MASS MEDIA

The third aspect of the hypothesis of the two-step flow of communication states that opinion leaders are more exposed to the mass media than are those whom they influence. In *The People's Choice* this is supported by reference to the media behavior of leaders and non-leaders.

The Decatur study corroborated this finding, and went on to explore two additional aspects of the same idea.[38] First of all, it was shown that leaders in a given sphere (fashions, public affairs, etc.) were particularly likely to be exposed to the media appropriate to that sphere. This is essentially a corroboration of the Rovere findings that those who proved influential with regard to "cosmopolitan" matters were more likely to be readers of national news magazines, but that this was not at all the case for those influential with regard to "local" matters. Secondly, the Decatur study shows that at least in the realm of fashions, the leaders are not only more exposed to the mass media, but are also more affected by them in their own decisions. This did not appear to be the case in other realms, where opinion leaders, though more exposed to the media than non-leaders, nevertheless reported personal influence as the major factor in their decisions. This suggests that in some spheres considerably longer chains of person-to-person influence than the dyad may have to be traced back before one encounters any decisive influence by the mass media, even though their contributory influence may be perceived at many points. This was suggested by the Elmira study too. It found that the leaders, though more exposed to the media, also more often reported that they sought information and advice from other persons.[39]

Similarly, the drug study showed that the influential doctors were more likely to be readers of a large number of professional journals and valued them more highly than did doctors of lesser influence. But at the same time, they were as likely as others to say that local colleagues were an important source of information and advice in their reaching particular decisions.

[37] Bryce Ryan and Neal Gross, *Acceptance and Diffusion of Hybrid Seed Corn in Two Iowa Communities*, Ames, Iowa: Iowa State College of Agriculture and Mechanic Arts, Research Bulletin 372, pp. 706–707. For a general summary, see Ryan and Gross, "The Diffusion of Hybrid Seed Corn in Two Iowa Communities," *Rural Sociology*, Vol. 8 (1942), pp. 15–24. An article, now in preparation, will point out some of the parallels in research design and in findings between this study and the drug study.

[38] Katz and Lazarsfeld, *op. cit.*, pp. 309–320.

[39] Berelson, Lazarsfeld and McPhee, *op. cit.*, p. 110.

Finally, the drug study demonstrated that the more influential doctors could be characterized by their greater attention not only to medical journals, but to out-of-town meetings and contacts as well. This finding has already been discussed in the previous section treating the *strategic location* of the opinion leader with respect to "the world outside" his group. Considering it again under the present heading suggests that the greater exposure of the opinion leader to the mass media may only be a special case of the more general proposition that opinion leaders serve to relate their groups to relevant parts of the environment through whatever media happen to be appropriate. This more general statement makes clear the similar functions of big city newspapers for the Decatur fashion leader; of national news magazines for the "cosmopolitan" influentials of Rovere; of out-of-town media meetings for the influential doctor; and of contact with the city for the farmer-innovator in Iowa[40] as well as for the newly-risen, young opinion leaders in underdeveloped areas throughout the world.[41]

CONCLUSION

Despite the diversity of subject matter with which they are concerned, the studies reviewed here constitute an example of continuity and cumulation both in research design and theoretical commitment. Piecing together the findings of the latter-day studies in the light of the original statement of the two-step flow hypothesis suggests the following picture.

Opinion leaders and the people whom they influence are very much alike and typically belong to the same primary groups of family, friends and co-workers. While the opinion leader may be more interested in the particular sphere in which he is influential, it is highly unlikely that the persons influenced will be very far behind the leader in their level of interest. Influential and influencees may exchange roles in different spheres of influence. Most spheres focus the group's attention on some related part of the world outside the group, and it is the opinion leader's function to bring the group into touch with this relevant part of its environment through whatever media are appropriate. In every case, influentials have been found to be more exposed to these points of contact with the outside world. Nevertheless, it is also true that, despite their greater exposure to the media, most opinion leaders are primarily affected not by the communication media but by still other people.

[40] Ryan and Gross, *op. cit.*, choose to explain "trips to the city" as another index of the non-traditional orientation of which innovation itself is also an index. In the case of the drug out-of-town meetings, trips to out-of-town centers of learning, etc., but the latter were also mentioned as key sources of advice by doctors who were innovators and influentials.

[41] See the forthcoming book by Lerner, *et. al* cited above.

The main emphasis of the two-step flow hypothesis appears to be on only one aspect of interpersonal relations—interpersonal relations as channels of communication. But from the several studies reviewed, it is clear that these very same interpersonal relations influence the making of decisions in at least two additional ways. In addition to serving as networks of communication, interpersonal relations are also sources of pressure to conform to the group's way of thinking and acting, as well as sources of social support. The workings of group pressure are clearly evident in the homogeneity of opinion and action observed among voters and among doctors in situations of unclarity or uncertainty. The social support that comes from being integrated in the medical community may give a doctor the confidence required to carry out a resolution to adopt a new drug. Thus, interpersonal relations are (1) channels of information, (2) sources of social pressure, and (3) sources of social support, and each relates interpersonal relations to decision-making in a somewhat different way.[42]

The central methodological problem in each of the studies reviewed has been how to take account of interpersonal relations and still preserve the economy and representativeness which the random, cross-sectional sample affords. Answers to this problem range from asking individuals in the sample to describe the others with whom they interacted (Elmira), to conducting "snowball" interviews with influential-influencee dyads (Decatur), to interviewing an entire community (drug study). Future studies will probably find themselves somewhere in between. For most studies, however, the guiding principle would seem to be to build larger or smaller social molecules around each individual atom in the sample.[43]

RETROSPECTIVE COMMENT

Katz's "two-step flow of communication" served a very useful role in focusing the attention of marketers on the importance of personal in-

---

[42] These different dimensions of interpersonal relations can be further illustrated by reference to studies which represent the "pure type" of each dimension. Studies of rumor flow illustrate the "channels" dimension; see, for example, Jacob L. Moreno, *Who Shall Survive*, Beacon, N.Y.: Beacon House, 1953, pp. 440–450. The study by Leon Festinger, Stanley Schachter and Kurt Back, *Social Pressures in Informal Groups*, New York: Harper and Bros., 1950, illustrates the second dimension, Blau, *op. cit.*, pp. 126–129, illustrates the "social support" dimension.

[43] Various ways of accomplishing this have been discussed for the past two years in a staff seminar on "relational analysis" at the Bureau of Applied Social Research. The recent study by Seymour M. Lipset, Martin A. Trow and James S. Coleman, *Union Democracy*, Glencoe, Ill.: The Free Press, 1956, illustrates one approach in its study of printers within the varying social contexts of the shops in which they are employed. The study by Riley and Riley, *op. cit.*, is another good example.

fluence. Nevertheless, the two-step model is highly simplistic in nature and does not account for the range of personal influence which is possible. The Katz view is that influence is a one-way verbal process from a dominant opinion leader to a passive follower. However, personal influence is indeed multidimensional in nature and can occur in a number of ways:

1. Personal influence may be initiated by the influence *source* or by the influence *recipient*. An individual can give information or seek information. The "two-step" model only takes into account source-initiated influence.

2. Personal influence may be *one-way* or *two-way*; that is, either or both parties to the communication transaction may come away influenced. Again, the "two-step" model only accounts for one-way influence.

3. Personal influence may occur through *verbal* or *visual* communication. Perhaps most influence is actually due to observation (fashion, for example) rather than verbal communication.

In refining the "two-step flow of communication," therefore, we must enrich our conceptualization to include all of the various forms of personal influence.—*Thomas S. Robertson*, Professor of Marketing at The Wharton School, University of Pennsylvania

26. The Adoption Process

Francis S. Bourne

For many products, the process of adoption follows a rather uniform pattern, from the time the new product is developed until it is widely accepted by the ultimate consumers. More is known about the adoption of agricultural products and practices than about others. Rural sociologists have been concerned with the introduction of new practices and with new product adoption in agriculture for a number of years, and they have systematically studied the process by which change takes place. In addition, some studies have been made of other kinds of innovation, including the adoption by doctors of new wonder drugs for treatment,[1] the adoption of new educational practices by school systems[2] and the adoption of color television.[3] The process of adoption in all these cases has been quite similar. There are exceptions to the pattern; for example, black and white television. The general pattern appears so widely, however, that it is the central theme of this report.

Researchers have charted the course of a new product by determining *when* people adopt it. The curve which results is a simple one, the well known probability curve, in cumulative form.[4] A few people adopt a product at first, then a few more, followed by a rather sharp increase and finally a leveling off when most of the potential consumers have adopted the product.

Such a curve is presented in general form in Figure 1. No scale is given for the time dimension, because this differs from product to product. A number of studies indicate, however, the *form* of the curve remains constant, and therefore that knowledge of the time required for a first

[1] E. Katz, "The Two-step Flow of Communication: an Up-to-date Report on an Hypothesis," *Public Opinion Quarterly* (1957), pp. 61–78; and H. Menzel and E. Katz, "Social Relations and Innovation in the Medical Profession: The Epidemiology of a New Drug," *Public Opinion Quarterly* (1955–56), 337–352.

[2] R. Mort and T. M. Pierce, *A Time Scale for Measuring the Adaptability of School Systems* (New York: Metropolitan School Study Council, 1947).

[3] Batton, Barton, Durstine and Osborn, *Colortown.*

[4] North Central Rural Sociology Committee, *The Diffusion Process* (Ames: Agricultural Extension Service, Iowa State College, Special Report No. 18, 1957).

Reprinted by permission from the Foundation for Research on Human Behavior, The Adoption of New Products *(1959), pp. 1–8.*

relatively small group to adopt a new product will, by establishing the time scale for that product, make possible fairly accurate prediction of the rate of adoption by the rest of the applicable universe.

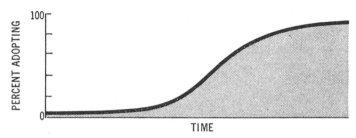

Figure 26.1.

THE KIND OF CHANGE

The time it takes from introduction to wide-spread acceptance depends, in part at least, on the kind of change involved. The adoption of a new product can be viewed as a special case of attitude change. Almost by definition, such a change encounters resistance. The new product or method usually alters or replaces something which is already part of the individual's pattern of thought. If the change under consideration is a really major one, it is quite likely that the attitudes and feelings associated with the old way are strongly held and will account for a great deal of resistance. On the other hand, if the change is trivial, the associated attitudes may be taken on easily. (They may also be cast off easily, of course.) Most new products or practices probably encounter resistance somewhere between these two extremes.

When new products are being adopted, there are different levels of *complexity* of change. The greater the complexity, the more resistance is aroused, and the longer the period required for adoption. Researchers have listed four levels of complexity in the changes usually confronting farmers who are adopting new products or practices.[5] Least complex is a simple change in materials or equipment. Such a change might be the decision to try another brand of fertilizer or to increase the amount already being used. A change in technique is slightly more complex. The farmer must learn to use the new method and this may involve more risk. An example might be applying fertilizer along planted rows, instead of broadcast over the field. The third level involves both a change in materials and a change in technique. A farmer who has never used fertilizer

[5] E. A. Wilkening, "The Role of Communicating Agents in Technological Change in Agriculture," *Social Forces* (1956), pp. 361–367.

faces such a change. He must adopt the new material, acquire the equipment to apply it, and learn how to use the equipment. The most complex change is a change of enterprise; for example, a change from cotton growing to dairying.

Obviously there are shadings in complexity among these four types of change, and other kinds of new products may involve a wider range of complexities than do farming practices. However, the level of complexity is an important factor in determining the time it takes for a new product to be adopted. Fifteen years elapsed between the introduction of hybrid seed corn and its adoption by almost 98 per cent of the farmers.[6] Other changes take longer. The adoption of new educational practices by school systems took 50 years.[7] Some changes take place quickly.

It is not always easy to tell how complex a change is involved in a new product. Hybrid corn is one example. Initially, this seemed like a simple change in materials. Actually, it was a far more complex change. Farmers feared the total reliance on commercial sources for seed corn, something they had previously produced for themselves. Furthermore, many farmers took pride in their ability to select good seed corn from their own crop, and they were accorded status for this skill. The new hybrid corn not only made the farmer feel more dependent, it also did away with an important source of prestige. A large majority of farmers had probably adopted hybrid corn within five years of the initial distribution, but it took fifteen years before almost all farmers were using it. Now, when a new hybrid variety of anything is introduced, it is adopted much more quickly. Examples are hybrid chickens and hybrid hogs.

The complexity of the change is also one important factor in determining the time required for adoption. There are others. For instance, *cost* is important. The more costly the item, the longer it takes before it is widely adopted. *Rate of return* and *visibility* of return are also important. A change which has rapid and obvious results is adopted more quickly than a change with slower, less visible results. In the long run, of course, the change which produces slower results may return more, but it still is not adopted as quickly. A new fertilizer is likely to be adopted more quickly, for example, than soil conservation practices.

THE INDIVIDUAL ADOPTION PROCESS

The decision to adopt a new product is not simply a "yes" or "no" decision, nor is it something that happens all at once. When an individual

[6] B. Ryan and N. C. Gross, "The Diffusion of Hybrid Seed Corn in Two Iowa Communities," *Rural Sociology* (1943), pp. 15–24; and B. Ryan and N. C. Gross, *Acceptance and Diffusion of Hybrid Seed Corn in Two Iowa Communities* (Ames: Iowa Agricultural Experiment Station, Research Bulletin 372, 1950).

[7] P. R. Mort and T. M. Pierce, *op. cit.*

is confronted with the possibility of change, he goes through several mental stages before he finally makes up his mind to adopt or not to adopt. Five stages in the decision-making process may be distinguished. Farmers readily recognized these stages when questioned regarding their decisions to make changes and adopt new products.

Awareness comes first. At this point, the farmer learns about the new product. He knows it exists, but he has only general information about it. The *interest or information* stage follows. If interested, the farmer begins to collect more specific information about the new product. If his interest continues to grow, he wants to know the potentialities of the new product for him; whether or not it will increase his income or contribute to other ends considered by him to be important. The next step is the *mental application or evaluation* stage. The farmer goes through the change mentally and asks himself, "How would I do it? Can I do it? If I do it, will I be better off?" The final stage before adoption is the *trial* stage. At this point the farmer tries the product out on a small scale if this is possible. Many farmers purchased a small can of weed spray and used it on their gardens before they used it on their crops on a large scale. A great many farmers planted six acres of hybrid seed corn the first year, the acreage one bushel of the new seed would sow. Some products cannot be tried out on a small scale, and it seems quite reasonable to expect such products to require a longer adoption time. However, people seem to be quite ingenious at finding ways to try new ideas. Some housewives prepared small amounts of food for freezing, and either rented locker space or used a neighbor's freezer before they gave up traditional canning methods and bought the necessary equipment for themselves. Marketing people have been aware of the value of free trials for many years. The trial stage appears to play a crucial role in the decision-making process. However, the other stages are important too, and probably give meaning to this final step before adoption. They should not be ignored.

The last stage is the *adoption* stage. At this point the farmer decides to adopt the new product and begins using it on a full scale. Presumably he is a "satisfied customer," at least until some other product comes along to replace it and the adoption process starts again.

ADOPTER CATEGORIES

Obviously, not all people adopt a new product at the same time. The adoption curve illustrates this point and suggests that some people arrive at a decision more quickly than others. Some people adopt very quickly. Others wait a long time before they take up the new product, and still others never adopt. There has been a great deal of interest in these individual differences and a great deal of speculation about "innovators," those who are first in a community to adopt a new product. To explore these individual differences, the Iowa State researchers took the data from a number of independent studies of new product adoption by farmers. They divided people into groups according to time of adoption,[8] and then studied each group. Significant differences appeared among them. These were the groups they distinguished and studied:

People Adopting			Cumulative Total Adopting
First	2.5%	Innovators	2.5%
Next	13.5%	Early adopters	16.0%
Next	34.0%	Early majority	50.0%
Next	34.0%	Late majority	84.0%
Last	16.0%	Laggards	100.0%

"Innovators" are arbitrarily defined here as the first 2.5 per cent to adopt the new product. Based on the data compiled, these generalizations appear for farm innovators.[9]

They have larger than average farms, are well educated and usually come from well established families. They usually have a relatively high net worth and—probably more important—a large amount of risk capital. They can afford and do take calculated risks on new products. They are respected for being successful, but ordinarily do not enjoy the highest prestige in the community. Because innovators adopt new ideas so much sooner than the average farmer, they are sometimes ridiculed by their conservative neighbors. This neighborhood group pressure is largely ignored by the innovators, however. The innovators are watched by their neighbors, but they are not followed immediately in new practices.

The activities of innovators often transcend local community boundaries. Rural innovators frequently belong to formal organizations at the county, regional, state, or national level. In addition, they are likely to have many informal contacts outside the community; they may visit with others many miles away who are also trying a new technique or product, or who are technical experts.

[8] For convenience in making comparative studies, researchers used standard deviations of a normal distribution to establish the percentage breaks between categories. People who fall within one standard deviation above the mean are considered in the early majority; people who are between one and two standard deviations above the mean are early adopters. Similarly, people within one standard deviation below the mean are late majority, etc.

[9] North Central Rural Sociology Committee, *How Farm People Accept New Ideas* (Ames: Iowa Agricultural Extension Service, Iowa State College, Special Report No. 15, 1955); and E. M. Rogers, "Categorizing the Adopters of Agricultural Practices," *Rural Sociology* (1943), pp. 15–24.

The "early adopters" are defined as the next 13.5 per cent of the people who adopt the new product. According to the researchers, early adopter farmers have the following characteristics.

They are younger than the average farmer, but not necessarily younger than the innovators. They also have a higher than average education, and participate more in the formal activities of the community through such organizations as churches, the PTA, and farm organizations. They participate more than the average in agricultural cooperatives and in government agency programs in the community (such as Extension Service or Soil Conservation). In fact, there is some evidence that this group furnishes a disproportionate amount of the formal leadership (elected officers) in the community. The early adopters are also respected as good sources of new farm information by their neighbors.

The third category of adopters is the "early majority," the 34 per cent of people who bring the total adoption to 50 per cent. The number of adoptions increases rapidly after this group begins to adopt.

The early majority are slightly above average in age, education, and farming experience. They have medium high social and economic status. They are less active in formal groups than innovators or early adopters, but more active than those who adopt later. In many cases they are not formal leaders in the community organizations, but they are active members in these organizations. They also attend Extension meetings and farm demonstrations.

The people in this category are most likely to be informal rather than elected leaders. They have a following insofar as people respect their opinions, their "high morality and sound judgment." They are "just like their following, only more so." They must be sure an idea will work before they adopt it. If the informal leader fails two or three times, his following looks elsewhere for information and guidance. Because the informal leader has more limited resources than the early adopters and innovators, he cannot afford to make poor decisions; the social and economic costs are too high.

These people tend to associate mainly in their own community. When people in the community are asked to name neighbors and friends with whom they talk over ideas, these early majority are named disproportionally frequently. On their part, they value highly the opinions their neighbors and friends hold about them, for this is their main source of status and prestige. The early majority may look to the early adopters for their new farm information.

The "late majority" are the fourth category. These are the 34 per cent of farmers who have adopted the new product after the average farmer is already using it.

Those in this group have less education and are older than the average farmer. While they participate less actively in formal groups, they probably form the bulk of the membership in these formal organizations. Individually they belong to fewer organizations, are less active in organizational work, and take fewer leadership roles than the earlier adopters. They do not participate in as many activities outside the community as do people who adopt earlier.

The last category, the final 16 per cent of those who adopt a new idea, are the "laggards." This group may include the "non-adopters" as well if the new product is not used by everyone.

They have the least education and are the oldest. They participate least in formal organizations, cooperatives, and government agency programs. They have the smallest farms and the least capital. Many are suspicious of county Extension agents and agricultural salesmen.

These are some of the important differences among the adopter categories. They may provide useful guidelines for further exploration. For example, each of these categories plays an important role for the others in the adoption process. Innovators are the pioneers, and early adopters wait to see the innovators' results before trying the new product themselves. The early adopters, in turn, often influence the early majority. In addition, each of these categories seems to rely on different sources of information and influence, other than the sources already described.

RETROSPECTIVE COMMENT

In many ways this classic article can be viewed as providing an impetus for much of the research on innovations—including diffusion research and adoption process research—that we currently think of as being marketing oriented. In this pioneering work Bourne not only initiated a research terminology unfamiliar to most marketers, but also introduced many concepts which even yet have not been fully investigated. If, though, Bourne were to rewrite this classic today, it would undoubtedly possess a markedly different flavor.

Perhaps most importantly, when this work was published there was no marketing tradition in adoption research. Because of this Bourne was able to refer to less than a dozen relevant publications, the majority of which relied heavily upon agriculturally-based research. With perhaps one or two exceptions, no marketing research had been conducted on the adoption process. Since then, especially beginning in the mid 1960's, there has been a plethora of marketing-oriented research studies conducted on the adoption process. In the past decade there have been well over one hundred research studies reported in the marketing literature alone. Hence, today Bourne would be able to draw many of his conclusions directly from the marketing literature, and would not have to make "inferential leaps" from other research disciplines.

At the same time, though, so many other disciplines have become involved in adoption process research that Bourne would be able to draw up a wide variety of research perspectives in synthesizing information on the adoption process. For example, E. M. Rogers, a well-known adoption process researcher, recently identified nearly two dozen distinct disciplines in which more than two thousand research studies have been conducted on the adoption process.

Finally, were Bourne writing this work now, he would probably make two related modifications. He would simultaneously develop a systematic framework for discussing all aspects of the adoption process research literature, and he would relate findings from this research to the broader areas of consumer behavior research and marketing management. Given recent advances in adoption research the former would perhaps occur naturally as a matter of course. However, it is in the latter area, especially, that Bourne would be expected to concentrate because of his long-standing interest in *applied* consumer behavior research. Moreover, he would probably conclude this rewriting by predicting future trends in adoption process research which could be expected in the next decade.—*Dr. Robert A. Peterson*, Associate Professor of Marketing, University of Texas at Austin

27. Class and Conservatism in the Adoption of Innovations

Saxon Graham

Several writers have posited a relationship between social class affiliation and conservatism or liberalism in accepting change.[1] Such statements have usually described the upper classes as upholders of the *status quo* and the lower strata as the innovators. It is the purpose of this paper to report on research undertaken to evaluate this conception and in general to examine the relation between stratification and change.[2] Conclusions that can be drawn from earlier findings in the fields of change and stratification indicate that while there could be an association between conservatism and stratum affiliation, such an association demands much more investigation than it has received in the past.

To take the factor of conservatism by itself, both sociologists and anthropologists have noted the importance of the culture base and the fact that the innovation must be compatible with it in order to be acceptable. Each innovation has a unique combination of characteristics; to be useful, each requires that certain ideas, behavior, and material apparatus should be a part of the equipment of potential accepters.[3] And as each innovation is unique, each requires that a different combination of cultural characteristics should be present in the group before adoption can take place. A group is conservative or liberal, therefore, in terms of how closely its culture can meet the test of compatibility with each of the

[1] W. F. Ogburn (14), Newell L. Sims (15), Kimball Young (20), and H. G. Barnett (1, pp. 404–7). Each of the above authors characterizes the upper classes as conservative, usually in relation to economic or political change. W. G. Sumner (17) sees the upper classes as innovators and the middle strata as conservative. R. S. and H. M. Lynd (11) indicate that in leisure pursuits the upper classes are usually the innovators. An excellent comprehensive treatment of adoption is found in Barnett, op. cit., Part IV.

[2] Discussion with Professors Maurice R. Davie and A. B. Hollingshead, and with the late Professor Ralph Linton, aided materially in the formulation and execution of this project; grateful thanks are here tendered.

[3] Cf. Hornell Hart (6), B. Malinowski (12), Ralph Linton (10), Bernard J. Stern (16), Joseph H. Greenberg (5, pp. 86–90), A. G. Keller (9), W. F. Ogburn (13).

Reprinted by permission from Human Relations, *Vol. 9 (1956), pp. 91–100.*

This research was carried out as the writer's Ph.D. dissertation study, "Selection and Social Stratification: Factors in the Acceptance and Rejection of Five Innovations by Social Strata in New Haven, Connecticut" (3).

innovations presented to it. Inasmuch as innovational characteristics differ, it might be hypothesized that no single group is wholly liberal or conservative in reacting to all innovations. This should apply to social class groupings as well as to any others.

This is particularly likely because social strata are distinguishable in large part by their special, differing configurations of cultural characteristics.[4] Thus, no single class or classes will be conservative or liberal in reacting to all innovations. Depending upon innovational characteristics in various instances, the upper classes would accept at one time and reject at another. The same could be said for the middle and lower classes. As each class, because of its peculiar cultural pattern, would be compatible with a given innovation in differing degree, we could expect the classes to vary in the degree to which they would accept. Or, if the classes were to accept in equal degree, they would do so because of their common sharing of some aspects of the culture of their society.

RESEARCH PROCEDURES

To examine the validity of the foregoing statements, it was necessary to determine the reaction of social classes to a group of innovations. After examining several score possibilities, five innovations appeared to meet the criteria demanded by the study. It was necessary that they should be of varied types, that they should be such that their acceptance could be readily discovered, and that they should have been sufficiently recently introduced for large numbers of people to be still in the process of adopting them. It was also required that they should be available for acceptance by all parts of the population, and that the individual should have ultimate control over their acceptance or rejection. This necessarily eliminated such innovations as a new printing device or the atom bomb. The innovations that most closely met the criteria and that were employed in this research were television, canasta, super markets, and two forms of health insurance.

In order to examine the reaction of social classes to these innovations, a sample of 150 families in New Haven, Connecticut, was developed. These were distributed in equal numbers into each of six strata, class membership being determined by occupation according to the Edwards scheme adapted to urban areas. The basic unit of investigation was the family, and, because of the suspected importance of age as a factor in conservatism,[5] families in the sample were limited to those whose male heads were between thirty and forty.

4 See, for example, John Useem, Pierre Tangent, and Ruth Useem (18), W. Lloyd Warner and Paul S. Lunt (19), and A. B. Hollingshead (8).

5 Cf. for example, J. O. Hertzler (7) and H. G. Barnett, op. cit., pp. 385-7.

In generating the sample, approximately 1,000 telephone interviews were conducted to elicit the information required on marital status, age, and occupation. From the resultant group of families meeting the criteria of the study, twenty-five were chosen for distribution into each of the four upper classes. To avoid the bias inherent in obtaining interviewees through telephoning, twenty-five cases representing each of the two lower strata were selected from the inactive files of the Connecticut State Employment Service. Intensive interviews were then conducted.

ANALYSIS

The hypothesis with which this study is concerned is that *social classes will accept innovations to the extent that the innovational features and the cultural characteristics of the classes are compatible. Because they vary in many aspects of their culture, different classes will possibly adopt a given innovation in varying degrees. But because they share some aspects of the common culture, they may accept in no significantly different degree. Finally, because each innovation requires that those who would use it should possess different physical, mental, and behavioral equipment, no class could be said to be conservative or liberal in reacting to all.*

In the analysis of this hypothesis several steps were necessary. First, the innovation had to be analysed to reveal the material equipment, mental sets, and behavioral patterns that a group must possess in order to use it. Second, the sample was examined without regard to class affiliation to determine whether accepters possess any of the above characteristics in significantly greater degree than rejecters. Those traits shown to be associated with acceptance were assumed to be crucial in determining the compatibility of innovation and group. Next, classes were compared to reveal whether they varied in their possession of the crucial culture elements. And finally the degree of acceptance of each innovation by each class was ascertained to show, first, whether classes vary in their acceptance of a single innovation, and second, whether any class was conservative in its reaction to all innovations.

Families who accepted television were operationally defined as those who possessed a receiving set, accepters of canasta as those who had played the game more than once, accepters of super markets as those who used them for over half of their food-shopping, and accepters of Blue Cross and Medical Service as policy holders in these plans.

Very briefly, the analysis upheld the hypothesis. As Table 1 shows, the classes did vary in their acceptance of three of the five innovations investigated in this study. But none of the strata proved to be consistently conservative or liberal.

Table 27.1. PERCENTAGE OF FAMILIES ACCEPTING AND REJECTING INNOVATIONS, BY
SOCIAL CLASS

Innovation	I	II	III	IV	V	VI	χ^2 Probability Level
	(upper)		(middle)		(lower)		
Television	%	%	%	%	%	%	
Accepters	24	44	48	52	84	72	
							$P<0.001$
Rejecters	76	56	52	48	16	28	
	100	100	100	100	100	100	
Canasta							
Accepters	72	72	44	20	32	12	
							$P<0.001$
Rejecters	28	28	56	80	68	88	
	100	100	100	100	100	100	
Super Markets							
Accepters	52	80	56	80	52	48	
							$P\approx0.04$
Rejecters	48	20	44	20	48	52	
	100	100	100	100	100	100	
Blue Cross							
Accepters	88	96	100	88	92	76	
							$P\approx0.25$
Rejecters	12	4	0	12	8	24	
	100	100	100	100	100	100	
Medical Service							
Accepters	20	48	40	24	36	20	
							$P\approx0.15$
Rejecters	80	52	60	76	64	80	
	100	100	100	100	100	100	

[1] For each class, $N = 25$.

Thus:

1. The upper classes were conservative in accepting television.
2. The lower classes were conservative in adopting canasta.
3. Both upper and lower strata reacted conservatively to super markets, with the greatest number of accepters found in the groups between the extreme ends of the class scale.
4. No class was conservative to a statistically significant degree in responding to the two innovations in health insurance.

It is clear, then, that the relation between stratification and conservatism is much more complex than heretofore supposed. The relationships discovered may be explained in part at least by the factor of innovational and cultural compatibility, and the variance in this from class to class. In the case of television, for example, compatibility was found to differ among the strata in a manner similar to variations in the pattern of acceptance. To analyse compatibility, television was examined in terms of the cultural equipment possibly required for its use. It was hypothesized that this would include the possession of an "average" education, a minimum income, and a *penchant* for passive recreation of the spectator sort. Accepters of television in the sample were then compared with rejecters, and it was found that the culture patterns of families who had adopted the innovation did include such characteristics. Rejecters, on the other hand, diverged.[6]

Thus, accepters were distinguished from rejecters by the large proportion having grammar and high-school education as opposed to college training ($P < 0.001$).[7] Accepters usually had moderate or low incomes and a feeling that television was a necessity, while rejecters ($P \approx 0.02$) were more apt to have higher incomes and the attitude that, as one expressed it, "television is an extravagance."

But it was the area of culture more directly related to television—recreational behavior—that was most crucial in acceptance. Rejecters differed greatly from accepters in that they preferred active, creative recreational activities, such as *participation* in sports, visiting, get-togethers, and serious reading. In the matter of reading habits specifically, rejecters were the readers of serious fiction and non-fiction, while accepters confined their efforts to fiction, a cursory inspection of the newspaper, or to no reading at all ($P < 0.001$). Again, accepters were more often active in a number of voluntary organizations than were rejecters ($P < 0.001$).

In the two activities most closely akin to television viewing—attendance at motion pictures and listening to radio programs—there were further significant differences. The families who accepted television were most often those who previouly had been avid devotees of radio and screen ($P \approx 0.03$, and $P < 0.001$, respectively). Thus the variables pertaining to recreation, voluntary association membership, income, and education appeared to be the ones most crucial in the process of acceptance. A number of others were examined, but were not found to be significantly related.

Once crucial factors in acceptance had been discovered, it remained to determine whether the classes varied in their possession of them. Statistical analysis revealed that they did so, and in a way similar to their acceptance pattern. Thus, moving-picture attendance increased in inci-

[6] A more complete report of this particular phase of the investigation appears in (4).

[7] Probability levels distinguishing accpters from rejecters throughout this paper are arrived at through the chi-square test.

dence as class status decreased. The same was true of sports, passive reading, other forms of passive recreation, and the appropriate educational and income characteristics.[8] As Table 1 reveals, television acceptance followed a similar pattern. These findings regarding compatibility offer a possible partial explanation for the conservatism of the upper classes and for the liberalism of the lower classes in accepting television.

The factor of compatibility also helped to explain the reaction of the classes to the canasta card-game. Crucial characteristics distinguishing accepters of the game from rejecters included their greater interest in active recreation, their being equipped with more numerous and varied games in their homes, their greater participation in card-playing, their ownership of more decks of cards, their more frequent gathering together with friends for social purposes, and their past history of accepting other innovations in card-games, such as gin rummy and, earlier, bridge. In addition, accepters were much more likely to have had some college training and to participate in a number of voluntary organizations.[9] Analysis of the classes to determine their possession of these crucial characteristics revealed that, in all but one case—the frequency with which subjects played cards—the strata varied significantly.[10] Thus, for example, upper-class spouses were the ones who were interested in active recreation, who had the best equipment for playing games, and who had previously accepted innovations in games. Table 1 shows that they were also the couples who accepted canasta to the greatest degree.

Another factor that may help to explain lower-class conservatism towards canasta is the relative lack of effective contact with the game among lower-class individuals. Canasta, unlike television, cannot be adopted simply by purchasing an apparatus. One must learn to play it, and in almost all cases in this sample this was accomplished through being taught by another person. The contact of accepters was further increased by the fact that their friends were often acquainted with the game and frequently urged them to play (on each factor, $P<0.001$). It was found that lower-class individuals had less contact with persons who could instruct them in the game than was true in the upper classes ($P<0.001$). Similarly, lower-class couples were much less frequently urged to play the game by their acquaintances ($P<0.001$).

This finding conforms with the rather scanty evidence in popular literature suggesting that the game was introduced by upper-class individuals who, having learned it in fashionable clubs in Buenos Aires,

[8] The probability level distinguishing the classes in the matter of motion-picture attendance was .001. In the case of all other variables the level was <0.001.

[9] The probability level distinguishing accepters from rejecters in the matter of getting together with friends for social purposes was 0.06. In all other cases it was <0.001.

[10] The probability level distinguishing classes in each case with the one exception noted was <0.001.

taught it to their upper-class friends in the United States. These two variables, the social distance separating the upper and lower classes and the necessity of teaching the game to achieve its diffusion also help to explain why the lower classes were slow to accept.

In the case of super markets, indications were that the accepting classes were those which had most contact with them, either through residing near to them, through prior use of chain stores (the organizations most prominent in the introduction of super markets), or through friends who had used them. But statistical tests on these and other factors were inconclusive, and the above statements indicate suggestions only. The finding of greatest interest regarding super markets is that accepters were not concentrated in the upper or lower classes, as was the case with canasta and television respectively, but were found mainly in Classes II and IV.

Table 1 reveals that in its reaction to medical insurance plans no class proved to be significantly more conservative than another. Two innovations were studied, Blue Cross and Medical Service.[11] The first was well on its way to complete acceptance; the second, having been instituted thirteen years later, in 1949, was still in the early stages of adoption. Blue Cross offers the traditional coverage of such plans, paying within certain limits the hospital expenses incurred by subscribers. Medical Service is operated in the same way to reimburse surgeons' fees to members. Subscriptions in Medical Service are available only to members of Blue Cross.

It was found that Blue Cross was accepted by 90 per cent of the members of the sample, while not quite one-third of the families adopted Medical Service. Thus, even though they were similar innovations, the difference in the length of time they were in contact with potential accepters contributed to the differential in the degree of their acceptance. Other factors promoting this differential were the added costs of Medical Service, and the feeling on the part of some couples that surgical coverage was not as important as, for example, provision for expenses of dental work or physicians' house calls.

Because of the almost unanimous acceptance of Blue Cross in this sample, and because membership in Medical Service depends on prior holding of a Blue Cross policy, no effective statistical comparison of accepters and rejecters was possible. Nevertheless, there is some evidence as to reasons for the adoption of the two innovations and for the slight variations detected in class reactions to them.

Table 1 shows that in the case of both innovations, Classes I, IV, and VI accept to a slightly smaller degree than others. This is accounted for in part by the fact that frequently husbands in these families are inde-

[11] Known officially as Connecticut Hospital Service and Connecticut Medical Service respectively.

pendent workers. They are thus unaffiliated with any group that is approached by the insurance organizations for membership recruitment. The offering of subscriptions to individuals not associated with a group has been so recent as to have had little effect on members of this sample.

Class I families also rejected occasionally because they felt no particular financial pressure to have the protection offered by the insurance plans. The Class VI families who rejected often did so on the opposite grounds. They were not as impressed with the need for insurance relative to other necessities. Especially was this true in their response to Medical Service. As a Class VI laborer said: "It's just too expensive for what you get. There are more things around, and they say everything just costs a few cents a day. It's a few cents here and a few there, and I just can't afford it. If you had six kids and made forty dollars a week, could you?"

The almost complete acceptance of Blue Cross is largely accounted for by the nearly universal desire to avoid the devastating costs of today's treatment for illness. The majority of upper-class families, just like those in lower strata, accepted with this factor in mind. A Class I housewife said: "The Blue Cross and Medical Service are a safe-guard for when you're least able to take it financially. You never can plan sickness, but at least you can protect yourself slightly with something like this." And a Class V machine operator noted: "It's an ace in the hole, you know. I got so many kids—I can't save money, anyway. This way, you got the Blue Cross—you got something behind."

Table 2 shows the three most mentioned reasons for accepting Blue Cross are all economic. A similar pattern was discovered in reasons given for subscribing to Medical Service.

Other motives cited revealed more of a class bias. Thus, some upper-class families were in favor of Blue Cross because they felt it would give workers more security. Others saw it as a means of stabilizing the financial position of hospitals, or as a bulwark against socialized medicine. Lower-class interviewees, on the other hand, were attracted by the instalment-payment feature of the health plans. But the reason that dominated the thinking of accepters in all classes was the desire to alleviate the great economic burden of modern therapy.

Table 27.2. REASONS GIVEN BY SUBJECTS FOR ACCEPTANCE OF BLUE CROSS, BY CLASS, IN PERCENTAGES

| | Class | | | | | |
Reasons	I	II	III	IV	V	VI
Impending hospitalization	40	12	12	16	8	8
Security	40	68	76	76	68	52
Low cost	44	40	32	20	40	28

A factor thus emerges from the investigation of health insurance that did not appear significant in the analyses of super markets and the recreational innovations. In the earlier cases it was found that differences in the cultural equipment of classes were crucial in explaining variations in acceptance. It must be emphasized, however, that the strata, while varying in some respects, nevertheless partake of the common culture of New Haven and, in some instances, in fairly equal degrees. The universal desire to avoid the tremendous costs of illness is a case in point. The fact that this desire was present in all classes may help to explain the lack of difference in their reactions to health insurance.

CONCLUSION

The association between conservatism in accepting innovations and social class affiliation has been examined as it existed in the adoption of five new items of different types. The research revealed that the amount of contact between innovation and potential accepters was crucial in determining degree of acceptance. Of equal importance was the extent to which innovational characteristics and the culture of the receiving group were compatible. It was found that as each innovation is unique, each is compatible in different degrees with the culture of a given group. Therefore, each is accepted in differing degrees by that group. Contrary to the statements of some writers, e.g. Joseph H. Greenberg, then, at the present state of our knowledge the degree of acceptance of any single innovation could not be an index to the acceptance of others. Further, it was discovered that no single class in the sample displayed conservatism in reacting to all five innovations. The upper classes were conservative in one case, the lower in another, and both in a third instance. And no one of the classes displayed more conservatism than another in reacting to the innovations in health insurance. In the light of these findings, it may be concluded that the relation between class and conservatism is much more complex than traditionally supposed.

RETROSPECTIVE COMMENT

Compatibility between various aspects of the culture of potential receivers of an innovation and the ideas and behavior required for the use of the innovation continues to be of interest because as such compatibility increases, the likelihood of acceptance of the innovation increases. If the compatibility is characteristic of the culture of a given social class, we can assume that the class will accept the innovation; class is interesting only to the extent that it is equatable with compatibility.

Another facet of compatibility, on a more social-psychological level, is the notion of cogency. Focusing on the individual, if he or she believes the innovation will solve a recognized problem and if further, he or she believes it will solve his or her own particular version of that problem, the innovation will more likely be accepted.

The time has long since past when we should go beyond *ex post facto* studies to experimental work, utilizing various methods of fostering contact with the innovation and seeking to understand bases on which it can be made compatible. More understanding needs to be obtained through experiments with various types of influentials, ranging from county agricultural agents, to health guides, to the development of lay influentials, to the use of institutionalization of innovations. In experimentation lies the interest of the future.—*Saxon Graham*

REFERENCES

BARNETT, H. G. *Innovation.* New York: McGraw-Hill, 1953.

EDWARDS, ALBA M. *Population: Comparative Occupation Statistics for the United States, 1870–1940.* Washington: U.S. Government Printing Office, 1943.

GRAHAM, SAXON. "Selection and Social Stratification: Factors in the Acceptance and Rejection of Five Innovations by Social Strata in New Haven, Connecticut." New Haven: Yale University Library, 1951.

GRAHAM, SAXON. "Cultural Compatibility in the Adoption of Television." *Soc. Forces*, 1954, Vol. 33, pp. 166–70.

GREENBERG, JOSEPH H. "Social Variables in Acceptance and Rejection of Artificial Insemination." *Amer. sociol. Rev.*, 1951, Vol. 6, pp. 86–90, 91.

HART, HORNELL. *Technique of Social Progress.* New York: Henry Holt, 1931, p. 607.

HERTZLER, J. O. *Social Institutions.* Lincoln: University of Nebraska Press, 1946, pp. 243–4.

HOLLINGSHEAD, A. B. *Elmtown's Youth.* New York: John Wiley and Sons, 1949.

KELLER, A. G. *Societal Evolution.* New Haven: Yale University Press, 1931.

LINTON, RALPH. *The Study of Man.* New York: D. Appleton-Century Co., 1936, Chs. 18, 19.

LYND, R. S., and Lynd, H. M. *Middletown.* New York: Harcourt Brace, 1929, p. 218.

MALINOWSKI, B. *Dynamics of Culture Change.* New Haven: Yale University Press, 1945, pp. 52, 56.

OGBURN, W. F. *Social Change.* New York: The Viking Press, 1928.

OGBURN, W. F. "Social Change." In Seligman, E. P. A., and Johnson, Alvin (Eds.), *Encyclopaedia of the Social Sciences*, Vol. 3. New York: The Macmillan Company, 1937.

SIMS, NEWELL L. *The Problem of Social Change*. New York: Thomas Y. Crowell, 1939, p. 45.

STERN, BERNARD J. "Resistance to the Adoption of Technical Innovations." Sub-committee on Technology of the National Resources Committee: *Technological Trends and National Policy*. Washington: U.S. Government Printing Office, 1937, pp. 36–67.

SUMNER, W. G. *Folkways*. Boston: Ginn and Company, 1906, pp. 45–6.

USEEM, JOHN, Tangent, Pierre, and Useem, Ruth. "Stratification in a Prairie Town." *Amer. sociol. Rev.*, 1942, Vol. 7, pp. 341–2.

WARNER, W. LLOYD, and Lunt, Paul S. *The Social Life of a Modern Community*. New Haven: Yale University Press, 1941.

YOUNG, KIMBALL. *Sociology*. New York: The American Book Company, 1942, p. 116.

PART IV.   QUESTIONS FOR DISCUSSION

1. What is the "two-step" flow of communication?

2. Suggest some positive actions to accelerate the rate of adoption.

3. What types of innovations are most likely to be first accepted by lower-class shoppers? By upper-class shoppers?

Part V.
Putting the Pieces Together

The selections in *Classics in Consumer Behavior* represent the wealth of research findings regarding decision making. Some focus on selective perception; others evaluate the influence of personality; still others treat the importance of culture. In order to implement the application of research findings on specific aspects of the consumer decision process, models, or theories, of consumer behavior are needed.

Three comprehensive, integrative models have been developed since 1966: the Nicosia model,[1] the model of Engel, Kollat, and Blackwell,[2] and the Howard-Sheth model.[3] A summary of the Howard-Sheth model is included in this final selection.

---

[1] F. M. Nicosia, *Consumer Decision Processes* (Englewood Cliffs, New Jersey: Prentice-Hall, Inc., 1966).

[2] J. F. Engel, D. T. Kollat, and R. D. Blackwell, *Consumer Behavior* (New York: Holt, Rinehart & Winston, Inc., 1973).

[3] J. A. Howard and J. N. Sheth, *The Theory of Buyer Behavior* (New York: John Wiley & Sons, Inc., 1969).

28. Theory of Buyer Behavior

John A. Howard and J. N. Sheth

In the last fifteen years, considerable research on consumer behavior both at the conceptual and empirical levels has accumulated. This can be gauged by reviews of the research.[1] As a consequence we believe that sufficient research exists in both the behavioral sciences and consumer behavior to attempt a comprehensive theory of buyer behavior. Furthermore, broadly speaking, there are two major reasons at the basic research level which seem to have created the need to take advantage of this opportunity. The first reason is that a great variety exists in today's effort to understand the consumer, and unfortunately there is no integration of this variety. The situation resembles the seven blind men touching different parts of the elephant and making inferences about the animal which differ, and occasionally contradict one another. A comprehensive theory of buyer behavior would hopefully not only provide a framework for integrating the existing variety but also would prepare the researcher to adopt appropriate research designs which would control sources of influence other than those he is immediately interested in. The difficulty of replicating a study and the possibility of getting contradictory findings will be minimized accordingly.

The second major basic research reason for a comprehensive theory is the potential application of research in buying behavior to human behavior in general. In asserting the need to validate psychological propositions in a real world context Sherif has repeatedly and eloquently argued for applied research.[2] Also, McGuire argues that social psychology is moving toward theory-oriented research in *natural settings* because a number of forces are encouraging the movement away from

---

[1] Theodore Levitt, *Innovation in Marketing: New Perspectives for Growth* (New York: McGraw-Hill Book Company, 1962).

[2] Jack B. McKitterick, "What is the Marketing Management Concept?" in Frank M. Bass (ed.) *The Frontiers of Marketing Thought and Science* (Chicago: American Marketing Association, 1957), pp. 71–82.

Reprinted by permission of the authors and publishers from Reed Moyer (ed.), Changing Marketing Systems, published by the American Marketing Association (1967), pp. 253–262.

laboratory research, and he cites the current work in buyer behavior as one of these forces.[3]

Again, one way that we can contribute to "pure" areas of behavioral science is by attempting a comprehensive theory which would help to identify and to iron out our own inconsistencies and contradictions. Such an attempt looks ambitious on the surface, but after several years of work and drawing upon earlier work,[4] we are confident that it can be achieved.

A BRIEF SUMMARY OF THE THEORY

Before we describe each component of the theory in detail, it will be helpful to discuss briefly the essentials of our view of the consumer choice process.

Much of buying behavior is more or less repetitive brand choice decisions. During his life cycle, the buyer establishes purchase cycles for various products which determine how often he will buy a given product. For some products, this cycle is very lengthy, as for example in buying durable appliances, and, therefore, he buys the product quite infrequently. For many other products, however, the purchase cycle is short and he buys the product frequently as is the case for many grocery and personal care items. Since there is usually the element of repeat buying, we must present a theory which incorporates the dynamics of purchase behavior over a period of time if we wish to capture the central elements of the empirical process.

In the face of repetitive brand choice decisions, the consumer simplifies his decision process by storing relevant information and routinizing his decision process. What is crucial, therefore, is to identify the elements of decision making, to observe the structural or substantive changes that occur in them over time due to the repetitive nature, and show how a combination of the decision elements affect search processes and the incorporation of information from the buyer's commercial and social environment.

The buyer, having been motivated to buy a product class, is faced with a brand choice decision. The elements of his decision are: (1) a set of motives, (2) several courses of action, and (3) decision mediators by which the motives are matched with the alternatives. Motives are specific to a product class, and they reflect the underlying needs of the buyer. The alternative courses of actions are the purchase of one of the various brands with their potential to satisfy the buyer's motives. There are two important notions involved in the definition of alternatives as brands.

[3] George Katona, *The Powerful Consumer* (New York: McGraw-Hill Book Company, 1960).

[4] John A. Howard, *Marketing Theory* (Boston: Allyn and Bacon, 1965), Chapter 1.

First, the brands which are alternatives of the buyer's choice decision at any given time are generally a small number, collectively called his "evoked set." The size of the evoked set is only two or three, a fraction of the brands he is aware of and a still smaller fraction of the total number of brands actually available in the market. Second, any two consumers may have quite different alternatives in their evoked sets.

The decision mediators are a set of rules that the buyer employs to match his motives and his means of satisfying those motives. They serve the function of ordering and structuring the buyer's motives and then ordering and structuring the various brands based on their potential to satisfy these ordered motives. The decision mediators develop by the process of learning about the buying situation. They are, therefore, influenced by information from the buyer's environment and even more importantly by the actual experience of purchasing and consuming the brand.

When the buyer is just beginning to purchase a product class such as when a purchase is precipitated by a change in his life cycle, he lacks experience. In order, therefore, to develop the decision mediators, he *actively seeks information* from his commercial and social environments. The information that he either actively seeks or accidentally receives, is subjected to perceptual processes which not only limits the intake of information (magnitude of information is affected) but modifies it to suit his own frame of reference (quality of information is affected). These modifications are significant since they distort the neat "marketing stimulus-consumer response" relation.

Along with active search for information, the buyer may, to some extent, generalize from past similar experiences. Such generalization can be due to physical similarity of the new product class to the old product class. For example, in the initial purchases of Scotch whisky, the buyer may generalize his experiences in buying of gin. Generalization can also occur even when the two product classes are physically dissimilar but have a common meaning such as deriving from a company-wide brand name. For example, the buyer could generalize his experiences in buying a refrigerator or range to his first purchase of a dishwasher of the same brand.

Whatever the source, the buyer develops sufficient decision mediators to enable him to choose a brand which seems to have the best potential for satisfying his motives. If the brand proves satisfactory, the potential of that brand to satisfy his motives is increased. The result is that the probability of buying that brand is likewise increased. With repeated satisfactory purchases of one or more brands, the buyer is likely to manifest a routinized decision process whereby the sequential steps in buying are well structured so that some event which triggers the process may actually complete the choice decision. Routinized purchasing implies that his decision mediators are well established, and that the buyer has strong brand preferences.

The phase of repetitive decision making, in which the buyer reduces the complexity of a buying situation with the help of information and experience is called the *psychology of simplification*. Decision-making can be divided into three stages and used to illustrate the psychology of simplification: Extensive Problem Solving, Limited Problem Solving and Routinized Response Behavior. The further he is along in simplifying his environment, the less is the tendency toward active search behavior. The environmental stimuli related to the purchase situation become more meaningful and less ambiguous. Furthermore, the buyer establishes more cognitive consistency among the brands as he moves toward routinization and the incoming information is then screened both with regard to its magnitude and quality. He becomes less attentive to stimuli which do not fit his cognitive structure and he distorts those stimuli which are forced upon him.

A surprising phenomenon, we believe, occurs in many instances of frequently purchased products such as in grocery and personal care items. The buyer, after attaining routinization of his decision process, may find himself in too simple a situation. He is likely to feel the monotony or boredom associated with such repetitive decision-making. It is also very likely that he is satisfied with even the most preferred brand. In both cases, he may feel that all existing alternatives including the preferred brand are unacceptable. He therefore, feels a need to *complicate* his buying situation by considering new brands, and this process can be called the *psychology of complication*. The new situation causes him to identify a new brand, and so he begins again to simplify in the manner described earlier. Thus with a frequently-purchased item buying is a continuing process with its ups and downs in terms of information seeking analogous to the familiar cyclical fluctuations in economic activity.

ELEMENTS OF THEORY

Any theory of human behavior needs some means for explaining individual differences. The marketing manager also is interested in differentiated masses of buyers. He wants to understand and separate individual differences so that he can classify or segment the total market based upon individual differences. By understanding the psychology of the individual buyer we may achieve this classification. Depending on the internal state of the buyer, a given stimulus may result in a given response. For example, one buyer who urgently needs a product may respond to the ad of a brand in that product class by buying it whereas another buyer who does not need the product may simply notice the ad and store the information or ignore the ad. A construct such as "level of motivation" will then explain the divergent reactions to the same stimulus. Alternatively, two buyers may both urgently need a product, but they buy two different brands. This can be explained by another construct: predisposition toward a brand.

Figure 1 represents the theory of buyer behavior. The central rectangular box isolates the various internal state variables and processes which combined together show the state of the buyer. The inputs to the rectangular box are the stimuli from the marketing and social environments. The outputs are a variety of responses that the buyer is likely to manifest based on the interaction between the stimuli and his internal state. Besides the inputs and outputs, there are a set of seven influences which affect the variables in the rectangular box.[5] These variables appear at the top of the diagram and are labelled "exogenous variables." Their function is to provide a means of adjusting for the interpersonal differences discussed above. The variables within the rectangular box serve the role of endogenous variables in the sense that changes in them are explained but they are something less than endogenous variables. They are not well defined and hence are not measurable. They are hypothetical constructs. Their values are inferred from relations among the output intervening variables. Several of the exogenous variables such as personality, social class and culture have traditionally been treated as part of the endogenous variables. We believe that they affect more specific variables, and by conceptualizing their effect as via the hypothetical constructs, we can better understand their role.

Thus it will be seen that the theory of buyer behavior has four major components: the stimulus variables, the response variables, the hypothetical constructs and the exogenous variables. We will elaborate on each of the components below both in terms of their substance and their interrelationships.

STIMULUS VARIABLES

At any point in time, the hypothetical constructs which reflect the buyer's internal state are affected by numerous stimuli from the environment. The environment is classified as Commercial or Social. The commercial environment is the marketing activities of various firms by which they attempt to communicate to the buyer. From the buyer's point of

[5] Lester Guest, "Consumer Analysis" *Annual Review of Psychology* Vol. 13 (1962), pp. 315–344; Frederick May, "Buying Behavior: Some Research Findings" *Journal of Business* (October 1965), pp. 379–396; Dik Warren Twedt, "Consumer Psychology" *Annual Review of Psychology* Vol. 16 (1965), pp. 265–294; Jagdish N. Sheth, "A Review of Buyer Behavior" *Management Science* Vol. 13 (August 1967), pp. B718–B756.

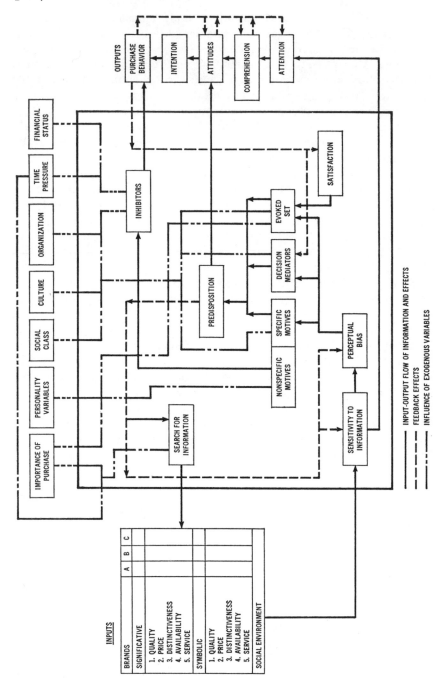

Figure 28.1. A THEORY OF BUYER BEHAVIOR.

view, these communications basically come either via the physical brands themselves or some linguistic or pictorial representations of the attributes of the brands. If the elements of the brands such as price, quality, service, distinctiveness or availability are communicated through the physical brands (significates) then the stimuli are defined and classified as significative stimuli. If, on the other hand, the attributes are communicated in linguistic or pictorial symbols such as in mass media, billboards, catalogs, salesmen, etc. then the stimuli from commercial sources are classified as symbolic stimuli. We view the marketing mix as the optimum allocation of funds between the two major channels of communication—significative or symbolic—to the buyer.

Each commercial input variable is hypothesized to be multivariate. Probably the five major dimensions of a brand—price, quality, distinctiveness, availability and service—summarize the various attributes. The same dimensions are present in both significative or symbolic communication which become the input stimuli for the buyer. However, certain dimensions may be more appropriately conveyed by significative rather than symbolic communication and vice versa. For example, price is easily communicated by both channels; shape may best be communicated by two-dimensional pictures rather than verbal communication. Finally, size may not be easily communicated by any symbolic representation: the physical product (significate) may be necessary.

The third stimulus input variable is social stimuli. It refers to the information that the buyer's social environment provides regarding a purchase decision. The most obvious is word of mouth communication.

The inputs to the buyer's mental state from the three major sources are then processed and stored by their interaction with a series of hypothetical constructs, and the buyer may react immediately or later.

HYPOTHETICAL CONSTRUCTS

The hypothetical constructs and their interrelationships are the result of an integration of Hull's learning theory,[6] Osgood's cognitive theory,[7] and Berlyne's theory of exploratory behavior[8] along with other ideas.

We may classify the constructs into two classes; those that have to do with perception, and those having to do with learning. Perceptual constructs serve the function of information processing while the learning constructs serve the function of concept formation. It is interesting that,

[6] Jagdish N. Seth, *op. cit.*, p. B742.

[7] Muzafer Sherif and Carolyn Sherif, "Interdisciplinary Coordination as a Validity Check: Retrospect and Prospects" in M. Sherif (ed.) *Problems of Interdisciplinary Relationships in the Social Sciences* (Aldine Publishing Company, to be published in 1968).

[8] William J. McGuire, "Some Impending Reorientations in Social Psychology" *Journal of Experimental Social Psychology* Vol. 3 (1967), pp. 124–139.

after years of experience in advertising, Reeves has a very similar classification:[9] his "penetration" is analogous to perceptual variables and his "unique selling propositions" in analogous to learning variables. We will at first describe the learning constructs since they are the major components of decision making; the perceptual constructs which serve the important role of obtaining and processing information are more complex and will be described later.

Learning Constructs. The learning constructs are labeled as: (1) Motives—Specific and Nonspecific, (2) Brand Potential of Evoked Set, (3) Decision Mediators, (4) Predisposition toward the brands, (5) Inhibitors, and (6) Satisfaction with the purchase of the brand.

1. Motive is the impetus to action. Motives or goals may be thought of as constituting a means-end chain and hence, as being general or specific depending upon their position in the chain. Motives can refer to the buyer's specific goals in purchasing a product class. The buyer is motivated by the expectation or anticipation due to past learning of outcome from the purchase of each of the brands in his evoked set.

The specific motives—lower level motives in the means-end chain—are very closely anchored to the attributes of a product class and in this way they become purchase criteria. Examples of specific motives for buying a dietary product such as Metrecal or Sego are low calories, nutrition, taste, and value.

Very often, several specific motives are nothing more than indicators of some underlying more general motive, that is, some motive that is higher in the means-end chain. In the above example, the specific motives of nutrition and low calories might be merely indicators of the common motive of good health.

Motives also serve the important function of raising the buyer's general motivational state or arousal and thereby tuning up the buyer, causing him to pay attention to environmental stimuli. Examples of nonspecific motives are probably anxiety, fear, many of the personality variables such as authoritarianism, exhibitionism, aggressiveness, etc., and social motives of power, status, prestige, etc. Although they are nonspecific, they are not innate, but rather learned, mostly due to acculturation. The nonspecific motives also possess a hierarchy within themselves. For example, anxiety is considered to be the source of another motive, that of the need of money.[10]

9 Patrick Suppes, *Information Processing and Choice Behavior* (Technical Paper No. 9: Institute for Mathematical Studies in the Social Sciences, Stanford University, January 31, 1966), p. 27.

10 John A. Howard, *Marketing Management* (Revised edition: R. D. Irwin, Inc., 1963); J. A. Howard, *Marketing: Executive and Buyer Behavior* (Columbia University Press, 1963).

2. Brand Potential of Evoked Set. A buyer who is familiar with a product class has an evoked set of alternatives to satisfy his motives. The elements of his *evoked set* are some of the brands that make up the product class. The concept is important because for this buyer the brands in his evoked set constitute competition for the seller.

A brand is, of course, a class concept like many other objects or things. The buyer attaches a *word* to his concept—a label—which is the brand name such as "Campbell's Tomato Soup". Whenever he sees a can of Campbell's Tomato Soup or hears the phrase, the image conveys to him certain satisfactions, procedures for preparation, etc. In short, it conveys certain meaning including its potential to satisfy his motives.

Various brands in the buyer's evoked set will generally satisfy the goal structure differently. One brand may possess potential to the extent that it is an ideal brand for the buyer. Another brand, on the other hand, may satisfy motives just enough to be part of his evoked set. By the process of learning the buyer obtains, and stores knowledge regarding each brand's potential and then rank orders them in terms of their want-satisfying potential. The evoked set, in short, is a set of alternatives with each alternative's payoff. Predisposition mentioned below enables the buyer to choose one among them.

3. Decision Mediator brings together motives and alternatives. The brand potential of each of the brands in his evoked set are the decision alternatives with their payoffs. Decision mediators are the buyer's mental rules for matching the alternatives with his motives, for rank-ordering them in terms of their want-satisfying capacity. As mental rules, they exhibit reasoning wherein the cognitive elements related to the alternatives and the motives are structured. The words that he uses to describe these attributes are also the words that he thinks with and that he finds are easy to remember. The criterial attributes are important to the manufacturer because if he knows them he can deliberately build into his brand and promotion, those characteristics which will differentiate his brand from competing brands.

The decision mediators thus represent enduring cognitive rules established by the process of learning, and their function is to obtain meaningful and congruent relations among brands so that the buyer can manifest goal-directed behavior. The aim of the theory of buyer behavior is not just the identification of motives and the respective brands but to show their structure as well. It is the decision mediators which provide this structure.

In view of the fact that decision mediators are learned, principles of learning become crucial in their development and change over time. There are two broad sources of learning: (1) actual experience, and (2) information. Actual experience can be either with the same buying situation in the past or with a *similar* buying situation. The latter is generally labelled as generalization as discussed earlier. Similarly, information as a source of learning can be from: (1) the buyer's commercial environment, or (2) his social environment. Later, we will elaborate on each of the sources of learning.

4. Predisposition is the summary effect of the previous three constructs. It refers to the buyer's preference toward brands in his evoked set. It is, in fact, an aggregate index which is reflected in attitude which, in turn, is measured by attitude scales. It might be visualized as the "place" where brands in Evoked Set are compared with Mediator's choice criteria to yield a judgment on the relative contribution of the brands to the buyer's motives. This judgment includes not only an estimate of the value of the brand to him but also an estimate of the confidence with which he holds that position. This uncertainty aspect of Predisposition can be called "brand ambiguity", in that, the more confident he holds it, the less ambiguous is the connotative meaning of the brand to the buyer and the more likely he is to buy it.[11]

5. Inhibitors are forces in the environment which create important disruptive influences in the actual purchase of a brand even when the buyer has reasoned out that that brand will best satisfy his motives. In other words, when the buyer is both predisposed to buy a brand, and has the motivation to buy some brand in the product class, he may not buy it because several environmental forces inhibit its purchase and prevent him from satisfying his preferences.

We postulate at least four types of inhibitors. They are: (1) high price of the brand, (2) lack of availability of the brand, (3) time pressure on the buyer, and (4) the buyer's financial status. The first two are part of the environmental stimuli, and therefore, they are part of the input system. The last two come from the two exogenous variables of the same name. It should be pointed out that social constraints emanating from other exogenous variables may also create temporary barriers to the purchase of a brand.

An essential feature of all inhibitors is that they are *not internalized* by the buyer because their occurrence is random and strictly situational. However, some of the inhibitors may persist systematically over time as they concern a given buyer. If they persist long enough, the buyer is likely to incorporate them as part of his decision mediators and thus to internalize them. The consequence is that they may affect even the structure of alternatives and motives.

[11] James G. March and Herbert A. Simon, *Organizations* (New York: John Wiley & Sons, 1958).

6. Satisfaction, the last of the learning constructs, refers to the degree of congruence between the actual consequences from purchase and consumption of a brand and what was expected from it by the buyer at the time of purchase. If the actual outcome is adjudged by the buyer as *at least* equal to the expected, the buyer will feel satisfied. If, on the other hand, the actual outcome is adjudged as less than what he expected, the buyer will feel dissatisfied and his attitude will be less favorable. Satisfaction or dissatisfaction with a brand can exist with respect to any one of the different attributes. If the brand proves more satisfactory than he expected, the buyer has a tendency to enhance the attractiveness of the brand. Satisfaction will, therefore, affect the reordering of the brands in the evoked set for the next buying decision.

Relations Among Learning Constructs.   Underlying Predisposition toward the brands and related variables, several important notions are present. The simplest way to describe them is to state that we may classify a decision process as either Extensive Problem Solving, Limited Problem Solving or Routinized Response Behavior depending on the strength of Predisposition toward the brands. In the early phases of buying, the buyer has not yet developed decision mediators well enough; specifically his product class concept is not well formed and predisposition is low. As he acquires information and gains experience in buying and consuming the brand, Decision Mediators become firm and Predisposition toward a brand is generally high.

In Extensive Problem Solving, Predisposition towards the brands is low. None of the brands is discriminated enough based on their criterial attributes for the buyer to show greater brand preference toward any one brand. At this stage of decision making, brand ambiguity is high with the result that the buyer actively seeks information from his environment. Due to greater search for information, there exists a greater *latency of response*—the time interval from the initiation of a decision to its completion. Similarly, deliberation or reasoning will be high since he lacks a well-defined product class concept which is the denotative aspect of mediator. He is also likely to consider many brands as part of Evoked Set, and stimuli coming from the commercial environment are less likely to trigger any immediate purchase reaction.

When Predisposition toward the brands is moderate, the buyer's decision process can be called Limited Problem Solving. There still exists brand ambiguity since the buyer is not able to discriminate and compare brands so that he may prefer one brand over others. He is likely to seek information but not to the extent that he seeks it in Extensive Problem Solving. More importantly, he seeks information more on a relative basis to compare and discriminate various brands rather than to compare them absolutely on each of the brands. His deliberation or thinking is much less since Decision Mediators are tentatively well defined. Evoked Set will consist of a small number of brands, each having about the same degree of preference.

In Routinized Response Behavior, the buyer will have a high level of Predisposition toward brands in his evoked set. Furthermore, he has now accumulated sufficient experience and information to have little brand ambiguity. He will in fact discriminate among brands enough to show a strong preference toward one or two brands in the evoked set. He is unlikely to actively seek any information from his environment since such information is not needed. Also, whatever information he passively or accidentally receives, he will subject it to selective perceptual processes so that only congruent information is allowed. Very often, the congruent information will act as "triggering cues" to motivate him to manifest purchase behavior. Much of impulse purchase, we believe, is really the outcome of a strong predisposition and such a facilitating commercial stimulus as store display. The buyer's evoked set will consist of a few brands toward which he is highly predisposed. However, he will have greater preference toward one or two brands in his evoked set and less towards others.

As mentioned earlier, Predisposition is an aggregate index of decision components. Thus, any changes in the components due to learning from experience or information imply some change in Predisposition. The greater the learning, the more the predisposition toward the brands in the evoked set. The exact nature of learning will be described later when we discuss the dynamics of buying behavior.

Perceptual Constructs.　Another set of constructs serve the function of information procurement and processing relevant to a purchase decision. As mentioned earlier, information can come from any one of the three stimulus inputs—significative commercial stimuli, symbolic commercial stimuli, and social stimuli. Once again we will here only describe the constructs; their utilization by the buyer will be explained when we discuss the dynamics of buying behavior. The perceptual constructs in Figure 1 are: (1) Sensitivity to information, (2) Perceptual Bias, and (3) Search for Information.

A perceptual phenomenon implies either ignoring a physical event which could be a stimulus, seeing it attentively or sometimes imagining what is not present in reality. All perceptual phenomena essentially create some change in quantity or quality of objective information.

1. Sensitivity to information refers to the opening and closing of sensory receptors which control the intake of information. The manifestation of this phenomenon is generally called perceptual vigilance

(paying attention) or perceptual defense (ignoring the information). Sensitivity to Information, therefore, primarily serves as a gate keeper to information entering into the buyer's mental state. It thus controls the quantity of information input.

Sensitivity to information, according to Berlyne,[12] is a function of the degree of ambiguity of the stimuli to which the buyer is exposed. If the stimulus is very familiar or too simple, the ambiguity is low and the buyer will not pay attention unless he is predisposed to such information from past learning. Furthermore, if ambiguity of the stimulus continues to be low, the buyer feels a sense of monotony and actually seeks other information, and this act can be said to *complicate* his environment. If the stimulus is very complex and ambiguous, the buyer finds it hard to comprehend and, therefore, he ignores it by resorting to perceptual defense. Only if the stimulus is in the moderate range of ambiguity is the buyer motivated to pay attention and to freely absorb the objective information.

In a single communication, the buyer may at first find the communication complex and ambiguous and so he will resort to perceptual defense and tend to ignore it. As some information enters, however, he finds that it is really at the medium level of ambiguity and so pays attention. On the other hand, it might be that the more he pays attention to it, the more he finds the communication too simple and, therefore ignores it as the process of communication progresses.

A second variable which governs Sensitivity to Information is the buyer's predisposition toward the brand about which the information is concerned. The more interesting the information, the more likely the buyer is to open up his receptors and therefore to pay attention to the information. Hess has recently measured this by obtaining the strength of pupil dilation.

2. Perceptual Bias. The buyer not only selectively attends to information, but he may actually distort it once it enters his mental state. In other words, quality of information can be altered by the buyer. This aspect of the perceptual process is summarized in Perceptual Bias. The buyer may distort the cognitive elements contained in information to make them congruent with his own frame of reference as determined by

[12] Terminology in a problem area that cuts across both economics and psychology is different because each discipline has often defined its terms differently from the other. We find the economist's definitions of exogenous versus endogenous, and theory versus model more useful than those of the psychologist. The psychologist's distinction of hypothetical constructs and intervening variables, however, provides a helpful breakdown of endogenous variables. Finally, for the sake of exposition we have often here not clearly distinguished between the theory and its empirical counterparts. Although this practice encourages certain ambiguities, and we lay ourselves open to the charge of reifying our theory, we believe that for most readers it will simplify the task of comprehending the material.

the amount of information he already has stored. A series of cognitive consistency theories have been recently developed to explain how this congruency is established and what the consequences are in terms of the distortion of information that we might expect.[13] Most of the qualitative change in information arises because of feedback from various decision components such as Motives, Evoked Set and Decision Mediators. These relations are too complex, however, to describe in the summary.

The perceptual phenomena described above are likely to be less operative if the information is received from the buyer's social environment. This is because: (i) the source of social information, such as a friend, is likely to be favorably regarded by the buyer and therefore proper, undistorted reception of information will occur, and (ii) the information itself is modified by the social environment (the friend) so that it conforms to the needs of the buyer and, therefore, further modification is less essential.

3. Search for Information. During the total buying phase which extends over time and involves several repeat purchases of a product class, there are stages when the buyer *actively* seeks information. It is very important to distinguish the times when he passively receives information from the situations where he actively seeks it. We believe that perceptual distortion is less operative in the latter instances, and that a commercial communication, therefore, at that stage has a high probability of influencing the buyer.

The active seeking of information occurs when the buyer senses ambiguity of the brands in his evoked set. As we saw earlier, this happens in the Extensive Problem Solving and Limited Problem Solving phases of the decision process. The ambiguity of brand exists because the buyer is not certain of the outcomes from each brand. In other words, he has not yet learned enough about the alternatives to establish an expectancy of potential of the brands to satisfy his motives. The type of brand ambiguity is essentially confined to initial buyer behavior which we have called Extensive Problem Solving. However, ambiguity may still exist despite knowledge of the potential of alternative brands. This ambiguity is with respect to his inability to discriminate between alternatives. The buyer may be unable to discriminate because his motives are not well structured: he does not know how to order them. He may then seek information which will resolve the conflict among goals, a resolution that is implied in his learning of the appropriate product class aspect of decision mediators that we discussed earlier.

There is yet another stage of total buying behavior in which the buyer is likely to seek information. It is when the buyer has not only routinized

---

[13] Clark E. Hull, *Principles of Behavior* (New York: Appleton-Century-Crofts, Inc., 1943); Clark C. Hull, *A Behavior System* (New York: Yale University Press, 1952).

his decision process but he is so familiar and satiated with repeat buying that he feels bored. Then, all the existing alternatives in his evoked set including the most preferred brand become unacceptable to him. He seeks change or variety in that buying situation. In order to obtain this change, he actively searches for information on other alternatives (brands) that he never considered before. At this stage, he is particularly receptive to any information about new brands. Incidentally, here is an explanation for advertising in a highly stable industry. This phenomena has long baffled both the critics and defenders of the institution of advertising. Newcomers to the market and forgetting do not provide a plausible explanation.

We have so far described the stimulus input variables and the hypothetical constructs. Now we proceed to describe the output of the system —the responses of the buyer.

RESPONSE VARIABLES

The complexity of buyer behavior does not stop with the hypothetical constructs. Just as there is a variety of inputs, these exist a variety of buyer responses which becomes revelant for different areas of marketing strategy. This variety of consumer responses can be easily appreciated from the diversity of measures to evaluate advertising effectiveness. We have attempted to classify and order this diversity of buyer responses in the output variables. Most of the output variables are directly related to some and not other constructs. Each output variable serves different purposes both in marketing practice and fundamental research. Let us at first describe each variable and then provide a rationale for their interrelationships.

1. Attention is related to Sensitivity to Information. It is a response of the buyer which indicates the magnitude of his information intake. Attention is measured continuously during the time interval when the buyer receives information. There are several psychophysical methods of quantifying the degree of attention that the buyer pays to a message. The pupil dilation is one.

2. Comprehension refers to the store of knowledge about the brand that the buyer possesses at any point in time. This knowledge could vary from his simply being aware of a single brand's existence to a complete description of the attributes of the product class of which the brand is an element. It reflects the denotative meaning of the brand and in that sense it is strictly in the cognitive realm. It lacks the motivational aspects of behavior. Some of the standard measures of advertising effectiveness such as awareness, aided or unaided recall, and recognition may capture different aspects of the buyer's comprehension of the brand.

3. Attitude toward a brand is the buyer's evalution of the brand's potential to satisfy his motives. It, therefore, includes the connotative aspects of the brand concept; it contains those aspects of the brand which are relevant to the buyer's goals. Attitude is directly related to Predisposition and so it consists of both the evaluation of a brand in terms of the criteria of choice from Mediator and the confidence with which that evaluation is held.

4. Intention to buy is the buyer's forecast of his brand choice some time in the future. Like any forecast, it involves assumptions about future events including the likelihood of any perceived inhibitors creating barriers over the buyer's planning horizon. Intention to buy has been extensively used in the purchases of durable goods with some recent refinements in terms of the buyer's confidence in his own forecast: these studies are in terms of broadly defined product classes.[14] We may summarize this response of the buyer as something short of actual purchase behavior.

5. Purchase Behavior refers to the overt act of purchasing a brand. What becomes a part of company's sales or what the consumer records in a diary as a panel member, however, is only the terminal act in the sequence of shopping and buying. Very often, it is useful to observe the complete movement of the buyer from his home to the store and his purchase in the store. Yoell, for example, shows several case histories where a time and motion study of consumer's purchase behavior have useful marketing implications.[15] We think that at times it may be helpful to go so far as to incorporate the act of consumption into the definition of Purchase Behavior. We have, for example, developed and used the technique of sequential decision making where the buyer verbally describes the sequential pattern of his purchase behavior in a given buying situation. Out of this description a "flow chart" of decision making is obtained which reveals the number and the structure of the decision rules that the buyer employs.

Purchase Behavior is the overt manifestation of the buyer's Predisposition in conjunction with any Inhibitors that may be present. It differs from Attitude to the extent that Inhibitors are taken into consideration. It differs from Intention to the extent that it is the actual manifestation of behavior which the buyer only forecasted in his intention.

[14] Charles E. Osgood, "A Behavioristic Analysis of Perception and Meaning as Cognitive Phenomena" in *Symposium on Cognition, University of Colorado, 1955* (Cambridge, Harvard University Press, 1957), pp. 75–119; Charles E. Osgood "Motivational Dynamics of Language Behavior" in J. R. Jones (ed.) *Nebraska Symposium on Motivation,* 1957 (Lincoln: University of Nebraska Press, 1957), pp. 348–423.

[15] D. E. Berlyne, "Motivational Problems Raised by Exploratory and Epistemic Behavior" in Sigmund Koch (ed). *Psychology: A Study of a Science* Vol. 5 (New York: McGraw-Hill Book Company, 1963).

Several characteristics of Purchase Behavior become useful if we observe the buyer in a repetitive buying situation. These include the incidence of buying a brand, the quantity bought, and the purchase cycle. Several stochastic models of brand loyalty, for example, have been developed in recent years.[16] Similarly, we could take the magnitude purchased and compare light buyers with heavy buyers to determine if heavy buyers are more loyal buyers.

Interrelationship of Response Variables. In Figure 1, it will be seen that we have ordered the five response variables to create a hierarchy. The hierarchy is similar to the variety of hierarchies used in practice such as AIDA (Attention, Interest, Desire and Action), to the Lavidge and Steiner hierarchy of advertising effectiveness,[17] as well as to the different mental states that a person is alleged by the anthropologists and sociologists to pass through when he adopts an innovation.[18] There are, however, some important differences which we believe will clarify certain conceptual and methodological issues raised by Palda and others.[19]

First, we have added a response variable called Attention which is crucial since it reflects whether a communication is received by the buyer. Secondly, several different aspects of the cognitive realm of behavior such as awareness, recall, recognition, etc. are lumped into one category called Comprehension to suggest that they all are varying indicators of the buyer's storage of information about a brand which can be extended to *product class,* and in this way obtain leverage toward understanding buyer innovation. Third, we have defined Attitude to include both affective and conative aspects since any one who wants to establish causal relations between attitude and behavior must bring the motivational aspects into attitude. Furthermore, we separate the perceptual and the preference maps of the buyer into Comprehension and Attitude respectively. Fourth, we add another variable, Intention to Buy, because there are several product classes in both durable and semi-durable goods where properly defined and measured intentions have already proved useful. To the extent that Intention incorporates the buyer's forecast of his inhibitors, it might serve the useful function of informing the firm how to remove the inhibitors before the actual purchase behavior is manifested.

Finally, and most importantly, we have incorporated several feed-

16 Rosser Reeves, *Reality in Advertising* (New York: Alfred A. Knopf, Inc., 1961).

17 J. S. Brown, *The Motivation of Behavior* (New York: McGraw-Hill Book Company, 1961).

18 George S. Day, "Buyer Attitudes and Brand Choice Behavior" (unpublished Ph. D. Dissertation, Graduate School of Business, Columbia University, 1967).

19 Berlyne, *op. cit.*

back effects which were described when we discussed the hypothetical constructs. We will now show the relations as direct connections among response variables but the reader should bear in mind that these "outside" relations are merely the reflection of relations among the hypothetical constructs. For example, Purchase Behavior via Satisfaction entails some consequences which affect Decision Mediators and brand potential in Evoked Set; any change in them can produce change in Predisposition. Attitude is related to Predisposition and, therefore, it can also be changed in the period from pre-purchase to post-purchase. In incorporating this feedback, we are opening the way to resolving the controversy whether attitude causes purchase behavior or purchase behavior causes attitude. Over a period of time, the relation is interdependent, each affecting the other. Similarly, we have a feedback from Attitude to Comprehension and Attention, the rationale for which was given when we described the perceptual constructs.

DYNAMICS OF BUYING BEHAVIOR

Let us now explain the changes in the hypothetical constructs which occur due to learning.

The learning constructs are, of course, directly involved in the change that we label "learning." Since some of the learning constructs indirectly govern the perceptual constructs by way of feedbacks, there is also an indirect effect back upon the learning constructs themselves. As mentioned earlier, learning of Decision Mediators which structure Motives and Evoked Set of Brands which contain brand potentials, can occur from two broad sources: (i) past experience and (ii) information. Experience can be further classified as having been derived from buying a specified product or buying some similar product. Similarly, information can come from the buyer's commercial environment or his social environment, and if commercial, it can be significative or symbolic.

We will look at the development and change in learning constructs as due to: (i) generalization from similar buying situations, (ii) repeat buying of the same product class, and (iii) information.

GENERALIZATION FROM SIMILAR PURCHASE SITUATIONS

Some decision mediators are common across several product classes because many motives are common to a wide variety of purchasing activity. For example, a buyer may satisfy his health motive from many product classes by looking for nutrition. Similarly, many product classes are all bought at the same place which very often leads to spatial or contiguous generalization. The capacity to generalize provides the buyer with a truly enormous range of flexibility in adapting his purchase behavior to the myraid of varying market conditions he faces.

Generalization refers to the transfer of responses and of the relevance of stimuli from past situations to new situations which are similar. It saves the buyer time and effort in seeking information in the face of uncertainty that is inevitable in a new situation. Generalization can occur at any one of the several levels of purchase activity, but we are primarily interested in generalization of those decision mediators which only involve brand choice behavior in contrast to store choice or choice of shopping time and day. In other words, we are concerned with brand generalization.

REPEAT PURCHASE EXPERIENCES

Another source of change in the learning constructs is the repeated purchase of the same product class over a period of time.

In Figure 1 the purchase of a brand entails two types of feedbacks, one affecting the decision mediators and the other affecting the brand potential of the evoked set. First, the experience of buying with all its cognitive aspects of memory, reasoning, etc. has a learning effect on the decision mediators. This occurs irrespective of which specific brand the buyer chooses in any one purchase decision because the decision mediators like the motives are product–specific and not limited to any one brand. Hence every purchase has an incremental effect in firmly establishing the decision mediators. This is easy to visualize if we remember that buying behavior is a series of mental and motor steps while the actual choice is only its terminal act.

Purchase of a brand creates certain satisfactions for the buyer which the consumer compares with his expectations of the brand's potential and this expectation is the basis on which he made his decision in the first place. This comparison of expected and actual consequences causes him to be satisfied or dissatisfied with his purchase of the brand. Hence, the second feedback from Purchase Behavior to Satisfaction changes the attractiveness of the brand purchased. If the buyer is satisfied with his consumption, he enhances the potential of the broad and this is likely to result in greater probability of its repeat purchase. If he is dissatisfied, the potential of the brand is diminished, and its probability of repeat purchase is also similarly reduced.

If there are no inhibitory forces which influence him, the buyer will continue to buy a brand which proves satisfactory. In the initial stages of decision-making he may show some tendency to oscillate between brands in order to formulate his decision mediators. In other words, he may learn by trial-and-error at first and then settle on a brand and thereafter, he may buy the brand with such regularity to suggest that he is brand loyal. Unless a product is of very high risk, however, there is a limit as to how long this brand loyalty will continue: he may become bored with his preferred brand and look for something new.

INFORMATION AS A SOURCE OF LEARNING

The third major source by which the learning constructs are changed is information from the buyer's (i) commercial environment consisting of advertising, promotion, salesmanship and retail shelf display of the competing companies, and (ii) his social environment consisting of his family, friends, reference group and social class.

We will describe the influence of information at first as if the perceptual constructs were absent. In other words, we assume that the buyer receives information with perfect fidelity as it exists in the environment. Also, we will discuss separately the information from the commercial and social environments.

Commercial Environment. The company communicates about its offerings to the buyers either by the physical brand (significates) or by symbols (pictorial or linguistic) which represent the brand. In other words, significative and symbolic communication are the two major ways of interaction between the sellers and the buyers.

In Figure 1, the influence of information is shown on Motives, Decision Mediators, Evoked Set, and Inhibitors. We believe that the influence of commercial information on motives (specific and nonspecific) is limited. The main effect is primarily to *intensify* whatever motives the buyer has rather than to create new ones. For example, physical display of the brand may intensify his motives above the threshold level which combined with strong predisposition can result in impulse (unplanned) purchase. A similar reaction is possible when an ad creates sufficient intensity of motives to provide an impetus for the buyer to go to the store. A second way to influence motives is to show the *perceived instrumentality* of the brand and thereby make it a part of the buyer's defined set of alternatives. Finally, to a very limited extent, marketing stimuli may change the *content of the motives.* The general conception both among marketing men and laymen is that marketing stimuli change the buyer's motives. However, on a closer examination it would appear that what is changed is the *intensity* of buyer's motives already provided by the social environment. Many dormant or latent motives may become stimulated. The secret of success very often lies in identifying the change in motives created by social change and intensifying them as seems to be the case in the recent projection of youthfulness in many buying situations.

Marketing stimuli are also important in determining and changing the buyer's evoked set. Commercial information tells him of the existence of the brands (awareness), their identifying characteristics (Comprehension plus brand name) and their relevance to the satisfaction of the buyer's needs (attitude).

Marketing stimuli are also important in creating and changing the buyer's decision mediators. They become important sources for learning decision mediators when the buyer has no prior experience to rely upon. In other words, when he is in the extensive problem solving (EPS) stage, it is marketing and social stimuli which are the important sources of learning. Similarly, when the buyer actively seeks information because all the existing alternative are unacceptable to him, marketing stimuli become important in *changing* his decision mediators.

Finally, marketing stimuli can unwittingly create inhibitors. For example, a company feels the need to emphasize price-quality association, but it may result in high-price inhibition in the mind of the buyer. Similarly, in emphasizing the details of usage and consumption of a product, the communication may create the inhibition related to time pressure.

Social Environment. The social environment of the buyer—family, friends, reference groups—is another major source of information in his buying behavior. Most of the inputs are likely to be symbolic (linguistic) although at times the physical product may be shown to the buyer.

Information from his social environment also affects the four learning constructs: Motives, Decision Mediators, Evoked Set and Inhibitors. However, the effect of these constructs is different from that of the commercial environment. First, the information about the brands will be considerably modified by the social environment before it reaches the buyer. Most of the modifications are likely to be in the nature of adding connotative meanings to brand descriptions, and of the biasing effects of the communication's perceptual variables like Sensitivity to Information and Perceptual Bias. Second, the buyer's social environment will probably have a very strong influence on the content of his motives and their ordering to establish a goal structure. Several research studies have concentrated on such influences.[20] Third, the social environment may also affect his evoked set. This will be particularly true when the buyer lacks experience. Furthermore, if the product class is important to the buyer and he is technically incompetent or uncertain in evaluating the consequences of the brand for his needs, he may rely

20 S. Feldman (ed.) *Cognitive Consistency: Motivational Antecedents and Behavioral Consequents* (Academic Press, 1966); Martin Fishbein (ed.) *Readings in Attitude Theory and Measurement* (New York: John Wiley & Sons, 1967).

more on the social than on the marketing environment for information. This is well documented by several studies using the perceived risk hypothesis.[21]

EXOGENOUS VARIABLES

Earlier we mentioned that there are several influences operating on the buyer's decisions which we treat as exogenous, that is, we do not explain their formation and change. Many of these influences come from the buyer's social environment and we wish to separate the effects of his environment which has occurred in the past and not related to a specific decision from those which are current and directly affect the decisions that occur during the period the buyer is being observed. The inputs during the observation period provide information to the buyer to help his current decision-making. The past influences are already imbedded in the values of the perceptual and learning constructs. Strictly speaking, therefore, there is no need for some of the exogenous variables which have influenced the buyer in the past. We bring them out explicitly, however, for the sake of research design where the researcher may control or take into account individual differences among buyers due to such past influences. Incorporating the effects of these exogenous variables will reduce the size of the unexplained variance or error in estimation which it is particularly essential to control under field conditions. Figure 1 presents a set of exogenous variables which we believe provide the control essential to obtaining satisfactory predictive relations between the inputs and the outputs of the system. Let us briefly discuss each of the exogenous variables.

1. Importance of Purchase refers to differential degrees of ego-involvement or commitment in different product classes. It, therefore, provides a mechanism which must be carefully examined in inter-product studies. Importance of Purchase will influence the size of the Evoked Set and the magnitude of Search for Information. The more important the product class, the larger the Evoked Set.

2. Time Pressure is a current exogenous variable and, therefore, specific to a decision situation. It refers to the situation when a buyer feels pressed for time due to any of several environmental influences and so must allocate his time among alternative uses. In this process a re-allocation unfavorable to the purchasing activity can occur. Time pressure will create Inhibition as mentioned earlier. It will also unfavorably affect Search for Information.

[21] Thomas F. Juster, *Anticipations and Purchases: An Analysis of Consumer Behavior* (Princeton University Press, 1964).

3. Financial Status refers to the constraint the buyer may feel because of lack of financial resources. This affects his purchase behavior to the extent that it creates a barrier to purchasing the most preferred brand. For example, a buyer may want to purchase a Mercedes-Benz but lacks sufficient financial resources and therefore, he will settle for some low-priced American automobile such as a Ford or Chevrolet. Its effect is via Inhibitor.

4. Personality Traits take into consideration many of the variables such as self-confidence, self-esteem, authoritarianism and anxiety which have been researched to identify individual differences. It will be noted that these individual differences are "topic free" and, therefore, are supposed to exert their effect across product classes. We believe their effect is felt on: i) nonspecific Motives and (ii) Evoked Set. For example, the more anxious a person, the greater the motivational arousal; dominant personalities are more likely by a small margin to buy a Ford instead of a Chevrolet; the more authoritarian a person, the narrower the category width of his evoked set.

5. Social and Organizational Setting (Organization) takes us to the group, to a higher level of social organization than the individual. It includes both the informal social organization such as family and reference groups which are relevant for *consumer behavior* and the formal organization which constitutes much of the environment for *industrial purchasing*. Organizational variables are those of small group interaction such as power, status and authority. We believe that the underlying process of intergroup conflicts in both industrial and consumer buying behavior are in principle very similar, and that the differences are largely due to the formalization of industrial activity. Organization, both formal and social, is a crucial variable because it influences all the learning constructs.

6. Social Class refers to a still higher level of social organization, the social aggregate. Several indices are available to classify people into various classes. The most common perhaps is the Warner classification of people into upper-upper, lower-upper, upper-middle, lower-middle, upper-lower, and lower-lower classes. Social class mediates the relation between the input and the output by influencing: (i) specific Motives, (ii) Decision Mediators, (iii) Evoked Set, and (iv) Inhibitors. The latter influence is important particularly in the adoption of innovations.

7. Culture provides an even more comprehensive social framework than social class. Culture consists of patterns of behavior, symbols, ideas and their attached values. Culture will influence Motives, Decision Mediators, and Inhibitors.

CONCLUSION

In the preceding pages we have summarized a theory of buyer brand choice. It is complex. We strongly believe that complexity is essential to adequately describe buying behavior, from the point of view of both marketing practice and public policy.

We hope that the theory can provide new insights into past empirical data and to guide future research so as to instill with coherence and unity current research which now tends to be atomistic and unrelated. We are vigorously pursuing a large research program aimed at testing the validity of the theory. The research was designed in terms of the variables specified by the theory, and our most preliminary results causes us to believe that it was fruitful to use the theory in this way. Because it specifies a number of relationships, it has clearly been useful in interpreting the preliminary findings. Above all, it is an aid in communication among the researchers and with the companies involved.

Finally, a number of new ideas are set forth in the theory, but we would like to call attention to three in particular. The concept of evoked set provides a means of reducing the noise in many analyses of buying behavior. The product class concept offers a new dimension for incorporating many of the complexities of innovations and especially for integrating systematically the idea of innovation into a framework of psychological constructs. Anthropologists and sociologists have been pretty much content to deal with peripheral variables in their investigations of innovation. The habit-perception cycle in which perception and habit respond inversely offers hope for explaining a large proportion of the phenomenon that has long baffled both the critics and defenders of advertising: large advertising expenditures in a stable market where, on the surface, it would seem that people are already sated with information.

RETROSPECTIVE COMMENT

Since this article was written, there have been, on the surface, profound changes. Yet, most of these could be said to be implied in this article. First, the structure of some of the individual constructs have been more fully explored. The most striking has been the case of attitude, where Professor Sheth in particular has continued pioneering work. Second, the system has become more sharply articulated and fully specified. Later research has shown, for example, that the system is more complex the constructs are more interrelated—than shown here. Third, the system, in general, has moved more from a traditional learning point of view to information processing and concept formation. Fourth, it has become almost fully mathematized. The earliest attempt is described in Farley, Howard and Ring (eds.), *Consumer Behavior: Theory and Application*, Allyn and Bacon, 1974, with an introduction by the eminent sociologist Paul F. Lazarsfeld, who places this work in the mainstream of developments in social science. The earlier mathematization was linear in nature, but recently non-linear relations have been introduced. Still more recently, a non-linear dynamics system with feedbacks has been developed.

Finally, the work has moved much more in the direction of application. To ascertain the generality of the system, e.g. across cultures and products, it has been applied to the introduction of an instant breakfast (1966), to a perfumed soap in another culture (1969), and to a large consumer durable (1970). It has been articulated in the context of public policy, and criteria for socially evaluating marketing activity have been derived from it in Howard and Hulbert, *Advertising and the Public Interest: A Federal Trade Commission Report* (Crain Communications, Inc., 1973). In the area of social marketing, Professor Farley has applied it to population control problems in Kenya.—*John A. Howard*

Since publishing our theory of buyer behavior as a book in 1969 (J. A. Howard and J. N. Sheth, *The Theory of Buyer Behavior,* John Wiley and Sons), the theory has been widely accepted as a major scientific contribution to the development of marketing thought and practice. It provided impetus for a very large scale empirical research at Columbia University primarily to test the theory in its totality. Surprising to both of the authors, the theory has been utilized by marketing practitioners as a market research tool and perspective and some companies have even attempted to build their market research information systems based on the Howard-Sheth theory.

I have continued to extend the theory to more complicated areas of consumer behavior including family buying decisions and industrial buying decisions. The other author has extended it to provide a public policy viewpoint of advertising and its regulation. We are both continuing to empirically validate the theory by replicating studies.—*Jagdish N. Sheth*

PART V. QUESTIONS FOR DISCUSSION

1. What contributions should a "theory" of consumer behavior provide for students of consumer behavior?

2. Suggest some methods of empirically testing the Howard-Sheth model.

3. Refer to two or three other models of consumer behavior (e.g., Francesco Nicosia, *Consumer Decision Processes* (Englewood Cliffs, N.J.: Prentice-Hall, Inc., 1966); Alan R. Andreasen, "Attitudes and Customer Behavior: A Decision Model," in Lee E. Preston (ed.), *New Research in Marketing* (Berkeley, Calif.; University of California Press, 1965), pp. 1–16; James F. Engel, David T. Kollat, and Roger D. Blackwell, *Consumer Behavior* (New York: Holt, Rinehart & Winston, Inc., 1973). Contrast these models with the Howard-Sheth model.

Name Index

Subject Index